Microsoft® POWERPOINT® 2010

INTRODUCTORY

Gary B. Shelly

Susan L. Sebok

COURSE TECHNOLOGY
CENGAGE Learning

SHELLY CASHMAN SERIES®

Australia • Brazil • Japan • Korea • Mexico • Singapore • Spain • United Kingdom • United States

COURSE TECHNOLOGY
CENGAGE Learning™

Microsoft® PowerPoint® 2010:
Introductory
Gary B. Shelly, Susan L. Sebok

Vice President, Publisher: Nicole Pinard

Executive Editor: Kathleen McMahon

Product Manager: Jon Farnham

Associate Product Manager: Aimee Poirier

Editorial Assistant: Lauren Brody

Director of Marketing: Cheryl Costantini

Marketing Manager: Tristen Kendall

Marketing Coordinator: Stacey Leasca

Print Buyer: Julio Esperas

Director of Production: Patty Stephan

Senior Content Project Manager: Jill Braiewa

Development Editor: Deb Kaufmann

Copyeditor: Troy Lilly

Proofreader: Karen Annett

Indexer: Rich Carlson

QA Manuscript Reviewers: Chris Scriver, John Freitas, Serge Palladino, Susan Pedicini, Danielle Shaw

Art Director: Marissa Falco

Cover Designer: Lisa Kuhn, Curio Press, LLC

Cover Photo: Tom Kates Photography

Text Design: Joel Sadagursky

Compositor: PreMediaGlobal

For product information and technology assistance, contact us at
Cengage Learning Customer & Sales Support, 1-800-354-9706

For permission to use material from this text or product, submit all requests online at **cengage.com/permissions**
Further permissions questions can be emailed to
permissionrequest@cengage.com

Library of Congress Control Number: 2010929407
ISBN-13: 978-1-4390-7848-8
ISBN-10: 1-4390-7848-3

Course Technology
20 Channel Center Street
Boston, MA 02210
USA

Microsoft and the Office logo are either registered trademarks or trademarks of Microsoft Corporation in the United States and/or other countries. Course Technology, a part of Cengage Learning, is an independent entity from the Microsoft Corporation, and not affiliated with Microsoft in any manner.

Cengage Learning is a leading provider of customized learning solutions with office locations around the globe, including Singapore, the United Kingdom, Australia, Mexico, Brazil, and Japan. Locate your local office at:
international.cengage.com/region

Cengage Learning products are represented in Canada by Nelson Education, Ltd.

Visit our Web site **www.cengage.com/ct/shellycashman** to share and gain ideas on our textbooks!

To learn more about Course Technology, visit **www.cengage.com/coursetechnology**

Purchase any of our products at your local college bookstore or at our preferred online store **www.cengagebrain.com**

We dedicate this book to the memory of James S. Quasney (1940 – 2009), who for 18 years co-authored numerous books with Tom Cashman and Gary Shelly and provided extraordinary leadership to the Shelly Cashman Series editorial team. As series editor, Jim skillfully coordinated, organized, and managed the many aspects of our editorial development processes and provided unending direction, guidance, inspiration, support, and advice to the Shelly Cashman Series authors and support team members. He was a trusted, dependable, loyal, and well-respected leader, mentor, and friend. We are forever grateful to Jim for his faithful devotion to our team and eternal contributions to our series.

The Shelly Cashman Series Team

Printed in the United States of America
1 2 3 4 5 6 7 16 15 14 13 12 11 10

Microsoft POWERPOINT® 2010
INTRODUCTORY

Contents

Microsoft **PowerPoint 2010**

Appendices

Preface

The Shelly Cashman Series® offers the finest textbooks in computer education. We are proud that since Mircosoft Office 4.3, our series of Microsoft Office textbooks have been the most widely used books in education. With each new edition of our Office books, we make significant improvements based on the software and comments made by instructors and students. For this Microsoft PowerPoint 2010 text, the Shelly Cashman Series development team carefully reviewed our pedagogy and analyzed its effectiveness in teaching today's Office student. Students today read less, but need to retain more. They need not only to be able to perform skills, but to retain those skills and know how to apply them to different settings. Today's students need to be continually engaged and challenged to retain what they're learning.

With this Microsoft PowerPoint 2010 text, we continue our commitment to focusing on the user and how they learn best.

Objectives of This Textbook

Microsoft PowerPoint 2010: Introductory is intended for a first course on PowerPoint 2010. No experience with a computer is assumed, and no mathematics beyond the high school freshman level is required. The objectives of this book are:

- To offer an introduction to Microsoft PowerPoint 2010

- To expose students to practical examples of the computer as a useful tool

- To acquaint students with the proper procedures to create presentations suitable for coursework, professional purposes, and personal use

- To help students discover the underlying functionality of PowerPoint 2010 so they can become more productive

- To develop an exercise-oriented approach that allows learning by doing

New to this Edition

Microsoft PowerPoint 2010: Introductory offers a number of new features and approaches, which improve student understanding, retention, transference, and skill in using PowerPoint 2010. The following enhancements will enrich the learning experience:

- Office 2010 and Windows 7: Essential Concepts and Skills chapter presents basic Office 2010 and Windows 7 skills.

- Streamlined first chapter allows the ability to cover more advanced skills earlier.

- Chapter topic redistribution offers concise chapters that ensure complete skill coverage.

- New pedagogical elements enrich material creating an accessible and user-friendly approach.

  - Break Points, a new boxed element, identify logical stopping points and give students instructions regarding what they should do before taking a break.

  - Within step instructions, Tab | Group Identifiers, such as (Home tab | Bold button), help students more easily locate elements in the groups and on the tabs on the Ribbon.

  - Modified step-by-step instructions tell the student what to do and provide the generic reason why they are completing a specific task, which helps students easily transfer given skills to different settings.

The Shelly Cashman Approach

A Proven Pedagogy with an Emphasis on Project Planning

Each chapter presents a practical problem to be solved, within a project planning framework. The project orientation is strengthened by the use of Plan Ahead boxes, which encourage critical thinking about how to proceed at various points in the project. Step-by-step instructions with supporting screens guide students through the steps. Instructional steps are supported by the Q&A, Experimental Step, and BTW features.

A Visually Engaging Book that Maintains Student Interest

The step-by-step tasks, with supporting figures, provide a rich visual experience for the student. Call-outs on the screens that present both explanatory and navigational information provide students with information they need when they need to know it.

Supporting Reference Materials (Appendices and Quick Reference)

The appendices provide additional information about the Application at hand and include such topics as project planning guidelines and certification. With the Quick Reference, students can quickly look up information about a single task, such as keyboard shortcuts, and find page references of where in the book the task is illustrated.

Integration of the World Wide Web

The World Wide Web is integrated into the PowerPoint 2010 learning experience by (1) BTW annotations; (2) BTW, Q&A, and Quick Reference Summary Web pages; and (3) the Learn It Online section for each chapter.

End-of-Chapter Student Activities

Extensive end-of-chapter activities provide a variety of reinforcement opportunities for students where they can apply and expand their skills.

Instructor Resources

The Instructor Resources include both teaching and testing aids and can be accessed via CD-ROM or at www.cengage.com/login.

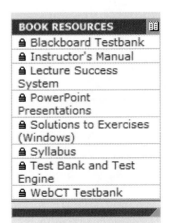

Instructor's Manual Includes lecture notes summarizing the chapter sections, figures and boxed elements found in every chapter, teacher tips, classroom activities, lab activities, and quick quizzes in Microsoft Word files.

Syllabus Easily customizable sample syllabi that cover policies, assignments, exams, and other course information.

Figure Files Illustrations for every figure in the textbook in electronic form.

PowerPoint Presentations A multimedia lecture presentation system that provides slides for each chapter. Presentations are based on chapter objectives.

Solutions to Exercises Includes solutions for all end-of-chapter and chapter reinforcement exercises.

Test Bank & Test Engine Test Banks include 112 questions for every chapter, featuring objective-based and critical thinking question types, and including page number references and figure references, when appropriate. Also included is the test engine, ExamView, the ultimate tool for your objective-based testing needs.

Data Files for Students Includes all the files that are required by students to complete the exercises.

Additional Activities for Students Consists of Chapter Reinforcement Exercises, which are true/false, multiple-choice, and short answer questions that help students gain confidence in the material learned.

SAM: Skills Assessment Manager

SAM 2010 is designed to help bring students from the classroom to the real world. It allows students to train on and test important computer skills in an active, hands-on environment.

SAM's easy-to-use system includes powerful interactive exams, training, and projects on the most commonly used Microsoft Office applications. SAM simulates the Microsoft Office 2010 application environment, allowing students to demonstrate their knowledge and think through the skills by performing real-world tasks such as bolding word text or setting up slide transitions. Add in live-in-the-application projects, and students are on their way to truly learning and applying skills to business-centric documents.

Designed to be used with the Shelly Cashman Series, SAM includes handy page references so that students can print helpful study guides that match the Shelly Cashman textbooks used in class. For instructors, SAM also includes robust scheduling and reporting features.

Content for Online Learning

Course Technology has partnered with the leading distance learning solution providers and class-management platforms today. To access this material, instructors will visit our password-protected instructor resources available at www.cengage.com/coursetechnology. Instructor resources include the following: additional case projects, sample syllabi, PowerPoint presentations per chapter, and more. For additional information or for an instructor user name and password, please contact your sales representative. For students to access this material, they must have purchased a WebTutor PIN-code specific to this title and your campus platform. The resources for students may include (based on instructor preferences), but are not limited to: topic review, review questions, and practice tests.

CourseNotes

Course Technology's CourseNotes are six-panel quick reference cards that reinforce the most important and widely used features of a software application in a visual and user-friendly format. CourseNotes serve as a great reference tool during and after the student completes the course. CourseNotes are available for software applications such as Microsoft Office 2010, Word 2010, Excel 2010, Access 2010, PowerPoint 2010, and Windows 7. Topic-based CourseNotes are available for Best Practices in Social Networking, Hot Topics in Technology, and Web 2.0. Visit www.cengage.com/ct/coursenotes to learn more!

A Guided Tour

Add excitement and interactivity to your classroom with "*A Guided Tour*" product line. Play one of the brief mini-movies to spice up your lecture and spark classroom discussion. Or, assign a movie for homework and ask students to complete the correlated assignment that accompanies each topic. "*A Guided Tour*" product line takes the prep work out of providing your students with information about new technologies and applications and helps keep students engaged with content relevant to their lives; all in under an hour!

About Our Covers

The Shelly Cashman Series is continually updating our approach and content to reflect the way today's students learn and experience new technology. This focus on student success is reflected on our covers, which feature real students from the University of Rhode Island using the Shelly Cashman Series in their courses, and reflect the varied ages and backgrounds of the students learning with our books. When you use the Shelly Cashman Series, you can be assured that you are learning computer skills using the most effective courseware available.

Textbook Walk-Through

The Shelly Cashman Series Pedagogy: Project-Based — Step-by-Step — Variety of Assessments

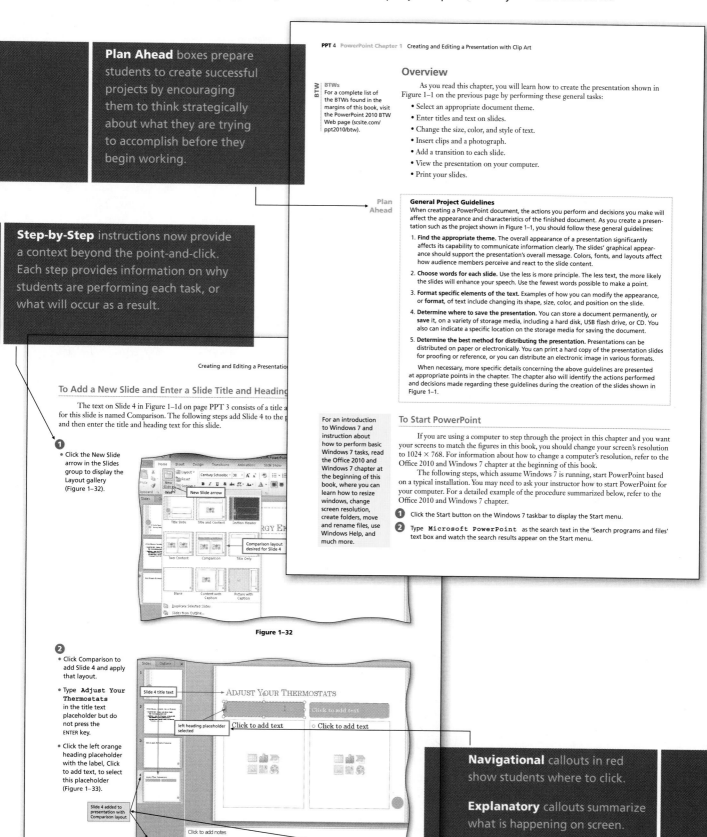

Plan Ahead boxes prepare students to create successful projects by encouraging them to think strategically about what they are trying to accomplish before they begin working.

Step-by-Step instructions now provide a context beyond the point-and-click. Each step provides information on why students are performing each task, or what will occur as a result.

Navigational callouts in red show students where to click.

Explanatory callouts summarize what is happening on screen.

BTW

BTWs
For a complete list of the BTWs found in the margins of this book, visit the PowerPoint 2010 BTW Web page (scsite.com/ppt2010/btw).

Overview

As you read this chapter, you will learn how to create the presentation shown in Figure 1–1 on the previous page by performing these general tasks:

- Select an appropriate document theme.
- Enter titles and text on slides.
- Change the size, color, and style of text.
- Insert clips and a photograph.
- Add a transition to each slide.
- View the presentation on your computer.
- Print your slides.

Plan Ahead

General Project Guidelines

When creating a PowerPoint document, the actions you perform and decisions you make will affect the appearance and characteristics of the finished document. As you create a presentation such as the project shown in Figure 1–1, you should follow these general guidelines:

1. **Find the appropriate theme.** The overall appearance of a presentation significantly affects its capability to communicate information clearly. The slides' graphical appearance should support the presentation's overall message. Colors, fonts, and layouts affect how audience members perceive and react to the slide content.

2. **Choose words for each slide.** Use the less is more principle. The less text, the more likely the slides will enhance your speech. Use the fewest words possible to make a point.

3. **Format specific elements of the text.** Examples of how you can modify the appearance, or **format**, of text include changing its shape, size, color, and position on the slide.

4. **Determine where to save the presentation.** You can store a document permanently, or **save** it, on a variety of storage media, including a hard disk, USB flash drive, or CD. You also can indicate a specific location on the storage media for saving the document.

5. **Determine the best method for distributing the presentation.** Presentations can be distributed on paper or electronically. You can print a hard copy of the presentation slides for proofing or reference, or you can distribute an electronic image in various formats.

When necessary, more specific details concerning the above guidelines are presented at appropriate points in the chapter. The chapter also will identify the actions performed and decisions made regarding these guidelines during the creation of the slides shown in Figure 1–1.

For an introduction to Windows 7 and instruction about how to perform basic Windows 7 tasks, read the Office 2010 and Windows 7 chapter at the beginning of this book, where you can learn how to resize windows, change screen resolution, create folders, move and rename files, use Windows Help, and much more.

To Start PowerPoint

If you are using a computer to step through the project in this chapter and you want your screens to match the figures in this book, you should change your screen's resolution to 1024 × 768. For information about how to change a computer's resolution, refer to the Office 2010 and Windows 7 chapter at the beginning of this book.

The following steps, which assume Windows 7 is running, start PowerPoint based on a typical installation. You may need to ask your instructor how to start PowerPoint for your computer. For a detailed example of the procedure summarized below, refer to the Office 2010 and Windows 7 chapter.

1 Click the Start button on the Windows 7 taskbar to display the Start menu.

2 Type **Microsoft PowerPoint** as the search text in the 'Search programs and files' text box and watch the search results appear on the Start menu.

Creating and Editing a Presentation

To Add a New Slide and Enter a Slide Title and Heading

The text on Slide 4 in Figure 1–1d on page PPT 3 consists of a title a for this slide is named Comparison. The following steps add Slide 4 to the p and then enter the title and heading text for this slide.

1
- Click the New Slide arrow in the Slides group to display the Layout gallery (Figure 1–32).

Figure 1–32

2
- Click Comparison to add Slide 4 and apply that layout.

- Type **Adjust Your Thermostats** in the title text placeholder but do not press the ENTER key.

- Click the left orange heading placeholder with the label, Click to add text, to select this placeholder (Figure 1–33).

Figure 1–33

Textbook Walk-Through

To Move Manually through Slides in a Slide Show

After you begin Slide Show view, you can move forward or backward through the slides. PowerPoint allows you to advance through the slides manually or automatically. During a slide show, each slide in the presentation shows on the screen, one slide at a time. Each time you click the mouse button, the next slide appears. The following steps move manually through the slides.

1
- Click each slide until Slide 5 (Be Green) is displayed (Figure 1–73).

Q&A I see a small toolbar in the lower-left corner of my slide. What is this toolbar?

The Slide Show toolbar appears when you begin running a slide show and then move the mouse pointer. The buttons on this toolbar allow you to navigate to the next slide, the previous slide, to mark up the current slide, or to change the current display.

Figure 1–73

2
- Click the More button (Design tab | Themes group) to expand the gallery, which shows more Built-In theme gallery options (Figure 1–3).

Experiment
- Point to various document themes in the Themes gallery and watch the colors and fonts change on the title slide.

Q&A Are the themes displayed in a specific order?

Yes. They are arranged in alphabetical order running from left to right. If you point to a theme, a ScreenTip with the theme's name appears on the screen.

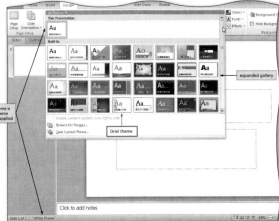

Figure 1–3

Q&A What if I change my mind and do not want to select a new theme?

Click anywhere outside the All Themes gallery to close the gallery.

3
- Click the Oriel theme to apply this theme to Slide 1 (Figure 1–4).

Q&A If I decide at some future time that this design does not fit the theme of my presentation, can I apply a different design?

Yes. You can repeat these steps at any time while creating your presentation.

Figure 1–4

Break Points identify logical breaks in the chapter if students need to stop before completing the project.

Break Point: If you wish to take a break, this is a good place to do so. You can quit PowerPoint now (refer to page PPT 50 for instructions). To resume at a later time, start PowerPoint (refer to pages PPT 4 and PPT 5 for instructions), open the file called Saving Energy (refer to pages PPT 50 and PPT 51 for instructions), and continue following the steps from this location forward.

Resizing Clip Art and Photographs

To Quit PowerPoint

The project now is complete. The following steps quit PowerPoint. For a detailed example of the procedure summarized below, refer to the Office 2010 and Windows 7 chapter at the beginning of this book.

1 If you have one PowerPoint document open, click the Close button on the right side of the title bar to close the document and quit PowerPoint; or if you have multiple PowerPoint documents open, click File on the Ribbon to open the Backstage view and then click Exit in the Backstage view to close all open documents and quit PowerPoint.

2 If a Microsoft Office PowerPoint dialog box appears, click the Save button to save any changes made to the document since the last save.

Chapter Summary A concluding paragraph, followed by a listing of the tasks completed within a chapter together with the pages on which the step-by-step, screen-by-screen explanations appear.

Chapter Summary

In this chapter you have learned how to apply a document theme, create a title slide and text slides with a bulleted list, clip art, and a photograph, size and move clip art and a photograph, format and edit text, add a slide transition, and print slides as handouts. The items listed below include all the new chapter.

20. Insert a Clip from the Clip Organizer into the Title Slide (PPT 27)
21. Insert a Clip from the Clip Organizer into a Content Placeholder (PPT 30)
22. Insert a Photograph from the Clip Organizer into a Slide without a Content Placeholder (PPT 32)
23. Resize Clip Art (PPT 33)
24. Move Clips (PPT 36)
25. Duplicate a Slide (PPT 38)
26. Arrange a Slide (PPT 39)
27. Delete Text in a Placeholder (PPT 41)
28. Add a Transition between Slides (PPT 43)
29. Change Document Properties (PPT 46)
30. Save an Existing Presentation with the Same File Name (PPT 47)
31. Start Slide Show View (PPT 47)
32. Move Manually through Slides in a Slide Show (PPT 49)
33. Quit PowerPoint (PPT 50)
34. Open a Document from PowerPoint (PPT 50)
35. Print a Presentation (PPT 51)

Learn It Online

Test your knowledge of chapter content and key terms.

Instructions: To complete the Learn It Online exercises, start your browser, click the Address bar, and then enter the Web address **scsite.com/ppt2010/learn**. When the PowerPoint 2010 Learn It Online page is displayed, click the link for the exercise you want to complete and then read the instructions.

Chapter Reinforcement TF, MC, and SA
A series of true/false, multiple choice, and short answer questions that test your knowledge of the chapter content.

Flash Cards
An interactive learning environment where you identify chapter key terms associated with displayed definitions.

Practice Test
A series of multiple choice questions that test your knowledge of chapter content and key terms.

Who Wants To Be a Computer Genius?
An interactive game that challenges your knowledge of chapter content in the style of a television quiz show.

Wheel of Terms
An interactive game that challenges your knowledge of chapter key terms in the style of the television show *Wheel of Fortune*.

Crossword Puzzle Challenge
A crossword puzzle that challenges your knowledge of key terms presented in the chapter.

Apply Your Knowledge

Reinforce the skills and apply the concepts you learned in this chapter.

Modifying Character Formats and Paragraph Levels and Moving a Clip
Note: To complete this assignment, you will be required to use the Data Files for Students. See the inside back cover of this book for instructions on downloading the Data Files for Students, or contact your instructor for information about accessing the required files.

Instructions: Start PowerPoint. Open the presentation, Apply 1-1 Flu Season, from the Data Files for Students.

The two slides in the presentation discuss ways to avoid getting or spreading the flu. The document you open is an unformatted presentation. You are to modify the document theme, indent the paragraphs, resize and move the clip art, and format the text so the slides look like Figure 1–77 on the next page.

Continued >

Learn It Online   Every chapter features a Learn It Online section that is comprised of six exercises. These exercises include True/False, Multiple Choice, Short Answer, Flash Cards, Practice Test, and Learning Games.

Apply Your Knowledge This exercise usually requires students to open and manipulate a file from the Data Files that parallels the activities learned in the chapter. To obtain a copy of the Data Files for Students, follow the instructions on the inside back cover of this text.

Textbook Walk-Through

Extend Your Knowledge

Extend the skills you learned in this chapter and experiment with new skills. You may need to use Help to complete the assignment.

Changing Slide Theme, Layout, and Text

Note: To complete this assignment, you will be required to use the Data Files for Students. See the inside back cover of this book for instructions on downloading the Data Files for Students, or contact your instructor for information about accessing the required files.

Instructions: Start PowerPoint. Open the presentation that you are going to prepare for your dental hygiene class, Extend 1–1 Winning Smile, from the Data Files for Students.
  You will choose a theme, format slides, and create a closing slide.

Perform the following tasks:
1. Apply an appropriate document theme.
2. On Slide 1, use your name in place of Student Name. Format the text on this slide using techniques you learned in this chapter, such as changing the font size and color and also bolding and italicizing words.
3. On Slide 2, change the slide layout and adjust the paragraph levels so that the lines of text are arranged under two headings: Discount Dental and Dental Insurance (Figure 1–78).
4. On Slide 3, create paragraphs and adjust the paragraph levels to create a bulleted list. Edit the text so that the slide meets the 7 × 7 rule, which states that each line should have a maximum of seven words, and each slide should have a maximum of seven lines.
5. Create an appropriate closing slide using the title slide as a guide.
6. The slides contain a variety of clips downloaded from the Microsoft Clip Organizer. Size and move them when necessary.
7. Apply an appropriate transition to all slides.
8. Change the document properties, as specified by your instructor. Save the presentation using the file name, Extend 1–1 Dental Plans.
9. Submit the revised document in the format specified by your instr

Extend Your Knowledge projects at the end of each chapter allow students to extend and expand on the skills learned within the chapter. Students use critical thinking to experiment with new skills to complete each project.

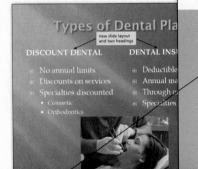

new slide layout
and two headings

Figure 1–78

Make It Right

Analyze a presentation and correct all errors and/or improve the design.

Correcting Formatting and List Levels

Note: To complete this assignment, you will be required to use the Data Files for Students. See the inside back cover of this book for instructions on downloading the Data Files for Students, or contact your instructor for information about accessing the required files.

Instructions: Start PowerPoint. Open the presentation, Make It Right 1–1 Air Ducts, from the Data Files for Students.
  Members of your homeowners' association are having their semiannual meeting, and each member of the board is required to give a short presentation on the subject of energy savings. You have decided to discuss the energy-saving benefits of maintaining the air ducts in your home. Correct the formatting problems and errors in the presentation while keeping in mind the guidelines presented in this chapter.

Perform the following tasks:
1. Change the document theme from Origin, shown in Figure 1–79, to Module.
2. On Slide 1, replace the words, Student Name, with your name. Format your name so that it displays prominently on the slide.
3. Increase the size of the clip on Slide 1 and move it to the upper-right corner.
4. Move Slide 2 to the end of the presentation so that it becomes the new Slide 3.
5. On Slide 2, correct the spelling errors and then increase the font size of the Slide 2 title text, Check Hidden Air Ducts, to 54 point. Increase the size of the clip and move it up to fill the white space on the right of the bulleted list.
6. On Slide 3, correct the spelling errors and then change the font size of the title text, Energy Savings, to 54 point. Increase the indent levels for paragraphs 2 and 4. Increase the size of the clips. Center the furnace clip at the bottom of the slide.
7. Change the document properties, as specified by your instructor. Save the presentation using the file name, Make It Right 1–1 Ducts Presentation.
8. Apply the same transition and duration to all slides.
9. Submit the revised document in the format specified by your instructor.

Make It Right projects call on students to analyze a file, discover errors in it, and fix them using the skills they learned in the chapter.

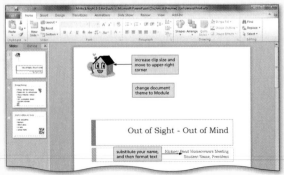

increase clip size and move to upper-right corner

change document theme to Module

Out of Sight - Out of Mind

substitute your name, and then format text

Figure 1–79

PowerPoint Chapter 1

STUDENT ASSIGNMENTS

In the Lab

Design and/or create a presentation using the guidelines, concepts, and skills presented in this chapter. Labs 1, 2, and 3 are listed in order of increasing difficulty.

Lab1: Creating a Presentation with Bulleted Lists, a Closing Slide, and Clips

Problem: You are working with upper-level students to host a freshmen orientation seminar. When you attended this seminar, you received some helpful tips on studying for exams. Your contribution to this year's seminar is to prepare a short presentation on study skills. You develop the outline shown in Figure 1–80 and then prepare the PowerPoint presentation shown in Figures 1–81a through 1–81d.

Studying for an Exam
Freshmen Orientation Seminar
Sarah Jones

Prepare in Advance
Location
Quiet, well-lit
Timing
15-minute breaks every hour
Material
Quiz yourself

Exam Time
Day of Exam
Rest properly
Eat a good meal
Wear comfy clothes
Be early
Be confident

Perform the following tasks:

1. Create a new presentation using the Aspect document theme.
2. Using the typed notes illustrated in Figure 1–80, create the title slide shown in Figure 1–81a, using your name in place of Sarah Jones. Italicize your name and increase the font size to 24 point. Increase the font size of the title text paragraph, Hit the Books, to 48 point. Increase the font size of the first paragraph of the subtitle text, Studying for an Exam, to 28 point.

In the Lab Three all new in-depth assignments per chapter require students to utilize the chapter concepts and techniques to solve problems on a computer.

Cases & Places exercises call on students to create open-ended projects that reflect academic, personal, and business settings.

STUDENT ASSIGNMENTS

Cases and Places

Apply your creative thinking and problem-solving skills to design and implement a solution.

Note: To complete these assignments, you may be required to use the Data Files for Students. See the inside back cover of this book for instructions on downloading the Data Files for Students, or contact your instructor for information about accessing the required files.

As you design the presentations, remember to use the 7 × 7 rule: a maximum of seven words on a line and a maximum of seven lines on one slide.

1: Design and Create a Presentation about Galileo

Academic

Italian-born Galileo is said to be the father of modern science. After the invention of the telescope by a Dutch eyeglass maker named Hans Lippershey, Galileo made his own telescope and made many discoveries. You decide to prepare a PowerPoint presentation to accompany a speech that is required in your Astronomy class. You create the outline shown in Figure 1–88 about Galileo. Use this outline, along with the concepts and techniques presented in this chapter, to develop and format a slide show with a title slide and three text slides with bulleted lists. Add photographs and clip art from the Microsoft Clip Organizer and apply a transition. Submit your assignment in the format specified by your instructor.

Galileo Galilei
Father of Modern Science
Astronomy 201
Sandy Wendt

Major Role in Scientific Revolution
February 15, 1564 - January 8, 1642
Physicist
Mathematician
Astronomer
Philosopher

Galileo's Research Years
1581 - Studied medicine
1589-1592 - Studied math and physics
1592-1607 - Padua University
Developed Law of Inertia
1609 - Built telescope
Earth's moon
Jupiter's moons

Galileo's Later Years
Dialogue - Two Chief World Systems
Controversy develops
1633 - Rome
Heresy trial
Imprisoned
1642 - Dies

Figure 1–88

Office 2010 and Windows 7: Essential Concepts and Skills

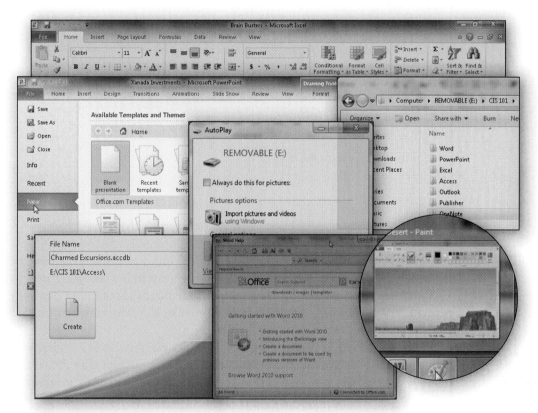

Objectives

You will have mastered the material in this chapter when you can:

- Perform basic mouse operations
- Start Windows and log on to the computer
- Identify the objects on the Windows 7 desktop
- Identify the programs in and versions of Microsoft Office
- Start a program
- Identify the components of the Microsoft Office Ribbon

- Create folders
- Save files
- Change screen resolution
- Perform basic tasks in Microsoft Office programs
- Manage files
- Use Microsoft Office Help and Windows Help

Office 2010 and Windows 7: Essential Concepts and Skills

Office 2010 and Windows 7

This introductory chapter covers features and functions common to Office 2010 programs, as well as the basics of Windows 7.

Overview

As you read this chapter, you will learn how to perform basic tasks in Windows and Office programs by performing these general activities:

- Start programs using Windows.
- Use features common across Office programs.
- Organize files and folders.
- Change screen resolution.
- Quit Office programs.

Introduction to the Windows 7 Operating System

Windows 7 is the newest version of Microsoft Windows, which is the most popular and widely used operating system. An **operating system** is a computer program (set of computer instructions) that coordinates all the activities of computer hardware such as memory, storage devices, and printers, and provides the capability for you to communicate with the computer.

The Windows 7 operating system simplifies the process of working with documents and programs by organizing the manner in which you interact with the computer. Windows 7 is used to run **application software**, which consists of programs designed to make users more productive and/or assist them with personal tasks, such as word processing.

Windows 7 has two interface variations, Windows 7 Basic and Windows 7 Aero. Computers with up to 1 GB of RAM display the Windows 7 Basic interface (Figure 1a). Computers with more than 1 GB of RAM also can display the Windows Aero interface (Figure 1b), which provides an enhanced visual appearance. The Windows 7 Professional, Windows 7 Enterprise, Windows 7 Home Premium, and Windows 7 Ultimate editions have the capability to use Windows Aero.

Using a Mouse

Windows users work with a mouse that has at least two buttons. For a right-handed user, the left button usually is the primary mouse button, and the right mouse button is the secondary mouse button. Left-handed people, however, can reverse the function of these buttons.

Figure 1 (a) Windows 7 Basic interface

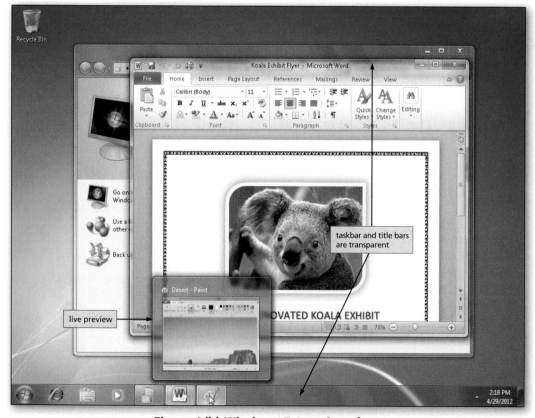

Figure 1 (b) Windows 7 Aero interface

Table 1 explains how to perform a variety of mouse operations. Some programs also use keys in combination with the mouse to perform certain actions. For example, when you hold down the CTRL key while rolling the mouse wheel, text on the screen becomes larger or smaller based on the direction you roll the wheel. The function of the mouse buttons and the wheel varies depending on the program.

Table 1 Mouse Operations		
Operation	Mouse Action	Example*
Point	Move the mouse until the pointer on the desktop is positioned on the item of choice.	Position the pointer on the screen.
Click	Press and release the primary mouse button, which usually is the left mouse button.	Select or deselect items on the screen or start a program or program feature.
Right-click	Press and release the secondary mouse button, which usually is the right mouse button.	Display a shortcut menu.
Double-click	Quickly press and release the left mouse button twice without moving the mouse.	Start a program or program feature.
Triple-click	Quickly press and release the left mouse button three times without moving the mouse.	Select a paragraph.
Drag	Point to an item, hold down the left mouse button, move the item to the desired location on the screen, and then release the left mouse button.	Move an object from one location to another or draw pictures.
Right-drag	Point to an item, hold down the right mouse button, move the item to the desired location on the screen, and then release the right mouse button.	Display a shortcut menu after moving an object from one location to another.
Rotate wheel	Roll the wheel forward or backward.	Scroll vertically (up and down).
Free-spin wheel	Whirl the wheel forward or backward so that it spins freely on its own.	Scroll through many pages in seconds.
Press wheel	Press the wheel button while moving the mouse.	Scroll continuously.
Tilt wheel	Press the wheel toward the right or left.	Scroll horizontally (left and right).
Press thumb button	Press the button on the side of the mouse with your thumb.	Move forward or backward through Web pages and/or control media, games, etc.

*Note: the examples presented in this column are discussed as they are demonstrated in this chapter.

Scrolling

A **scroll bar** is a horizontal or vertical bar that appears when the contents of an area may not be visible completely on the screen (Figure 2). A scroll bar contains **scroll arrows** and a **scroll box** that enable you to view areas that currently cannot be seen. Clicking the up and down scroll arrows moves the screen content up or down one line. You also can click above or below the scroll box to move up or down a section, or drag the scroll box up or down to move up or down to move to a specific location.

Shortcut Keys

In many cases, you can use the keyboard instead of the mouse to accomplish a task. To perform tasks using the keyboard, you press one or more keyboard keys, sometimes identified as

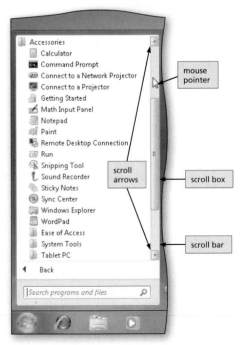

Figure 2

a **shortcut key** or **keyboard shortcut**. Some shortcut keys consist of a single key, such as the F1 key. For example, to obtain help about Windows 7, you can press the F1 key. Other shortcut keys consist of multiple keys, in which case a plus sign separates the key names, such as CTRL+ESC. This notation means to press and hold down the first key listed, press one or more additional keys, and then release all keys. For example, to display the Start menu, press CTRL+ESC, that is, hold down the CTRL key, press the ESC key, and then release both keys.

Starting Windows 7

It is not unusual for multiple people to use the same computer in a work, educational, recreational, or home setting. Windows 7 enables each user to establish a **user account**, which identifies to Windows 7 the resources, such as programs and storage locations, a user can access when working with a computer.

Each user account has a user name and may have a password and an icon, as well. A **user name** is a unique combination of letters or numbers that identifies a specific user to Windows 7. A **password** is a private combination of letters, numbers, and special characters associated with the user name that allows access to a user's account resources. A **user icon** is a picture associated with a user name.

When you turn on a computer, an introductory screen consisting of the Windows logo and copyright messages is displayed. The Windows logo is animated and glows as the Windows 7 operating system is loaded. After the Windows logo appears, depending on your computer's settings, you may or may not be required to log on to the computer. **Logging on** to a computer opens your user account and makes the computer available for use. If you are required to log on to the computer, the **Welcome screen** is displayed, which shows the user names of users on the computer (Figure 3). Clicking the user name or picture begins the process of logging on to the computer.

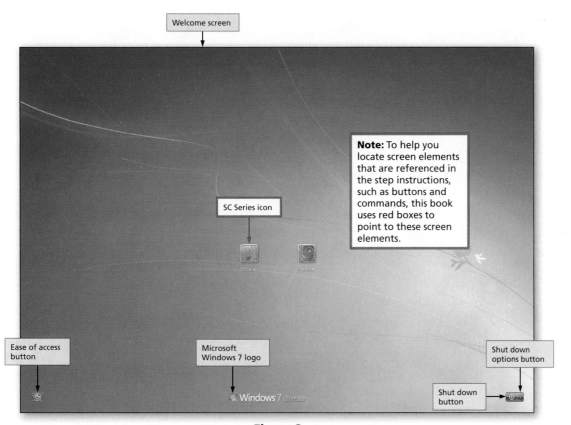

Welcome screen

Note: To help you locate screen elements that are referenced in the step instructions, such as buttons and commands, this book uses red boxes to point to these screen elements.

SC Series icon

Ease of access button

Microsoft Windows 7 logo

Shut down options button

Shut down button

Figure 3

At the bottom of the Welcome screen is the 'Ease of access' button, Windows 7 logo, a Shut down button, and a 'Shut down options' button. The following list identifies the functions of the buttons and commands that typically appear on the Welcome screen:

- Clicking the 'Ease of access' button displays the Ease of Access Center, which provides tools to optimize your computer to accommodate the needs of the mobility, hearing, and vision impaired users.
- Clicking the Shut down button shuts down Windows 7 and the computer.
- Clicking the 'Shut down options' button, located to the right of the Shut down button, provides access to a menu containing commands that perform actions such as restarting the computer, putting the computer in a low-powered state, and shutting down the computer. The commands available on your computer may differ.
  - The **Restart command** closes open programs, shuts down Windows 7, and then restarts Windows 7 and displays the Welcome screen.
  - The **Sleep command** waits for Windows 7 to save your work and then turns off the computer fans and hard disk. To wake the computer from the Sleep state, press the power button or lift a notebook computer's cover, and log on to the computer.
  - The **Shut down command** shuts down and turns off the computer.

To Log On to the Computer

After starting Windows 7, you might need to log on to the computer. The following steps log on to the computer based on a typical installation. You may need to ask your instructor how to log on to your computer. This set of steps uses SC Series as the user name. The list of user names on your computer will be different.

①

- Click the user icon (SC Series, in this case) on the Welcome screen (shown in Figure 3 on the previous page); depending on settings, this either will display a password text box (Figure 4) or will log on to the computer and display the Windows 7 desktop.

Q&A Why do I not see a user icon?

Your computer may require you to type a user name instead of clicking an icon.

Q&A What is a text box?

A text box is a rectangular box in which you type text.

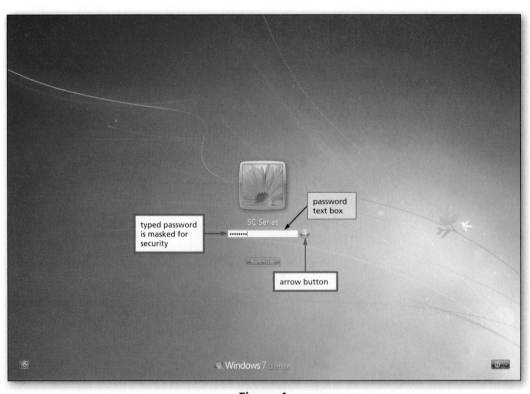

Figure 4

Q&A Why does my screen not show a password text box?

Your account does not require a password.

2

● If Windows 7 displays a password text box, type your password in the text box and then click the arrow button to log on to the computer and display the Windows 7 desktop (Figure 5).

Q&A

Why does my desktop look different from the one in Figure 5?

The Windows 7 desktop is customizable, and your school or employer may have modified the desktop to meet its needs. Also, your screen resolution, which affects the size of the elements on the screen, may differ from the screen resolution used in this book. Later in this chapter, you learn how to change screen resolution.

Figure 5

The Windows 7 Desktop

The Windows 7 desktop (Figure 5) and the objects on the desktop emulate a work area in an office. Think of the Windows desktop as an electronic version of the top of your desk. You can perform tasks such as placing objects on the desktop, moving the objects around the desktop, and removing items from the desktop.

When you start a program in Windows 7, it appears on the desktop. Some icons also may be displayed on the desktop. For instance, the icon for the **Recycle Bin**, the location of files that have been deleted, appears on the desktop by default. A **file** is a named unit of storage. Files can contain text, images, audio, and video. You can customize your desktop so that icons representing programs and files you use often appear on your desktop.

Introduction to Microsoft Office 2010

Microsoft Office 2010 is the newest version of Microsoft Office, offering features that provide users with better functionality and easier ways to work with the various files they create. These features include enhanced design tools, such as improved picture formatting tools and new themes, shared notebooks for working in groups, mobile versions of Office programs, broadcast presentation for the Web, and a digital notebook for managing and sharing multimedia information.

Microsoft Office 2010 Programs

Microsoft Office 2010 includes a wide variety of programs such as Word, PowerPoint, Excel, Access, Outlook, Publisher, OneNote, InfoPath, SharePoint Workspace, Communicator, and Web Apps:

- **Microsoft Word 2010**, or Word, is a full-featured word processing program that allows you to create professional-looking documents and revise them easily.
- **Microsoft PowerPoint 2010**, or PowerPoint, is a complete presentation program that allows you to produce professional-looking presentations.
- **Microsoft Excel 2010**, or Excel, is a powerful spreadsheet program that allows you to organize data, complete calculations, make decisions, graph data, develop professional-looking reports, publish organized data to the Web, and access real-time data from Web sites.
- **Microsoft Access 2010**, or Access, is a database management system that allows you to create a database; add, change, and delete data in the database; ask questions concerning the data in the database; and create forms and reports using the data in the database.
- **Microsoft Outlook 2010**, or Outlook, is a communications and scheduling program that allows you to manage e-mail accounts, calendars, contacts, and access to other Internet content.
- **Microsoft Publisher 2010**, or Publisher, is a desktop publishing program that helps you create professional-quality publications and marketing materials that can be shared easily.
- **Microsoft OneNote 2010**, or OneNote, is a note taking program that allows you to store and share information in notebooks with other people.
- **Microsoft InfoPath 2010**, or InfoPath, is a form development program that helps you create forms for use on the Web and gather data from these forms.
- **Microsoft SharePoint Workspace 2010**, or SharePoint, is collaboration software that allows you access and revise files stored on your computer from other locations.
- **Microsoft Communicator** is communications software that allows you to use different modes of communications such as instant messaging, video conferencing, and sharing files and programs.
- **Microsoft Web Apps** is a Web application that allows you to edit and share files on the Web using the familiar Office interface.

Microsoft Office 2010 Suites

A **suite** is a collection of individual programs available together as a unit. Microsoft offers a variety of Office suites. Table 2 lists the Office 2010 suites and their components.

Programs in a suite, such as Microsoft Office, typically use a similar interface and share features. In addition, Microsoft Office programs use **common dialog boxes** for performing actions such as opening and saving files. Once you are comfortable working with these elements and this interface and performing tasks in one program, the similarity can help you apply the knowledge and skills you have learned to another Office program(s). For example, the process for saving a file in Word is the same in PowerPoint, Excel, and the other Office programs. While briefly showing how to use several Office programs, this chapter illustrates some of the common functions across the programs and also identifies the characteristics unique to these programs.

Table 2 Microsoft Office 2010 Suites	Microsoft Office Professional Plus 2010	Microsoft Office Professional 2010	Microsoft Office Home and Business 2010	Microsoft Office Standard 2010	Microsoft Office Home and Student 2010
Microsoft Word 2010	✔	✔	✔	✔	✔
Microsoft PowerPoint 2010	✔	✔	✔	✔	✔
Microsoft Excel 2010	✔	✔	✔	✔	✔
Microsoft Access 2010	✔	✔	✗	✗	✗
Microsoft Outlook 2010	✔	✔	✔	✔	✗
Microsoft Publisher 2010	✔	✔	✗	✔	✗
Microsoft OneNote 2010	✔	✔	✔	✔	✔
Microsoft InfoPath 2010	✔	✗	✗	✗	✗
Microsoft SharePoint Workspace 2010	✔	✗	✗	✗	✗
Microsoft Communicator	✔	✗	✗	✗	✗

Starting and Using a Program

To use a program, you must instruct the operating system to start the program. Windows 7 provides many different ways to start a program, one of which is presented in this section (other ways to start a program are presented throughout this chapter). After starting a program, you can use it to perform a variety of tasks. The following pages use Word to discuss some elements of the Office interface and to perform tasks that are common to other Office programs.

Word

Word is a full-featured word processing program that allows you to create many types of personal and business documents, including flyers, letters, memos, resumes, reports, fax cover sheets, mailing labels, and newsletters. Word also provides tools that enable you to create Web pages and save these Web pages directly on a Web server. Word has many features designed to simplify the production of documents and add visual appeal. Using Word, you easily can change the shape, size, and color of text. You also can include borders, shading, tables, images, pictures, charts, and Web addresses in documents.

To Start a Program Using the Start Menu

Across the bottom of the Windows 7 desktop is the taskbar. The taskbar contains the **Start button**, which you use to access programs, files, folders, and settings on a computer. A **folder** is a named location on a storage medium that usually contains related documents. The taskbar also displays a button for each program currently running on a computer.

Clicking the Start button displays the Start menu. The **Start menu** allows you to access programs, folders, and files on the computer and contains commands that allow you to start programs, store and search for documents, customize the computer, and obtain help about thousands of topics. A **menu** is a list of related items, including folders, programs, and commands. Each **command** on a menu performs a specific action, such as saving a file or obtaining help.

The following steps, which assume Windows 7 is running, use the Start menu to start an Office program based on a typical installation. You may need to ask your instructor how to start Office programs for your computer. Although the steps illustrate starting the Word program, the steps to start any Office program are similar.

1
- Click the Start button on the Windows 7 taskbar to display the Start menu (Figure 6).

Q&A Why does my Start menu look different?

It may look different depending on your computer's configuration. The Start menu may be customized for several reasons, such as usage requirements or security restrictions.

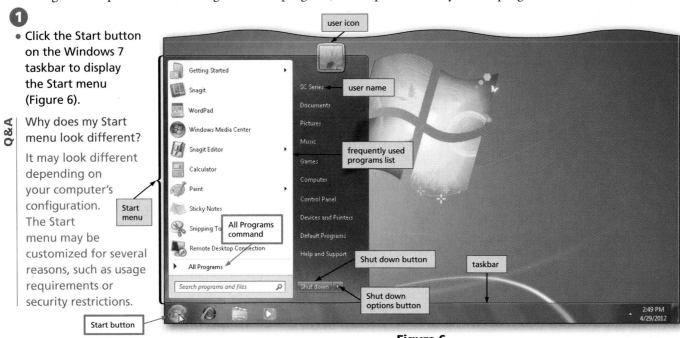

Figure 6

2
- Click All Programs at the bottom of the left pane on the Start menu to display the All Programs list (Figure 7).

Q&A What is a pane?

A **pane** is an area of a window that displays related content. For example, the left pane on the Start menu contains a list of frequently used programs, as well as the All Programs command.

Q&A Why might my All Programs list look different?

Most likely, the programs installed on your computer will differ from those shown in Figure 7. Your All Programs list will show the programs that are installed on your computer.

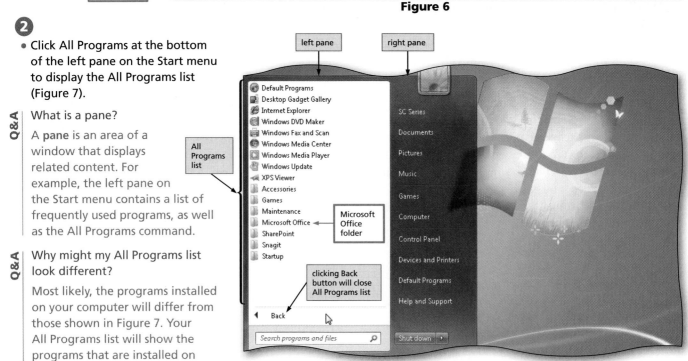

Figure 7

3

- If the program you wish to start is located in a folder, click or scroll to and then click the folder (Microsoft Office, in this case) in the All Programs list to display a list of the folder's contents (Figure 8).

Q&A

Why is the Microsoft Office folder on my computer?

During installation of Microsoft Office 2010, the Microsoft Office folder was added to the All Programs list.

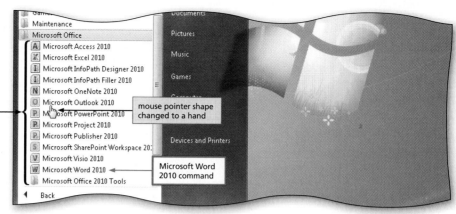

Figure 8

4

- Click, or scroll to and then click, the program name (Microsoft Word 2010, in this case) in the list to start the selected program (Figure 9).

Q&A

What happens when you start a program?

Many programs initially display a blank document in a program window, as shown in the Word window in Figure 9; others provide a means for you to create a blank document. A **window** is a rectangular area that displays data and information. The top of a window has a **title bar**, which is a horizontal space that contains the window's name.

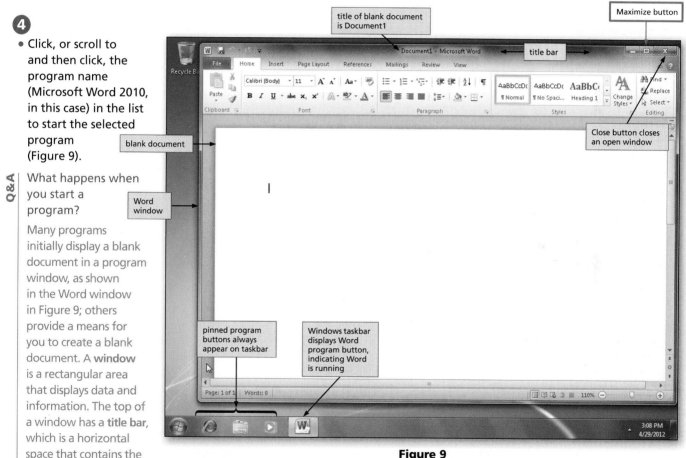

Figure 9

Q&A

Why is my program window a different size?

The Word window shown in Figure 9 is not maximized. Your Word window already may be maximized. The next steps maximize a window.

Other Ways	
1. Double-click program icon on desktop, if one is present	3. Display Start menu, type program name in search box, click program name
2. Click program name in left pane of Start menu, if present	4. Double-click file created using program you want to start

To Maximize a Window

Sometimes content is not visible completely in a window. One method of displaying the entire contents of a window is to **maximize** it, or enlarge the window so that it fills the entire screen. The following step maximizes the Word window; however, any Office program's window can be maximized using this step.

1

- If the program window is not maximized already, click the Maximize button (shown in Figure 9 on the previous page) next to the Close button on the window's title bar (the Word window title bar, in this case) to maximize the window (Figure 10).

Q&A What happened to the Maximize button?

It changed to a Restore Down button, which you can use to return a window to its size and location before you maximized it.

Q&A How do I know whether a window is maximized?

A window is maximized if it fills the entire display area and the Restore Down button is displayed on the title bar.

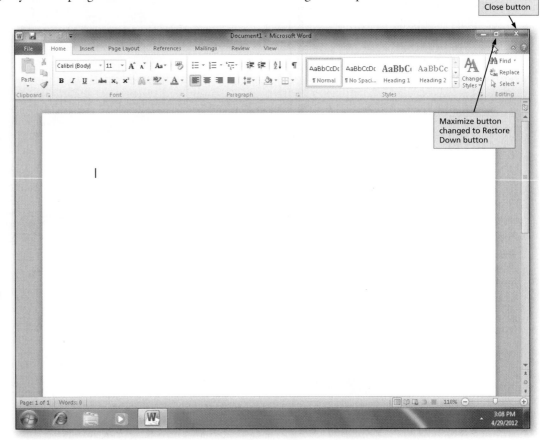

Close button

Maximize button changed to Restore Down button

Figure 10

Other Ways

1. Double-click title bar
2. Drag title bar to top of screen

The Word Document Window, Ribbon, and Elements Common to Office Programs

The Word window consists of a variety of components to make your work more efficient and documents more professional. These include the document window, Ribbon, Mini toolbar, shortcut menus, and Quick Access Toolbar. Most of these components are common to other Microsoft Office 2010 programs; others are unique to Word.

You view a portion of a document on the screen through a **document window** (Figure 11). The default (preset) view is **Print Layout view**, which shows the document on a mock sheet of paper in the document window.

Scroll Bars You use a scroll bar to display different portions of a document in the document window. At the right edge of the document window is a vertical scroll bar. If a document is too wide to fit in the document window, a horizontal scroll bar also appears at the bottom of the document window. On a scroll bar, the position of the scroll box reflects the location of the portion of the document that is displayed in the document window.

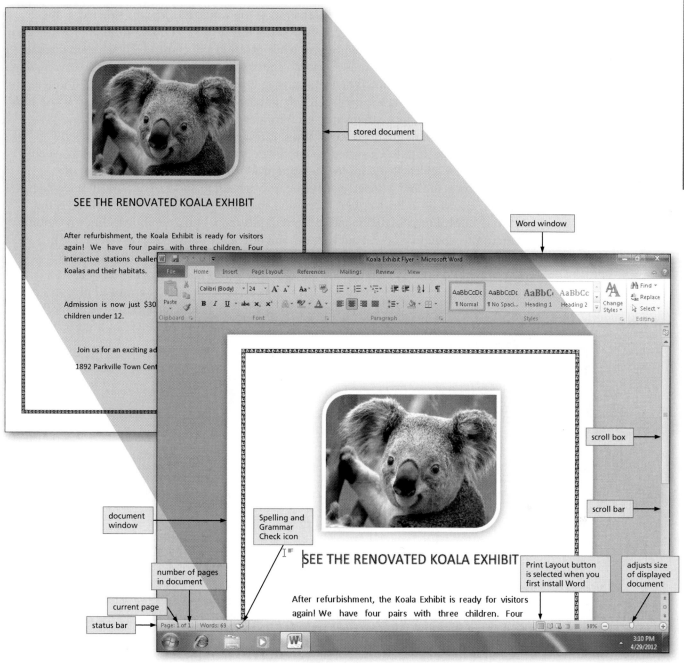

Figure 11

Status Bar   The **status bar**, located at the bottom of the document window above the Windows 7 taskbar, presents information about the document, the progress of current tasks, and the status of certain commands and keys; it also provides controls for viewing the document. As you type text or perform certain tasks, various indicators and buttons may appear on the status bar.

The left side of the status bar in Figure 11 shows the current page followed by the total number of pages in the document, the number of words in the document, and an icon to check spelling and grammar. The right side of the status bar includes buttons and controls you can use to change the view of a document and adjust the size of the displayed document.

Ribbon The Ribbon, located near the top of the window below the title bar, is the control center in Word and other Office programs (Figure 12). The Ribbon provides easy, central access to the tasks you perform while creating a document. The Ribbon consists of tabs, groups, and commands. Each **tab** contains a collection of groups, and each **group** contains related functions. When you start an Office program, such as Word, it initially displays several main tabs, also called default tabs. All Office programs have a **Home tab**, which contains the more frequently used commands.

In addition to the main tabs, Office programs display **tool tabs**, also called contextual tabs (Figure 13), when you perform certain tasks or work with objects such as pictures or tables. If you insert a picture in a Word document, for example, the Picture Tools tab and its related subordinate Format tab appear, collectively referred to as the Picture Tools Format tab. When you are finished working with the picture, the Picture Tools Format tab disappears from the Ribbon. Word and other Office programs determine when tool tabs should appear and disappear based on tasks you perform. Some tool tabs, such as the Table Tools tab, have more than one related subordinate tab.

Items on the Ribbon include buttons, boxes (text boxes, check boxes, etc.), and galleries (Figure 12). A **gallery** is a set of choices, often graphical, arranged in a grid or in a list. You can scroll through choices in an in-Ribbon gallery by clicking the gallery's scroll arrows. Or, you can click a gallery's More button to view more gallery options on the screen at a time.

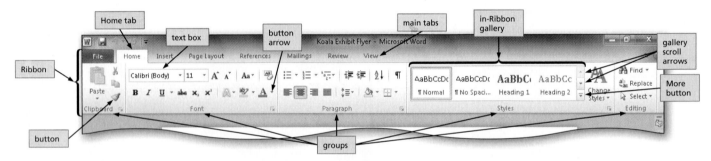

Figure 12

Some buttons and boxes have arrows that, when clicked, also display a gallery; others always cause a gallery to be displayed when clicked. Most galleries support **live preview**, which is a feature that allows you to point to a gallery choice and see its effect in the document — without actually selecting the choice (Figure 13).

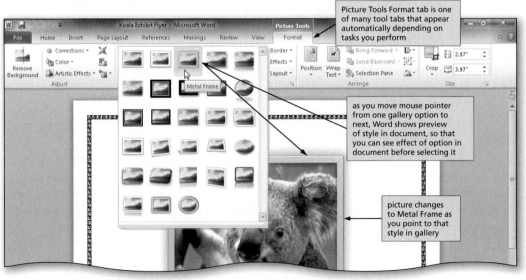

Figure 13

Some commands on the Ribbon display an image to help you remember their function. When you point to a command on the Ribbon, all or part of the command glows in shades of yellow and orange, and an Enhanced ScreenTip appears on the screen. An **Enhanced ScreenTip** is an on-screen note that provides the name of the command, available keyboard shortcut(s), a description of the command, and sometimes instructions for how to obtain help about the command (Figure 14). Enhanced ScreenTips are more detailed than a typical ScreenTip, which usually displays only the name of the command.

Some groups on the Ribbon have a small arrow in the lower-right corner, called a **Dialog Box Launcher**, that when clicked, displays a dialog box or a task pane with additional options for the group (Figure 15). When presented with a dialog box, you make selections and must close the dialog box before returning to the document. A **task pane**, in contrast to a dialog box, is a window that can remain open and visible while you work in the document.

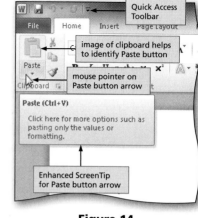

Figure 14

Mini Toolbar   The **Mini toolbar**, which appears automatically based on tasks you perform, contains commands related to changing the appearance of text in a document. All commands on the Mini toolbar also exist on the Ribbon. The purpose of the Mini toolbar is to minimize mouse movement.

When the Mini toolbar appears, it initially is transparent (Figure 16a). If you do not use the transparent Mini toolbar, it disappears from the screen. To use the Mini toolbar, move the mouse pointer into the toolbar, which causes the Mini toolbar to change

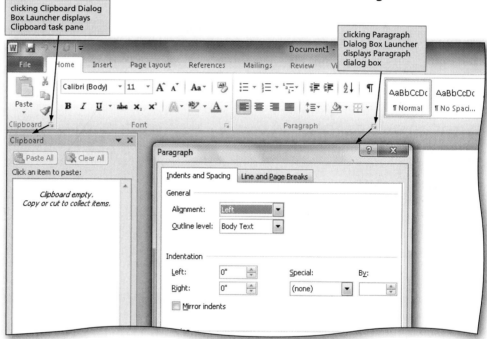

Figure 15

from a transparent to bright appearance (Figure 16b). If you right-click an item in the document window, Word displays both the Mini toolbar and a shortcut menu, which is discussed in a later section in this chapter.

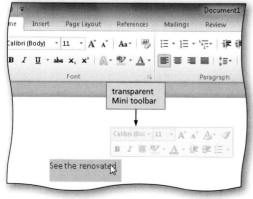

(a) transparent Mini toolbar

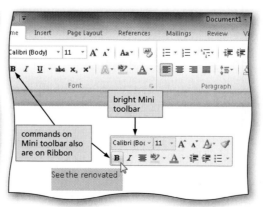

(b) bright Mini toolbar

Figure 16

BTW

Turning Off the Mini Toolbar
If you do not want the Mini toolbar to appear, click File on the Ribbon to open the Backstage view, click Options in the Backstage view, click General (Options dialog box), remove the check mark from the Show Mini Toolbar on selection check box, and then click the OK button.

Quick Access Toolbar   The **Quick Access Toolbar**, located initially (by default) above the Ribbon at the left edge of the title bar, provides convenient, one-click access to frequently used commands (Figure 14 on the previous page). The commands on the Quick Access Toolbar always are available, regardless of the task you are performing. The Quick Access Toolbar is discussed in more depth later in the chapter.

KeyTips   If you prefer using the keyboard instead of the mouse, you can press the ALT key on the keyboard to display **KeyTips**, or keyboard code icons, for certain commands (Figure 17). To select a command using the keyboard, press the letter or number displayed in the KeyTip, which may cause additional KeyTips related to the selected command to appear. To remove KeyTips from the screen, press the ALT key or the ESC key until all KeyTips disappear, or click the mouse anywhere in the program window.

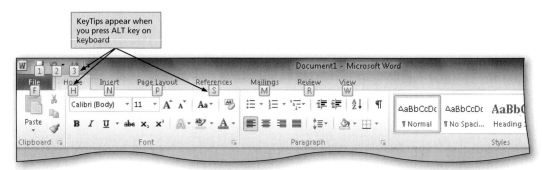

Figure 17

To Display a Different Tab on the Ribbon

When you start Word, the Ribbon displays eight main tabs: File, Home, Insert, Page Layout, References, Mailings, Review, and View. The tab currently displayed is called the **active tab**.

The following step displays the Insert tab, that is, makes it the active tab.

1

• Click Insert on the Ribbon to display the Insert tab (Figure 18).

 Experiment

• Click the other tabs on the Ribbon to view their contents. When you are finished, click the Insert tab to redisplay the Insert tab.

 If I am working in a different Office program, such as PowerPoint or Access, how do I display a different tab on the Ribbon?

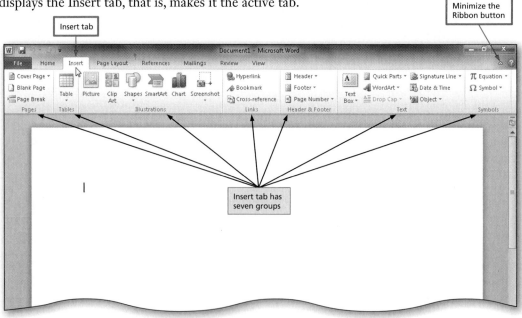

Figure 18

Follow this same procedure; that is, click the desired tab on the Ribbon.

To Minimize, Display, and Restore the Ribbon

To display more of a document or other item in the window of an Office program, some users prefer to minimize the Ribbon, which hides the groups on the Ribbon and displays only the main tabs. Each time you start an Office program, the Ribbon appears the same way it did the last time you used that Office program. The chapters in this book, however, begin with the Ribbon appearing as it did at the initial installation of the software.

The following steps minimize, display, and restore the Ribbon in an Office program.

- Click the Minimize the Ribbon button on the Ribbon (shown in Figure 18) to minimize the Ribbon (Figure 19).

Q&A

What happened to the groups on the Ribbon?

When you minimize the Ribbon, the groups disappear so that the Ribbon does not take up as much space on the screen.

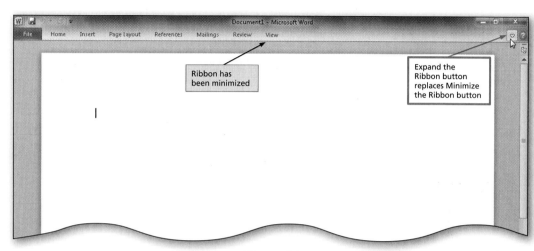

Figure 19

Q&A

What happened to the Minimize the Ribbon button?

The Expand the Ribbon button replaces the Minimize the Ribbon button when the Ribbon is minimized.

- Click Home on the Ribbon to display the Home tab (Figure 20).

Q&A

Why would I click the Home tab?

If you want to use a command on a minimized Ribbon, click the main tab to display the groups for that tab. After you select a command on the Ribbon, the groups will be hidden once again. If you decide not to use a command on the Ribbon, you can hide the groups by clicking the same main tab or clicking in the program window.

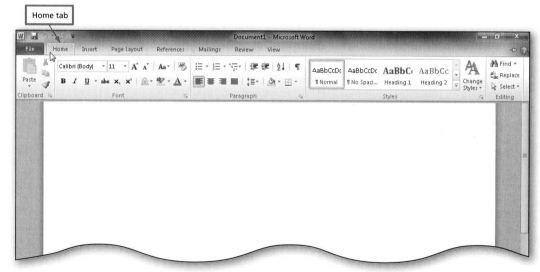

Figure 20

- Click Home on the Ribbon to hide the groups again (shown in Figure 19).
- Click the Expand the Ribbon button on the Ribbon (shown in Figure 19) to restore the Ribbon.

Other Ways

1. Double-click Home on the Ribbon
2. Press CTRL+F1

To Display and Use a Shortcut Menu

When you right-click certain areas of the Word and other program windows, a shortcut menu will appear. A **shortcut menu** is a list of frequently used commands that relate to the right-clicked object. When you right-click a scroll bar, for example, a shortcut menu appears with commands related to the scroll bar. When you right-click the Quick Access Toolbar, a shortcut menu appears with commands related to the Quick Access Toolbar. You can use shortcut menus to access common commands quickly. The following steps use a shortcut menu to move the Quick Access Toolbar, which by default is located on the title bar.

- Right-click the Quick Access Toolbar to display a shortcut menu that presents a list of commands related to the Quick Access Toolbar (Figure 21).

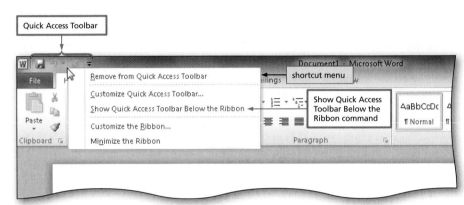

Figure 21

- Click Show Quick Access Toolbar Below the Ribbon on the shortcut menu to display the Quick Access Toolbar below the Ribbon (Figure 22).

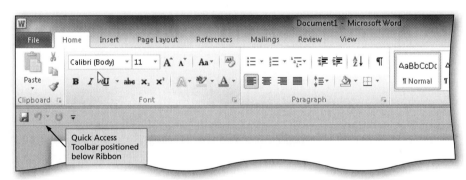

Figure 22

- Right-click the Quick Access Toolbar to display a shortcut menu (Figure 23).

- Click Show Quick Access Toolbar Above the Ribbon on the shortcut menu to return the Quick Access Toolbar to its original position (shown in Figure 21).

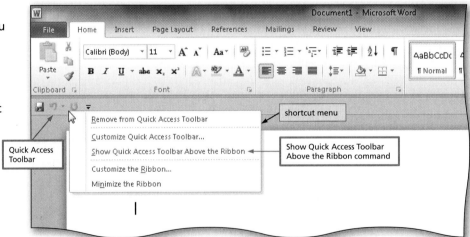

Figure 23

To Customize the Quick Access Toolbar

The Quick Access Toolbar provides easy access to some of the more frequently used commands in Office programs. By default, the Quick Access Toolbar contains buttons for the Save, Undo, and Redo commands. You can customize the Quick Access Toolbar by changing its location in the window, as shown in the previous steps, and by adding more buttons to reflect commands you would like to access easily. The following steps add the Quick Print button to the Quick Access Toolbar.

1

- Click the Customize Quick Access Toolbar button to display the Customize Quick Access Toolbar menu (Figure 24).

Q&A Which commands are listed on the Customize Quick Access Toolbar menu?

It lists commands that commonly are added to the Quick Access Toolbar.

Q&A What do the check marks next to some commands signify?

Check marks appear next to commands that already are on the Quick Access Toolbar. When you add a button to the Quick Access Toolbar, a check mark will be displayed next to its command name.

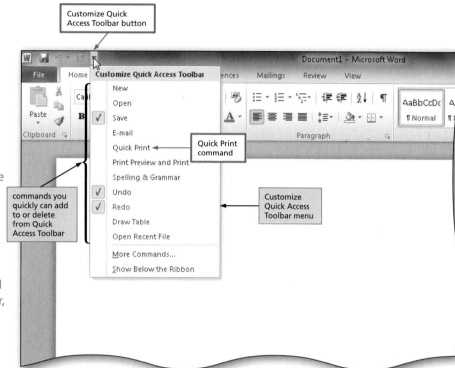

Figure 24

2

- Click Quick Print on the Customize Quick Access Toolbar menu to add the Quick Print button to the Quick Access Toolbar (Figure 25).

Q&A How would I remove a button from the Quick Access Toolbar?

You would right-click the button you wish to remove and then click Remove from Quick Access Toolbar on the shortcut menu.

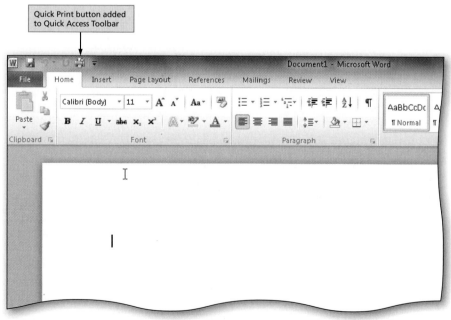

Figure 25

To Enter Text in a Document

The first step in creating a document is to enter its text by typing on the keyboard. By default, Word positions text at the left margin as you type. To begin creating a flyer, for example, you type the headline in the document window. The following steps type this first line of text, a headline, in a document.

1

- Type **SEE THE RENOVATED KOALA EXHIBIT** as the text (Figure 26).

Q&A What is the blinking vertical bar to the right of the text?

The insertion point. It indicates where text, graphics, and other items will be inserted in the document. As you type, the insertion point moves to the right, and when you reach the end of a line, it moves downward to the beginning of the next line.

Q&A What if I make an error while typing?

You can press the BACKSPACE key until you have deleted the text in error and then retype the text correctly.

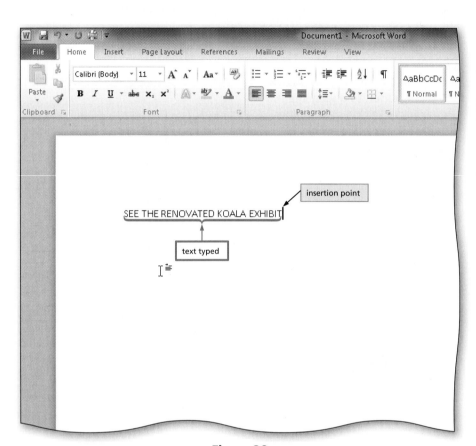

Figure 26

2

- Press the ENTER key to move the insertion point to the beginning of the next line (Figure 27).

Q&A Why did blank space appear between the entered text and the insertion point?

Each time you press the ENTER key, Word creates a new paragraph and inserts blank space between the two paragraphs.

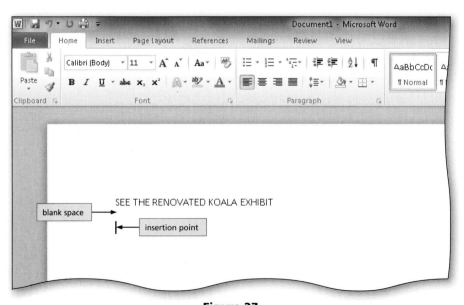

Figure 27

Saving and Organizing Files

While you are creating a document, the computer stores it in memory. When you save a document, the computer places it on a storage medium such as a hard disk, USB flash drive, or optical disc. A saved document is referred to as a file. A **file name** is the name assigned to a file when it is saved. It is important to save a document frequently for the following reasons:

- The document in memory might be lost if the computer is turned off or you lose electrical power while a program is running.
- If you run out of time before completing a project, you may finish it at a future time without starting over.

When saving files, you should organize them so that you easily can find them later. Windows 7 provides tools to help you organize files.

BTW

File Type
Depending on your Windows 7 settings, the file type .docx may be displayed immediately to the right of the file name after you save the file. The file type .docx is a Word 2010 document.

Organizing Files and Folders

A file contains data. This data can range from a research paper to an accounting spreadsheet to an electronic math quiz. You should organize and store these files in folders to avoid misplacing a file and to help you find a file quickly.

If you are a freshman taking an introductory computer class (CIS 101, for example), you may want to design a series of folders for the different subjects covered in the class. To accomplish this, you can arrange the folders in a hierarchy for the class, as shown in Figure 28.

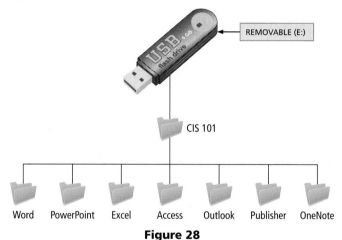

Figure 28

The hierarchy contains three levels. The first level contains the storage device, in this case a USB flash drive. Windows 7 identifies the storage device with a letter, and, in some cases, a name. In Figure 28, the USB flash drive is identified as REMOVABLE (E:). The second level contains the class folder (CIS 101, in this case), and the third level contains seven folders, one each for a different Office program that will be covered in the class (Word, PowerPoint, Excel, Access, Outlook, Publisher, and OneNote).

When the hierarchy in Figure 28 is created, the USB flash drive is said to contain the CIS 101 folder, and the CIS 101 folder is said to contain the separate Office folders (i.e., Word, PowerPoint, Excel, etc.). In addition, this hierarchy easily can be expanded to include folders from other classes taken during additional semesters.

The vertical and horizontal lines in Figure 28 form a pathway that allows you to navigate to a drive or folder on a computer or network. A **path** consists of a drive letter (preceded by a drive name when necessary) and colon, to identify the storage device, and one or more folder names. Each drive or folder in the hierarchy has a corresponding path.

BTW

Saving Online
Instead of saving files on a USB flash drive, some people prefer to save them online so that they can access the files from any computer with an Internet connection. For more information, read Appendix C.

Table 3 shows examples of paths and their corresponding drives and folders.

Table 3 Paths and Corresponding Drives and Folders	
Path	**Drive and Folder**
Computer ▶ REMOVABLE (E:)	Drive E (REMOVABLE (E:))
Computer ▶ REMOVABLE (E:) ▶ CIS 101	CIS 101 folder on drive E
Computer ▶ REMOVABLE (E:) ▶ CIS 101 ▶ Word	Word folder in CIS 101 folder on drive E

The following pages illustrate the steps to organize the folders for this class and save a file in one of those folders:

1. Create the folder identifying your class.
2. Create the Word folder in the folder identifying your class.
3. Create the remaining folders in the folder identifying your class (one each for PowerPoint, Excel, Access, Outlook, Publisher, and OneNote).
4. Save a file in the Word folder.
5. Verify the location of the saved file.

To Create a Folder

When you create a folder, such as the CIS 101 folder shown in Figure 28 on the previous page, you must name the folder. A folder name should describe the folder and its contents. A folder name can contain spaces and any uppercase or lowercase characters, except a backslash (\), slash (/), colon (:), asterisk (*), question mark (?), quotation marks ("), less than symbol (<), greater than symbol (>), or vertical bar (|). Folder names cannot be CON, AUX, COM1, COM2, COM3, COM4, LPT1, LPT2, LPT3, PRN, or NUL. The same rules for naming folders also apply to naming files.

To store files and folders on a USB flash drive, you must connect the USB flash drive to an available USB port on a computer. The following steps create your class folder (CIS 101, in this case) on a USB flash drive.

1

- Connect the USB flash drive to an available USB port on the computer to open the AutoPlay window (Figure 29).

Q&A Why does the AutoPlay window not open?

Some computers are not configured to open an AutoPlay window. Instead, they might display the contents of the USB flash drive automatically, or you might need to access contents of the USB flash drive using the Computer window. To use the Computer window to display the USB flash drive's contents, click the Start button, click Computer on the Start menu, and then click the icon representing the USB flash drive.

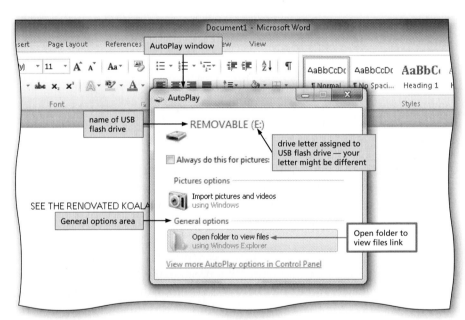

Figure 29

Q&A Why does the AutoPlay window look different from the one in Figure 29?

The AutoPlay window that opens on your computer might display different options. The type of USB flash drive, its contents, and the next available drive letter on your computer all will determine which options are displayed in the AutoPlay window.

2

- Click the 'Open folder to view files' link in the AutoPlay window to open the USB flash drive window (Figure 30).

Q&A

Why does Figure 30 show REMOVABLE (E:) for the USB flash drive?

REMOVABLE is the name of the USB flash drive used to illustrate these steps. The (E:) refers to the drive letter assigned by Windows 7 to the USB flash drive. The name and drive letter of your USB flash drive probably will be different.

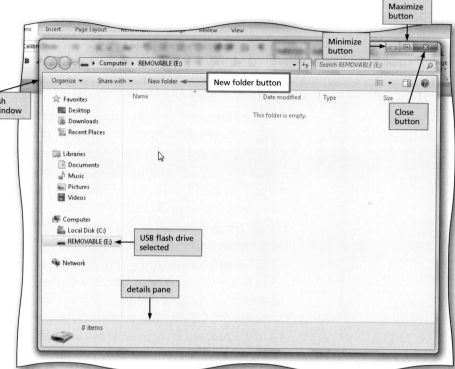

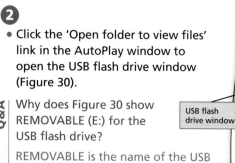

Figure 30

3

- Click the New folder button on the toolbar to display a new folder icon with the name, New folder, selected in a text box.

- Type **CIS 101** (or your class code) in the text box to name the folder.

- Press the ENTER key to create a folder identifying your class on the selected drive (Figure 31). If the CIS 101 folder does not appear in the navigation pane, double-click REMOVABLE (E:) in the navigation pane to display the folder just added.

Q&A

What happens when I press the ENTER key?

The class folder (CIS 101, in this case) is displayed in the File list, which contains the folder name, date modified, type, and size.

Q&A

Why is the folder icon displayed differently on my computer?

Windows might be configured to display contents differently on your computer.

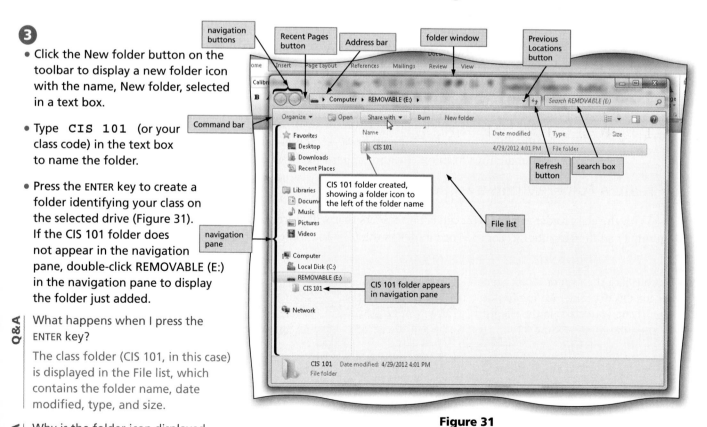

Figure 31

Folder Windows

The USB flash drive window (shown in Figure 31 on the previous page) is called a folder window. Recall that a folder is a specific named location on a storage medium that contains related files. Most users rely on **folder windows** for finding, viewing, and managing information on their computer. Folder windows have common design elements, including the following (Figure 31).

- The **Address bar** provides quick navigation options. The arrows on the Address bar allow you to visit different locations on the computer.
- The buttons to the left of the Address bar allow you to navigate the contents of the left pane and view recent pages. Other buttons allow you to specify the size of the window.
- The **Previous Locations button** saves the locations you have visited and displays the locations when clicked.
- The **Refresh button** on the right side of the Address bar refreshes the contents of the right pane of the folder window.
- The **search box** to the right of the Address bar contains the dimmed word, Search. You can type a term in the search box for a list of files, folders, shortcuts, and elements containing that term within the location you are searching. A **shortcut** is an icon on the desktop that provides a user with immediate access to a program or file.
- The **Command bar** contains five buttons used to accomplish various tasks on the computer related to organizing and managing the contents of the open window.
- The **navigation pane** on the left contains the Favorites area, Libraries area, Computer area, and Network area.
- The **Favorites area** contains links to your favorite locations. By default, this list contains only links to your Desktop, Downloads, and Recent Places.
- The **Libraries area** shows links to files and folders that have been included in a library.

A **library** helps you manage multiple folders and files stored in various locations on a computer. It does not store the files and folders; rather, it displays links to them so that you can access them quickly. For example, you can save pictures from a digital camera in any folder on any storage location on a computer. Normally, this would make organizing the different folders difficult; however, if you add the folders to a library, you can access all the pictures from one location regardless of where they are stored.

To Create a Folder within a Folder

With the class folder created, you can create folders that will store the files you create using each Office program. The following steps create a Word folder in the CIS 101 folder (or the folder identifying your class).

- Double-click the icon or folder name for the CIS 101 folder (or the folder identifying your class) in the File list to open the folder (Figure 32).

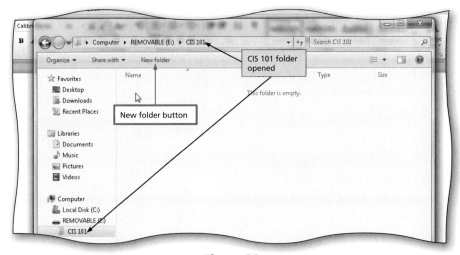

Figure 32

2

- Click the New folder button on the toolbar to display a new folder icon and text box for the folder.

- Type **Word** in the text box to name the folder.

- Press the ENTER key to create the folder (Figure 33).

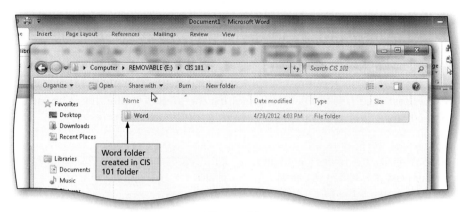

Figure 33

To Create the Remaining Folders

The following steps create the remaining folders in the folder identifying your class (in this case, CIS 101).

1 Click the New folder button on the toolbar to display a new folder icon and text box.

2 Type **PowerPoint** in the text box to name the folder.

3 Repeat Steps 1 and 2 to create each of the remaining folders, using the names Excel, Access, Outlook, Publisher, and OneNote as the folder names (Figure 34).

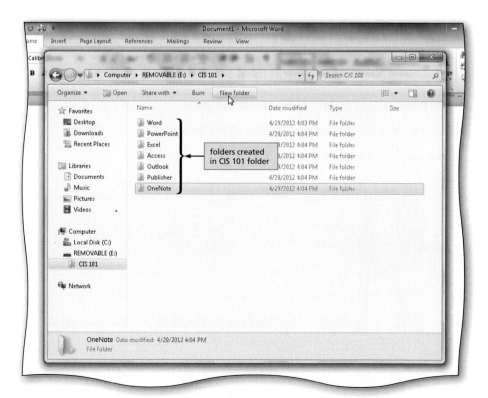

Figure 34

To Expand a Folder, Scroll through Folder Contents, and Collapse a Folder

Folder windows display the hierarchy of items and the contents of drives and folders in the right pane. You might want to expand a drive in the navigation pane to view its contents, scroll through its contents, and collapse it when you are finished viewing its contents. When a folder is expanded, it lists all the folders it contains. By contrast, a collapsed folder does not list the folders it contains. The following steps expand, scroll through, and then collapse the folder identifying your class (CIS 101, in this case).

1

- Double-click the folder identifying your class (CIS 101, in this case), which expands the folder to display its contents and displays a black arrow to the left of the folder icon (Figure 35).

Q&A Why are the subject folders indented below the CIS 101 folder in the navigation pane?

It shows that the folders are contained within the CIS 101 folder.

Q&A Why did a scroll bar appear in the navigation pane?

When all contents cannot fit in a window or pane, a scroll bar appears. As described earlier, you can view areas currently not visible by (1) clicking the scroll arrows, (2) clicking above or below the scroll bar, and (3) dragging the scroll box.

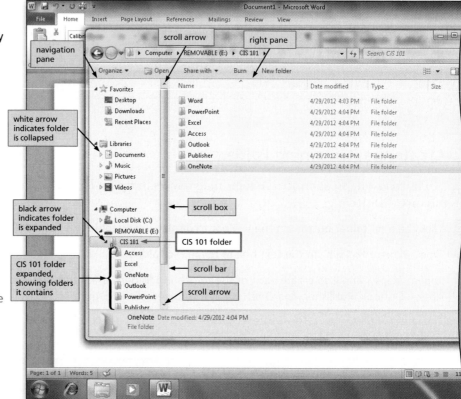

Figure 35

 Experiment

- Click the down scroll arrow on the vertical scroll bar to display additional folders at the bottom of the navigation pane.

- Click the scroll bar above the scroll box to move the scroll box to the top of the navigation pane.

- Drag the scroll box down the scroll bar until the scroll box is halfway down the scroll bar.

2

- Double-click the folder identifying your class (CIS 101, in this case) to collapse the folder (Figure 36).

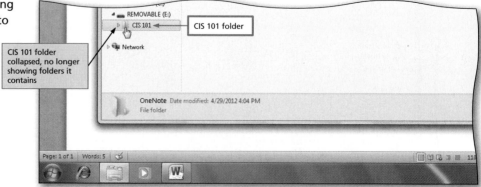

Figure 36

Other Ways

1. Point in navigation pane to display arrows, click white arrow to expand or click black arrow to collapse

2. Select folder to expand or collapse using arrow keys, press RIGHT ARROW to expand; press LEFT ARROW to collapse.

To Switch from One Program to Another

The next step is to save the Word file containing the headline you typed earlier. Word, however, currently is not the active window. You can use the program button on the taskbar and live preview to switch to Word and then save the document in the Word document window.

If Windows Aero is active on your computer, Windows displays a live preview window whenever you move your mouse on a button or click a button on the taskbar. If Aero is not supported or enabled on your computer, you will see a window title instead of a live preview. The steps below use the Word program; however, the steps are the same for any active Office program currently displayed as a program button on the taskbar.

The following steps switch to the Word window.

1

• Point to the Word program button on the taskbar to see a live preview of the open document(s) or the window title(s) of the open document(s), depending on your computer's configuration (Figure 37).

2

• Click the program button or the live preview to make the program associated with the program button the active window (shown in Figure 27 on page OFF 20).

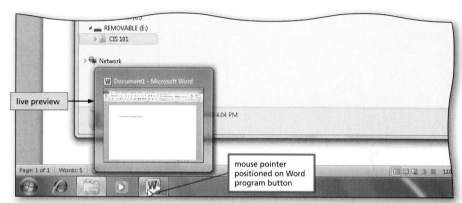

Figure 37

Q&A
What if multiple documents are open in a program?

If Aero is enabled on your computer, click the desired live preview. If Aero is not supported or not enabled, click the window title.

To Save a File in a Folder

Now that you have created the folders for storing files, you can save the Word document. The following steps save a file on a USB flash drive in the Word folder contained in your class folder (CIS 101, in this case) using the file name, Koala Exhibit.

1

• With a USB flash drive connected to one of the computer's USB ports, click the Save button on the Quick Access Toolbar to display the Save As dialog box (Figure 38).

Q&A
Why does a file name already appear in the File name text box?

Word automatically suggests a file name the first time you save a document. The file name normally consists of the first few words contained in the document. Because the suggested file name is selected, you do not need to delete it; as soon as you begin typing, the new file name replaces the selected text.

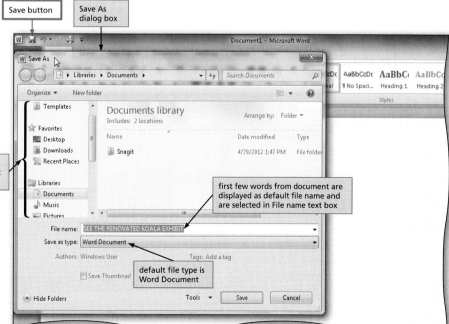

Figure 38

• Type **Koala Exhibit** in the File name text box (Save As dialog box) to change the file name. Do not press the ENTER key after typing the file name because you do not want to close the dialog box at this time (Figure 39).

Q&A

What characters can I use in a file name?

The only invalid characters are the backslash (\), slash (/), colon (:), asterisk (*), question mark (?), quotation mark ("), less than symbol (<), greater than symbol (>), and vertical bar (|).

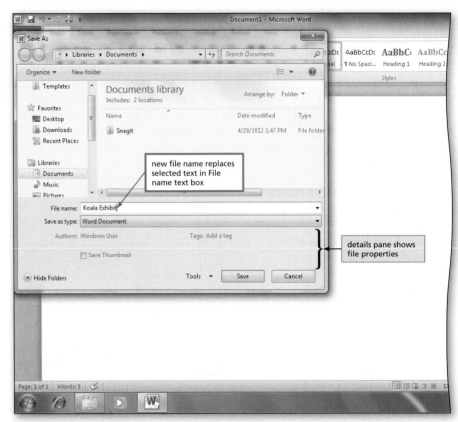

Figure 39

• Navigate to the desired save location (in this case, the Word folder in the CIS 101 folder [or your class folder] on the USB flash drive) by performing the tasks in Steps 3a, 3b, and 3c.

• If the navigation pane is not displayed in the dialog box, click the Browse Folders button to expand the dialog box.

• If Computer is not displayed in the navigation pane, drag the navigation pane scroll bar until Computer appears.

• If Computer is not expanded in the navigation pane, double-click Computer to display a list of available storage devices in the navigation pane.

• If necessary, scroll through the dialog box until your USB flash drive appears in the list of available storage devices in the navigation pane (Figure 40).

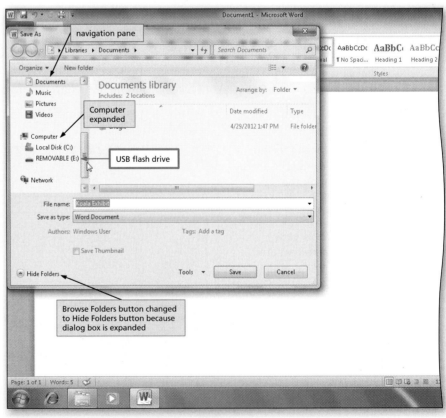

Figure 40

- If your USB flash drive is not expanded, double-click the USB flash drive in the list of available storage devices in the navigation pane to select that drive as the new save location and display its contents in the right pane.

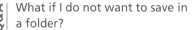

- If your class folder (CIS 101, in this case) is not expanded, double-click the CIS 101 folder to select the folder and display its contents in the right pane.

Q&A

What if I do not want to save in a folder?

Although storing files in folders is an effective technique for organizing files, some users prefer not to store files in folders. If you prefer not to save this file in a folder, skip all instructions in Step 3c and proceed to Step 4.

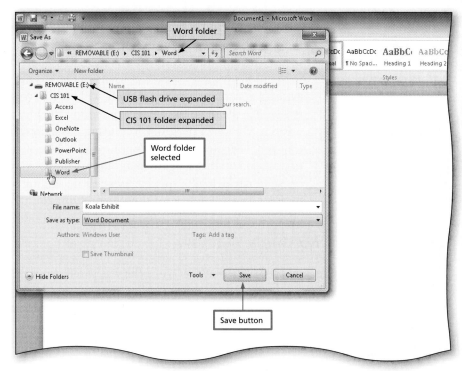

Figure 41

- Click the Word folder to select the folder and display its contents in the right pane (Figure 41).

- Click the Save button (Save As dialog box) to save the document in the selected folder on the selected drive with the entered file name (Figure 42).

Q&A

How do I know that the file is saved?

While an Office program is saving a file, it briefly displays a message on the status bar indicating the amount of the file saved. In addition, the USB flash drive may have a light that flashes during the save process.

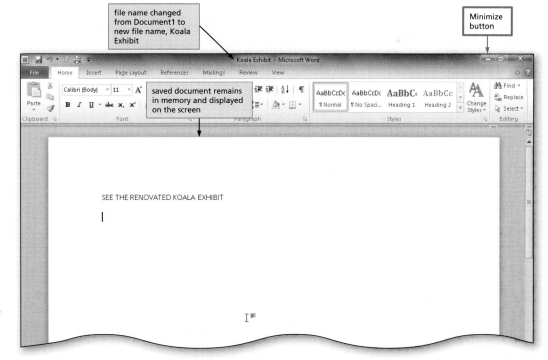

Figure 42

Other Ways

1. Click File on Ribbon, click Save, type file name, navigate to desired save location, click Save button

2. Press CTRL+S or press SHIFT+F12, type file name, navigate to desired save location, click Save button

Navigating in Dialog Boxes

Navigating is the process of finding a location on a storage device. While saving the Koala Exhibit file, for example, Steps 3a – 3c in the previous set of steps navigated to the Word folder located in the CIS 101 folder. When performing certain functions in Windows programs, such as saving a file, opening a file, or inserting a picture in an existing document, you most likely will have to navigate to the location where you want to save the file or to the folder containing the file you want to open or insert. Most dialog boxes in Windows programs requiring navigation follow a similar procedure; that is, the way you navigate to a folder in one dialog box, such as the Save As dialog box, is similar to how you might navigate in another dialog box, such as the Open dialog box. If you chose to navigate to a specific location in a dialog box, you would follow the instructions in Steps 3a – 3c on pages OFF 28 and OFF 29.

To Minimize and Restore a Window

Before continuing, you can verify that the Word file was saved properly. To do this, you will minimize the Word window and then open the USB flash drive window so that you can verify the file is stored on the USB flash drive. A **minimized window** is an open window hidden from view but that can be displayed quickly by clicking the window's program button on the taskbar.

In the following example, Word is used to illustrate minimizing and restoring windows; however, you would follow the same steps regardless of the Office program you are using.

The following steps minimize the Word window, verify that the file is saved, and then restore the minimized window.

- Click the Minimize button on the program's title bar (shown in Figure 42 on the previous page) to minimize the window (Figure 43).

 Is the minimized window still available?

The minimized window, Word in this case, remains available but no longer is the active window. It is minimized as a program button on the taskbar.

- If necessary, click the Windows Explorer program button on the taskbar to open the USB flash drive window.

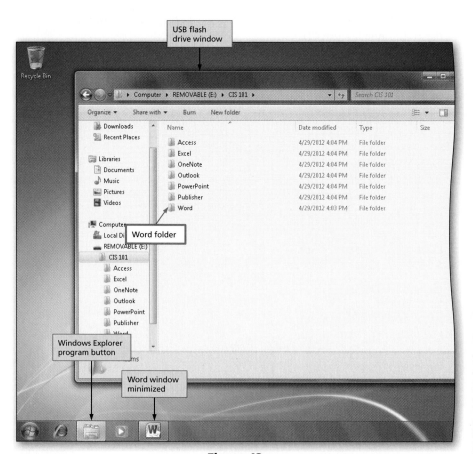

Figure 43

2

- Double-click the Word folder to select the folder and display its contents (Figure 44).

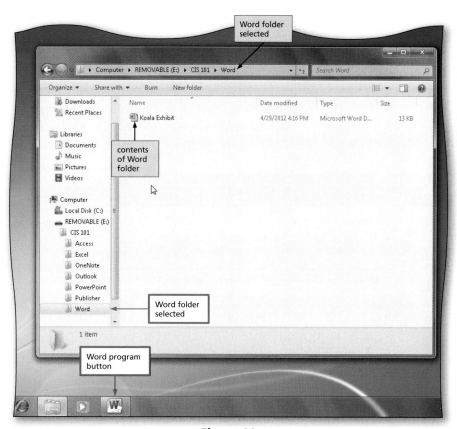

Figure 44

Q&A

Why does the Windows Explorer button on the taskbar change?

The button changes to reflect the status of the folder window (in this case, the USB flash drive window). A selected button indicates that the folder window is active on the screen. When the button is not selected, the window is open but not active.

3

- After viewing the contents of the selected folder, click the Word program button on the taskbar to restore the minimized window (as shown in Figure 42 on page OFF 29).

Other Ways
1. Right-click title bar, click Minimize on shortcut menu, click taskbar button in taskbar button area   2. Press WINDOWS+M, press WINDOWS+SHIFT+M

Screen Resolution

Screen resolution indicates the number of pixels (dots) that the computer uses to display the letters, numbers, graphics, and background you see on the screen. When you increase the screen resolution, Windows displays more information on the screen, but the information decreases in size. The reverse also is true: as you decrease the screen resolution, Windows displays less information on the screen, but the information increases in size.

Screen resolution usually is stated as the product of two numbers, such as 1024 × 768 (pronounced "ten twenty-four by seven sixty-eight"). A 1024 × 768 screen resolution results in a display of 1,024 distinct pixels on each of 768 lines, or about

786,432 pixels. Changing the screen resolution affects how the Ribbon appears in Office programs. Figure 45 shows the Word Ribbon at screen resolutions of 1024 × 768 and 1280 × 800. All of the same commands are available regardless of screen resolution. Word, however, makes changes to the groups and the buttons within the groups to accommodate the various screen resolutions. The result is that certain commands may need to be accessed differently depending on the resolution chosen. A command that is visible on the Ribbon and available by clicking a button at one resolution may not be visible and may need to be accessed using its Dialog Box Launcher at a different resolution.

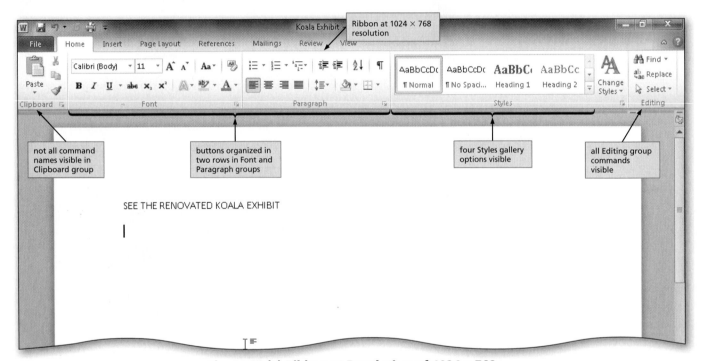

Figure 45 (a) Ribbon at Resolution of 1024 x 768

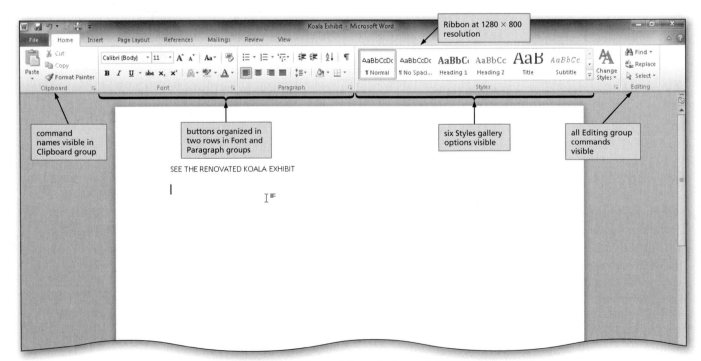

Figure 45 (b) Ribbon at Resolution of 1280 x 800

Comparing the two Ribbons in Figure 45, notice the changes in content and layout of the groups and galleries. In some cases, the content of a group is the same in each resolution, but the layout of the group differs. For example, the same gallery and buttons appear in the Styles groups in the two resolutions, but the layouts differ. In other cases, the content and layout are the same across the resolution, but the level of detail differs with the resolution. In the Clipboard group, when the resolution increases to 1280 × 800, the names of all the buttons in the group appear in addition to the buttons themselves. At the lower resolution, only the buttons appear.

To Change the Screen Resolution

If you are using a computer to step through the chapters in this book and you want your screen to match the figures, you may need to change your screen's resolution. The figures in this book use a screen resolution of 1024 × 768. The following steps change the screen resolution to 1024 × 768. Your computer already may be set to 1024 × 768 or some other resolution. Keep in mind that many computer labs prevent users from changing the screen resolution; in that case, read the following steps for illustration purposes.

1

• Click the Show desktop button on the taskbar to display the Windows 7 desktop.

• Right-click an empty area on the Windows 7 desktop to display a shortcut menu that displays a list of commands related to the desktop (Figure 46).

Q&A

Why does my shortcut menu display different commands?

Depending on your computer's hardware and configuration, different commands might appear on the shortcut menu.

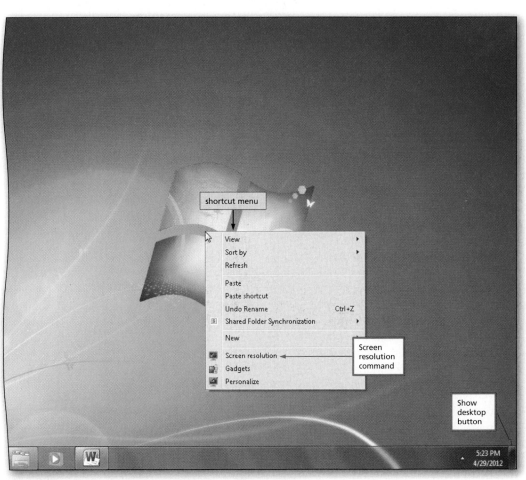

Figure 46

● Click Screen resolution on the shortcut menu to open the Screen Resolution window (Figure 47).

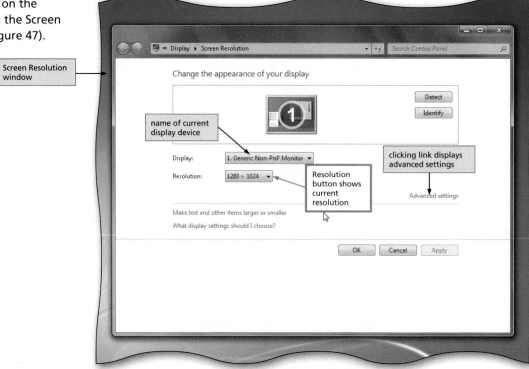

Figure 47

● Click the Resolution button in the Screen Resolution window to display the resolution slider.

Q&A | What is a slider?

A **slider** is an object that allows users to choose from multiple predetermined options. In most cases, these options represent some type of numeric value. In most cases, one end of the slider (usually the left or bottom) represents the lowest of available values, and the opposite end (usually the right or top) represents the highest available value.

● If necessary, drag the resolution slider until the desired screen resolution (in this case, 1024 × 768) is selected (Figure 48).

Q&A | What if my computer does not support the 1024 × 768 resolution?

Some computers do not support the 1024 × 768 resolution. In this case, select a resolution that is close to the 1024 × 768 resolution.

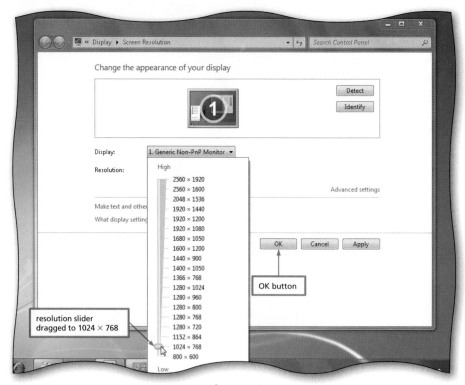

Figure 48

5

- Click an empty area of the Screen Resolution window to close the resolution slider.

- Click the OK button to change the screen resolution and display the Display Settings dialog box (Figure 49).

- Click the Keep changes button (Display Settings dialog box) to accept the new screen resolution.

Q&A Why does a message display stating that the image quality can be improved?

Some computer monitors are designed to display contents better at a certain screen resolution, sometimes referred to as an optimal resolution.

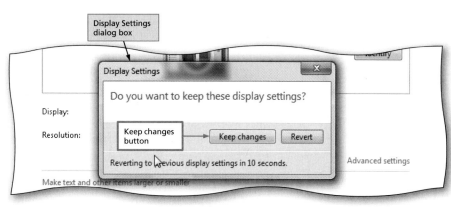

Figure 49

To Quit an Office Program with One Document Open

When you quit an Office program, such as Word, if you have made changes to a file since the last time the file was saved, the Office program displays a dialog box asking if you want save the changes you made to the file before it closes the program window. The dialog box contains three buttons with these resulting actions: the Save button saves the changes and then quits the Office program, the Don't Save button quits the Office program without saving changes, and the Cancel button closes the dialog box and redisplays the file without saving the changes.

If no changes have been made to an open document since the last time the file was saved, the Office program will close the window without displaying a dialog box.

The following steps quit an Office program. In the following example, Word is used to illustrate quitting an Office program; however, you would follow the same steps regardless of the Office program you were using.

1

- If necessary, click the Word program button on the taskbar to display the Word window on the desktop.

- Point to the Close button on the right side of the program's title bar, Word in this case (Figure 50).

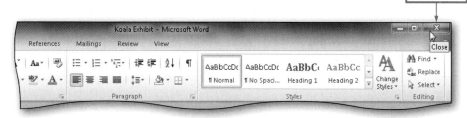

Figure 50

2

- Click the Close button to close the document and quit Word.

Q&A What if I have more than one document open in an Office program?

You would click the Close button for each open document. When you click the last open document's Close button, the Office program also quits. As an alternative, you could click File on the Ribbon to open the Backstage view and then click Exit in the Backstage view to close all open documents and quit the Office program.

Q&A What is the Backstage view?

The **Backstage view** contains a set of commands that enable you to manage documents and data about the documents. The Backstage view is discussed in more depth later in this chapter.

3

- If a Microsoft Word dialog box appears, click the Save button to save any changes made to the document since the last save.

Other Ways

1. Right-click the Office program button on Windows 7 taskbar, click Close window or 'Close all windows' on shortcut menu

2. Press ALT + F4

Break Point: If you wish to take a break, this is a good place to do so. To resume at a later time, continue to follow the steps from this location forward.

Additional Microsoft Office Programs

The previous section used Word to illustrate common features of Office and some basic elements unique to Word. The following sections present elements unique to PowerPoint, Excel, and Access, as well as illustrate additional common features of Office.

In the following pages, you will learn how to do the following:

1. Start an Office program (PowerPoint) using the search box.
2. Create two small documents in the same Office program (PowerPoint).
3. Close one of the documents.
4. Reopen the document just closed.
5. Create a document in a different Office program (Excel).
6. Save the document with a new file name.
7. Create a file in a different Office program (Access).
8. Close the file and then open the file.

PowerPoint

PowerPoint is a complete presentation program that allows you to produce professional-looking presentations (Figure 51). A PowerPoint **presentation** also is called a **slide show**. PowerPoint contains several features to simplify creating a slide show. To make presentations more impressive, you can add diagrams, tables, pictures, video, sound, and animation effects. Additional PowerPoint features include the following:

- **Word processing** — Create bulleted lists, combine words and images, find and replace text, and use multiple fonts and font sizes.
- **Outlining** — Develop a presentation using an outline format. You also can import outlines from Microsoft Word or other word processing programs, including single-level and multilevel lists.
- **Charting** — Create and insert charts into presentations and then add effects and chart elements.
- **Drawing** — Create and modify diagrams using shapes such as arcs, arrows, cubes, rectangles, stars, and triangles. Then, customize and add effects to the diagrams, and arrange these objects by sizing, scaling, and rotating them.
- **Inserting multimedia** — Insert artwork and multimedia effects into a slide show. The Microsoft Clip Organizer, included with Office programs, contains hundreds of media files, including pictures, sounds, and movies.
- **Saving to the Web** — Save presentations or parts of a presentation so that they can be viewed in a Web browser. You can publish your slide show to the Internet or to an intranet.
- **E-mailing** — Send an entire slide show as an attachment to an e-mail message.
- **Collaborating** — Share a presentation with friends and coworkers. Ask them to review the slides and then insert comments that offer suggestions to enhance the presentation.
- **Preparing delivery** — Rehearse integrating PowerPoint slides into your speech by setting timings, using presentation tools, showing only selected slides in a presentation, and packaging the presentation for an optical disc.

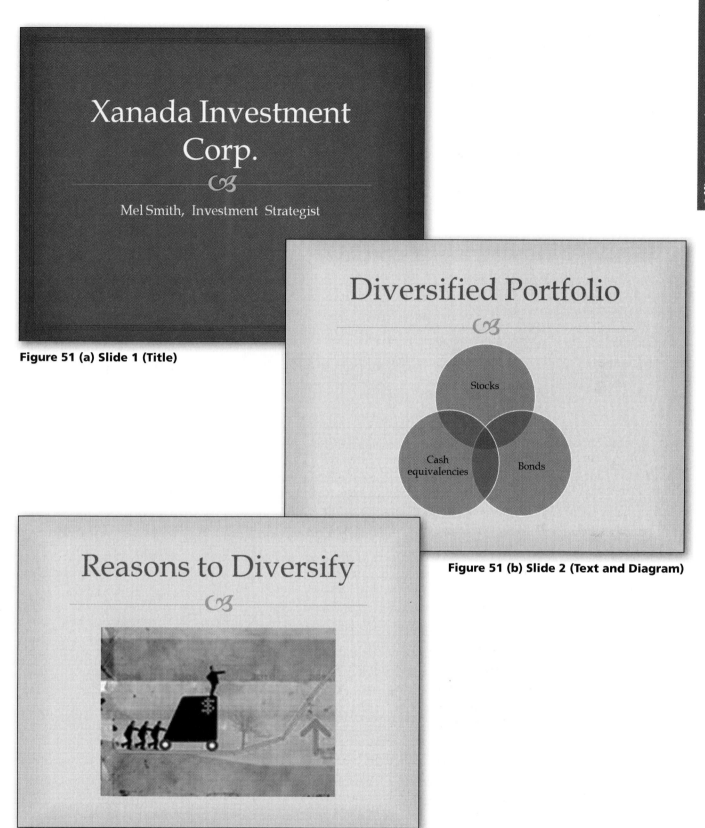

Figure 51 (a) Slide 1 (Title)

Figure 51 (b) Slide 2 (Text and Diagram)

Figure 51 (c) Slide 3 (Text and Picture)

To Start a Program Using the Search Box

The steps on the next page, which assume Windows 7 is running, use the search box to start the PowerPoint Office program based on a typical installation; however, you would follow similar steps to start any Office program. You may need to ask your instructor how to start programs for your computer.

1

• Click the Start button on the Windows 7 taskbar to display the Start menu.

2

• Type **Microsoft PowerPoint** as the search text in the 'Search programs and files' text box and watch the search results appear on the Start menu (Figure 52).

Q&A Do I need to type the complete program name or correct capitalization?

No, just enough of it for the program name to appear on the Start menu. For example, you may be able to type PowerPoint or powerpoint, instead of Microsoft PowerPoint.

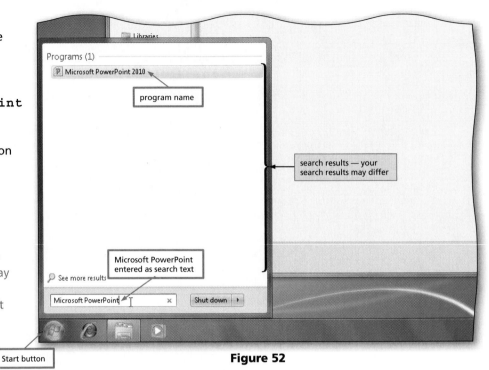

Figure 52

3

• Click the program name, Microsoft PowerPoint 2010 in this case, in the search results on the Start menu to start PowerPoint and display a new blank presentation in the PowerPoint window.

• If the program window is not maximized, click the Maximize button on its title bar to maximize the window (Figure 53).

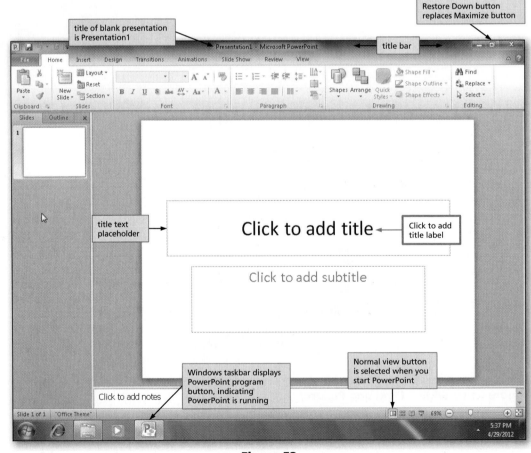

Figure 53

The PowerPoint Window and Ribbon

The PowerPoint window consists of a variety of components to make your work more efficient and documents more professional: the window, Ribbon, Mini toolbar, shortcut menus, and Quick Access Toolbar. Many of these components are common to other Office programs and have been discussed earlier in this chapter. Other components, discussed in the following paragraphs and later in subsequent chapters, are unique to PowerPoint.

The basic unit of a PowerPoint presentation is a **slide**. A slide may contain text and objects, such as graphics, tables, charts, and drawings. **Layouts** are used to position this content on the slide. When you create a new presentation, the default **Title Slide** layout appears (Figure 54). The purpose of this layout is to introduce the presentation to the audience. PowerPoint includes eight other built-in standard layouts.

The default slide layouts are set up in **landscape orientation**, where the slide width is greater than its height. In landscape orientation, the slide size is preset to 10 inches wide and 7.5 inches high when printed on a standard sheet of paper measuring 11 inches wide and 8.5 inches high.

BTW

Portrait Orientation
If your slide content is dominantly vertical, such as a skyscraper or a person, consider changing the slide layout to a portrait orientation. To change the orientation to portrait, click the Slide Orientation button (Design tab | Page Setup group) and then click Portrait. You can use both landscape and portrait orientation in the same slide show.

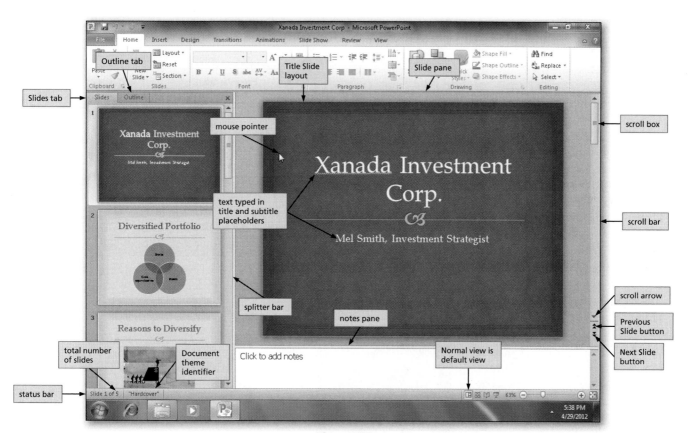

Figure 54

Placeholders   **Placeholders** are boxes with dotted or hatch-marked borders that are displayed when you create a new slide. All layouts except the Blank slide layout contain placeholders. Depending on the particular slide layout selected, title and subtitle placeholders are displayed for the slide title and subtitle; a content text placeholder is displayed for text, art, or a table, chart, picture, graphic, or movie. The title slide in Figure 53 has two text placeholders for the main heading, or title, of a new slide and the subtitle.

Ribbon The Ribbon in PowerPoint is similar to the one in Word and the other Microsoft Office programs. When you start PowerPoint, the Ribbon displays nine main tabs: File, Home, Insert, Design, Transitions, Animations, Slide Show, Review, and View.

To Enter Content in a Title Slide

With the exception of a blank slide and a slide with a picture and caption, PowerPoint assumes every new slide has a title. Many of PowerPoint's layouts have both a title text placeholder and at least one content placeholder. To make creating a presentation easier, any text you type after a new slide appears becomes title text in the title text placeholder. As you begin typing text in the title text placeholder, the title text also is displayed in the Slide 1 thumbnail in the Slides tab. The presentation title for this presentation is Xanada Investments. The following steps enter a presentation title on the title slide.

- Click the label 'Click to add title' located inside the title text placeholder (shown in Figure 53 on page OFF 38) to select the placeholder (Figure 55).

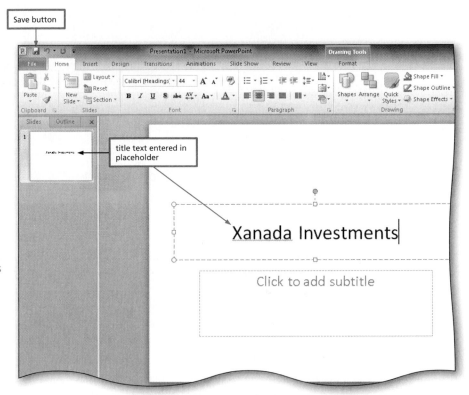

Figure 55

- Type **Xanada Investments** in the title text placeholder. Do not press the ENTER key because you do not want to create a new line of text (Figure 56).

Q&A

What are the white squares and circles that appear around the title text placeholder as I type the presentation title?

The white squares and circles are sizing handles, which you can drag to change the size of the title text placeholder. Sizing handles also can be found around other placeholders and objects within a presentation.

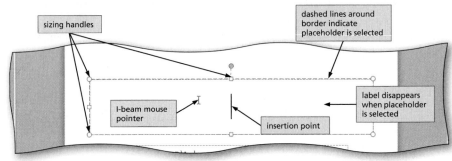

Figure 56

To Save a File in a Folder

The following steps save the presentation in the PowerPoint folder in the class folder (CIS 101, in this case) on a USB flash drive using the file name, Xanada Investments.

1 With a USB flash drive connected to one of the computer's USB ports, click the Save button on the Quick Access Toolbar to display the Save As dialog box.

2 If necessary, type **Xanada Investments** in the File name text box to change the file name. Do not press the ENTER key after typing the file name because you do not want to close the dialog box at this time.

3 Navigate to the desired save location (in this case, the PowerPoint folder in the CIS 101 folder [or your class folder] on the USB flash drive). For specific instructions, perform the tasks in Steps 3a through 3g.

3a If a navigation pane is not displayed in the Save As dialog box, click the Browse Folders button to expand the dialog box.

3b If Computer is not displayed in the navigation pane, drag the navigation pane scroll bar (Save As dialog box) until Computer appears.

3c If Computer is not expanded in the navigation pane, double-click Computer to display a list of available storage devices in the navigation pane.

3d If necessary, scroll through the Save As dialog box until your USB flash drive appears in the list of available storage devices in the navigation pane.

3e If your USB flash drive is not expanded, double-click the USB flash drive in the list of available storage devices in the navigation pane to select that drive as the new save location and display its contents in the right pane.

3f If your class folder (CIS 101, in this case) is not expanded, double-click the CIS 101 folder to select the folder and display its contents.

3g Click the PowerPoint folder to select it as the new save location and display its contents in the right pane.

4 Click the Save button (Save As dialog box) to save the presentation in the selected folder on the selected drive with the entered file name.

To Create a New Office Document from the Backstage View

As discussed earlier, the Backstage view contains a set of commands that enable you to manage documents and data about the documents. From the Backstage view in PowerPoint, for example, you can create, open, print, and save presentations. You also can share documents, manage versions, set permissions, and modify document properties. In other Office 2010 programs, the Backstage view may contain features specific to those programs. The steps on the following pages create a file, a blank presentation in this case, from the Backstage view.

①

- Click File on the Ribbon to open the Backstage view (Figure 57).

Q&A

What is the purpose of the File tab?

The **File** tab is used to display the Backstage view for each Office program.

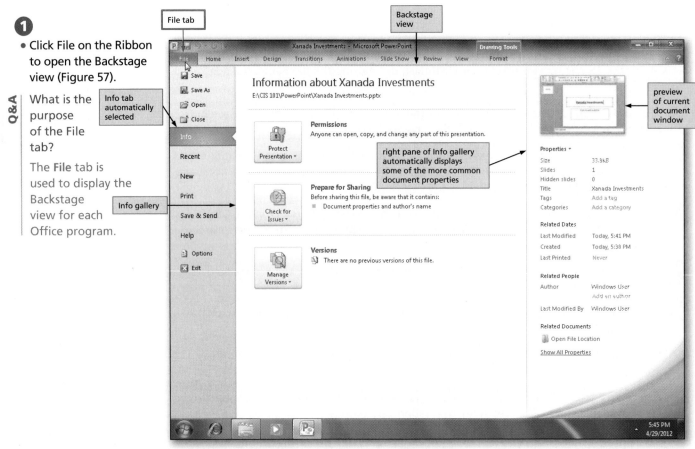

Figure 57

②

- Click the New tab in the Backstage view to display the New gallery (Figure 58).

Q&A

Can I create documents through the Backstage view in other Office programs?

Yes. If the Office program has a New tab in the Backstage view, the New gallery displays various options for creating a new file.

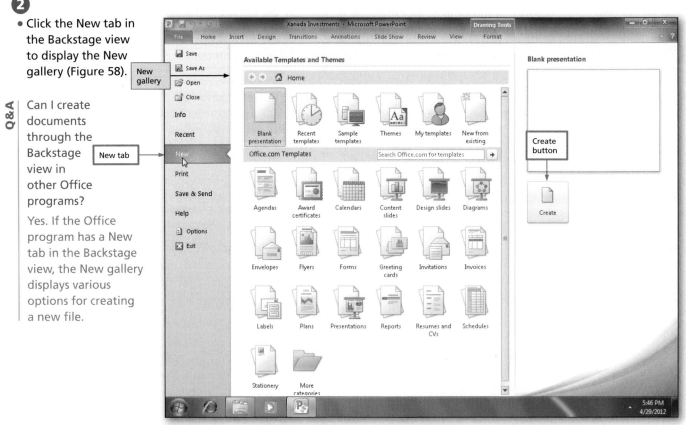

Figure 58

3

● Click the Create button in the New gallery to create a new presentation (Figure 59).

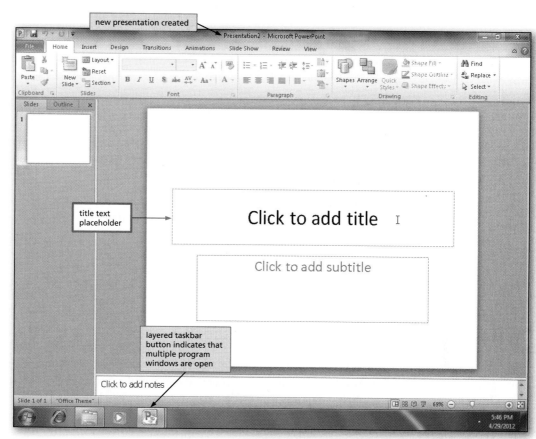

Figure 59

Other Ways

1. Press CTRL+N

To Enter Content in a Title Slide of a Second PowerPoint Presentation

The presentation title for this presentation is Koala Exhibit Gala. The following steps enter a presentation title on the title slide.

1 Click the title text placeholder (shown in Figure 59) to select it.

2 Type **Koala Exhibit Gala** in the title text placeholder. Do not press the ENTER key (Figure 60).

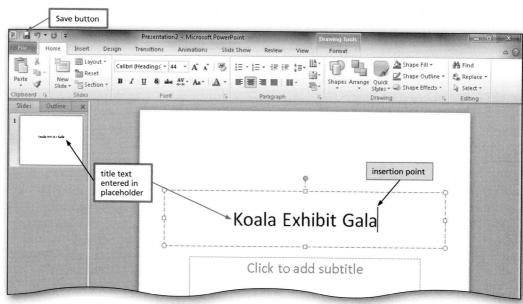

Figure 60

To Save a File in a Folder

The following steps save the second presentation in the PowerPoint folder in the class folder (CIS 101, in this case) on a USB flash drive using the file name, Koala Exhibit Gala.

1 With a USB flash drive connected to one of the computer's USB ports, click the Save button on the Quick Access Toolbar to display the Save As dialog box.

2 If necessary, type **Koala Exhibit Gala** in the File name text box to change the file name. Do not press the ENTER key after typing the file name because you do not want to close the dialog box at this time.

3 If necessary, navigate to the desired save location (in this case, the PowerPoint folder in the CIS 101 folder [or your class folder] on the USB flash drive).

4 Click the Save button (Save As dialog box) to save the presentation in the selected folder on the selected drive with the entered file name.

To Close an Office File Using the Backstage View

Sometimes, you may want to close an Office file, such as a PowerPoint presentation, entirely and start over with a new file. You also may want to close a file when you are finished working with it so that you can begin a new file. The following steps close the current active Office file, that is, the Koala Exhibit Gala presentation, without quitting the active program (PowerPoint in this case).

1
- Click File on the Ribbon to open the Backstage view (Figure 61).

2
- Click Close in the Backstage view to close the open file (Koala Exhibit Gala, in this case) without quitting the active program.

Q&A What if the Office program displays a dialog box about saving?

Click the Save button if you want to save the changes, click the Don't Save button if you want to ignore the changes since the last time you saved, and click the Cancel button if you do not want to close the document.

Q&A Can I use the Backstage view to close an open file in other Office programs, such as Word and Excel?

Yes.

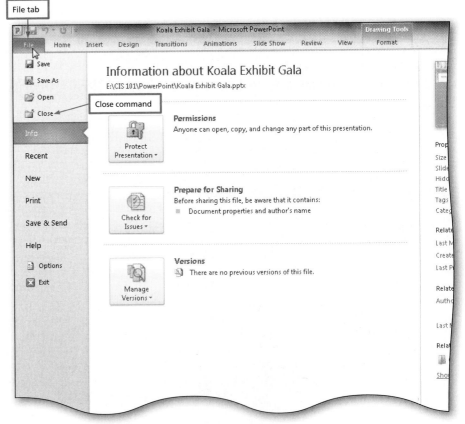

Figure 61

To Open a Recent Office File Using the Backstage View

You sometimes need to open a file that you recently modified. You may have more changes to make such as adding more content or correcting errors. The Backstage view allows you to access recent files easily. The following steps reopen the Koala Exhibit Gala file just closed.

1

- Click File on the Ribbon to open the Backstage view.

- Click the Recent tab in the Backstage view to display the Recent gallery (Figure 62).

2

- Click the desired file name in the Recent gallery, Koala Exhibit Gala in this case, to open the file (shown in Figure 60 on page OFF 43).

Q&A

Can I use the Backstage view to open a recent file in other Office programs, such as Word and Excel?

Yes, as long as the file name appears in the list of recent files in the Recent gallery.

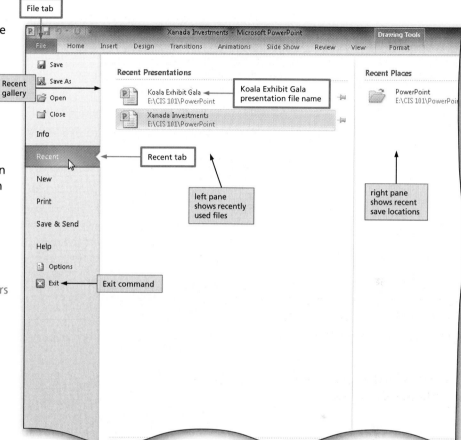

Figure 62

Other Ways

1. Click Start button, point to program name, click file name on submenu
2. Click File on Ribbon, click Open in Backstage view, navigate to file (Open dialog box), click Open button

To Quit an Office Program

You are finished using PowerPoint. Thus, you should quit this Office program. The following steps quit PowerPoint.

1 If you have one Office document open, click the Close button on the right side of the title bar to close the document and quit the Office program; or if you have multiple Office documents open, click File on the Ribbon to open the Backstage view and then click Exit in the Backstage view to close all open documents and quit the Office program.

2 If a dialog box appears, click the Save button to save any changes made to the document since the last save.

Excel

Excel is a powerful spreadsheet program that allows users to organize data, complete calculations, make decisions, graph data, develop professional-looking reports (Figure 63), publish organized data to the Web, and access real-time data from Web sites. The four major parts of Excel are:

- **Workbooks and Worksheets** - A **workbook** is like a notebook. Inside the workbook are sheets, each of which is called a **worksheet**. In other words, a workbook is a collection of worksheets. Worksheets allow users to enter, calculate, manipulate, and analyze data such as numbers and text. The terms worksheet and spreadsheet are interchangeable.

- **Charts** - Excel can draw a variety of charts.

- **Tables** - Tables organize and store data within worksheets. For example, once a user enters data into a worksheet, an Excel table can sort the data, search for specific data, and select data that satisfies defined criteria.

- **Web Support -** Web support allows users to save Excel worksheets or parts of a worksheet in HTML format, so that a user can view and manipulate the worksheet using a browser. Excel Web support also provides access to real-time data, such as stock quotes, using Web queries.

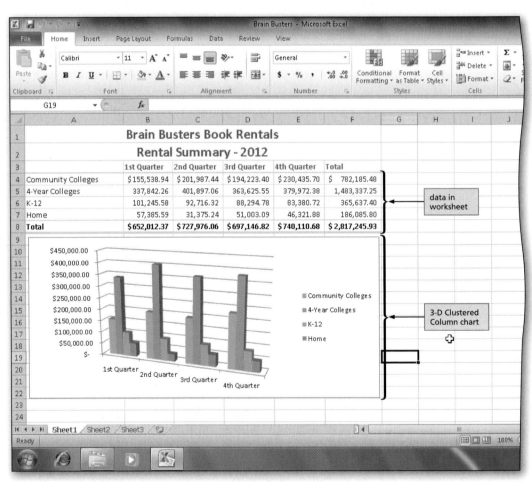

Figure 63

To Create a New Blank Office Document from Windows Explorer

Windows Explorer provides a means to create a blank Office document without ever starting an Office program. The following steps use Windows Explorer to create a blank Excel document.

1

- If necessary, click the Windows Explorer program button on the taskbar to make the folder window the active window in Windows Explorer.

- Double-click your class folder (CIS 101, in this case) in the navigation pane to display the contents of the selected folder.

- Double-click the Excel folder to display its contents in the right pane.

- With the Excel folder selected, right-click an open area in the right pane to display a shortcut menu.

- Point to New on the shortcut menu to display the New submenu (Figure 64).

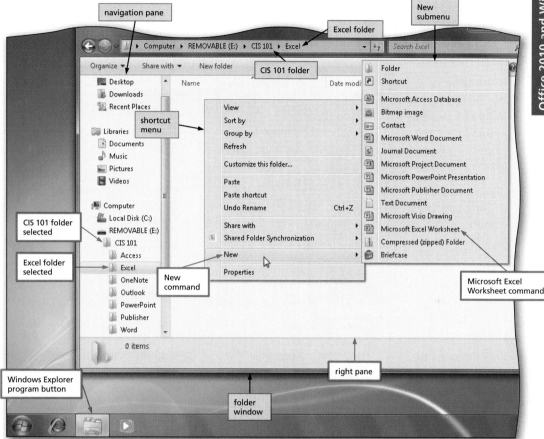

Figure 64

2

- Click Microsoft Excel Worksheet on the New submenu to display an icon and text box for a new file in the current folder window (Figure 65).

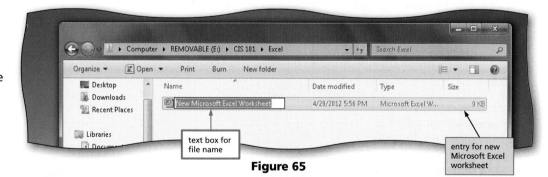

Figure 65

3

- Type **Brain Busters** in the text box and then press the ENTER key to assign a name to the new file in the current folder (Figure 66).

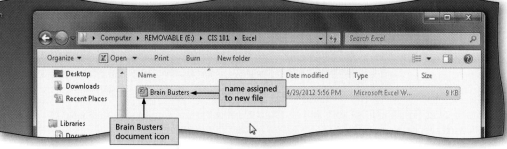

Figure 66

To Start a Program from Windows Explorer and Open a File

Previously, you learned how to start an Office program using the Start menu and the search box. Another way start an Office program is to open an existing file from Windows Explorer, which causes the program in which the file was created to start and then open the selected file. The following steps, which assume Windows 7 is running, use Windows Explorer to start the Excel Office program based on a typical installation. You may need to ask your instructor how to start Office programs for your computer.

1

- If necessary, display the file to open in the folder window in Windows Explorer (shown in Figure 66 on the previous page).

- Right-click the file icon or file name (Brain Busters, in this case) to display a shortcut menu (Figure 67).

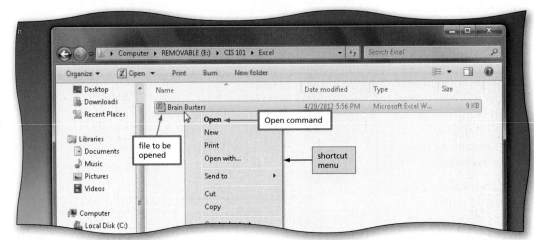

Figure 67

2

- Click Open on the shortcut menu to open the selected file in the program used to create the file, Microsoft Excel in this case (Figure 68).

- If the program window is not maximized, click the Maximize button on the title bar to maximize the window.

- For Excel users, if the worksheet window in Excel is not maximized, click the worksheet window Maximize button to maximize the worksheet window within Excel.

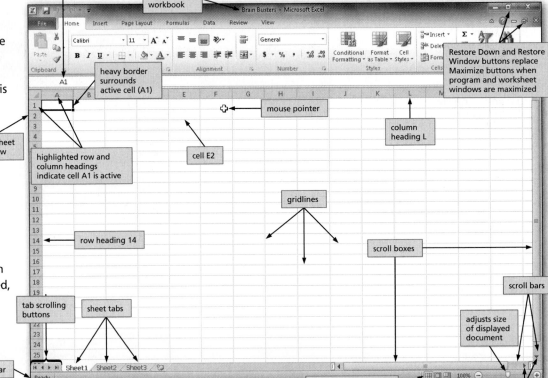

Figure 68

Q&A

Instead of using Windows Explorer, can I start Excel using the same method shown previously for Word and PowerPoint?

Yes, you can use any method of starting an Office program to start Excel.

Unique Features of Excel

The Excel window consists of a variety of components to make your work more efficient and worksheets more professional. These include the document window, Ribbon, Mini toolbar and shortcut menus, Quick Access Toolbar, and the Backstage view. Some of these components are common to other Microsoft Office 2010 programs; others are unique to Excel.

Excel opens a new workbook with three worksheets. If necessary, you can add additional worksheets as long as your computer has enough memory to accommodate them.

Each worksheet has a sheet name that appears on a **sheet tab** at the bottom of the workbook. For example, Sheet1 is the name of the active worksheet displayed in the Brain Busters workbook. If you click the sheet tab labeled Sheet2, Excel displays the Sheet2 worksheet.

The Worksheet   The worksheet is organized into a rectangular grid containing vertical columns and horizontal rows. A column letter above the grid, also called the **column heading**, identifies each column. A row number on the left side of the grid, also called the **row heading**, identifies each row. With the screen resolution set to 1024 × 768 and the Excel window maximized, Excel displays 15 columns (A through O) and 25 rows (1 through 25) of the worksheet on the screen, as shown in Figure 68.

The intersection of each column and row is a cell. A **cell** is the basic unit of a worksheet into which you enter data. Each worksheet in a workbook has 16,384 columns and 1,048,576 rows for a total of 17,179,869,180 cells. Only a small fraction of the active worksheet appears on the screen at one time.

A cell is referred to by its unique address, or **cell reference**, which is the coordinates of the intersection of a column and a row. To identify a cell, specify the column letter first, followed by the row number. For example, cell reference E2 refers to the cell located at the intersection of column E and row 2 (Figure 68).

One cell on the worksheet, designated the **active cell**, is the one into which you can enter data. The active cell in Figure 68 is A1. The active cell is identified in three ways. First, a heavy border surrounds the cell; second, the active cell reference shows immediately above column A in the Name box; and third, the column heading A and row heading 1 are highlighted so it is easy to see which cell is active (Figure 68).

The horizontal and vertical lines on the worksheet itself are called **gridlines**. Gridlines make it easier to see and identify each cell in the worksheet. If desired, you can turn the gridlines off so that they do not show on the worksheet, but it is recommended that you leave them on for now.

The mouse pointer in Figure 68 has the shape of a block plus sign. The mouse pointer appears as a block plus sign whenever it is located in a cell on the worksheet. Another common shape of the mouse pointer is the block arrow. The mouse pointer turns into the block arrow when you move it outside the worksheet or when you drag cell contents between rows or columns. The other mouse pointer shapes are described when they appear on the screen.

Ribbon   When you start Excel, the Ribbon displays eight main tabs: File, Home, Insert, Page Layout, Formulas, Data, Review, and View. The Formulas and Data tabs are specific to Excel. The Formulas tab allows you to work with Excel formulas, and the Data tab allows you to work with data processing features such as importing and sorting data.

BTW

The Worksheet Size and Window
The 16,384 columns and 1,048,576 rows in Excel make for a huge worksheet that – if you could imagine – takes up the entire side of a building to display in its entirety. Your computer screen, by comparison, is a small window that allows you to view only a minute area of the worksheet at one time. While you cannot see the entire worksheet, you can move the window over the worksheet to view any part of it.

BTW

Customizing the Ribbon
In addition to customizing the Quick Access Toolbar, you can add items to and remove items from the Ribbon. To customize the Ribbon, click File on the Ribbon to open the Backstage view, click Options in the Backstage view, and then click Customize Ribbon in the left pane of the Options dialog box. More information about customizing the Ribbon is presented in a later chapter.

Formula Bar   The formula bar appears below the Ribbon (Figure 69). As you type, Excel displays the entry in the **formula bar**. You can make the formula bar larger by dragging the sizing handle at the bottom of the formula bar or clicking the expand button to the right of the formula bar. Excel also displays the active cell reference in the **Name box** on the left side of the formula bar.

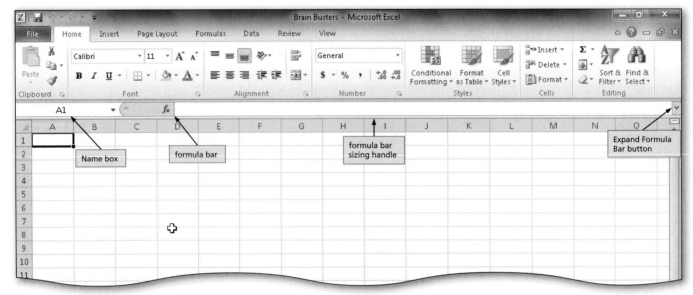

Figure 69

To Enter a Worksheet Title

To enter data into a cell, you first must select it. The easiest way to select a cell (make it active) is to use the mouse to move the block plus sign mouse pointer to the cell and then click. An alternative method is to use the arrow keys that are located just to the right of the typewriter keys on the keyboard. An arrow key selects the cell adjacent to the active cell in the direction of the arrow on the key.

In Excel, any set of characters containing a letter, hyphen (as in a telephone number), or space is considered text. **Text** is used to place titles, such as worksheet titles, column titles, and row titles, on the worksheet. The following steps enter the worksheet title in cell A1.

- If it is not already the active cell, click cell A1 to make it the active cell (Figure 70).

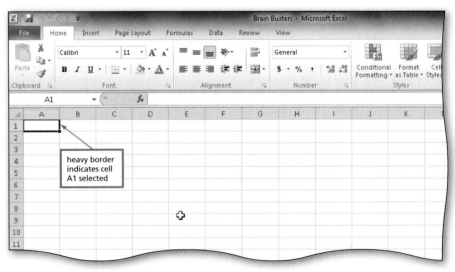

Figure 70

2

- Type **Brain Buster Book Rentals** in cell A1 (Figure 71).

Q&A

Why did the appearance of the formula bar change?

Excel displays the title in the formula bar and in cell A1. When you begin typing a cell entry, Excel displays two additional boxes in the formula bar: the Cancel box and the Enter box. Clicking the Enter box completes an entry. Clicking the Cancel box cancels an entry.

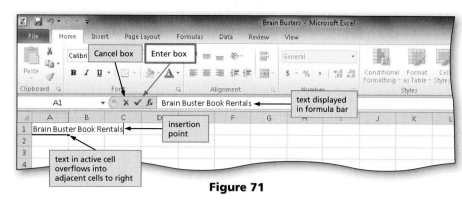

Figure 71

3

- Click the Enter box to complete the entry and enter the worksheet title in cell A1 (Figure 72).

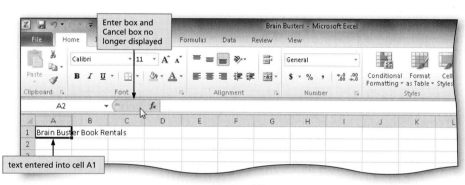

Figure 72

Other Ways		
1. To complete entry, click any cell other than active cell	2. To complete entry, press ENTER, HOME, PAGE UP, PAGE DOWN, END,	UP, DOWN, LEFT ARROW, or RIGHT ARROW

To Save an Existing Office Document with the Same File Name

Saving frequently cannot be overemphasized. You have made modifications to the file (spreadsheet) since you created it. Thus, you should save again. Similarly, you should continue saving files frequently so that you do not lose your changes since the time you last saved the file. You can use the same file name, such as Brain Busters, to save the changes made to the document. The following step saves a file again.

1

- Click the Save button on the Quick Access Toolbar to overwrite the previously saved file (Brain Busters, in this case) on the USB flash drive (Figure 73).

Q&A

Why did the Save As dialog box not appear?

Office programs, including Excel, overwrite the document using the setting specified the first time you saved the document.

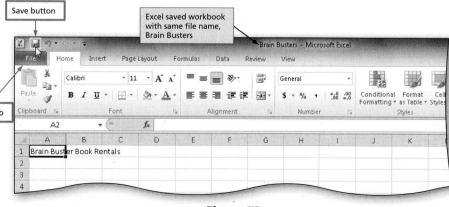

Figure 73

Other Ways
1. Press CTRL+S or press SHIFT+F12

To Use Save As to Change the Name of a File

You might want to save a file with a different name and even to a different location. For example, you might start a homework assignment with a data file and then save it with a final file name for submitting to your instructor, saving it to a location designated by your instructor. The following steps save a file with a different file name.

1 With your USB flash drive connected to one of the computer's USB ports, click File on the Ribbon to open the Backstage view.

2 Click Save As in the Backstage view to display the Save As dialog box.

3 Type **Brain Busters Rental Summary** in the File name text box (Save As dialog box) to change the file name. Do not press the ENTER key after typing the file name because you do not want to close the dialog box at this time.

4 Navigate to the desired save location (the Excel folder in the CIS 101 folder [or your class folder] on the USB flash drive, in this case). For specific instructions, perform the tasks in steps 4a through 4g.

4a If a navigation pane is not displayed in the Save As dialog box, click the Browse Folders button to expand the dialog box.

4b If Computer is not displayed in the navigation pane, drag the navigation pane scroll bar (Save As dialog box) until Computer appears.

4c If Computer is not expanded in the navigation pane, double-click Computer to display a list of available storage devices in the navigation pane.

4d If necessary, scroll through the Save As dialog box until your USB flash drive appears in the list of available storage devices in the navigation pane.

4e If your USB flash drive is not expanded, double-click the USB flash drive in the list of available storage devices in the navigation pane to select that drive as the new save location and display its contents in the right pane.

4f If your class folder (CIS 101, in this case) is not expanded, double-click the CIS 101 folder to select the folder and display its contents.

4g Double-click the Excel folder to select it and display its contents in the right pane.

5 Click the Save button (Save As dialog box) to save the file in the selected folder on the selected drive with the new file name.

To Quit an Office Program

You are finished using Excel. The following steps quit Excel.

1 If you have one Office document open, click the Close button on the right side of the title bar to close the document and quit the Office program; or if you have multiple Office documents open, click File on the Ribbon to open the Backstage view and then click Exit in the Backstage view to close all open documents and quit the Office program.

2 If a dialog box appears, click the Save button to save any changes made to the file since the last save.

Access

The term **database** describes a collection of data organized in a manner that allows access, retrieval, and use of that data. **Microsoft Access 2010**, usually referred to as simply **Access,** is a database management system. A **database management system** is software that allows you to use a computer to create a database; add, change, and delete data in the database; create queries that allow you to ask questions concerning the data in the database; and create forms and reports using the data in the database.

To Start a Program

The following steps, which assume Windows 7 is running, start the Access program based on a typical installation. You may need to ask your instructor how to start programs for your computer.

1 Click the Start button on the Windows 7 taskbar to display the Start menu.

2 Type the name of the program, **Microsoft Access** in this case, as the search text in the 'Search programs and files' text box and watch the search results appear on the Start menu.

3 Click the name of the program, Microsoft Access 2010 in this case, in the search results on the Start menu to start Access.

4 If the program window is not maximized, click the Maximize button on its title bar to maximize the window (Figure 74).

Q&A Do I have to start Access using these steps?

No. You can use any previously discussed method of starting an Office program to start Access.

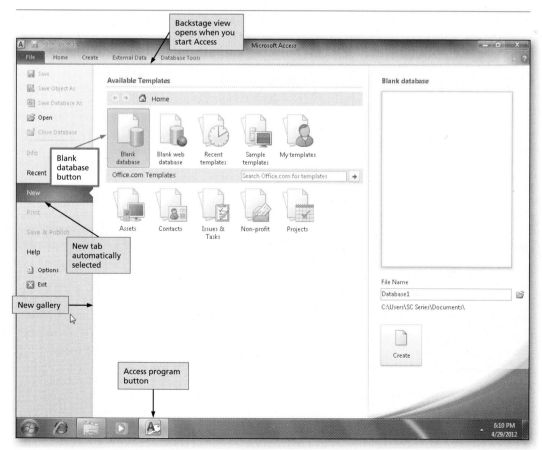

Figure 74

Unique Elements in Access

You work on objects such as tables, forms, and reports in the **Access work area**. In Figure 74, the Access window contains no open objects. Figure 75 shows a work area with multiple objects open. **Object tabs** for the open objects appear at the top of the work area. You select an open object by clicking its tab. In the figure, the Suppliers Split Form is the selected object. To the left of the work area is the Navigation Pane, which contains a list of all the objects in the database. You use this pane to open an object. You also can customize the way objects are displayed in the Navigation Pane.

Because the Navigation Pane can take up space in the window, you may not have as much open space for working as you would with Word or Excel. You can use the Shutter Bar Open/Close button to minimize the Navigation Pane when you are not using it, which allows more space to work with tables, forms, reports, and other database elements.

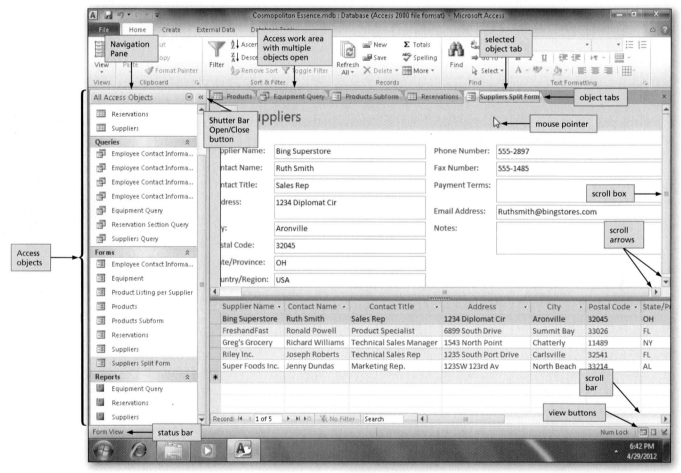

Figure 75

Ribbon When you start Access, the Ribbon displays five main tabs: File, Home, Create, External Data, and Database Tools. Access has unique groupings such as Sort & Filter and Records that are designed specifically for working with databases. Many of the formatting options are reserved for the tool tabs that appear when you are working with forms and reports.

To Create an Access Database

Unlike the other Office programs, Access saves a database when you first create it. When working in Access, you will add data to an Access database. As you add data to a database, Access automatically saves your changes rather than waiting until you manually save the database or quit Access. Recall that in Word and Excel, you entered the data first and then saved it.

Because Access automatically saves the database as you add and change data, you do not have to always click the Save button. In fact, the Save button in Access is used for saving the objects (including tables, queries, forms, reports, and other database objects) a database contains. You can use either the Blank Database option or a template to create a new database. If you already know the organization of your database, you would use the Blank Database option. If not, you can use a template. Templates can guide you by suggesting some commonly used database organizations.

The following steps use the Blank Database option to create a database named Charmed Excursions in the Access folder in the class folder (CIS 101, in this case) on a USB flash drive.

 1

- If necessary, click the Blank database button in the New gallery (shown in Figure 74 on page OFF 53) in the Backstage view to select the template type.

- Click the File Name text box to select the default database name.

- Type **Charmed Excursions** in the File Name text box to enter the new file name. Do not press the ENTER key after typing the file name because you do not want to create the database at this time (Figure 76).

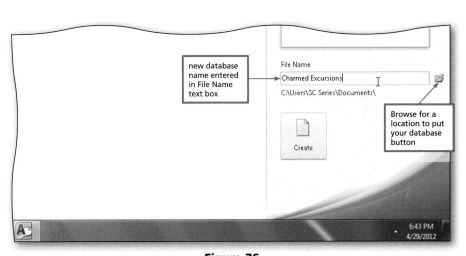

Figure 76

Q&A Why is the Backstage view automatically open when you start Access?

Unlike other Office programs, you first must save a database before adding any data. For this reason, the Backstage view opens automatically when you start Access.

2

- Click the 'Browse for a location to put your database' button to display the File New Database dialog box.

- Navigate to the location for the database, that is, the USB flash drive, then to the folder identifying your class (CIS 101, in this case), and then to the Access folder (Figure 77). For detailed steps about navigating, see Steps 3a – 3c on pages OFF 28 and OFF 29.

Q&A Why does the 'Save as type' box say Microsoft Access 2007 Databases?

Microsoft Access database formats change with some new versions of Microsoft Access. The most recent format is the Microsoft Access 2007 Databases format, which was released with Access 2007.

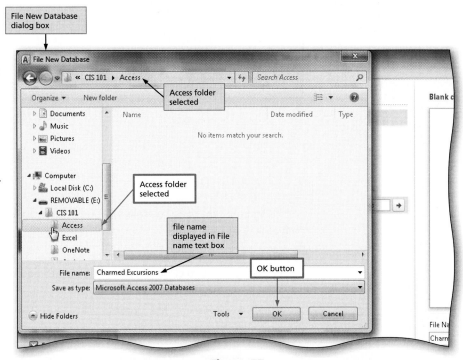

Figure 77

3

- Click the OK button (File New Database dialog box) to select the Access folder as the location for the database and close the dialog box (Figure 78).

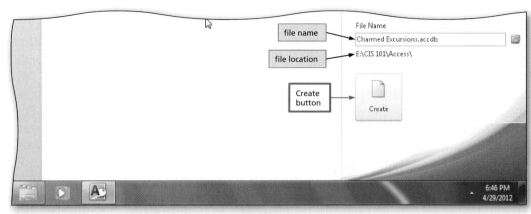

Figure 78

4

- Click the Create button in the Backstage view to create the database on the selected drive in the selected folder with the file name, Charmed Excursions. If necessary, click the Enable Content button (Figure 79).

Q&A

How do I know that the Charmed Excursions database is created?

The name of the database appears on the title bar.

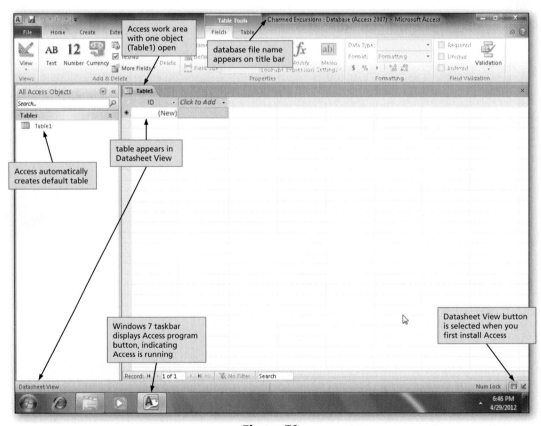

Figure 79

To Close an Office File

Assume you need to close the Access database and return to it later. The following step closes an Office file.

1 Click File on the Ribbon to open the Backstage view and then click Close Database in the Backstage view to close the open file (Charmed Excursions, in this case) without quitting the active program.

Q&A

Why is Access still on the screen?

When you close a database, the program remains open.

To Open an Existing Office File

Assume you wish to continue working on an existing file, that is, a file you previously saved. Earlier in this chapter, you learned how to open a recently used file through the Backstage view. The following steps open a database, specifically the Charmed Excursions database, from the USB flash drive.

1

- With your USB flash drive connected to one of the computer's USB ports, if necessary, click File on the Ribbon to open the Backstage view.

- Click Open in the Backstage view to display the Open dialog box (Figure 80).

2

- Navigate to the location of the file to be opened (in this case, the USB flash drive, then to the CIS 101 folder [or your class folder], and then to the Access folder). For detailed steps about navigating, see Steps 3a – 3c on pages OFF 28 and OFF 29.

Q&A

What if I did not save my file in a folder?

If you did not save your file in a folder, the file you wish to open should be displayed in the Open dialog box before navigating to any folders.

Figure 80

3

- Click the file to be opened, Charmed Excursions in this case, to select the file (Figure 81).

4

- Click the Open button (Open dialog box) to open the selected file and display the opened file in the current program window (shown in Figure 79).

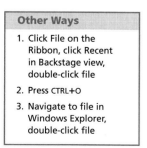

Other Ways

1. Click File on the Ribbon, click Recent in Backstage view, double-click file
2. Press CTRL+O
3. Navigate to file in Windows Explorer, double-click file

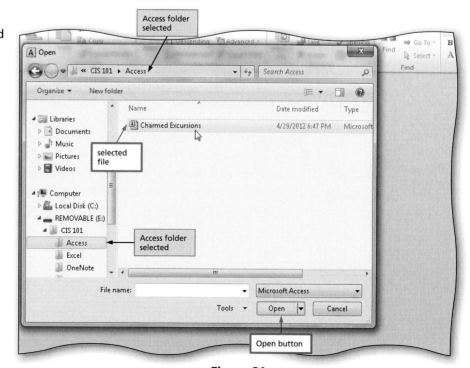

Figure 81

To Quit an Office Program

You are finished using Access. The following step quits Access.

1 Click the Close button on the right side of the title bar to close the file and quit the Office program.

Other Office Programs

In addition to the Office programs discussed thus far, three other programs are useful when collaborating and communicating with others: Outlook, Publisher, and OneNote.

Outlook

Outlook is a powerful communications and scheduling program that helps you communicate with others, keep track of contacts, and organize your calendar. Personal information manager (PIM) programs such as Outlook provide a way for individuals and workgroups to organize, find, view, and share information easily. Outlook allows you to send and receive electronic mail (e-mail) and permits you to engage in real-time messaging with family, friends, or coworkers using instant messaging. Outlook also provides a means to organize contacts. Users can track e-mail messages, meetings, and notes related to a particular contact. Outlook's Calendar, Contacts, Tasks, and Notes components aid in this organization. Contact information readily is available from the Outlook Calendar, Mail, Contacts, and Task components by accessing the Find a Contact feature.

Electronic mail (e-mail) is the transmission of messages and files over a computer network. E-mail has become an important means of exchanging information and files between business associates, classmates and instructors, friends, and family. Businesses find that using e-mail to send documents electronically saves both time and money. Parents with students away at college or relatives who live across the country find that communicating by e-mail is an inexpensive and easy way to stay in touch with their family members. Exchanging e-mail messages is one of the more widely used features of the Internet.

The Outlook Window Figure 82 shows an Outlook window, which is divided into six panes: the Favorites folder pane, Mail folder pane, and Navigation Pane on the left side of the window, the Inbox message pane to the left of center, the Reading Pane to the right of center, and the People Pane just below the Reading Pane.

When an e-mail message is open in Outlook, it is displayed in a Message window (Figure 83). When you open a message, the Message window Ribbon displays the Message tab, which contains the more frequently used commands.

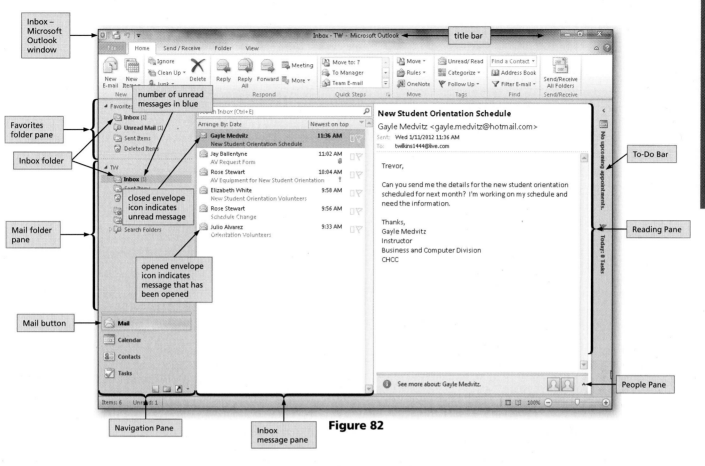

Figure 82

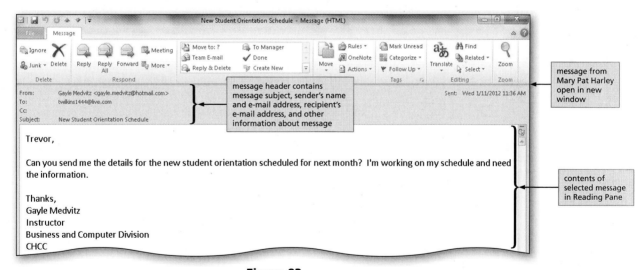

Figure 83

Publisher

Publisher is a powerful desktop publishing (DTP) program that assists you in designing and producing professional-quality documents that combine text, graphics, illustrations, and photos. DTP software provides additional tools beyond those typically found in word processing programs, including design templates, graphic manipulation tools, color schemes or libraries, advanced layout and printing tools, and Web components. For large jobs, businesses use DTP software to design publications that are camera ready, which means the files are suitable for outside commercial printing. In addition, DTP software can be used to create Web pages and interactive Web forms.

Publisher is used by people who regularly produce high-quality color publications, such as newsletters, brochures, flyers, logos, signs, catalogs, cards, and business forms. Saving publications as Web pages or complete Web sites is a powerful component of Publisher. All publications can be saved in a format that easily is viewed and manipulated using a browser.

Publisher has many features designed to simplify production and make publications visually appealing. Using Publisher, you easily can change the shape, size, and color of text and graphics. You can include many kinds of graphical objects, including mastheads, borders, tables, images, pictures, charts, and Web objects in publications, as well as integrate spreadsheets and databases.

The Publisher Window On the right side of the Backstage view, Publisher displays the New template gallery, which includes a list of publication types. **Publication types** are typical publications used by desktop publishers. The more popular types are displayed in the center of the window. Each publication type is a link to display various templates and blank publications from which you may choose.

Once you select a publication type, the window changes to allow you to select a specific template (Figure 84). Some templates are installed with Publisher, and others are available online. Clicking a publication type causes template previews to be displayed in the center of the window. The templates are organized by purpose (for example, Sales) and then alphabetically by design type. On the right, Publisher will display a larger preview of the selected template, along with some customization options if the template is installed or a download option if the template is online. In Figure 84, the installed Arrows template is selected so that the customize options appear.

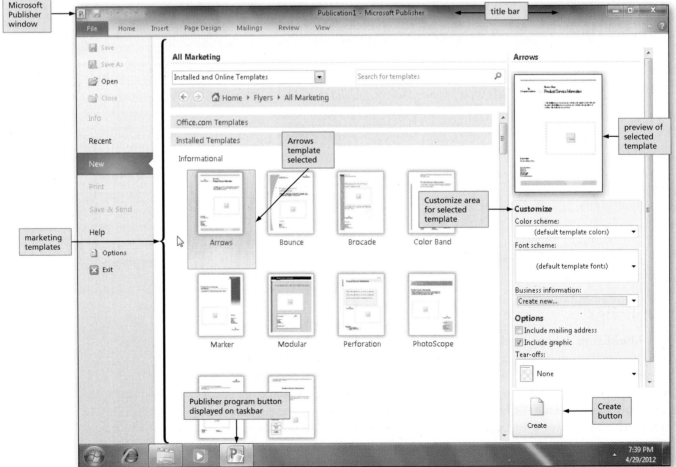

Figure 84

When you click the Create button, Publisher creates the document and sets it up for you to edit. Figure 85 shows the Arrows document that Publisher creates when default options are selected.

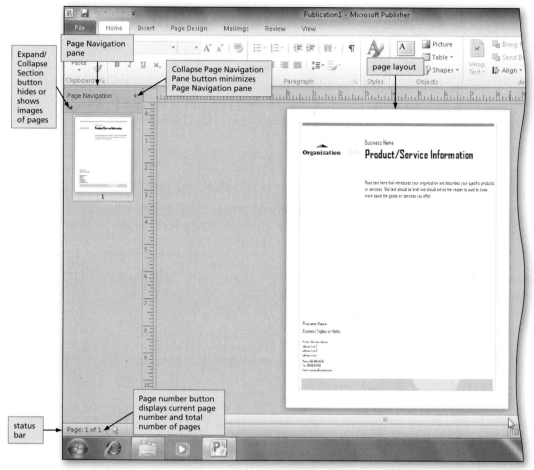

Figure 85

OneNote

OneNote is a note taking program that assists you in entering, saving, organizing, searching, and using notes. It enables you to create pages, which are organized in sections, just as in a physical notebook. In OneNote, you can type notes anywhere on a page and then easily move the notes around on the page. You can create lists and outlines, use handwriting to enter notes, and create drawings. If you use a Tablet PC to add handwritten notes to a document, OneNote can convert the handwriting to text. It also can perform searches on the handwritten entries. Pictures and data from other programs easily are incorporated in your notes.

In addition to typing and handwriting, you can take audio notes. For example, you could record conversations during a meeting or lecture. As you record, you can take additional notes. When you play back the audio notes, you can synchronize the additional notes you took; that is, OneNote will show you during playback the exact points at which you added the notes. A variety of note flags, which are symbols that call your attention to notes on a page, enable you to flag notes as being important. You then can use the Note Flags summary to view the flagged notes, which can be sorted in a variety of ways.

OneNote includes tools to assist you with organizing a notebook and navigating its contents. It also includes a search facility, making it easy to find the specific notes in which you are interested. For short notes that you always want to have available readily, you can use Side Notes, which are used much like the sticky notes that you might use in a physical notebook.

OneNote Window   All activity in OneNote takes place in the **notebook** (Figure 86). Like a physical notebook, the OneNote notebook consists of notes that are placed on **pages**. The pages are grouped into **sections**, which can be further grouped into **folders**. (No folders are shown in the notebook in the figure.) You can use the Search All Notebooks box to search for specific text in your notes.

You can add pages to the notebook using the New Page button in the Page Tabs pane. If Page Tabs are displayed, then you can switch to a page by clicking its tab. Figure 86 shows the Top Uses page being displayed for the General notebook.

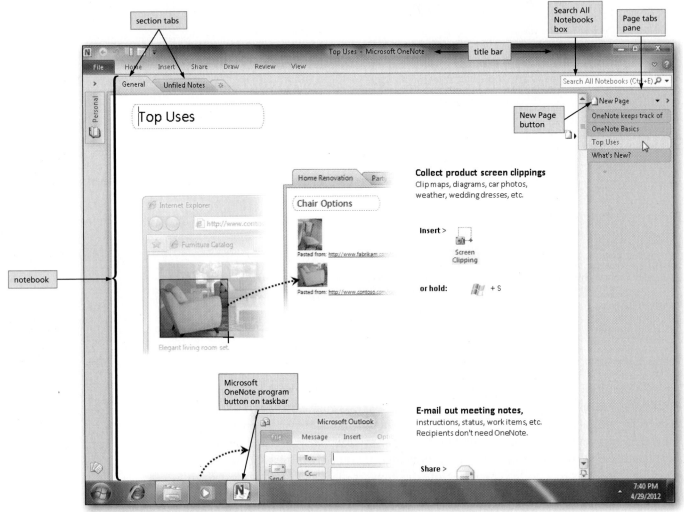

Figure 86

Break Point: If you wish to take a break, this is a good place to do so. To resume at a later time, continue to follow the steps from this location forward.

Moving, Renaming, and Deleting Files

Earlier in this chapter, you learned how to organize files in folders, which is part of a process known as **file management**. The following sections cover additional file management topics including renaming, moving, and deleting files.

To Rename a File

In some circumstances, you may want to change the name of, or rename, a file or a folder. For example, you may want to distinguish a file in one folder or drive from a copy of a similar file, or you may decide to rename a file to better identify its contents. The Word folder shown in Figure 87 contains the Word document, Koala Exhibit. The following steps change the name of the Koala Exhibit file in the Word folder to Koala Exhibit Flyer.

1

- If necessary, click the Windows Explorer program button on the taskbar to display the folder window in Windows Explorer.

- Navigate to the location of the file to be renamed (in this case, the Word folder in the CIS 101 [or your class folder] folder on the USB flash drive) to display the file(s) it contains in the right pane.

- Right-click the Koala Exhibit icon or file name in the right pane to select the Koala Exhibit file and display a shortcut menu that presents a list of commands related to files (Figure 87).

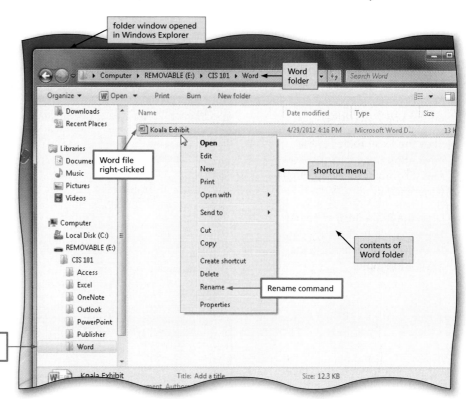

Figure 87

2

- Click Rename on the shortcut menu to place the current file name in a text box.

- Type **Koala Exhibit Flyer** in the text box and then press the ENTER key (Figure 88).

Q&A Are any risks involved in renaming files that are located on a hard disk?

If you inadvertently rename a file that is associated with certain programs, the programs may not be able to find the file and, therefore, may not execute properly. Always use caution when renaming files.

Q&A Can I rename a file when it is open?

No, a file must be closed to change the file name.

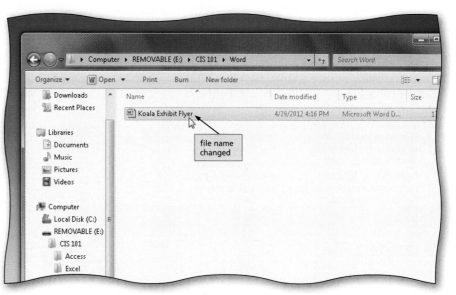

Figure 88

Other Ways
1. Select file, press F2, type new file name, press ENTER

To Move a File

At some time, you may want to move a file from one folder, called the source folder, to another, called the destination. When you move a file, it no longer appears in the original folder. If the destination and the source folders are on the same disk drive, you can move a file by dragging it. If the folders are on different disk drives, then you will need to right-drag the file. The following step moves the Brain Busters Rental Summary file from the Excel folder to the OneNote folder.

- In Windows Explorer, navigate to the location of the file to be moved (in this case, the Excel folder in the CIS 101 folder [or your class folder] on the USB flash drive).

- Click the Excel folder in the navigation pane to display the files it contains in the right pane (Figure 89).

- Drag the Brain Busters Rental Summary file in the right pane to the OneNote folder in the navigation pane.

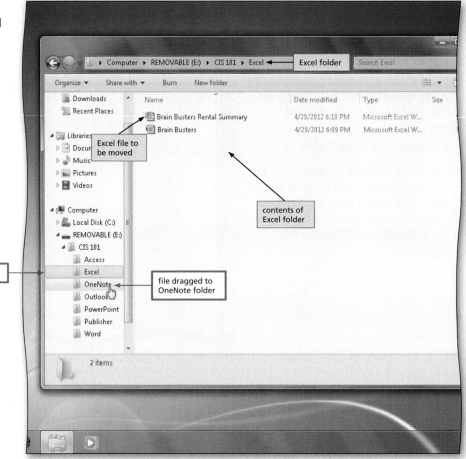

Figure 89

Other Ways
1. Right-click file, drag file to destination folder, click Move here	folder, click Paste on shortcut menu
2. Right-click file to copy, click Cut on shortcut menu, right-click destination	3. Select file to copy, press CTRL+X, select destination folder, press CTRL+V

To Delete a File

A final task you may want to perform is to delete a file. Exercise extreme caution when deleting a file or files. When you delete a file from a hard disk, the deleted file is stored in the Recycle Bin where you can recover it until you empty the Recycle Bin. If you delete a file from removable media, such as a USB flash drive, the file is deleted permanently. The next steps delete the Koala Exhibit Gala file from the PowerPoint folder.

1

- In Windows Explorer, navigate to the location of the file to be deleted (in this case, the PowerPoint folder in the CIS 101 folder [or your class folder] on the USB flash drive).

- Click the PowerPoint folder in the navigation pane to display the files it contains in the right pane.

- Right-click the Koala Exhibit Gala icon or file name in the right pane to select the file and display a shortcut menu (Figure 90).

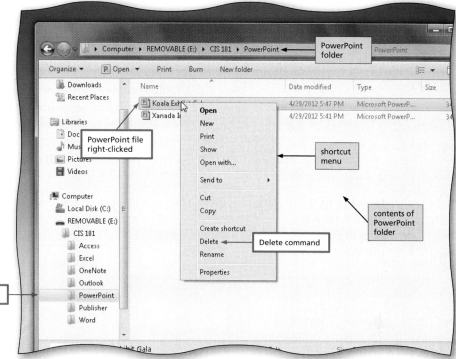

Figure 90

2

- Click Delete on the shortcut menu to display the Delete File dialog box (Figure 91).

- Click the Yes button (Delete File dialog box) to delete the selected file.

Q&A

Can I use this same technique to delete a folder?

Yes. Right-click the folder and then click Delete on the shortcut menu. When you delete a folder, all of the files and folders contained in the folder you are deleting, together with any files and folders on lower hierarchical levels, are deleted as well.

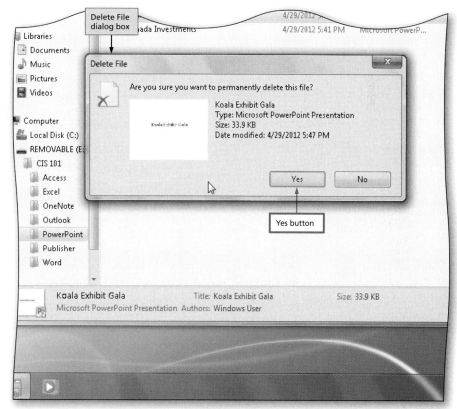

Figure 91

Other Ways

1. Select icon, press DELETE

Microsoft Office and Windows Help

At any time while you are using one of the Microsoft Office 2010 programs, you can use Office Help to display information about all topics associated with the program. To illustrate the use of Office Help, this section uses Word. Help in other Office 2010 programs operates in a similar fashion.

In Office 2010, Help is presented in a window that has Web-browser-style navigation buttons. Each Office 2010 program has its own Help home page, which is the starting Help page that is displayed in the Help window. If your computer is connected to the Internet, the contents of the Help page reflect both the local help files installed on the computer and material from Microsoft's Web site.

To Open the Help Window in an Office Program

The following step opens the Word Help window.

1

- Start an Office program, in this case Word.

- Click the Office program's Help button near the upper-right corner of the program window (the Microsoft Word Help button, in this case) to open the program's Help window (Figure 92).

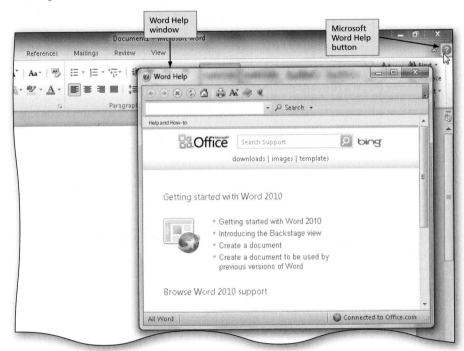

Figure 92

Other Ways
1. Press F1

Moving and Resizing Windows

Up to this point, this chapter has used minimized and maximized windows. At times, however, it is useful, or even necessary, to have more than one window open and visible on the screen at the same time. You can resize and move these open windows so that you can view different areas of and elements in the window. In the case of the Help window, for example, it could be covering document text in the Word window that you need to see.

To Move a Window by Dragging

You can move any open window that is not maximized to another location on the desktop by dragging the title bar of the window. The following step drags the Word Help window to the top left of the desktop.

• Drag the window title bar (the Word Help window title bar, in this case) so that the window moves to the top left of the desktop, as shown in Figure 93.

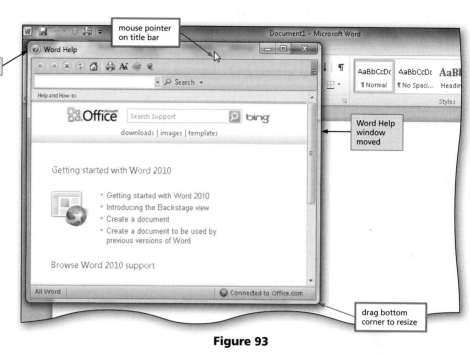

Other Ways

1. Right-click title bar, click Move on shortcut menu, drag window

Figure 93

To Resize a Window by Dragging

Sometimes, information is not visible completely in a window. A method used to change the size of the window is to drag the window borders. The following step changes the size of the Word Help window by dragging its borders.

• Point to the lower-right corner of the window (the Word Help window, in this case) until the mouse pointer changes to a two-headed arrow.

• Drag the bottom border downward to display more of the active window (Figure 94).

Q&A Can I drag other borders on the window to enlarge or shrink the window?

Yes, you can drag the left, right, and top borders and any window corner to resize a window.

Q&A Will Windows 7 remember the new size of the window after I close it?

Yes. When you reopen the window, Windows 7 will display it at the same size it was when you closed it.

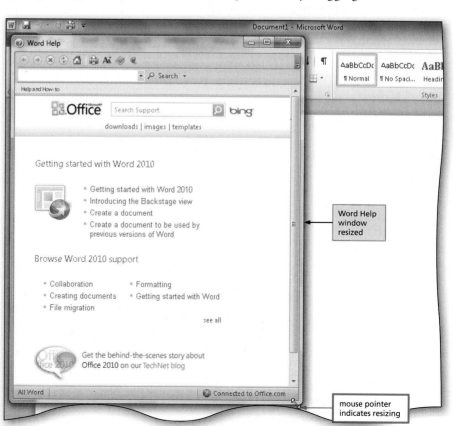

Figure 94

Using Office Help

Once an Office program's Help window is open, several methods exist for navigating Help. You can search for help by using any of the three following methods from the Help window:

1. Enter search text in the 'Type words to search for' text box
2. Click the links in the Help window
3. Use the Table of Contents

To Obtain Help Using the 'Type words to search for' Text Box

Assume for the following example that you want to know more about the Backstage view. The following steps use the 'Type words to search for' text box to obtain useful information about the Backstage view by entering the word, Backstage, as search text.

1

- Type **Backstage** in the 'Type words to search for' text box at the top of the Word Help window to enter the search text.

- Click the Search button arrow to display the Search menu (Figure 95).

- If it is not selected already, click All Word on the Search menu, so that Help performs the most complete search of the current program (Word, in this case). If All Word already is selected, click the Search button arrow again to close the Search menu.

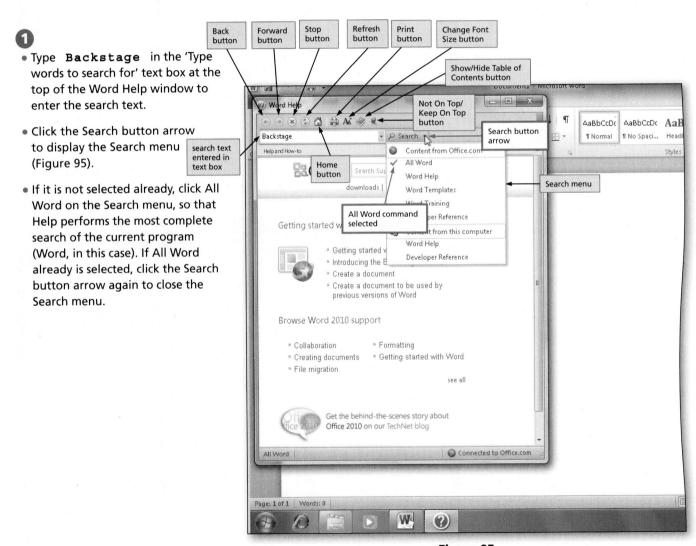

Figure 95

2

• Click the Search button to display the search results (Figure 96).

Q&A Why do my search results differ?

If you do not have an Internet connection, your results will reflect only the content of the Help files on your computer. When searching for help online, results also can change as material is added, deleted, and updated on the online Help Web pages maintained by Microsoft.

Q&A Why were my search results not very helpful?

When initiating a search, be sure to check the spelling of the search text; also, keep your search specific, with fewer than seven words, to return the most accurate results.

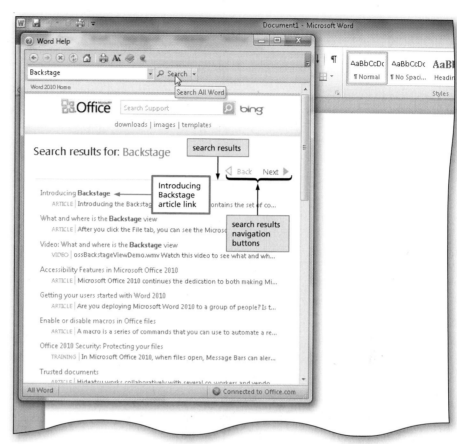

Figure 96

3

• Click the Introducing Backstage link to open the Help document associated with the selected topic (Figure 97).

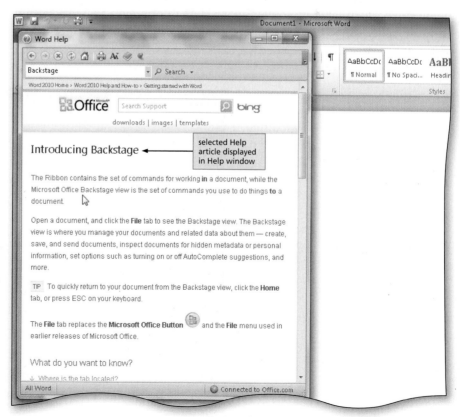

Figure 97

4

- Click the Home button on the toolbar to clear the search results and redisplay the Help home page (Figure 98).

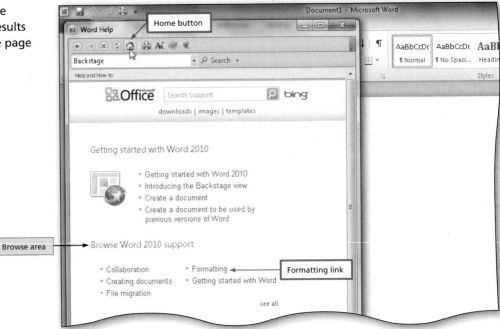

Figure 98

To Obtain Help Using the Help Links

If your topic of interest is listed in the Browse area of the Help window, you can click the link to begin browsing the Help categories instead of entering search text. You browse Help just as you would browse a Web site. If you know which category contains your Help information, you may wish to use these links. The following step finds the Formatting Help information using the category links from the Word Help home page.

1

- Click the Formatting link on the Help home page (shown in Figure 98) to display the Formatting page (Figure 99).

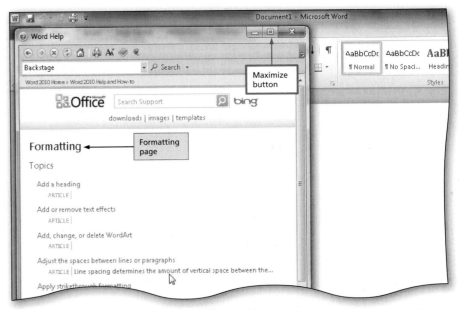

Figure 99

To Obtain Help Using the Help Table of Contents

A third way to find Help in Office programs is through the Help Table of Contents. You can browse through the Table of Contents to display information about a particular topic or to familiarize yourself with an Office program. The following steps access the Help information about themes by browsing through the Table of Contents.

1

- Click the Home button on the toolbar to display the Help home page.

- Click the Show Table of Contents button on the toolbar to display the Table of Contents pane on the left side of the Help window. If necessary, click the Maximize button on the Help title bar to maximize the window (Figure 100).

Q&A Why does the appearance of the Show Table of Contents button change?

When the Table of Contents is displayed in the Help window, the Hide Table of Contents button replaces the Show Table of Contents button.

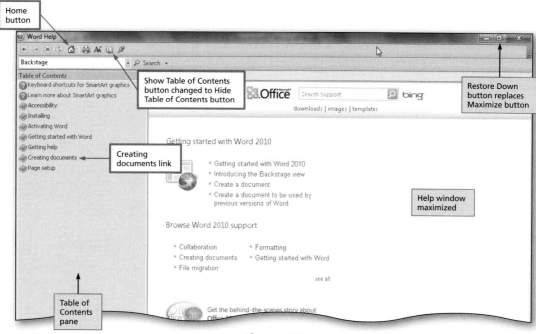

Figure 100

2

- Click the Creating documents link in the Table of Contents pane to view a list of Help subtopics.

- Click the Apply themes to Word documents link in the Table of Contents pane to view the selected Help document in the right pane (Figure 101).

- After reviewing the page, click the Close button to quit Help.

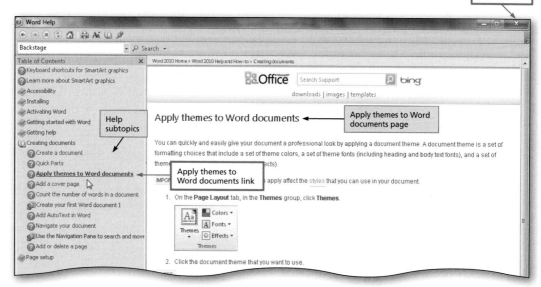

Figure 101

- Click the Office program's Close button (Word, in this case) to quit the Office program.

Q&A How do I remove the Table of Contents pane when I am finished with it?

The Show Table of Contents button acts as a toggle. When the Table of Contents pane is visible, the button changes to Hide Table of Contents. Clicking it hides the Table of Contents pane and changes the button to Show Table of Contents.

Obtaining Help while Working in an Office Program

Help in the Office programs provides you with the ability to obtain help directly, without the need to open the Help window and initiate a search. For example, you may be unsure about how a particular command works, or you may be presented with a dialog box that you are not sure how to use.

Figure 102 shows one option for obtaining help while working in Word. If you want to learn more about a command, point to the command button and wait for the Enhanced ScreenTip to appear. If the Help icon appears in the Enhanced ScreenTip, press the F1 key while pointing to the command to open the Help window associated with that command.

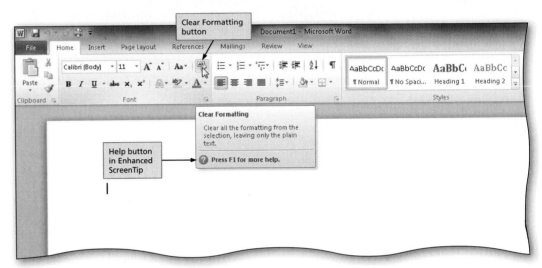

Figure 102

Figure 103 shows a dialog box that contains a Help button. Pressing the F1 key while the dialog box is displayed opens a Help window. The Help window contains help about that dialog box, if available. If no help file is available for that particular dialog box, then the main Help window opens.

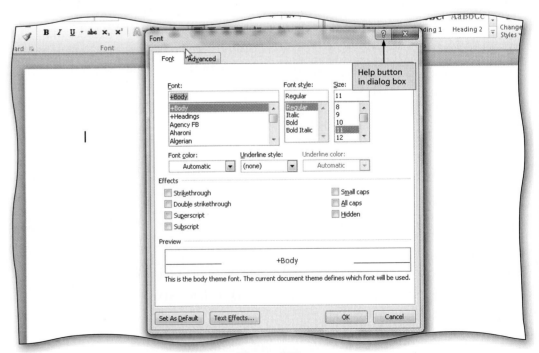

Figure 103

Using Windows Help and Support

One of the more powerful Windows 7 features is Windows Help and Support. **Windows Help and Support** is available when using Windows 7 or when using any Microsoft program running under Windows 7. This feature is designed to assist you in using Windows 7 or the various programs. Table 4 describes the content found in the Help and Support Center. The same methods used for searching Microsoft Office Help can be used in Windows Help and Support. The difference is that Windows Help and Support displays help for Windows 7, instead of for Microsoft Office.

Table 4 Windows Help and Support Center Content Areas	
Area	**Function**
Find an answer quickly	This area contains instructions about how to do a quick search using the search box.
Not sure where to start?	This area displays three topics to help guide a user: How to get started with your computer, Learn about Windows Basics, and Browse Help topics. Clicking one of the options navigates to corresponding Help and Support pages.
More on the Windows Website	This area contains links to online content from the Windows Web site. Clicking the links navigates to the corresponding Web pages on the Web site.

To Start Windows Help and Support

The following steps start Windows Help and Support and display the Windows Help and Support window, containing links to more information about Windows 7.

- Click the Start button on the taskbar to display the Start menu (Figure 104).

Q&A

Why are the programs that are displayed on the Start menu different?

Windows adds the programs you have used recently to the left pane on the Start menu. You have started several programs while performing the steps in this chapter, so those programs now are displayed on the Start menu.

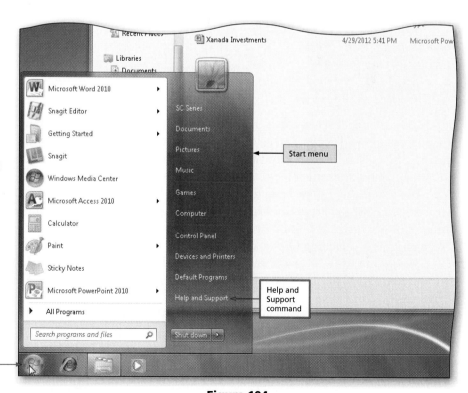

Figure 104

2

• Click Help and Support on the Start menu to open the Windows Help and Support window (Figure 105).

• After reviewing the Windows Help and Support window, click the Close button to quit Windows Help and Support.

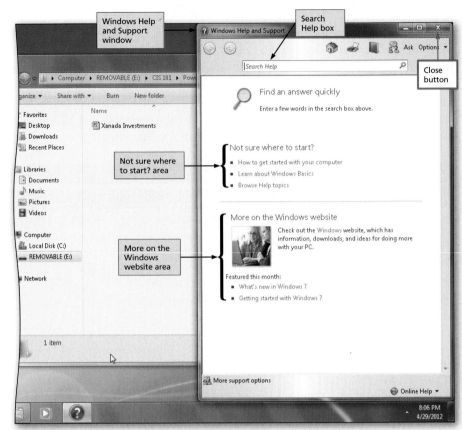

Figure 105

Other Ways

1. Press CTRL+ESC, press RIGHT ARROW, press UP ARROW, press ENTER

2. Press WINDOWS+F1

Chapter Summary

In this chapter, you learned about the Windows 7 interface. You started Windows 7, were introduced to the components of the desktop, and learned several mouse operations. You opened, closed, moved, resized, minimized, maximized, and scrolled a window. You used folder windows to expand and collapse drives and folders, display drive and folder contents, create folders, and rename and then delete a file.

You also learned some basic features of some Microsoft Office 2010 programs, including Word, PowerPoint, Excel, and Access. As part of this learning process, you discovered the common elements that exist among these different Office programs. You now can save basic document, presentation, spreadsheet, and database files. Additional Office programs, including Outlook, Publisher, and OneNote also were discussed.

Microsoft Office Help was demonstrated, and you learned how to use the Office Help window. You were introduced to the Windows 7 Help and Support Center and learned how to use it to obtain more information about Windows 7.

The items listed below include all of the new Windows 7 and Office 2010 skills you have learned in this chapter.

1. Log On to the Computer (OFF 6)
2. Start a Program Using the Start Menu (OFF 10)
3. Maximize a Window (OFF 12)
4. Display a Different Tab on the Ribbon (OFF 16)
5. Minimize, Display, and Restore the Ribbon (OFF 17)
6. Display and Use a Shortcut Menu (OFF 18)
7. Customize the Quick Access Toolbar (OFF 19)
8. Enter Text in a Document (OFF 20)

9. Create a Folder (OFF 22)
10. Create a Folder within a Folder (OFF 24)
11. Expand a Folder, Scroll through Folder Contents, and Collapse a Folder (OFF 26)
12. Switch from One Program to Another (OFF 27)
13. Save a File in a Folder (OFF 27)
14. Minimize and Restore a Window (OFF 30)
15. Change the Screen Resolution (OFF 33)

16. Quit an Office Program with One Document Open (OFF 35)
17. Start a Program Using the Search Box (OFF 37)
18. Enter Content in a Title Slide (OFF 40)
19. Create a New Office Document from the Backstage View (OFF 41)
20. Close an Office File Using the Backstage View (OFF 44)
21. Open a Recent Office File Using the Backstage View (OFF 45)
22. Create a New Blank Office Document from Windows Explorer (OFF 47)
23. Start a Program from Windows Explorer and Open a File (OFF 48)
24. Enter a Worksheet Title (OFF 50)
25. Save an Existing Document with the Same File Name (OFF 51)

26. Create an Access Database (OFF 55)
27. Open an Existing Office File (OFF 57)
28. Rename a File (OFF 63)
29. Move a File (OFF 64)
30. Delete a File (OFF 64)
31. Open the Help Window in an Office Program (OFF 66)
32. Move a Window by Dragging (OFF 66)
33. Resize a Window by Dragging (OFF 67)
34. Obtain Help Using the 'Type words to search for' Text Box (OFF 68)
35. Obtain Help Using the Help Links (OFF 70)
36. Obtain Help Using the Help Table of Contents (OFF 71)
37. Start Windows Help and Support (OFF 73)

 If you have a SAM 2010 user profile, your instructor may have assigned an autogradable version of this assignment. If so, log into the SAM 2010 Web site at www.cengage.com/sam2010 to download the instruction and start files.

Learn It Online

Test your knowledge of chapter content and key terms.

Instructions: To complete the Learn It Online exercises, start your browser, click the Address bar, and then enter the Web address **scsite.com/office2010/learn**. When the Office 2010 Learn It Online page is displayed, click the link for the exercise you want to complete and then read the instructions.

Chapter Reinforcement TF, MC, and SA
A series of true/false, multiple choice, and short answer questions that test your knowledge of the chapter content.

Flash Cards
An interactive learning environment where you identify chapter key terms associated with displayed definitions.

Practice Test
A series of multiple choice questions that test your knowledge of chapter content and key terms.

Who Wants To Be a Computer Genius?
An interactive game that challenges your knowledge of chapter content in the style of a television quiz show.

Wheel of Terms
An interactive game that challenges your knowledge of chapter key terms in the style of the television show *Wheel of Fortune*.

Crossword Puzzle Challenge
A crossword puzzle that challenges your knowledge of key terms presented in the chapter.

Apply Your Knowledge

Reinforce the skills and apply the concepts you learned in this chapter.

Creating a Folder and a Document

Instructions: You will create a Word folder and then create a Word document and save it in the folder.

Perform the following tasks:

1. Connect a USB flash drive to an available USB port and then open the USB flash drive window.

2. Click the New folder button on the toolbar to display a new folder icon and text box for the folder name.

3. Type `Word` in the text box to name the folder. Press the ENTER key to create the folder on the USB flash drive.

4. Start Word.

5. Enter the text shown in Figure 106.

6. Click the Save button on the Quick Access Toolbar. Navigate to the Word folder on the USB flash drive and then save the document using the file name, Apply 1 Class List.

7. If your Quick Access Toolbar does not show the Quick Print button, add the Quick Print button to the Quick Access Toolbar. Print the document using the Quick Print button on the Quick Access Toolbar. When you are finished printing, remove the Quick Print button from the Quick Access Toolbar.

8. Submit the printout to your instructor.

9. Quit Word.

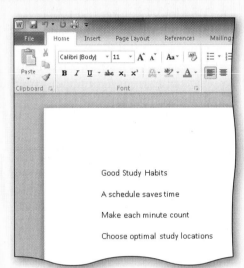

Figure 106

Extend Your Knowledge

Extend the skills you learned in this chapter and experiment with new skills. You will use Help to complete the assignment.

Using Help

Instructions: Use Office Help to perform the following tasks.

Perform the following tasks:

1. Start Word.

2. Click the Microsoft Word Help button to open the Word Help window (Figure 107).

3. Search Word Help to answer the following questions.

   a. What are the steps to add a new group to the Ribbon?

   b. What are Quick Parts?

4. With the Word program still running, start PowerPoint.

Figure 107

5. Click the Microsoft PowerPoint Help button on the title bar to open the PowerPoint Help window.

6. Search PowerPoint Help to answer the following questions.

   a. What is a slide master?

   b. How do you copy slides from another presentation into the existing presentation?

7. Quit PowerPoint.

8. Start Excel.

9. Click the Microsoft Excel Help button to open the Excel Help window.

10. Search Excel Help to answer the following questions.

    a. What are three different functions available in Excel?

    b. What are sparklines?

11. Quit Excel.

12. Start Access.

13. Click the Microsoft Access Help button to open the Access Help window.

14. Search Access Help to answer the following questions.

    a. What is SQL?

    b. What is a data macro?

15. Quit Access.

16. Type the answers from your searches in the Word document. Save the document with a new file name and then submit it in the format specified by your instructor.

17. Quit Word.

Make It Right

Analyze a file structure and correct all errors and/or improve the design.

Organizing Vacation Photos

Instructions: See the inside back cover of this book for instructions on downloading the Data Files for Students, or contact your instructor for information on accessing the required files.

Traditionally, you have stored photos from past vacations together in one folder. The photos are becoming difficult to manage, and you now want to store them in appropriate folders. You will create the folder structure shown in Figure 108. You then will move the photos to the folders so that they will be organized properly.

1. Connect a USB flash drive to an available USB port to open the USB flash drive window.

2. Using the techniques presented in the chapter, create the hierarchical folder structure shown in Figure 108.

3. Using the techniques presented in the chapter, move the vacation photos to their appropriate folders.

4. Submit your work in the format specified by your instructor.

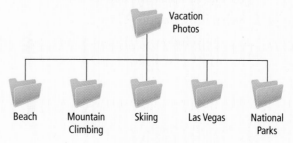

Figure 108

In the Lab

Use the guidelines, concepts, and skills presented in this chapter to increase your knowledge of Windows 7 and Office 2010. Labs are listed in order of increasing difficulty.

Lab 1: Using Windows Help and Support

Problem: You have a few questions about using Windows 7 and would like to answer these questions using Windows Help and Support.

Instructions: Use Windows Help and Support to perform the following tasks:

1. Display the Start menu and then click Help and Support to start Windows Help and Support.

2. Use the Help and Support Content page to answer the following questions.
   a. How do you reduce computer screen flicker?
   b. Which dialog box do you use to change the appearance of the mouse pointer?
   c. How do you minimize all windows?
   d. What is a VPN?

3. Use the Search Help text box in Windows Help and Support to answer the following questions.
   a. How can you minimize all open windows on the desktop?
   b. How do you start a program using the Run command?
   c. What are the steps to add a toolbar to the taskbar?
   d. What wizard do you use to remove unwanted desktop icons?

4. The tools to solve a problem while using Windows 7 are called **troubleshooters**. Use Windows Help and Support to find the list of troubleshooters (Figure 109), and answer the following questions.
   a. What problems does the HomeGroup troubleshooter allow you to resolve?
   b. List five Windows 7 troubleshooters that are not listed in Figure 109.

5. Use Windows Help and Support to obtain information about software licensing and product activation, and answer the following questions.
   a. What is genuine Windows?
   b. What is activation?
   c. What steps are required to activate Windows?
   d. What steps are required to read the Microsoft Software License Terms?
   e. Can you legally make a second copy of Windows 7 for use at home, work, or on a mobile computer or device?
   f. What is registration?

6. Close the Windows Help and Support window.

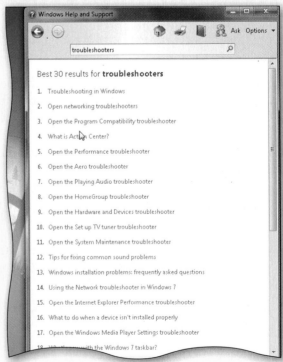

Figure 109

In the Lab

Lab 2: Creating Folders for a Pet Supply Store

Problem: Your friend works for Pete's Pet Supplies. He would like to organize his files in relation to the types of pets available in the store. He has five main categories: dogs, cats, fish, birds, and exotic. You are to create a folder structure similar to Figure 110.

Instructions: Perform the following tasks:
1. Connect a USB flash drive to an available USB port and then open the USB flash drive window.
2. Create the main folder for Pete's Pet Supplies.
3. Navigate to the Pete's Pet Supplies folder.
4. Within the Pete's Pet Supplies folder, create a folder for each of the following: Dogs, Cats, Fish, Birds, and Exotic.
5. Within the Exotic folder, create two additional folders, one for Primates and the second for Reptiles.
6. Submit the assignment in the format specified by your instructor.

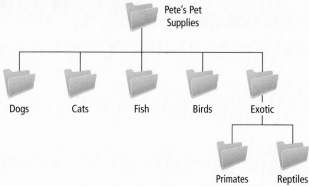

Figure 110

In the Lab

Lab 3: Creating Office Documents

Problem: You are taking a class that requires you to create a Word, PowerPoint, Excel, and Access file. You will save these files to folders named for four different Office programs (Figure 111).

Instructions: Create the folders shown in Figure 111. Then, using the respective Office program, create a small file to save in each folder (i.e., create a Word document to save in the Word folder, a PowerPoint presentation to save in the PowerPoint folder, and so on).

Figure 111

1. Connect a USB flash drive to an available USB port and then open the USB flash drive window.
2. Create the folder structure shown in Figure 111.
3. Navigate to the Word folder.
4. Create a Word document containing the text, My First Word Document, and then save it in the Word folder.
5. Navigate to the PowerPoint folder.
6. Create a PowerPoint presentation containing the title text, My First PowerPoint Presentation, and then save it in the PowerPoint folder.
7. Navigate to the Excel folder.

Continued >

In the Lab *continued*

8. Create an Excel spreadsheet containing the text, My First Excel Spreadsheet, in cell A1 and then save it in the Excel folder.

9. Navigate to the Access folder.

10. Save an Access database named, My First Database, in the Access folder.

11. Close all open Office programs.

12. Submit the assignment in the format specified by your instructor.

Cases and Places

Apply your creative thinking and problem solving skills to design and implement a solution.

Note: To complete these assignments, you may be required to use the Data Files for Students. See the inside back cover of this book for instructions on downloading the Data Files for Students, or contact your instructor for information about accessing the required files.

1: Creating Beginning Files for Classes

Academic

You are taking the following classes: Introduction to Engineering, Beginning Psychology, Introduction to Biology, and Accounting. Create folders for each of the classes. Use the following folder names: Engineering, Psychology, Biology, and Accounting, when creating the folder structure. In the Engineering folder, use Word to create a Word document with the name of the class and the class meeting location and time (MW 10:30 – 11:45, Room 317). In the Psychology folder, use PowerPoint to create your first lab presentation. It should begin with a title slide containing the text, Behavioral Observations. In the Biology folder, save a database named Research in the Biology folder. In the Accounting folder, create an Excel spreadsheet with the text, Tax Information, in cell A1. Use the concepts and techniques presented in this chapter to create the folders and files.

2: Using Help

Personal

Your parents enjoy working and playing games on their home computers. Your mother uses a notebook computer downstairs, and your father uses a desktop computer upstairs. They expressed interest in sharing files between their computers and sharing a single printer, so you offered to research various home networking options. Start Windows Help and Support, and search Help using the keywords, home networking. Use the link for installing a printer on a home network. Start Word and then type the main steps for installing a printer. Use the link for setting up a HomeGroup and then type the main steps for creating a HomeGroup in the Word document. Use the concepts and techniques presented in this chapter to use Help and create the Word document.

3: Creating Folders

Professional

Your boss at the bookstore where you work part-time has asked for help with organizing her files. After looking through the files, you decided upon a file structure for her to use, including the following folders: books, magazines, tapes, DVDs, and general merchandise. Within the books folder, create folders for hardback and paperback books. Within magazines, create folders for special issues and periodicals. In the tapes folder, create folders for celebrity and major release. In the DVDs folder, create a folder for book to DVD. In the general merchandise folder, create folders for novelties, posters, and games. Use the concepts and techniques presented in this chapter to create the folders.

1 | Creating and Editing a Presentation with Clip Art

Objectives

You will have mastered the material in this chapter when you can:

- Select a document theme
- Create a title slide and a text slide with a multi-level bulleted list
- Add new slides and change slide layouts
- Insert clips and pictures into a slide with and without a content placeholder
- Move and size clip art

- Change font size and color
- Bold and italicize text
- Duplicate a slide
- Arrange slides
- Select slide transitions
- View a presentation in Slide Show view
- Print a presentation

1 | Creating and Editing a Presentation with Clip Art

Introduction

A PowerPoint **presentation,** also called a **slide show**, can help you deliver a dynamic, professional-looking message to an audience. PowerPoint allows you to produce slides to use in an academic, business, or other environment. One of the more common uses of these slides is to enhance an oral presentation. A speaker may desire to convey information, such as urging students to volunteer at a fund-raising event, explaining changes in employee compensation packages, or describing a new laboratory procedure. The PowerPoint slides should reinforce the speaker's message and help the audience retain the information presented. Custom slides can fit your specific needs and contain diagrams, charts, tables, pictures, shapes, video, sound, and animation effects to make your presentation more effective. An accompanying handout gives audience members reference notes and review material for your presentation.

Project Planning Guidelines

The process of developing a presentation that communicates specific information requires careful analysis and planning. As a starting point, establish why the presentation is needed. Next, analyze the intended audience for the presentation and its unique needs. Then, gather information about the topic and decide what to include in the presentation. Finally, determine the presentation design and style that will be most successful at delivering the message. Details of these guidelines are provided in Appendix A. In addition, each project in this book provides practical applications of these planning considerations.

BTW

Energy-Saving Information
The U.S. Department of Energy's Web site has myriad information available on the topics of energy efficiency and renewable energy. These features can provide news and product research that you can share with audiences with the help of a PowerPoint presentation.

Project — Presentation with Bulleted Lists and Clip Art

In this chapter's project, you will follow proper design guidelines and learn to use PowerPoint to create, save, and print the slides shown in Figures 1–1a through 1–1e. The objective is to produce a presentation, called It Is Easy Being Green, to help consumers understand basic steps they can take to save energy in their homes. This slide show has a variety of clip art and visual elements to add interest and illustrate energy-cutting measures. Some of the text has formatting and color enhancements. Transitions help one slide flow gracefully into the next during a slide show. In addition, you will print a handout of your slides to distribute to audience members.

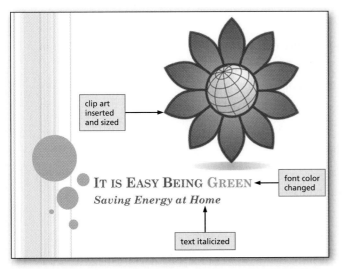

(a) Slide 1 (Title Slide with Clip Art)

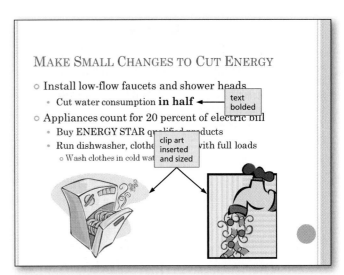

(b) Slide 2 (Multi-Level Bulleted List with Clip Art)

(c) Slide 3 (Title and Photograph)

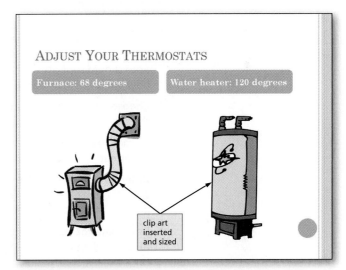

(d) Slide 4 (Comparison Layout and Clip Art)

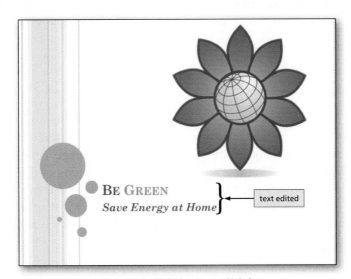

(e) Slide 5 (Closing Slide)

Figure 1–1

Overview

BTW
BTWs
For a complete list of the BTWs found in the margins of this book, visit the PowerPoint 2010 BTW Web page (scsite.com/ppt2010/btw).

As you read this chapter, you will learn how to create the presentation shown in Figure 1–1 on the previous page by performing these general tasks:

- Select an appropriate document theme.
- Enter titles and text on slides.
- Change the size, color, and style of text.
- Insert clips and a photograph.
- Add a transition to each slide.
- View the presentation on your computer.
- Print your slides.

Plan Ahead

General Project Guidelines

When creating a PowerPoint document, the actions you perform and decisions you make will affect the appearance and characteristics of the finished document. As you create a presentation such as the project shown in Figure 1–1, you should follow these general guidelines:

1. **Find the appropriate theme.** The overall appearance of a presentation significantly affects its capability to communicate information clearly. The slides' graphical appearance should support the presentation's overall message. Colors, fonts, and layouts affect how audience members perceive and react to the slide content.

2. **Choose words for each slide.** Use the less is more principle. The less text, the more likely the slides will enhance your speech. Use the fewest words possible to make a point.

3. **Format specific elements of the text.** Examples of how you can modify the appearance, or **format**, of text include changing its shape, size, color, and position on the slide.

4. **Determine where to save the presentation.** You can store a document permanently, or **save** it, on a variety of storage media, including a hard disk, USB flash drive, or CD. You also can indicate a specific location on the storage media for saving the document.

5. **Determine the best method for distributing the presentation.** Presentations can be distributed on paper or electronically. You can print a hard copy of the presentation slides for proofing or reference, or you can distribute an electronic image in various formats.

When necessary, more specific details concerning the above guidelines are presented at appropriate points in the chapter. The chapter also will identify the actions performed and decisions made regarding these guidelines during the creation of the slides shown in Figure 1–1.

For an introduction to Windows 7 and instruction about how to perform basic Windows 7 tasks, read the Office 2010 and Windows 7 chapter at the beginning of this book, where you can learn how to resize windows, change screen resolution, create folders, move and rename files, use Windows Help, and much more.

To Start PowerPoint

If you are using a computer to step through the project in this chapter and you want your screens to match the figures in this book, you should change your screen's resolution to 1024×768. For information about how to change a computer's resolution, refer to the Office 2010 and Windows 7 chapter at the beginning of this book.

The following steps, which assume Windows 7 is running, start PowerPoint based on a typical installation. You may need to ask your instructor how to start PowerPoint for your computer. For a detailed example of the procedure summarized below, refer to the Office 2010 and Windows 7 chapter.

1 Click the Start button on the Windows 7 taskbar to display the Start menu.

2 Type **Microsoft PowerPoint** as the search text in the 'Search programs and files' text box and watch the search results appear on the Start menu.

3 Click Microsoft PowerPoint 2010 in the search results on the Start menu to start PowerPoint and display a new blank document in the PowerPoint window.

4 If the PowerPoint window is not maximized, click the Maximize button next to the Close button on its title bar to maximize the window.

Choosing a Document Theme

You can give a presentation a professional and integrated appearance easily by using a document theme. A **document theme** provides consistency in design and color throughout the entire presentation by setting the color scheme, font set, and layout of a presentation. This collection of formatting choices includes a set of colors (the Theme Colors group), a set of heading and content text fonts (the Theme Fonts group), and a set of lines and fill effects (the Theme Effects group). These groups allow you to choose and change the appearance of all the slides or individual slides in your presentation. The left edge of the status bar in Figure 1–2 shows the current slide number followed by the total number of slides in the document and a document theme identifier.

Find the appropriate theme.
In the initial steps of this project, you will select a document theme by locating a particular built-in theme in the Themes group. You could, however, apply a theme at any time while creating the presentation. Some PowerPoint slide show designers create presentations using the default Office Theme. This blank design allows them to concentrate on the words being used to convey the message and does not distract them with colors and various text attributes. Once the text is entered, the designers then select an appropriate document theme.

Plan Ahead

To Choose a Document Theme

The document theme identifier shows the theme currently used in the slide show. PowerPoint initially uses the **Office Theme** until you select a different theme. The following steps change the theme for this presentation from the Office Theme to the Oriel document theme.

1

• Click Design on the Ribbon to display the Design tab (Figure 1–2).

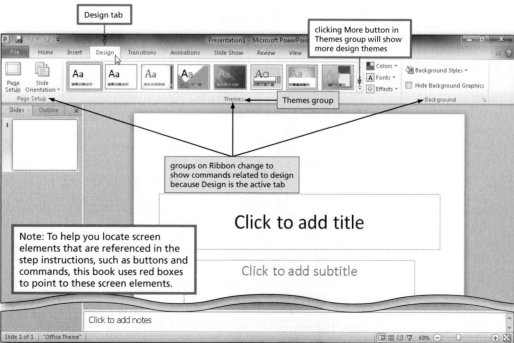

Figure 1–2

2

- Click the More button (Design tab | Themes group) to expand the gallery, which shows more Built-In theme gallery options (Figure 1–3).

🔍 **Experiment**

- Point to various document themes in the Themes gallery and watch the colors and fonts change on the title slide.

Q&A

Are the themes displayed in a specific order?

Yes. They are arranged in alphabetical order running from left to right. If you point to a theme, a ScreenTip with the theme's name appears on the screen.

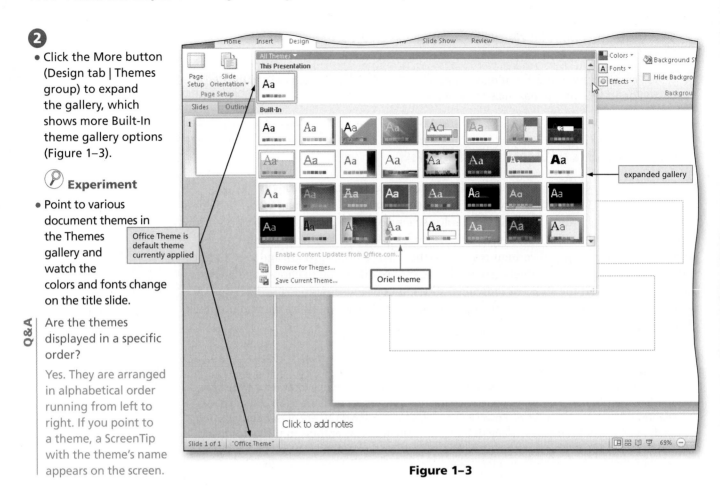

Figure 1–3

Q&A

What if I change my mind and do not want to select a new theme?

Click anywhere outside the All Themes gallery to close the gallery.

3

- Click the Oriel theme to apply this theme to Slide 1 (Figure 1–4).

Q&A

If I decide at some future time that this design does not fit the theme of my presentation, can I apply a different design?

Yes. You can repeat these steps at any time while creating your presentation.

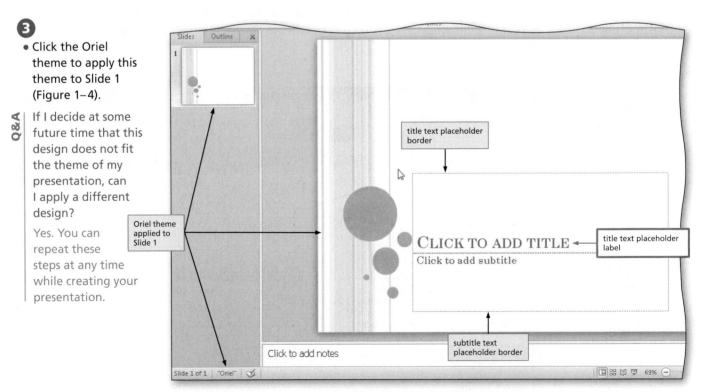

Figure 1–4

Creating a Title Slide

When you open a new presentation, the default **Title Slide** layout appears. The purpose of this layout is to introduce the presentation to the audience. PowerPoint includes eight other built-in standard layouts. The default (preset) slide layouts are set up in **landscape orientation**, where the slide width is greater than its height. In landscape orientation, the slide size is preset to 10 inches wide and 7.5 inches high when printed on a standard sheet of paper measuring 11 inches wide and 8.5 inches high.

Placeholders are boxes with dotted or hatch-marked borders that are displayed when you create a new slide. Most layouts have both a title text placeholder and at least one content placeholder. Depending on the particular slide layout selected, title and subtitle placeholders are displayed for the slide title and subtitle; a content text placeholder is displayed for text, art, or a table, chart, picture, graphic, or movie. The title slide has two text placeholders where you can type the main heading, or title, of a new slide and the subtitle.

With the exception of a blank slide, PowerPoint assumes every new slide has a title. To make creating a presentation easier, any text you type after a new slide appears becomes title text in the title text placeholder. The following steps create the title slide for this presentation.

Plan Ahead

Choose the words for the slide.
No doubt you have heard the phrase, "You get only one chance to make a first impression." The same philosophy holds true for a PowerPoint presentation. The title slide gives your audience an initial sense of what they are about to see and hear. It is, therefore, extremely important to choose the text for this slide carefully. Avoid stating the obvious in the title. Instead, create interest and curiosity using key ideas from the presentation.

Some PowerPoint users create the title slide as their last step in the design process so that it reflects the tone of the presentation. They begin by planning the final slide in the presentation so that they know where and how they want to end the slide show. All the slides in the presentation should work toward meeting this final slide.

To Enter the Presentation Title

The presentation title for Project 1 is It Is Easy Being Green. This title creates interest by introducing the concept of simple energy conservation tasks. The following step creates the slide show's title.

- Click the label, Click to add title, located inside the title text placeholder to select the placeholder (Figure 1–5).

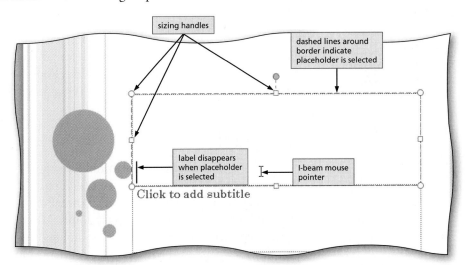

Figure 1–5

2

• Type **It Is Easy Being Green** in the title text placeholder. Do not press the ENTER key (Figure 1–6).

Why does the text display with capital letters despite the fact I am typing uppercase and lowercase letters?

The Oriel theme uses the Small Caps effect for the title text. This effect converts lowercase letters to uppercase and reduces their size.

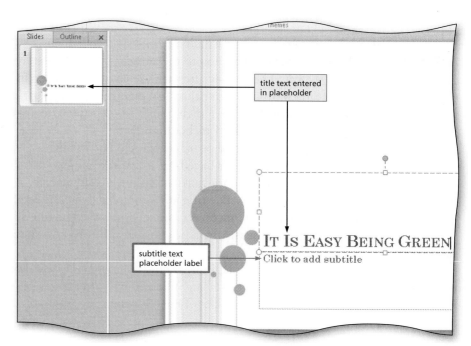

Figure 1–6

Correcting a Mistake When Typing

If you type the wrong letter, press the BACKSPACE key to erase all the characters back to and including the one that is incorrect. If you mistakenly press the ENTER key after typing the title and the insertion point is on the new line, simply press the BACKSPACE key to return the insertion point to the right of the letter n in the word, Green.

When you install PowerPoint, the default setting allows you to reverse up to the last 20 changes by clicking the Undo button on the Quick Access Toolbar. The ScreenTip that appears when you point to the Undo button changes to indicate the type of change just made. For example, if you type text in the title text placeholder and then point to the Undo button, the ScreenTip that appears is Undo Typing. For clarity, when referencing the Undo button in this project, the name displaying in the ScreenTip is referenced. You can reapply a change that you reversed with the Undo button by clicking the Redo button on the Quick Access Toolbar. Clicking the Redo button reverses the last undo action. The ScreenTip name reflects the type of reversal last performed.

Paragraphs

Text in the subtitle text placeholder supports the title text. It can appear on one or more lines in the placeholder. To create more than one subtitle line, you press the ENTER key after typing some words. PowerPoint creates a new line, which is the second paragraph in the placeholder. A **paragraph** is a segment of text with the same format that begins when you press the ENTER key and ends when you press the ENTER key again. This new paragraph is the same level as the previous paragraph. A **level** is a position within a structure, such as an outline, that indicates the magnitude of importance. PowerPoint allows for five paragraph levels.

For an introduction to Office 2010 and instruction about how to perform basic tasks in Office 2010 programs, read the Office 2010 and Windows 7 chapter at the beginning of this book, where you can learn how to start a program, use the Ribbon, save a file, open a file, quit a program, use Help, and much more.

To Enter the Presentation Subtitle Paragraph

The first subtitle paragraph links to the title by giving further detail that the presentation will focus on energy-saving measures at home. The following steps enter the presentation subtitle.

1

• Click the label, Click to add subtitle, located inside the subtitle text placeholder to select the placeholder (Figure 1–7).

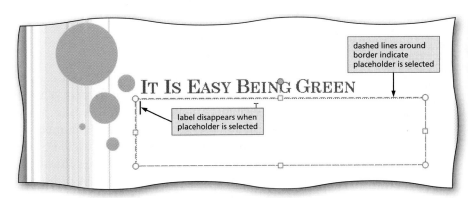

Figure 1–7

2

• Type **Saving Energy at Home** but do not press the ENTER key (Figure 1–8).

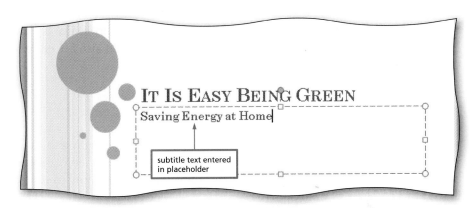

Figure 1–8

Identify how to format specific elements of the text.
Most of the time, you use the document theme's text attributes, color scheme, and layout. Occasionally, you may want to change the way a presentation looks, however, and still keep a particular document theme. PowerPoint gives you that flexibility.
Graphic designers use several rules when formatting text.

• Avoid all capital letters, if possible. Audiences have difficulty comprehending sentences typed in all capital letters, especially when the lines exceed seven words. All capital letters leaves no room for emphasis or inflection, so readers get confused about what material deserves particular attention. Some document themes, however, have a default title text style of all capital letters.

• Avoid text with a font size less than 30 point. Audience members generally will sit a maximum of 50 feet from a screen, and at this distance 30-point type is the smallest size text they can read comfortably without straining.

• Make careful color choices. Color evokes emotions, and a careless color choice may elicit the incorrect psychological response. PowerPoint provides a color gallery with hundreds of colors. The built-in document themes use complementary colors that work well together. If you stray from these themes and add your own color choices, without a good reason to make the changes, your presentation is apt to become ineffective.

Plan Ahead

Formatting Characters in a Presentation

Recall that each document theme determines the color scheme, font set, and layout of a presentation. You can use a specific document theme and then change the characters' formats any time before, during, or after you type the text.

BTW

Q&As

For a complete list of the Q&As found in many of the step-by-step sequences in this book, visit the PowerPoint 2010 Q&A Web page (scsite.com/ ppt2010/qa).

Fonts and Font Styles

Characters that appear on the screen are a specific shape and size. Examples of how you can modify the appearance, or **format**, of these typed characters on the screen and in print include changing the font, style, size, and color. The **font**, or typeface, defines the appearance and shape of the letters, numbers, punctuation marks, and symbols. **Style** indicates how the characters are formatted. PowerPoint's text font styles include regular, italic, bold, and bold italic. **Size** specifies the height of the characters and is gauged by a measurement system that uses points. A **point** is 1/72 of an inch in height. Thus, a character with a font size of 36 is 36/72 (or 1/2) of an inch in height. **Color** defines the hue of the characters.

This presentation uses the Oriel document theme, which uses particular font styles and font sizes. The Oriel document theme default title text font is named Century Schoolbook. It has a bold style with no special effects, and its size is 30 point. The Oriel document theme default subtitle text font also is Century Schoolbook with a font size of 18 point.

To Select a Paragraph

You can use many techniques to format characters. When you want to apply the same formats to multiple words or paragraphs, it is efficient to select the desired text and then make the desired changes to all the characters simultaneously. The first formatting change you will make will apply to the title slide subtitle. The following step selects this paragraph.

- Triple-click the paragraph, Saving Energy at Home, in the subtitle text placeholder to select the paragraph (Figure 1–9).

Q&A

Can I select the paragraph using a technique other than triple-clicking?

Yes. You can move your mouse pointer to the left of the first paragraph and then drag to the end of the line.

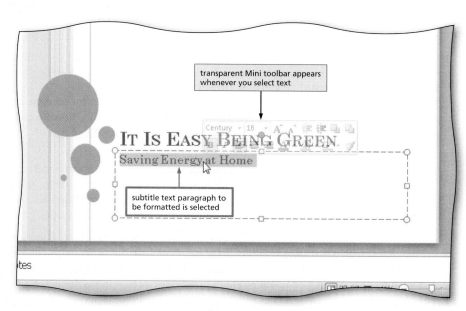

transparent Mini toolbar appears whenever you select text

IT IS EASY BEING GREEN

Saving Energy at Home

subtitle text paragraph to be formatted is selected

Figure 1–9

To Italicize Text

Different font styles often are used on slides to make them more appealing to the reader and to emphasize particular text. **Italicized** text has a slanted appearance. Used sparingly, it draws the readers' eyes to these characters. The following step adds emphasis to the second line of the subtitle text by changing regular text to italic text.

- With the subtitle text still selected, click the Italic button on the Mini toolbar to italicize that text on the slide (Figure 1–10).

Q&A

If I change my mind and decide not to italicize the text, how can I remove this style?

Click the Italic button a second time or immediately click the Undo button on the Quick Access Toolbar or press CTRL+Z.

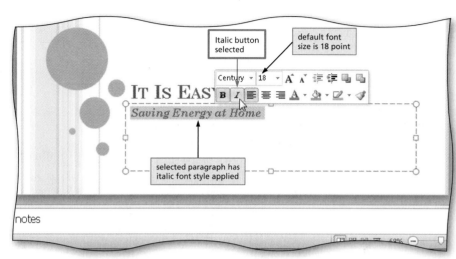

Figure 1–10

Other Ways		
1. Right-click selected text, click Font on shortcut menu, click Font tab (Font dialog box), click Italic in Font style list, click OK button	2. Select text, click Italic button (Home tab | Font group) 3. Click Font Dialog Box Launcher (Home tab | Font	group), click Font tab (Font dialog box), click Italic in Font style list, click OK button 4. Select text, press CTRL+I

To Increase Font Size

To add emphasis, you increase the font size for the subtitle text. The Increase Font Size button on the Mini toolbar increases the font size in preset increments. The following step uses this button to increase the font size.

- Click the Increase Font Size button on the Mini toolbar twice to increase the font size of the selected text from 18 to 24 point (Figure 1–11).

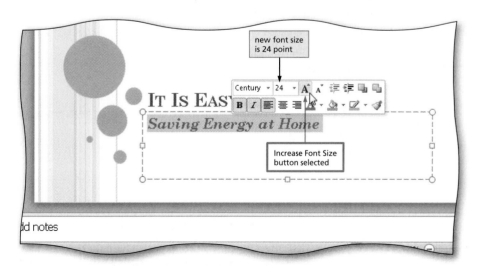

Figure 1–11

Other Ways		
1. Click Font Size box arrow on Mini toolbar, click desired font size in Font Size gallery	2. Click Increase Font Size button (Home tab | Font group) 3. Click Font Size box arrow (Home tab | Font group),	click desired font size in Font size gallery 4. Press CTRL+SHIFT+>

To Select a Word

PowerPoint designers use many techniques to emphasize words and characters on a slide. To add emphasis to the energy-saving concept of your slide show, you want to increase the font size and change the font color to green for the word, Green, in the title text. You could perform these actions separately, but it is more efficient to select the word and then change the font attributes. The following steps select a word.

1

• Position the mouse pointer somewhere in the word to be selected (in this case, in the word, Green) (Figure 1–12).

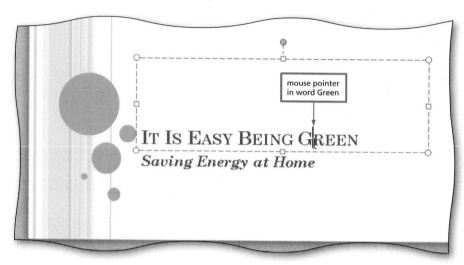

Figure 1–12

2

• Double-click the word to select it (Figure 1–13).

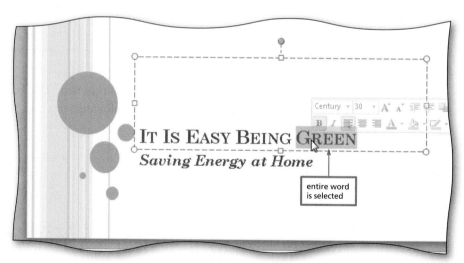

Figure 1–13

Other Ways

1. Position mouse pointer before first character, press CTRL+SHIFT+RIGHT ARROW

Plan Ahead

Format text colors.
When selecting text colors, try to limit using red. This color often is associated with dangerous or alarming situations. In addition, at least 15 percent of men have difficulty distinguishing varying shades of green or red. They also often see the color purple as blue and the color brown as green. This problem is more pronounced when the colors appear in small areas, such as slide paragraphs or line chart bars.

To Change the Text Color

PowerPoint allows you to use one or more text colors in a presentation. To add more emphasis to the word, Green, in the title slide text, you decide to change the color. The following steps add emphasis to this word by changing the font color from black to green.

1

• With the word, Green, selected, click the Font Color arrow on the Mini toolbar to display the gallery of Theme Colors and Standard Colors (Figure 1–14).

Q&A If the Mini toolbar disappears from the screen, how can I display it once again?

Right-click the text, and the Mini toolbar should appear.

 Experiment

• Point to various colors in the gallery and watch the word's font color change.

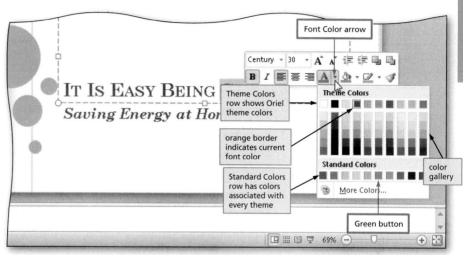

Figure 1–14

2

• Click the Green button in the Standard Colors row on the Mini toolbar (sixth color) to change the font color to green (Figure 1–15).

Q&A Why did I select the color Green?

Green is one of the 10 standard colors associated with every document theme, and it is a universal color to represent respecting natural resources. The color will emphasize the fact that the presentation focuses on green conservation measures.

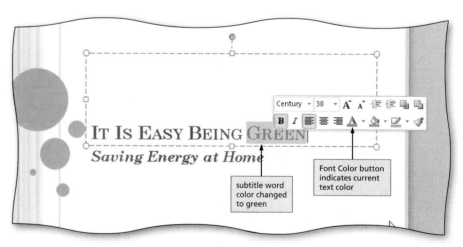

Figure 1–15

Q&A What is the difference between the colors shown in the Theme Colors area and the Standard Colors?

The 10 colors in the top row of the Theme Colors area are two text, two background, and six accent colors in the Oriel theme; the five colors in each column under the top row display different transparencies. These colors are available in every document theme.

3

• Click outside the selected area to deselect the word.

Other Ways	
1. Right-click selected text, click Font on shortcut menu, click Font Color button, click Green in Standard Colors row	2. Click Font Color arrow (Home tab | Font group), click Green in Standard Colors row

Organizing Files and Folders

You should organize and store files in folders so that you easily can find the files later. For example, if you are taking an introductory computer class called CIS 101, a good practice would be to save all PowerPoint files in a PowerPoint folder in a CIS 101 folder. For a discussion of folders and detailed examples of creating folders, refer to the Office 2010 and Windows 7 chapter at the beginning of this book.

To Save a Presentation

You have performed many tasks while creating this slide and do not want to risk losing work completed thus far. Accordingly, you should save the document.

The following steps assume you already have created folders for storing your files, for example, a CIS 101 folder (for your class) that contains a PowerPoint folder (for your assignments). Thus, these steps save the document in the PowerPoint folder in the CIS 101 folder on a USB flash drive using the file name, Saving Energy. For a detailed example of the procedure summarized below, refer to the Office 2010 and Windows 7 chapter at the beginning of this book.

1 With a USB flash drive connected to one of the computer's USB ports, click the Save button on the Quick Access Toolbar to display the Save As dialog box.

2 Type **Saving Energy** in the File name text box to change the file name. Do not press the ENTER key after typing the file name because you do not want to close the dialog box at this time.

3 Navigate to the desired save location (in this case, the PowerPoint folder in the CIS 101 folder [or your class folder] on the USB flash drive).

4 Click the Save button (Save As dialog box) to save the document in the selected folder on the selected drive with the entered file name.

Adding a New Slide to a Presentation

With the text for the title slide for the presentation created, the next step is to add the first text slide immediately after the title slide. Usually, when you create a presentation, you add slides with text, clip art, graphics, or charts. Some placeholders allow you to double-click the placeholder and then access other objects, such as media clips, charts, diagrams, and organization charts. You can change the layout for a slide at any time during the creation of a presentation.

To Add a New Text Slide with a Bulleted List

When you add a new slide, PowerPoint uses the Title and Content slide layout. This layout provides a title placeholder and a content area for text, art, charts, and other graphics. A vertical scroll bar appears in the Slide pane when you add the second slide so that you can move from slide to slide easily. A thumbnail of this slide also appears in the Slides tab. The following steps add a new slide with the Title and Content slide layout.

1

• Click Home on the Ribbon to display the Home tab (Figure 1–16).

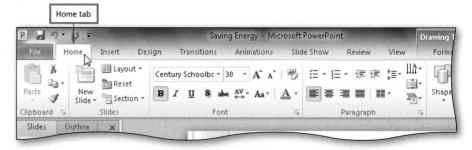

Figure 1–16

2

- Click the New Slide button (Home tab | Slides group) to insert a new slide with the Title and Content layout (Figure 1–17).

Q&A Why does the bullet character display an orange circle?

The Oriel document theme determines the bullet characters. Each paragraph level has an associated bullet character.

Q&A I clicked the New Slide arrow instead of the New Slide button. What should I do?

Click the Title and Content slide thumbnail in the layout gallery.

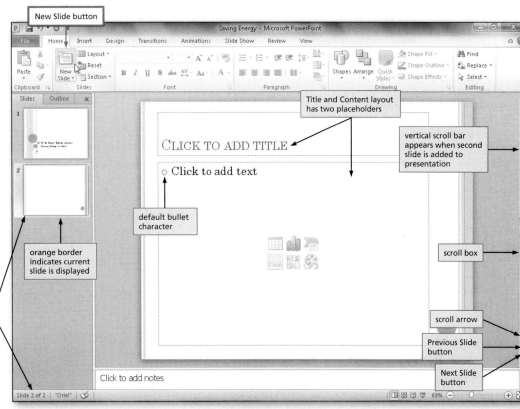

Figure 1–17

Other Ways

1. Press CTRL+M

Choose the words for the slide.

All presentations should follow the 7 × 7 rule, which states that each slide should have a maximum of seven lines, and each line should have a maximum of seven words. PowerPoint designers must choose their words carefully and, in turn, help viewers read the slides easily.

Avoid line wraps. Your audience's eyes want to stop at the end of a line. Thus, you must plan your words carefully or adjust the font size so that each point displays on only one line.

Creating a Text Slide with a Multi-Level Bulleted List

The information in the Slide 2 text placeholder is presented in a bulleted list with three levels. A **bulleted list** is a list of paragraphs, each of which is preceded by a bullet. A slide that consists of more than one level of bulleted text is called a **multi-level bulleted list slide**. In a multi-level bulleted list, a lower-level paragraph is a subset of a higher-level paragraph. It usually contains information that supports the topic in the paragraph immediately above it.

Two of the Slide 2 bullets appear at the same paragraph level, called the first level: Install low-flow faucets and shower heads, and Appliances count for 20 percent of electric bill. Beginning with the second level, each paragraph indents to the right of the preceding level and is pushed down to a lower level. For example, if you increase the indent of a first-level paragraph, it becomes a second-level paragraph. The second, fourth, and fifth paragraphs on Slide 2 are second-level paragraphs. The last paragraph, Wash clothes in cold water, is a third-level paragraph.

BTW

The Ribbon and Screen Resolution
PowerPoint may change how the groups and buttons within the groups appear on the Ribbon, depending on the computer's screen resolution. Thus, your Ribbon may look different from the ones in this book if you are using a screen resolution other than 1024 x 768.

Creating a text slide with a multi-level bulleted list requires several steps. Initially, you enter a slide title in the title text placeholder. Next, you select the content text placeholder. Then, you type the text for the multi-level bulleted list, increasing and decreasing the indents as needed. The next several sections add a slide with a multi-level bulleted list.

To Enter a Slide Title

PowerPoint assumes every new slide has a title. The title for Slide 2 is Make Small Changes to Cut Energy. The following step enters this title.

1

• Click the label, Click to add title, to select it and then type **Make Small Changes to Cut Energy** in the placeholder. Do not press the ENTER key (Figure 1–18).

Q&A What are those six icons grouped in the middle of the slide?

You can click one of the icons to insert a specific type of content: table, chart, SmartArt graphic, picture, clip art, or media clip.

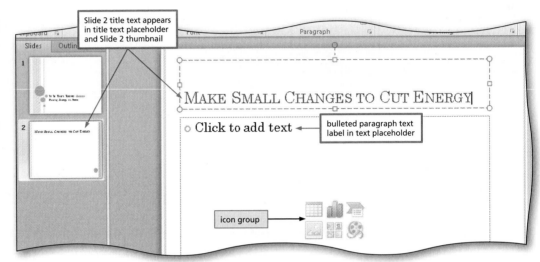

Figure 1–18

To Select a Text Placeholder

Before you can type text into the text placeholder, you first must select it. The following step selects the text placeholder on Slide 2.

1

• Click the label, Click to add text, to select the text placeholder (Figure 1–19).

Q&A Why does my mouse pointer have a different shape?

If you move the mouse pointer away from the bullet, it will change shape.

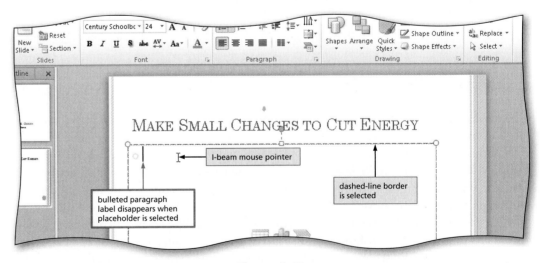

Figure 1–19

Other Ways

1. Press CTRL+ENTER

To Type a Multi-Level Bulleted List

The content placeholder provides an area for the text characters. When you click inside a placeholder, you then can type or paste text. As discussed previously, a bulleted list is a list of paragraphs, each of which is preceded by a bullet. A paragraph is a segment of text ended by pressing the ENTER key.

The content text placeholder is selected, so the next step is to type the multi-level bulleted list that consists of six paragraphs, as shown in Figure 1–1b on page PPT 3. Creating a lower-level paragraph is called **demoting** text; creating a higher-level paragraph is called **promoting** text. The following steps create a multi-level bulleted list consisting of three levels.

1

- Type **Install low-flow faucets and shower heads** and then press the ENTER key (Figure 1–20).

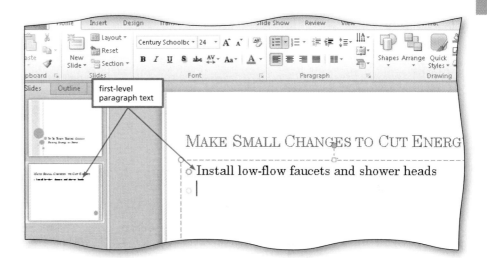

Figure 1–20

2

- Click the Increase List Level button (Home tab | Paragraph group) to indent the second paragraph below the first and create a second-level paragraph (Figure 1–21).

 Why does the bullet for this paragraph have a different size and color?

A different bullet is assigned to each paragraph level.

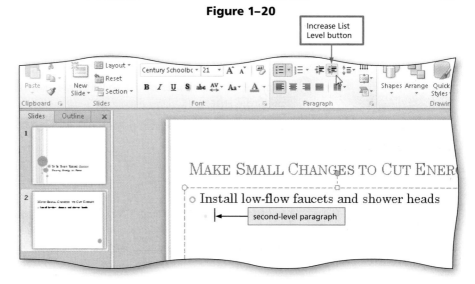

Figure 1–21

3

- Type **Cut water consumption in half** and then press the ENTER key (Figure 1–22).

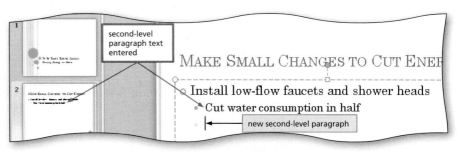

Figure 1–22

4

- Click the Decrease List Level button (Home tab | Paragraph group) so that the second-level paragraph becomes a first-level paragraph (Figure 1–23).

Q&A

Can I delete bullets on a slide?

Yes. If you do not want bullets to display in a particular paragraph, click the Bullets button (Home tab | Paragraph group) or right-click the paragraph and then click the Bullets button on the shortcut menu.

Other Ways

1. Press TAB to promote paragraph; press SHIFT+TAB to demote paragraph

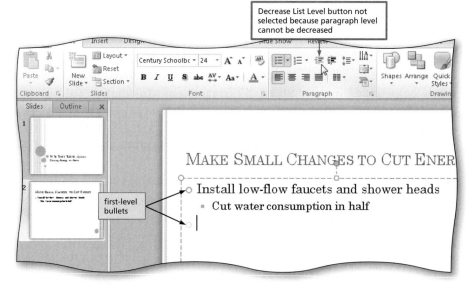

Figure 1–23

To Type the Remaining Text for Slide 2

The following steps complete the text for Slide 2.

1 Type `Appliances count for 20 percent of electric bill` and then press the ENTER key.

2 Click the Increase List Level button (Home tab | Paragraph group) to demote the paragraph to the second level.

3 Type `Buy ENERGY STAR qualified products` and then press the ENTER key to add a new paragraph at the same level as the previous paragraph.

4 Type `Run dishwasher, clothes washer with full loads` and then press the ENTER key.

5 Click the Increase List Level button (Home tab | Paragraph group) to demote the paragraph to the third level.

6 Type `Wash clothes in cold water` but do not press the ENTER key (Figure 1–24).

Q&A

I pressed the ENTER key in error, and now a new bullet appears after the last entry on this slide. How can I remove this extra bullet?

Press the BACKSPACE key twice.

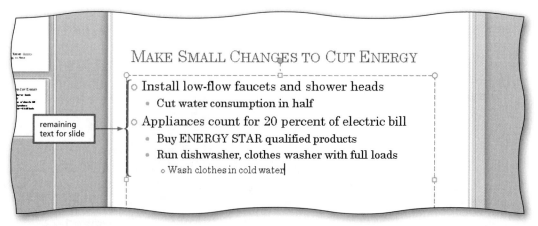

Figure 1–24

To Select a Group of Words

PowerPoint designers use many techniques to emphasize words and characters on a slide. To add emphasis to your slide show's concept of saving natural resources, you want to bold and increase the font size of the words, in half, in the body text. You could perform these actions separately, but it is more efficient to select the words and then change the font attributes. The following steps select two words.

1
- Position the mouse pointer immediately to the left of the first character of the text to be selected (in this case, the i in the word, in) (Figure 1–25).

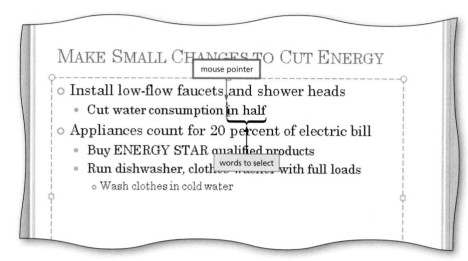

Figure 1–25

2
- Drag the mouse pointer through the last character of the text to be selected (in this case, the f in half) (Figure 1–26).

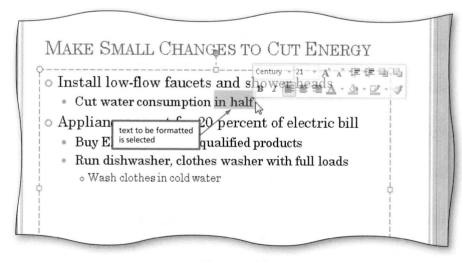

Figure 1–26

Other Ways
1. Press CTRL+SHIFT+RIGHT ARROW

To Bold Text

Bold characters display somewhat thicker and darker than those that display in a regular font style. Clicking the Bold button on the Mini toolbar is an efficient method of bolding text. To add more emphasis to the amount of water savings that can occur by installing low-flow faucets and shower heads, you want to bold the words, in half. The following step bolds this text.

1
- With the words, in half, selected, click the Bold button on the Mini toolbar to bold the two words (Figure 1–27).

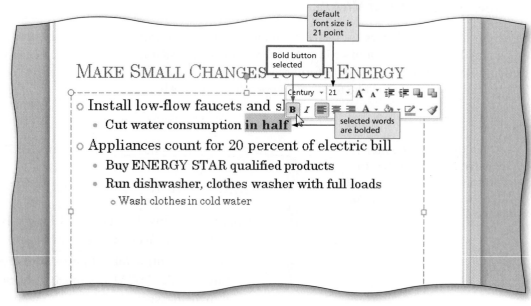

Figure 1–27

Other Ways
1. Click Bold button (Home tab | Font group)
2. Press CTRL+B

Formatting Words
To format one word, position the insertion point anywhere in the word. Then make the formatting changes you desire. The entire word does not need to be selected for the change to occur.

To Increase Font Size

To add emphasis, you increase the font size for the words, in half. The following step increases the font size from 21 to 24 point.

1 With the words, in half, still selected, click the Increase Font Size button on the Mini toolbar once (Figure 1–28).

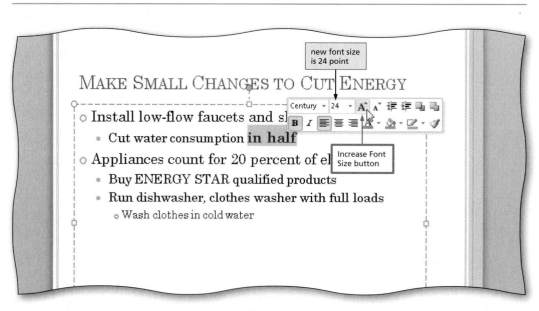

Figure 1–28

Adding New Slides and Changing the Slide Layouts

Slide 3 in Figure 1–1c on page PPT 3 contains a photograph and does not contain a bulleted list. When you add a new slide, PowerPoint applies the Title and Content layout. This layout along with the Title Slide layout for Slide 1 are the default styles. A **layout** specifies the arrangement of placeholders on a slide. These placeholders are arranged in various configurations and can contain text, such as the slide title or a bulleted list, or they can contain content, such as SmartArt graphics, pictures, charts, tables, shapes, and clip art. The placement of the text, in relationship to content, depends on the slide layout. You can specify a particular slide layout when you add a new slide to a presentation or after you have created the slide.

Using the **Layout gallery**, you can choose a slide layout. The nine layouts in this gallery have a variety of placeholders to define text and content positioning and formatting. Three layouts are for text: Title Slide, Section Header, and Title Only. Five are for text and content: Title and Content, Two Content, Comparison, Content with Caption, and Picture with Caption. The Blank layout has no placeholders. If none of these standard layouts meets your design needs, you can create a **custom layout**. A custom layout specifies the number, size, and location of placeholders, background content, and optional slide and placeholder-level properties.

When you change the layout of a slide, PowerPoint retains the text and objects and repositions them into the appropriate placeholders. Using slide layouts eliminates the need to resize objects and the font size because PowerPoint automatically sizes the objects and text to fit the placeholders.

BTW

Experimenting with Normal View
As you learn to use PowerPoint's features, experiment with using the Outline tab and with closing the Tabs pane to maximize the slide area. To close the Tabs pane, click the x to the right of the Outline tab. To redisplay the Tabs pane, click the View tab on the Ribbon and then click Normal in the Presentation Views group.

To Add a Slide with the Title Only Layout

The following steps add Slide 3 to the presentation with the Title Only slide layout style.

1
- If necessary, click Home on the Ribbon to display the Home tab.

- Click the New Slide arrow (Home tab | Slides group) to display the Layout gallery (Figure 1–29).

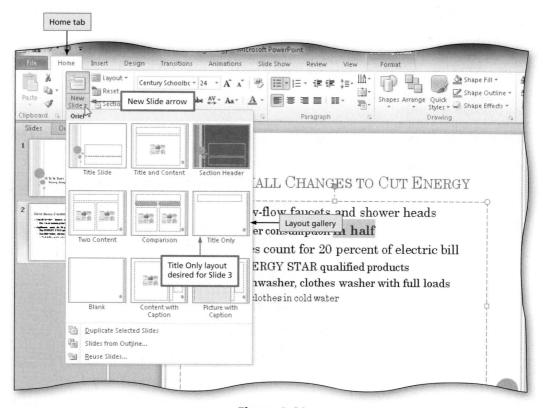

Figure 1–29

2

- Click Title Only to add a new slide and apply that layout to Slide 3 (Figure 1–30).

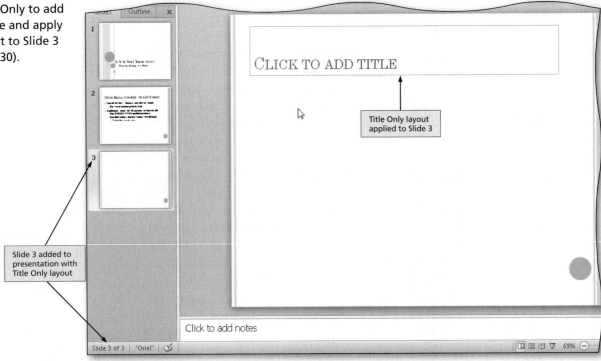

Figure 1–30

Other Ways
1. Press CTRL+M

To Enter a Slide Title

The only text on Slide 3 is the title. The following step enters the title text for this slide.

1 Type **Use Energy Efficient Lighting** as the title text but do not press the ENTER key (Figure 1–31).

Portrait Page Orientation
If your slide content is dominantly vertical, such as a skyscraper or a person, consider changing the slide layout to a portrait page orientation. To change the orientation, click the Slide Orientation button (Design tab | Page Setup group) and then click the desired orientation.

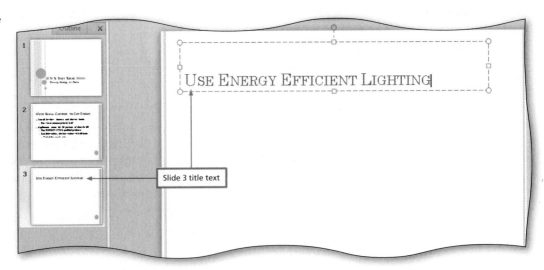

Figure 1–31

To Add a New Slide and Enter a Slide Title and Headings

The text on Slide 4 in Figure 1–1d on page PPT 3 consists of a title and two headings. The appropriate layout for this slide is named Comparison. The following steps add Slide 4 to the presentation with the Comparison layout and then enter the title and heading text for this slide.

1

- Click the New Slide arrow in the Slides group to display the Layout gallery (Figure 1–32).

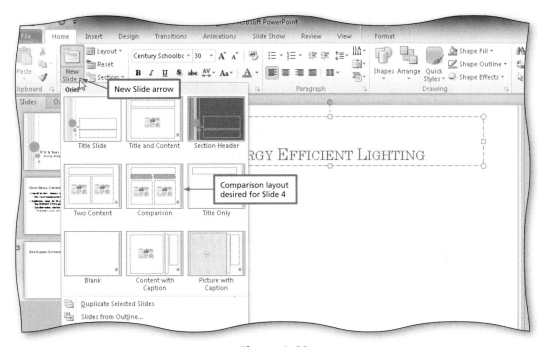

Figure 1–32

2

- Click Comparison to add Slide 4 and apply that layout.

- Type **Adjust Your Thermostats** in the title text placeholder but do not press the ENTER key.

- Click the left orange heading placeholder with the label, Click to add text, to select this placeholder (Figure 1–33).

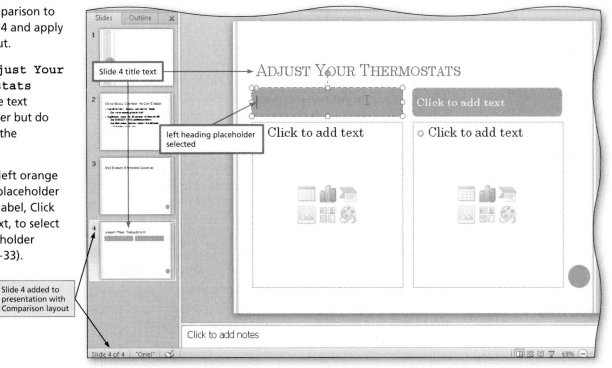

Figure 1–33

3

- Type **Furnace: 68 degrees** but do not press the ENTER key.

- Click the right orange heading placeholder and then type **Water heater: 120 degrees** but do not press the ENTER key (Figure 1–34).

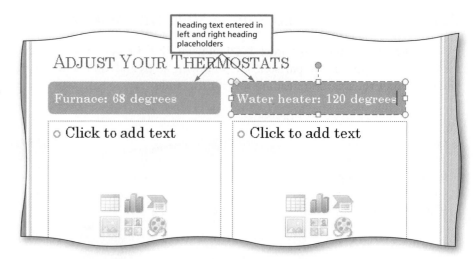

Figure 1–34

Break Point: If you wish to take a break, this is a good place to do so. You can quit PowerPoint now (refer to page PPT 50 for instructions). To resume at a later time, start PowerPoint (refer to pages PPT 4 and PPT 5 for instructions), open the file called Saving Energy (refer to pages PPT 50 and PPT 51 for instructions), and continue following the steps from this location forward.

PowerPoint Views

The PowerPoint window display varies depending on the view. A **view** is the mode in which the presentation appears on the screen. PowerPoint has four main views: Normal, Slide Sorter, Reading, and Slide Show. It also has another view, called Notes Page view, used for entering information about a slide.

The default view is **Normal view**, which is composed of three working areas that allow you to work on various aspects of a presentation simultaneously. The left side of the screen has a Tabs pane that consists of a **Slides tab** and an **Outline tab**. These tabs alternate between views of the presentation in a thumbnail, or miniature, view of the slides and an outline of the slide text. You can type the text of the presentation on the Outline tab and easily rearrange bulleted lists, paragraphs, and individual slides. As you type, you can view this text in the **Slide pane**, which shows a large view of the current slide on the right side of the window. You also can enter text, graphics, animations, and hyperlinks directly in the Slide pane. The **Notes pane** at the bottom of the window is an area where you can type notes and additional information. This text can consist of notes to yourself or remarks to share with your audience. If you want to work with your notes in full page format, you can display them in **Notes Page view**.

In Normal view, you can adjust the width of the Slide pane by dragging the **splitter bar** and the height of the Notes pane by dragging the pane borders. After you have created at least two slides, a scroll bar containing **scroll arrows** and **scroll boxes** will appear on the right edge of the window.

BTW

Using the Notes Pane
As you create your presentation, type comments to yourself in the Notes pane. This material can be used as part of the spoken information you will share with your audience as you give your presentation. You can print these notes for yourself or to distribute to your audience.

To Move to Another Slide in Normal View

When creating or editing a presentation in Normal view (the view you are currently using), you often want to display a slide other than the current one. Before continuing with developing this project, you want to display the title slide by dragging the scroll box on the vertical scroll bar. When you drag the scroll box, the **slide indicator** shows the number and title of the slide you are about to display. Releasing the mouse button shows the slide. The following steps move from Slide 4 to Slide 1 using the scroll box on the Slide pane.

1
- Position the mouse pointer on the scroll box.

- Press and hold down the mouse button so that Slide: 4 of 4 Adjust Your Thermostats appears in the slide indicator (Figure 1–35).

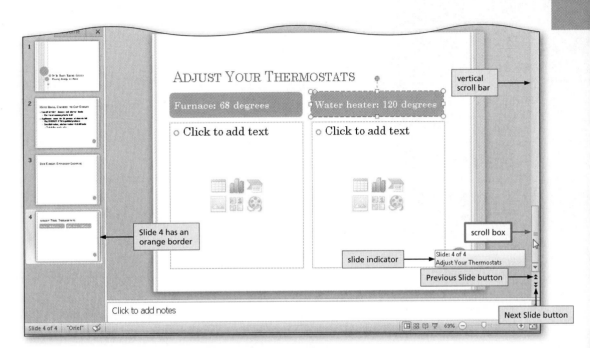

Figure 1–35

2
- Drag the scroll box up the vertical scroll bar until Slide: 1 of 4 It Is Easy Being Green appears in the slide indicator (Figure 1–36).

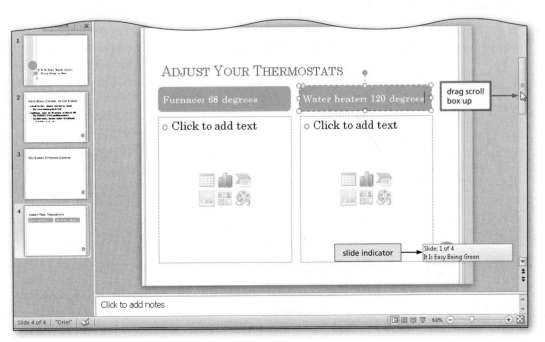

Figure 1–36

3

- Release the mouse button so that Slide 1 appears in the Slide pane and the Slide 1 thumbnail has an orange border in the Slides tab (Figure 1–37).

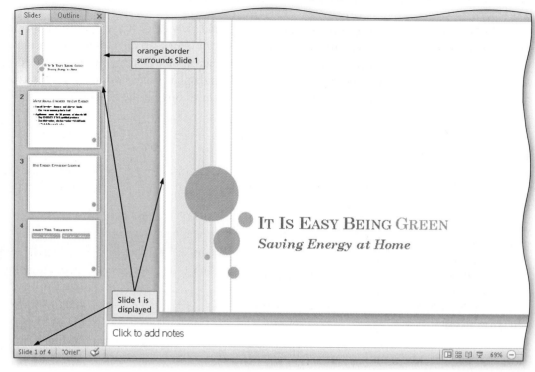

Figure 1–37

Other Ways

1. Click Next Slide button or Previous Slide button to move forward or back one slide
2. Click slide thumbnail on Slides tab
3. Press PAGE DOWN or PAGE UP to move forward or back one slide

BTW

Today's Clip
Each day, Microsoft features "today's clip," which reflects events or themes specific to this time. For example, the pictures, illustrations, and clip art have back-to-school images, winter scenes, and holiday characters.

Inserting Clip Art and Photographs into Slides

A **clip** is a single media file that can include art, sound, animation, or movies. Adding a clip can help increase the visual appeal of many slides and can offer a quick way to add professional-looking graphic images and sounds to a presentation without creating these files yourself. This art is contained in the **Microsoft Clip Organizer**, a collection of drawings, photographs, sounds, videos, and other media files shared among Microsoft Office applications. The **Office Collections** contains all these media files included with Microsoft Office.

You also can add your own clips to slides. You can insert these files directly from a storage medium, such as a USB flash drive. In addition, you can add them to the other files in the Clip Organizer so that you can search for and reuse these images, sounds, animations, and movies. When you create these media files, they are stored on your hard disk in **My Collections**. The Clip Organizer will find these files and create a new collection with these files. Two other locations for clips are Shared Collections and Web Collections. Files in the **Shared Collections** typically reside on a shared network file server and are accessible to multiple users. The **Web Collections** clips reside on the Microsoft Clip Art and Media Home page on the Microsoft Office Online Web site. They are available only if you have an active Internet connection.

The Clip Art Task Pane

You can add clips to your presentation in two ways. One way is by selecting one of the slide layouts that includes a content placeholder with a Clip Art button. A second method is by clicking the Clip Art button in the Images area on the Insert tab. Clicking the Clip Art button opens the Clip Art task pane. The **Clip Art task pane** allows you to search for clips by using descriptive keywords, file names, media file formats, and clip collections. Specific file formats could be for clip art, photographs, movies, and sounds.

Clips are organized in hierarchical **clip collections** that combine topic-related clips into categories, such as Academic, Business, and Technology.

Clips have one or more keywords associated with various entities, activities, labels, and emotions. In most instances, the keywords give the name of the clip and related categories. For example, an image of a cow in the Animals category has the keywords animals, cattle, cows, dairies, farms, and Holsteins. You can enter these keywords in the Search for text box to find clips when you know one of the words associated with the image. Otherwise, you might find it necessary to scroll through several categories to find an appropriate clip.

Depending on the installation of the Microsoft Clip Organizer on your computer, you might not have the clip art used in this chapter. Contact your instructor if you are missing clips used in the following steps. If you have an active connection to the Internet, clips from the Microsoft Office Online Web site will display automatically as the result of your search results.

Plan Ahead

Adhere to copyright regulations.
You have permission to use the clips from the Microsoft Clip Organizer. If you want to use a clip from another source, be certain you have the legal right to insert this file in your presentation. Read the copyright notices that may accompany the clip and may be posted on the Web site where you obtained the clip. The owners of these images and files often ask you to give them credit for using their work, which may be satisfied by stating where you obtained the images.

To Insert a Clip from the Clip Organizer into the Title Slide

Slide 1 uses the Title Slide layout, which has two placeholders for text but none for graphical content. You desire to place a graphic on Slide 1, so you will locate a clip art image of a green globe and flower and then insert it in this slide. Later in this chapter, you will size and position it in an appropriate location. The following steps add a clip to Slide 1.

1
- Click Insert on the Ribbon to display the Insert tab.

- Click the Clip Art button (Insert tab | Images group) to display the Clip Art task pane.

- Click the Search for text box in the Clip Art task pane, if necessary delete any letters that are present, and then type **green globe** in the Search for text box.

- If necessary, click the 'Include Office.com content' check box to select it (Figure 1–38).

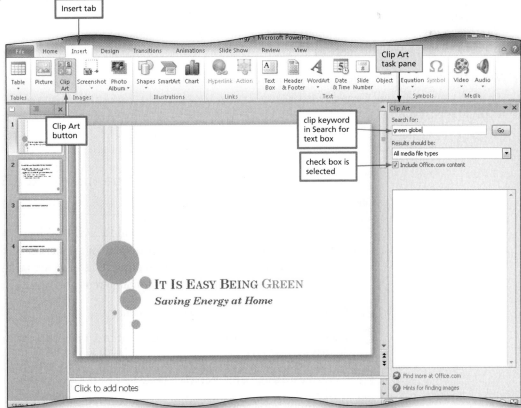

Figure 1–38

- Click the Go button so that the Microsoft Clip Organizer will search for and display all clips having the keywords, green globe.

- If necessary, click the Yes button if a Microsoft Clip Organizer dialog box appears asking if you want to include additional clip art images from Office.com.

- If necessary, scroll down the list to display the globe clip shown in Figure 1–39.

- Click the clip to insert it into the slide (Figure 1–39).

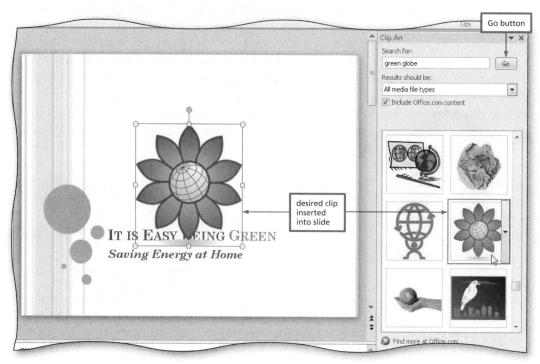

Figure 1–39

Q&A What if the globe image displayed in Figure 1–39 is not shown in my Clip Art task pane?

Select a similar clip. Your clips may be different depending on the clips installed on your computer and if you have an active connection to the Internet.

Q&A What is the yellow star image that displays in the lower-right corner of some clips in the Clip Art task pane?

The star indicates the image is animated and will move when the slide containing this clip is displayed during a slide show.

Q&A Why is this globe clip displayed in this location on the slide?

The slide layout does not have a content placeholder, so PowerPoint inserts the clip in the center of the slide.

To Insert a Clip from the Clip Organizer into a Slide without a Content Placeholder

The next step is to add two clips to Slide 2. Slide 2 has a bulleted list in the text placeholder, so the icon group does not display in the center of the placeholder. Later in this chapter, you will resize the inserted clips. The Clip Art task pane is displayed and will remain open until you close it. The following steps add one clip to Slide 2.

1 Click the Next Slide button to display Slide 2.

2 Click the Search for text box in the Clip Art task pane and then delete the letters in the Search for text box.

3 Type `faucets` and then click the Go button.

4 If necessary, scroll down the list to display the faucet clip shown in Figure 1–40 and then click the clip to insert it into Slide 2 (Figure 1–40).

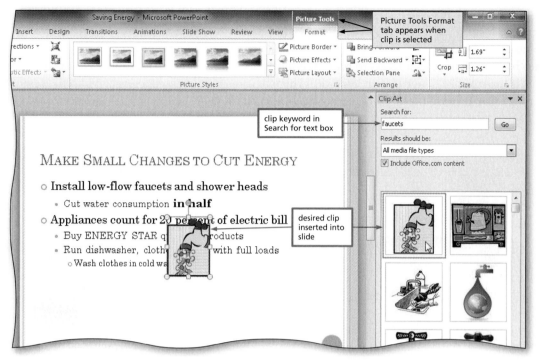

Figure 1–40

To Insert a Second Clip from the Clip Organizer into a Slide without a Content Placeholder

The following steps add a second clip to Slide 2. PowerPoint inserts this clip on top of the faucet clip in the center of the slide. Both clips will be moved and resized later in this project.

1 Click the Search for text box in the Clip Art task pane and then delete the letters in the text box.

2 Type **dishwasher**, click the Go button, locate the clip shown in Figure 1–41, and then click the clip to insert it into Slide 2 (Figure 1–41).

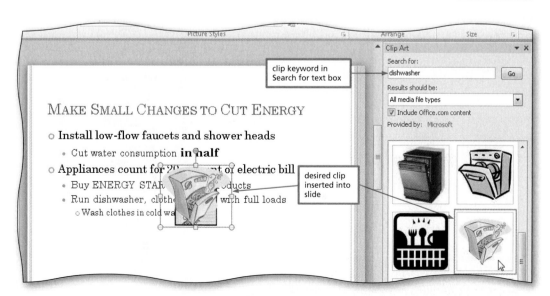

Figure 1–41

To Insert a Clip from the Clip Organizer into a Content Placeholder

Slide 4 uses the Comparison layout, which has a content placeholder below each of the two headings. You desire to insert clip art into both content placeholders to reinforce the concept that consumers should adjust the heating temperatures of their furnace and water heater. The following steps insert clip art of a furnace into the left content placeholder and a water heater into the right content placeholder on Slide 4.

• Click the Close button in the Clip Art task pane so that it no longer is displayed.

• Click the Next Slide button twice to display Slide 4.

• Click the Clip Art icon in the left content placeholder to select that placeholder and to open the Clip Art task pane (Figure 1–42).

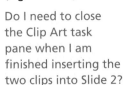

Q&A

Do I need to close the Clip Art task pane when I am finished inserting the two clips into Slide 2?

No. You can leave the Clip Art task pane open and then display Slide 4. It is often more convenient, however, to open this pane when you are working with a layout that has a content placeholder so that the clip is inserted in the desired location.

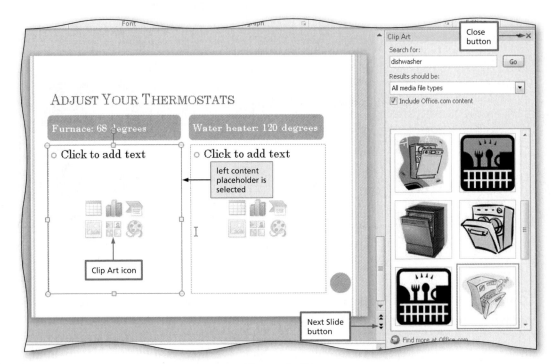

Figure 1–42

2

• Click the Search for text box in the Clip Art task pane, delete any letters that are present, type **furnace** in the Search for text box, and then click the Go button to search for and display all pictures having the keyword, furnace.

• If necessary, scroll down the list to display the furnace clip shown in Figure 1–43.

• Click the clip to insert it into the left content placeholder (Figure 1–43).

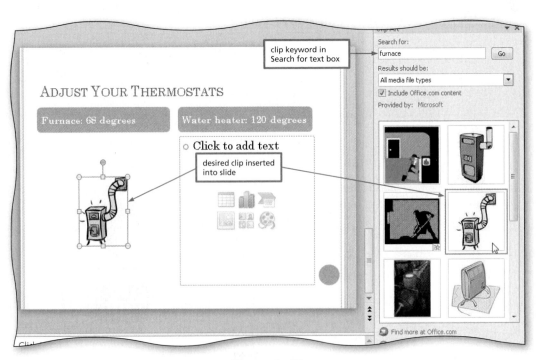

Figure 1–43

3

- Click anywhere in the right placeholder except one of the six icons to select the placeholder.

Q&A

I clicked the Clip Art icon by mistake, which closed the Clip Art task pane. How do I open it?

Click the Clip Art icon.

4

- Click the Search for text box in the Clip Art task pane, delete any letters that are present, type **water heater** in the Search for text box, and then click the Go button.

- If necessary, scroll down the list to display the water heater clip shown in Figure 1–44 and then click the clip to insert it into the right content placeholder (Figure 1–44).

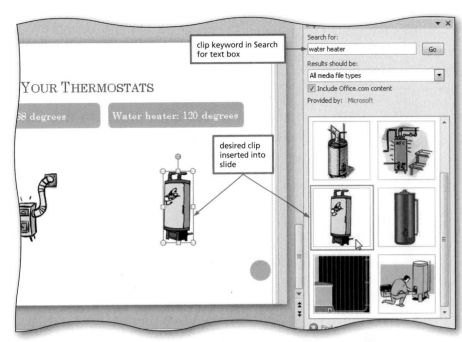

Figure 1–44

Photographs and the Clip Organizer

In addition to clip art, you can insert pictures into a presentation. These may include scanned photographs, line art, and artwork from storage media, such as USB flash drives, hard disks, optical discs, and memory cards. To insert a picture into a presentation, the picture must be saved in a format that PowerPoint can recognize. Table 1–1 identifies some of the formats PowerPoint recognizes.

BTW

Compressing File Size
When you add a picture to a presentation, PowerPoint automatically compresses this image. Even with this compression applied, a presentation that contains pictures usually has a large file size. To reduce this size, you can compress a picture further without affecting the quality of how it displays on the slide. To compress a picture, select the picture and then click the Compress Pictures button (Picture Tools Format tab | Adjust group). You can restore the picture's original settings by clicking the Reset Picture button (Picture Tools Format tab | Adjust group).

Table 1–1 Primary File Formats PowerPoint Recognizes	
Format	**File Extension**
Computer Graphics Metafile	.cgm
CorelDRAW	.cdr, .cdt, .cmx, and .pat
Encapsulated PostScript	.eps
Enhanced Metafile	.emf
FlashPix	.fpx
Graphics Interchange Format	.gif
Hanako	.jsh, .jah, and .jbh
Joint Photographic Experts Group (JPEG)	.jpg
Kodak PhotoCD	.pcd
Macintosh PICT	.pct
PC Paintbrush	.pcx
Portable Network Graphics	.png
Tagged Image File Format	.tif
Windows Bitmap	.bmp, .rle, .dib
Microsoft Windows Metafile	.wmf
WordPerfect Graphics	.wpg

BTW

Wrapping Text around a Picture
PowerPoint 2010 does not allow you to wrap text around a picture or other graphics, such as tables, shapes, charts, or graphics. This feature, however, is available in Word 2010.

You can import files saved with the .emf, .gif, .jpg, .png, .bmp, .rle, .dib, and .wmf formats directly into PowerPoint presentations. All other file formats require separate filters that are shipped with the PowerPoint installation software and must be installed separately. You can download additional filters from the Microsoft Office Online Web site.

To Insert a Photograph from the Clip Organizer into a Slide without a Content Placeholder

Next, you will add a photograph to Slide 3. You will not insert this picture into a content placeholder, so it will display in the center of the slide. Later in this chapter, you will resize this picture. To start the process of locating this photograph, you do not need to click the Clip Art button icon in the content placeholder because the Clip Art task pane already is displayed. The following steps add a photograph to Slide 3.

1 Click the Previous Slide button to display Slide 3.

2 Click the Search for text box in the Clip Art task pane, delete the letters in the text box, type **CFL**, and then click the Go button.

3 If necessary, scroll down the list to display the picture of a light bulb shown in Figure 1–45, and then click the photograph to insert it into Slide 2 (Figure 1–45).

Q&A Why is my photograph a different size from the one shown in Figure 1–1c on page PPT 3?
The photograph was inserted into the slide and not into a content placeholder. You will resize the picture later in this chapter.

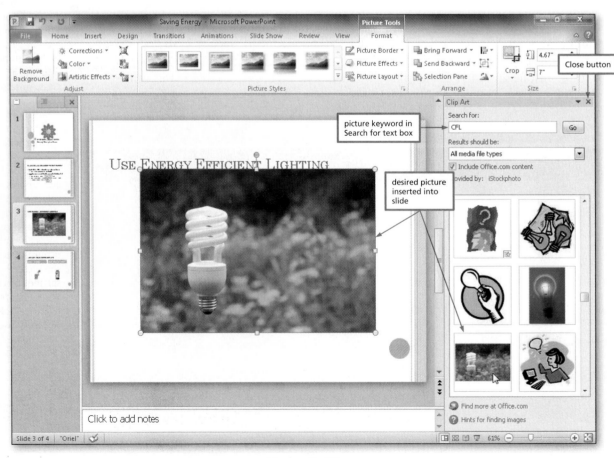

Figure 1–45

Break Point: If you wish to take a break, this is a good place to do so. You can quit PowerPoint now (refer to page PPT 50 for instructions). To resume at a later time, start PowerPoint (refer to pages PPT 4 and PPT 5 for instructions), open the file called Saving Energy (refer to pages PPT 50 and PPT 51 for instructions), and continue following the steps from this location forward.

Resizing Clip Art and Photographs

Sometimes it is necessary to change the size of clip art. **Resizing** includes enlarging or reducing the size of a clip art graphic. You can resize clip art using a variety of techniques. One method involves changing the size of a clip by specifying exact dimensions in a dialog box. Another method involves dragging one of the graphic's sizing handles to the desired location. A selected graphic appears surrounded by a **selection rectangle**, which has small squares and circles, called **sizing handles** or move handles, at each corner and middle location.

To Resize Clip Art

On Slides 1, 2, and 4, much space appears around the clips, so you can increase their sizes. Likewise, the photograph on Slide 3 can be enlarged to fill more of the space below the slide title. To change the size, drag the corner sizing handles to view how the clip will look on the slide. Using these corner handles maintains the graphic's original proportions. Dragging the square sizing handles alters the proportions so that the graphic's height and width become larger or smaller. The following steps increase the size of the Slide 1 clip using a corner sizing handle.

1

- Click the Close button in the Clip Art task pane so that it no longer is displayed.

- Click the Previous Slide button two times to display Slide 1.

- Click the globe clip to select it and display the selection rectangle.

- Point to the lower-left corner sizing handle on the clip so that the mouse pointer changes to a two-headed arrow (Figure 1–46).

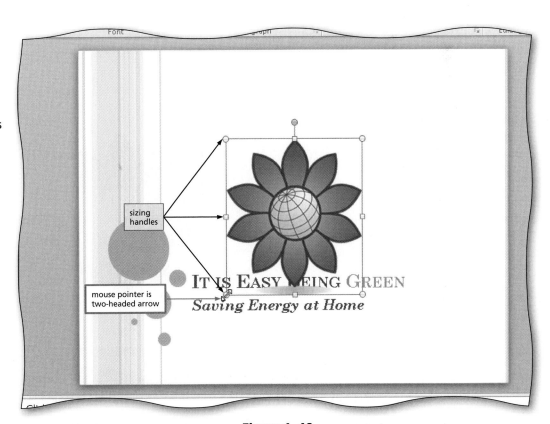

Figure 1–46

2

- Drag the sizing handle diagonally toward the lower-left corner of the slide until the mouse pointer is positioned approximately as shown in Figure 1–47.

Q&A

What if the clip is not the same size as the one shown in Figure 1–47?

Repeat Steps 1 and 2.

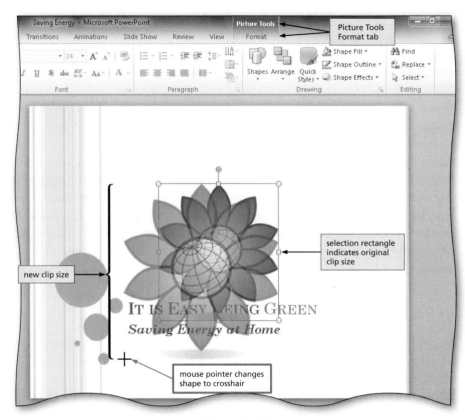

Figure 1–47

3

- Release the mouse button to resize the clip.
- Click outside the clip to deselect it (Figure 1–48).

Q&A

What happened to the Picture Tools Format tab?

When you click outside the clip, PowerPoint deselects the clip and removes the Picture Tools Format tab from the screen.

Q&A

What if I want to return the clip to its original size and start again?

With the graphic selected, click the Reset Picture button (Picture Tools Format tab | Adjust group).

Figure 1–48

To Resize Clips on Slide 4

The two clip art images on Slide 4 also can be enlarged to fill much of the white space below the headings. You will reposition the clips in a later step. The following steps resize these clips using a sizing handle.

1 Click the Next Slide button three times to display Slide 4.

2 Click the furnace clip to select it.

3 Drag the lower-left corner sizing handle on the clip diagonally outward until the clip is resized approximately as shown in Figure 1–49.

4 Click the water heater clip to select it.

5 Drag the lower-right corner sizing handle on the clip diagonally outward until the clip is resized approximately as shown in Figure 1–49.

Figure 1–49

To Resize a Photograph

The light bulb picture in Slide 3 can be enlarged slightly to fill much of the space below the slide title. You resize a photograph in the same manner that you resize clip art. The following steps resize this photograph using a sizing handle.

1 Click the Previous Slide button to display Slide 3.

2 Click the light bulb photograph to select it.

BTW

Minimalist Design
Resist the urge to fill your slides with clips from the Microsoft Clip Organizer. Minimalist style reduces clutter and allows the slide content to display prominently. This simple, yet effective design helps audience members with short attention spans to focus on the message.

3 Drag the lower-left corner sizing handle on the photograph diagonally outward until the photograph is resized approximately as shown in Figure 1–50.

light bulb picture resized

Figure 1–50

To Move Clips

After you insert clip art or a photograph on a slide, you might want to reposition it. The light bulb photograph on Slide 3 could be centered in the space between the slide title and the left and right edges of the slide. The clip on Slide 1 could be positioned in the upper-right corner of the slide. On Slide 4, the furnace and water heater clips could be centered under each heading. The following steps move these graphics.

1

- If necessary, click the light bulb photograph on Slide 3 to select it.

- Press and hold down the mouse button and then drag the photograph diagonally downward below the title text (Figure 1–51).

- If necessary, select the photograph and then use the ARROW keys to position it precisely as shown in Figure 1–51.

Q&A

The photograph still is not located exactly where I want it to display. What can I do to align the photograph?

Press the CTRL key while you press the ARROW keys. This key combination moves the clip in smaller increments than when you press only an ARROW key.

light bulb picture moved to desired location on Slide 3

Figure 1–51

- Click the Next Slide button to display Slide 4.

- Click the furnace clip to select it, press and hold down the mouse button, and then drag the clip to center it under the furnace heading.

- Click the water heater clip and then drag the clip to center it under the water heater heading (Figure 1–52).

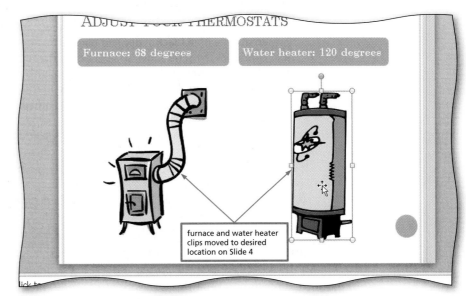

Figure 1–52

3

- Click the Previous Slide button twice to display Slide 2.

- Click the dishwasher clip, which is on top of the faucet clip, and then drag the clip to center it under the last bulleted paragraph, Wash clothes in cold water.

- Click the faucet clip and then drag the clip so that the faucet handle is centered under the words, full loads.

- Drag a corner sizing handle on the faucet clip diagonally outward until the clip is resized approximately as shown in Figure 1–53. You may need to drag the clip to position it in the desired location.

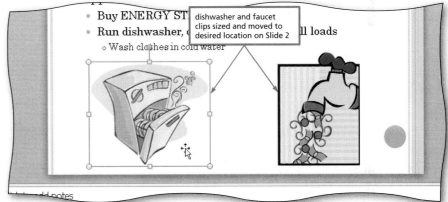

Figure 1–53

- Select the dishwasher clip and then resize and move it so that the clip displays approximately as shown in Figure 1–53.

4

- Click the Previous Slide button to display Slide 1.

- Click the globe clip and then drag it to the upper-right corner of the slide. You may want to adjust its size by selecting it and then dragging the corner sizing handles.

- Click outside the clip to deselect it (Figure 1–54).

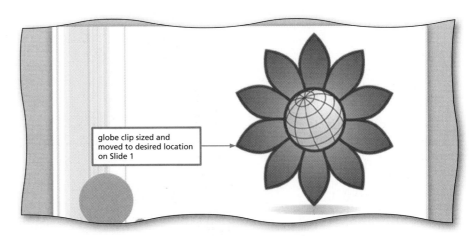

Figure 1–54

Plan
Ahead

Choose a closing slide.
After the last slide appears during a slide show, the default PowerPoint setting is to end the presentation with a **black slide.** This black slide appears only when the slide show is running and concludes the slide show, so your audience never sees the PowerPoint window. It is a good idea, however, to end the presentation with a final closing slide to display at the end of the presentation. This slide ends the presentation gracefully and should be an exact copy, or a very similar copy, of your title slide. The audience will recognize that the presentation is drawing to a close when this slide appears. It can remain on the screen when the audience asks questions, approaches the speaker for further information, or exits the room.

Ending a Slide Show with a Closing Slide

All the text for the slides in the Saving Energy slide show has been entered. This presentation thus far consists of a title slide, one text slide with a multi-level bulleted list, a third slide for a photograph, and a fourth slide with a Comparison layout. A closing slide that resembles the title slide is the final slide to create.

To Duplicate a Slide

When two slides contain similar information and have the same format, duplicating one slide and then making minor modifications to the new slide saves time and increases consistency.

Slide 5 will have the same layout and design as Slide 1. The most expedient method of creating this slide is to copy Slide 1 and then make minor modifications to the new slide. The following steps duplicate the title slide.

- With Slide 1 selected, click the New Slide arrow (Home tab | Slides group) to display the Oriel layout gallery (Figure 1–55).

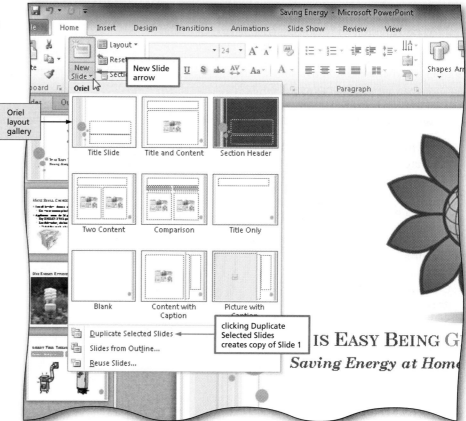

Figure 1–55

2
- Click Duplicate Selected Slides in the Oriel layout gallery to create a new Slide 2, which is a duplicate of Slide 1 (Figure 1–56).

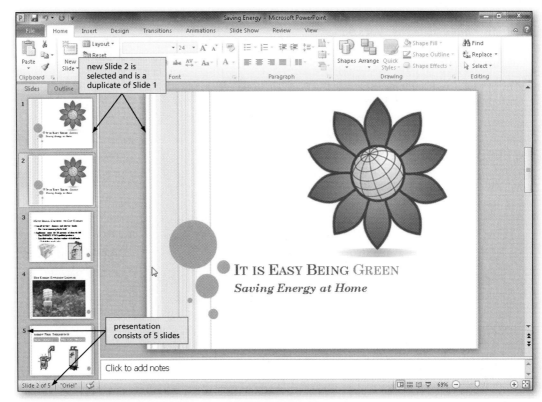

Figure 1–56

Break Point: If you wish to take a break, this is a good place to do so. You can quit PowerPoint now (refer to page PPT 50 for instructions). To resume at a later time, start PowerPoint (refer to pages PPT 4 and PPT 5 for instructions), open the file called Saving Energy (refer to pages PPT 50 and PPT 51 for instructions), and continue following the steps from this location forward.

To Arrange a Slide

The new Slide 2 was inserted directly below Slide 1 because Slide 1 was the selected slide. This duplicate slide needs to display at the end of the presentation directly after the final title and content slide.

Changing slide order is an easy process and is best performed in the Slides pane. When you click the slide thumbnail and begin to drag it to a new location, a line indicates the new location of the selected slide. When you release the mouse button, the slide drops into the desired location. Hence, this process of dragging and then dropping the thumbnail in a new location is called **drag and drop**. You can use the drag-and-drop method to move any selected item, including text and graphics. The following step moves the new Slide 2 to the end of the presentation so that it becomes a closing slide.

1

● With Slide 2 selected, drag the Slide 2 slide thumbnail in the Slides pane below the last slide thumbnail (Figure 1–57).

Q&A

The Slide 2 thumbnail is not visible in the Slides pane when I am dragging the thumbnail downward. How do I know it will be positioned in the desired location?

A blue horizontal bar indicates where the slide will move.

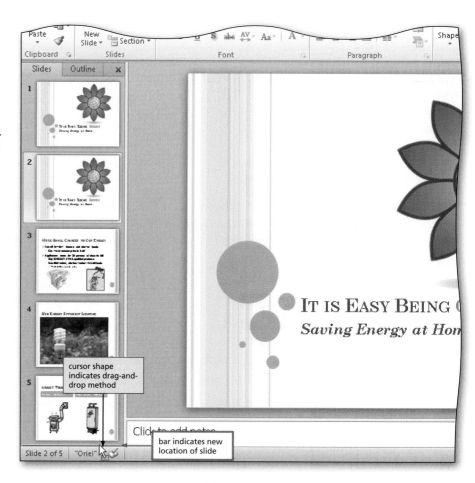

Figure 1–57

Other Ways

1. Click slide icon on Outline tab, drag icon to new location
2. Click Slide Sorter (View tab | Presentation Views group), click slide thumbnail, drag thumbnail to new location

Making Changes to Slide Text Content

After creating slides in a presentation, you may find that you want to make changes to the text. Changes may be required because a slide contains an error, the scope of the presentation shifts, or the style is inconsistent. This section explains the types of changes that commonly occur when creating a presentation.

You generally make three types of changes to text in a presentation: additions, replacements, and deletions.

BTW

Checking Spelling
As you review your slides, you should examine the text for spelling errors. In Chapter 3, you will learn to use PowerPoint's built-in spelling checker to help you perform this task.

- Additions are necessary when you omit text from a slide and need to add it later. You may need to insert text in the form of a sentence, word, or single character. For example, you may want to add the presenter's middle name on the title slide.

- Replacements are needed when you want to revise the text in a presentation. For example, you may want to substitute the word *their* for the word *there*.

- Deletions are required when text on a slide is incorrect or no longer is relevant to the presentation. For example, a slide may look cluttered. Therefore, you may want to remove one of the bulleted paragraphs to add more space.

Editing text in PowerPoint basically is the same as editing text in a word processing program. The following sections illustrate the most common changes made to text in a presentation.

Replacing Text in an Existing Slide

When you need to correct a word or phrase, you can replace the text by selecting the text to be replaced and then typing the new text. As soon as you press any key on the keyboard, the selected text is deleted and the new text is displayed.

PowerPoint inserts text to the left of the insertion point. The text to the right of the insertion point moves to the right (and shifts downward if necessary) to accommodate the added text.

Deleting Text

You can delete text using one of three methods. One is to use the BACKSPACE key to remove text just typed. The second is to position the insertion point to the left of the text you want to delete and then press the DELETE key. The third method is to drag through the text you want to delete and then press the DELETE or BACKSPACE key. Use the third method when deleting large sections of text.

To Delete Text in a Placeholder

To keep the ending slide clean and simple, you want to delete a few words in the slide show title and subtitle text. The following steps change It Is Easy Being Green to Be Green and then change Saving Energy at Home to Save Energy.

1

- With Slide 5 selected, position the mouse pointer immediately to the left of the first character of the text to be selected (in this case, the I in the word, It).

- Drag the mouse pointer through the last character of the text to be selected (in this case, the space after the y in Easy) (Figure 1–58).

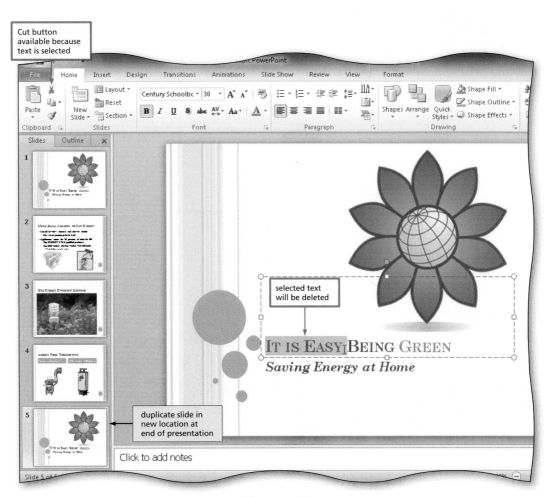

Figure 1–58

● Click the Cut button (Home tab |
Clipboard group) to delete all the
selected text (Figure 1–59).

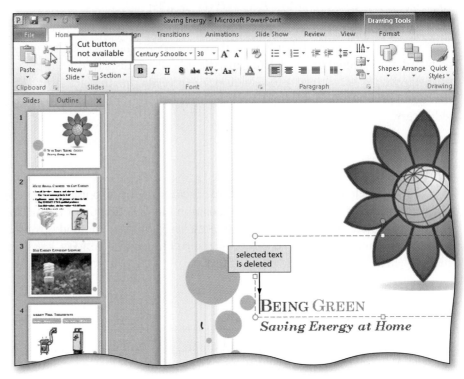

Figure 1–59

● Select the letters, ing, in the word,
Being.

● Click the Cut button (Figure 1–60).

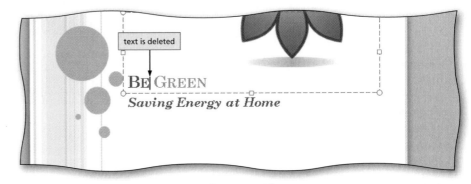

Figure 1–60

● Select the letters, ing, in the word,
Saving, and then click the Cut
button.

● Type e to change the word to
Save (Figure 1–61).

Other Ways

1. Right-click selected text,
   click Cut on shortcut
   menu

2. Select text, press DELETE
   or BACKSPACE key

3. Select text, press CTRL+X

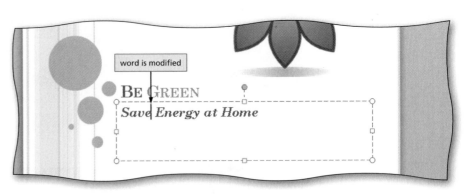

Figure 1–61

Adding a Transition

PowerPoint provides many animation effects to add interest and make a slide show presentation look professional. **Animation** includes special visual and sound effects applied to text or content. A **slide transition** is a special animation effect used to progress from one slide to the next in a slide show. You can control the speed of the transition effect and add a sound.

PowerPoint provides a variety of transitions arranged into three categories that describe the types of effects: Subtle, Exciting, and Dynamic Content.

To Add a Transition between Slides

In this presentation, you apply the Doors transition in the Exciting category to all slides and change the transition speed from 1.40 seconds to 2 seconds. The following steps apply this transition to the presentation.

1

- Click the Transitions tab on the Ribbon and then point to the More button (Transitions tab | Transition to This Slide group) (Figure 1–62).

Is a transition applied now?

No. The first slide icon in the Transitions group has an orange border, which indicates no transition has been applied.

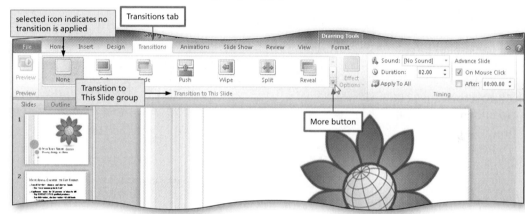

Figure 1–62

2

- Click the More button to expand the Transitions gallery.

- Point to the Doors transition in the Exciting category in the Transitions gallery (Figure 1–63).

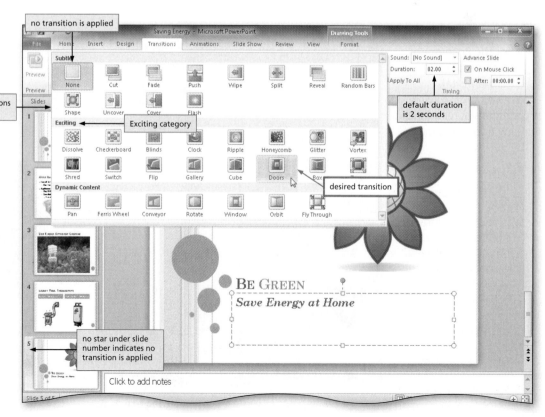

Figure 1–63

3

- Click Doors in the Exciting category in the Transitions gallery to apply this transition to the closing slide.

Q&A Why does a star appear next to Slide 5 in the Slides tab?

The star indicates that a transition animation effect is applied to that slide.

- Click the Duration up arrow (Transitions tab | Timing group) three times to change the transition speed from 01.40 seconds to 02.00 seconds (Figure 1–64).

Q&A Why did the time change?

Each transition has a default duration time. The Doors transition time is 1:40 seconds.

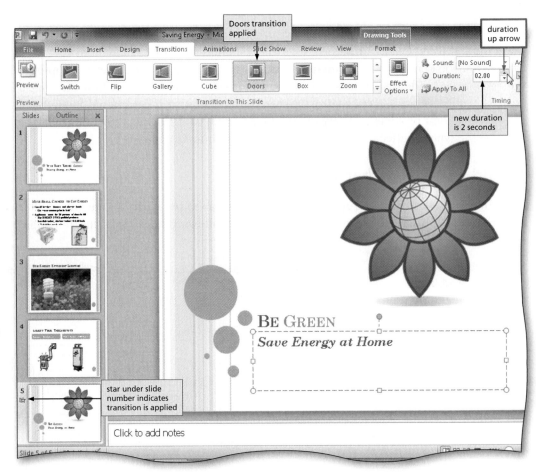

Figure 1–64

4

- Click the Preview Transitions button (Transitions tab | Preview area) to view the transition and the new transition time (Figure 1–65).

Q&A Can I adjust the duration time I just set?

Yes. Click the Duration up or down arrows or type a speed in the Duration text box and preview the transition until you find the time that best fits your presentation.

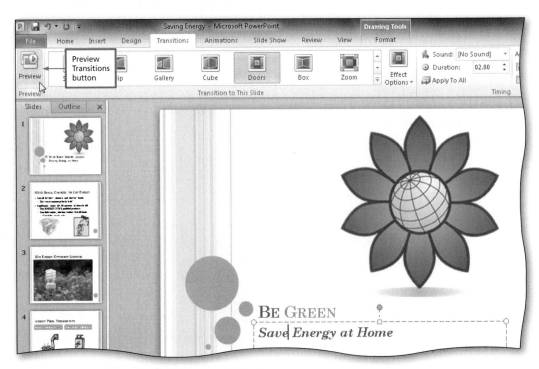

Figure 1–65

5

- Click the Apply To All button (Transitions tab | Timing group) to apply the Doors transition and the increased transition time to Slides 1 through 4 in the presentation (Figure 1–66).

Q&A

What if I want to apply a different transition and duration to each slide in the presentation?

Repeat Steps 2 and 3 for each slide individually.

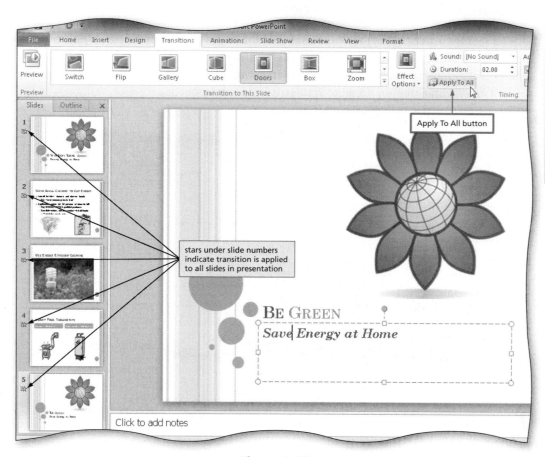

Figure 1–66

Changing Document Properties

PowerPoint helps you organize and identify your files by using **document properties**, which are the details about a file. Document properties, also known as **metadata**, can include information such as the project author, title, subject, and keywords. A **keyword** is a word or phrase that further describes the document. For example, a class name or document topic can describe the file's purpose or content.

Document properties are valuable for a variety of reasons:

- Users can save time locating a particular file because they can view a document's properties without opening the document.

- By creating consistent properties for files having similar content, users can better organize their documents.

- Some organizations require PowerPoint users to add document properties so that other employees can view details about these files.

Five different types of document properties exist, but the more common ones used in this book are standard and automatically updated properties. **Standard properties** are associated with all Microsoft Office documents and include author, title, and subject. **Automatically updated properties** include file system properties, such as the date you create or change a file, and statistics, such as the file size.

BTW

PowerPoint Help
At any time while using PowerPoint, you can find answers to questions and display information about various topics through PowerPoint Help. Used properly, this form of assistance can increase your productivity and reduce your frustrations by minimizing the time you spend learning how to use PowerPoint. For instruction about PowerPoint Help and exercises that will help you gain confidence in using it, read the Office 2010 and Windows 7 chapter at the beginning of this book.

To Change Document Properties

The **Document Information Panel** contains areas where you can view and enter document properties. You can view and change information in this panel at any time while you are creating a document. Before saving the presentation again, you want to add your name and course information as document properties. The following steps use the Document Information Panel to change document properties.

1

• Click File on the Ribbon to open the Backstage view.

• If necessary, click the Info tab in the Backstage view to display the Info gallery (Figure 1–67).

Q&A

How do I close the Backstage view?

Click File on the Ribbon or click the preview of the document in the Info gallery to return to the PowerPoint document window.

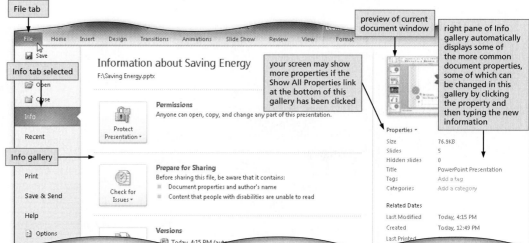

Figure 1–67

2

• Click the Properties button in the right pane of the Info gallery to display the Properties menu (Figure 1–68).

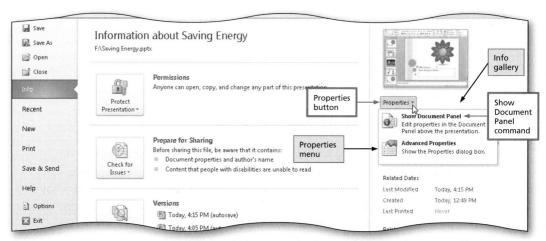

Figure 1–68

3

• Click Show Document Panel on the Properties menu to close the Backstage view and display the Document Information Panel in the PowerPoint document window (Figure 1–69).

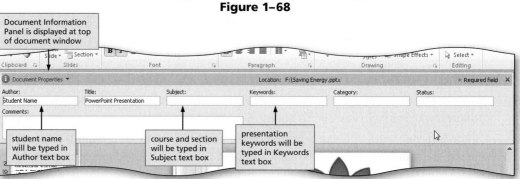

Figure 1–69

Q&A

Why are some of the document properties in my Document Information Panel already filled in?

The person who installed Microsoft Office 2010 on your computer or network may have set or customized the properties.

- Click the Author text box, if necessary, and then type your name as the Author property. If a name already is displayed in the Author text box, delete it before typing your name.

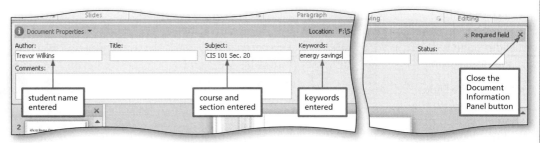

Figure 1–70

- Click the Subject text box, if necessary delete any existing text, and then type your course and section as the Subject property.

- If an AutoComplete dialog box appears, click its Yes button.

- Click the Keywords text box, if necessary delete any existing text, and then type **energy savings** as the Keywords property (Figure 1–70).

Q&A

What types of document properties does PowerPoint collect automatically?

PowerPoint records details such as time spent editing a document, the number of times a document has been revised, and the fonts and themes used in a document.

- Click the Close the Document Information Panel button so that the Document Information Panel no longer is displayed.

Other Ways

1. Click File on Ribbon, click Info in Backstage view, if necessary click Show All Properties link in Info gallery, click property to change and type new information, close Backstage view

To Save an Existing Presentation with the Same File Name

You have made several modifications to the presentation since you last saved it. Thus, you should save it again. The following step saves the document again. For an example of the step listed below, refer to the Office 2010 and Windows 7 chapter at the beginning of this book.

 Click the Save button on the Quick Access Toolbar to overwrite the previously saved file.

BTW

Saving in a Previous PowerPoint Format
To ensure that your presentation will open in PowerPoint 2003 or older versions of this software, you must save your file in PowerPoint 97-2003 format. These files will have the .ppt extension.

Viewing the Presentation in Slide Show View

The Slide Show button, located in the lower-right corner of the PowerPoint window above the status bar, allows you to show a presentation using a computer. The computer acts like a slide projector, displaying each slide on a full screen. The full-screen slide hides the toolbars, menus, and other PowerPoint window elements.

To Start Slide Show View

When making a presentation, you use **Slide Show view**. You can start Slide Show view from Normal view or Slide Sorter view. Slide Show view begins when you click the Slide Show button in the lower-right corner of the PowerPoint window above the status bar. PowerPoint then shows the current slide on the full screen without any of the PowerPoint window objects, such as the menu bar or toolbars. The following steps start Slide Show view.

1

- Click the Slide 1 thumbnail in the Slides pane to select and display Slide 1.

- Point to the Slide Show button in the lower-right corner of the PowerPoint window on the status bar (Figure 1–71).

Q&A Why did I need to select Slide 1?

When you run a slide show, PowerPoint begins the show with the currently displayed slide. If you had not selected Slide 1, then only Slide 5 would have displayed in the slide show.

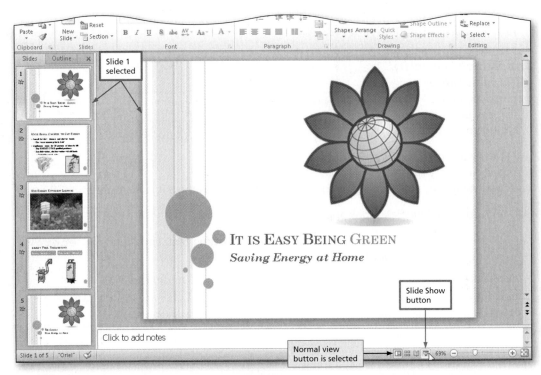

Figure 1–71

2

- Click the Slide Show button to display the title slide (Figure 1–72).

Q&A Where is the PowerPoint window?

When you run a slide show, the PowerPoint window is hidden. It will reappear once you end your slide show.

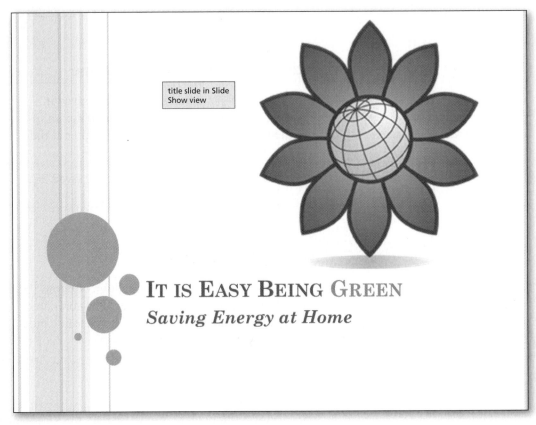

Figure 1–72

Other Ways

1. Click Slide Show From Beginning button (Slide Show tab | Start Slide Show group)
2. Press F5

To Move Manually through Slides in a Slide Show

After you begin Slide Show view, you can move forward or backward through the slides. PowerPoint allows you to advance through the slides manually or automatically. During a slide show, each slide in the presentation shows on the screen, one slide at a time. Each time you click the mouse button, the next slide appears. The following steps move manually through the slides.

1

- Click each slide until Slide 5 (Be Green) is displayed (Figure 1–73).

Q&A I see a small toolbar in the lower-left corner of my slide. What is this toolbar?

The Slide Show toolbar appears when you begin running a slide show and then move the mouse pointer. The buttons on this toolbar allow you to navigate to the next slide, the previous slide, to mark up the current slide, or to change the current display.

Slide 5 is displayed in Slide Show view

BE GREEN
Save Energy at Home

Figure 1–73

2

- Click Slide 5 so that the black slide appears with a message announcing the end of the slide show (Figure 1–74).

Q&A How can I end the presentation at this point?

Click the black slide to return to Normal view in the PowerPoint window or press the ESC key.

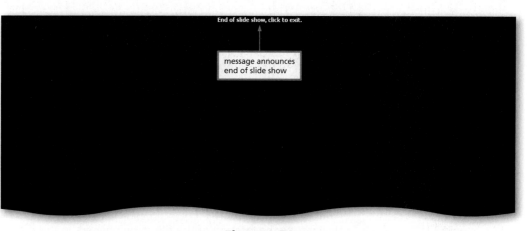

End of slide show, click to exit.

message announces end of slide show

Figure 1–74

Other Ways

| 1. Press PAGE DOWN to advance one slide at a time, or press PAGE UP to go back one slide at a time | 2. Press RIGHT ARROW or DOWN ARROW to advance one slide at a time, or press LEFT ARROW or UP ARROW to go back one slide at a time | 3. If Slide Show toolbar is displayed, click Next Slide or Previous Slide button on toolbar |

To Quit PowerPoint

This project now is complete. The following steps quit PowerPoint. For a detailed example of the procedure summarized below, refer to the Office 2010 and Windows 7 chapter at the beginning of this book.

1 If you have one PowerPoint presentation open, click the Close button on the right side of the title bar to close the document and quit PowerPoint; or if you have multiple PowerPoint presentations open, click File on the Ribbon to open the Backstage view and then click Exit in the Backstage view to close all open documents and quit PowerPoint.

2 If a Microsoft PowerPoint dialog box appears, click the Save button to save any changes made to the document since the last save.

BTW

Certification
The Microsoft Office Specialist (MOS) program provides an opportunity for you to obtain a valuable industry credential — proof that you have the PowerPoint 2010 skills required by employers. For more information, visit the PowerPoint 2010 Certification Web page (scsite.com/ppt2010/cert).

To Start PowerPoint

Once you have created and saved a document, you may need to retrieve it from your storage medium. For example, you might want to revise the presentation or print it. The following steps, which assume Windows 7 is running, start PowerPoint so that you can open and modify the presentation. You may need to ask your instructor how to start PowerPoint for your computer. For a detailed example of the procedure summarized below, refer to the Office 2010 and Windows 7 chapter at the beginning of this book.

1 Click the Start button on the Windows 7 taskbar to display the Start menu.

2 Type `Microsoft PowerPoint` as the search text in the 'Search programs and files' text box and watch the search results appear on the Start menu.

3 Click Microsoft PowerPoint 2010 in the search results on the Start menu to start PowerPoint and display a new blank document in the PowerPoint window.

4 If the PowerPoint window is not maximized, click the Maximize button next to the Close button on its title bar to maximize the window.

To Open a Document from PowerPoint

Earlier in this chapter you saved your project on a USB flash drive using the file name, Saving Energy. The following steps open the Saving Energy file from the PowerPoint folder in the CIS 101 folder on the USB flash drive. For a detailed example of the procedure summarized below, refer to the Office 2010 and Windows 7 chapter at the beginning of this book.

1 With your USB flash drive connected to one of the computer's USB ports, click File on the Ribbon to open the Backstage view.

2 Click Open in the Backstage view to display the Open dialog box.

3 Navigate to the location of the file to be opened (in this case, the USB flash drive, then to the CIS 101 folder [or your class folder], and then to the PowerPoint folder).

4 Click Saving Energy to select the file to be opened.

5 Click the Open button (Open dialog box) to open the selected file and display the opened document in the PowerPoint window.

Printing a Presentation

After creating a presentation, you may want to print the slides. Printing a presentation enables you to distribute the document to others in a form that can be read or viewed but typically not edited. It is a good practice to save a presentation before printing it, in the event you experience difficulties printing.

Determine the best method for distributing the presentation.
The traditional method of distributing a presentation uses a printer to produce a hard copy. A **hardcopy** or **printout** is information that exists on a physical medium such as paper. For users who can receive fax documents, you can elect to print a hard copy on a remote fax machine. Hard copies can be useful for the following reasons:

- Many people prefer proofreading a hard copy of a document rather than viewing it on the screen to check for errors and readability.

- Hard copies can serve as reference material if your storage medium is lost or becomes corrupted and you need to recreate the document.

    Instead of distributing a hard copy of a presentation slides, users can choose to distribute the presentation as an electronic image that mirrors the original document's appearance. The electronic image of the document can be e-mailed, posted on a Web site, or copied to a portable storage medium such as a USB flash drive. Two popular electronic image formats, sometimes called fixed formats, are PDF by Adobe Systems and XPS by Microsoft. In PowerPoint, you can create electronic image files through the Print tab in the Backstage view, the Save & Send tab in the Backstage view, and the Save As dialog box. Electronic images of documents, such as PDF and XPS, can be useful for the following reasons.

- Users can view electronic images of documents without the software that created the original document (e.g., PowerPoint). Specifically, to view a PDF file, you use a program called Acrobat Reader, which can be downloaded free from Adobe's Web site. Similarly, to view an XPS file, you use a program called an XPS Viewer, which is included in the latest versions of Windows and Internet Explorer.

- Sending electronic documents saves paper and printer supplies. Society encourages users to contribute to **green computing**, which involves reducing the environmental waste generated when using a computer.

Plan Ahead

To Print a Presentation

With the completed presentation saved, you may want to print it. If copies of the presentation are being distributed to audience members, you will print a hard copy of each individual slide on a printer. The following steps print a hard copy of the contents of the saved Saving Energy presentation.

1

- Click File on the Ribbon to open the Backstage view.

- Click the Print tab in the Backstage view to display the Print gallery (Figure 1–75).

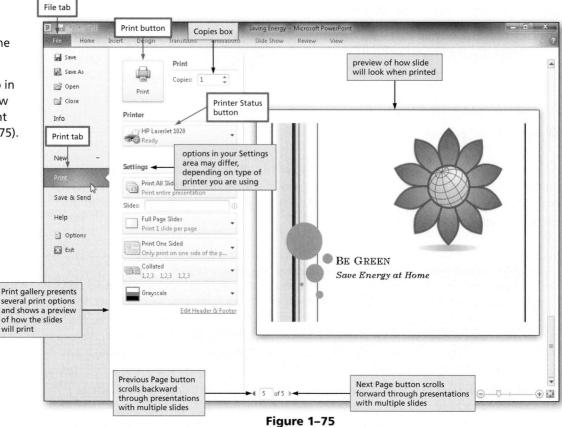

Figure 1–75

Q&A How do I preview Slides 2 through 5?

Click the Next Page button in the Print gallery to scroll forward through pages in the document; similarly, click the Previous Page button to scroll backward through pages.

Q&A How can I print multiple copies of my slides?

Increase the number in the Copies box in the Print gallery.

Q&A What if I decide not to print the document at this time?

Click File on the Ribbon to close the Backstage view and return to the PowerPoint document window.

2

- Verify the printer name that appears on the Printer box Status button will print a hard copy of the document. If necessary, click the Printer Status button to display a list of available printer options and then click the desired printer to change the currently selected printer.

BTW

Quick Reference
For a table that lists how to complete the tasks covered in this book using the mouse, Ribbon, shortcut menu, and keyboard, see the Quick Reference Summary at the back of this book, or visit the PowerPoint 2010 Quick Reference Web page (scsite.com/ppt2010/qr).

3

- Click the Print button in the Print gallery to print the document on the currently selected printer.

- When the printer stops, retrieve the hard copy (Figure 1–76).

Q&A

Do I have to wait until my document is complete to print it?

No, you can follow these steps to print a document at any time while you are creating it.

Q&A

What if I want to print an electronic image of a document instead of a hard copy?

You would click the Printer Status button in the Print gallery and then select the desired electronic image option such as a Microsoft XPS Document Writer, which would create an XPS file.

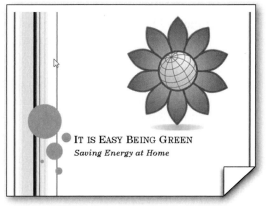

(a) Slide 1

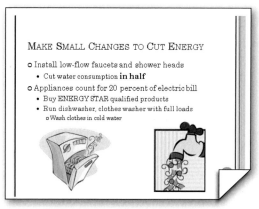

(b) Slide 2

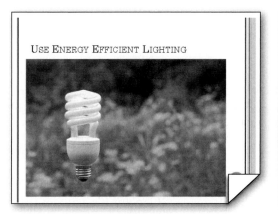

(c) Slide 3

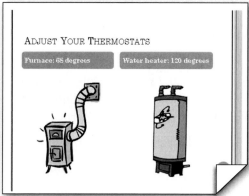

(d) Slide 4

(e) Slide 5

Figure 1–76

Other Ways
1. Press CTRL+P, press ENTER

To Quit PowerPoint

The project now is complete. The following steps quit PowerPoint. For a detailed example of the procedure summarized below, refer to the Office 2010 and Windows 7 chapter at the beginning of this book.

1 If you have one PowerPoint document open, click the Close button on the right side of the title bar to close the document and quit PowerPoint; or if you have multiple PowerPoint documents open, click File on the Ribbon to open the Backstage view and then click Exit in the Backstage view to close all open documents and quit PowerPoint.

2 If a Microsoft Office PowerPoint dialog box appears, click the Save button to save any changes made to the document since the last save.

Chapter Summary

In this chapter you have learned how to apply a document theme, create a title slide and text slides with a bulleted list, clip art, and a photograph, size and move clip art and a photograph, format and edit text, add a slide transition, view the presentation in Slide Show view, and print slides as handouts. The items listed below include all the new PowerPoint skills you have learned in this chapter.

1. Start PowerPoint (PPT 4)
2. Choose a Document Theme (PPT 5)
3. Enter the Presentation Title (PPT 7)
4. Enter the Presentation Subtitle Paragraph (PPT 9)
5. Select a Paragraph (PPT 10)
6. Italicize Text (PPT 11)
7. Increase Font Size (PPT 11)
8. Select a Word (PPT 12)
9. Change the Text Color (PPT 13)
10. Save a Presentation (PPT 14)
11. Add a New Text Slide with a Bulleted List (PPT 14)
12. Enter a Slide Title (PPT 16)
13. Select a Text Placeholder (PPT 16)
14. Type a Multi-Level Bulleted List (PPT 17)
15. Select a Group of Words (PPT 19)
16. Bold Text (PPT 19)
17. Add a Slide with the Title Only Layout (PPT 21)
18. Add a New Slide and Enter a Slide Title and Headings (PPT 23)
19. Move to Another Slide in Normal View (PPT 25)
20. Insert a Clip from the Clip Organizer into the Title Slide (PPT 27)
21. Insert a Clip from the Clip Organizer into a Content Placeholder (PPT 30)
22. Insert a Photograph from the Clip Organizer into a Slide without a Content Placeholder (PPT 32)
23. Resize Clip Art (PPT 33)
24. Move Clips (PPT 36)
25. Duplicate a Slide (PPT 38)
26. Arrange a Slide (PPT 39)
27. Delete Text in a Placeholder (PPT 41)
28. Add a Transition between Slides (PPT 43)
29. Change Document Properties (PPT 46)
30. Save an Existing Presentation with the Same File Name (PPT 47)
31. Start Slide Show View (PPT 47)
32. Move Manually through Slides in a Slide Show (PPT 49)
33. Quit PowerPoint (PPT 50)
34. Open a Document from PowerPoint (PPT 50)
35. Print a Presentation (PPT 51)

 If you have a SAM 2010 user profile, your instructor may have assigned an autogradable version of this assignment. If so, log into the SAM 2010 Web site at www.cengage.com/sam2010 to download the instruction and start files.

Learn It Online

Test your knowledge of chapter content and key terms.

Instructions: To complete the Learn It Online exercises, start your browser, click the Address bar, and then enter the Web address **scsite.com/ppt2010/learn**. When the PowerPoint 2010 Learn It Online page is displayed, click the link for the exercise you want to complete and then read the instructions.

Chapter Reinforcement TF, MC, and SA

A series of true/false, multiple choice, and short answer questions that test your knowledge of the chapter content.

Flash Cards

An interactive learning environment where you identify chapter key terms associated with displayed definitions.

Practice Test

A series of multiple choice questions that test your knowledge of chapter content and key terms.

Who Wants To Be a Computer Genius?

An interactive game that challenges your knowledge of chapter content in the style of a television quiz show.

Wheel of Terms

An interactive game that challenges your knowledge of chapter key terms in the style of the television show *Wheel of Fortune*.

Crossword Puzzle Challenge

A crossword puzzle that challenges your knowledge of key terms presented in the chapter.

Apply Your Knowledge

Reinforce the skills and apply the concepts you learned in this chapter.

Modifying Character Formats and Paragraph Levels and Moving a Clip

Note: To complete this assignment, you will be required to use the Data Files for Students. See the inside back cover of this book for instructions on downloading the Data Files for Students, or contact your instructor for information about accessing the required files.

Instructions: Start PowerPoint. Open the presentation, Apply 1-1 Flu Season, from the Data Files for Students.

The two slides in the presentation discuss ways to avoid getting or spreading the flu. The document you open is an unformatted presentation. You are to modify the document theme, indent the paragraphs, resize and move the clip art, and format the text so the slides look like Figure 1–77 on the next page.

Continued >

Apply Your Knowledge *continued*

Perform the following tasks:

1. Change the document theme to Urban. On the title slide, use your name in place of Student Name and bold and italicize your name. Increase the title text font size to 60 point. Resize and position the clip as shown in Figure 1–77a.

2. On Slide 2, increase the indent of the second, third, and fifth paragraphs (Cover mouth and nose with a tissue; No tissue? Use your elbow or sleeve; Use soap, warm water for 20 seconds) to second-level paragraphs. Then combine paragraphs six and seven (Drink fluids; Get plenty of rest) to read, Drink fluids and get plenty of rest, as shown in Figure 1–77b.

3. Change the document properties, as specified by your instructor. Save the presentation using the file name, Apply 1–1 Avoid the Flu. Submit the revised document in the format specified by your instructor.

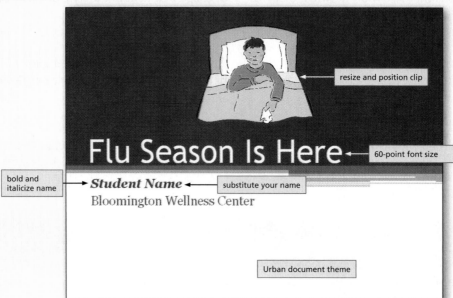

(a) Slide 1 (Title Slide with Clip Art)

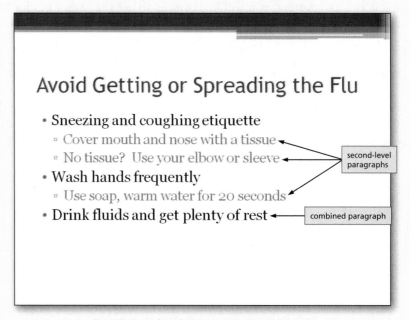

(b) Slide 2 (Multi-Level Bulleted List)

Figure 1–77

Extend Your Knowledge

Extend the skills you learned in this chapter and experiment with new skills. You may need to use Help to complete the assignment.

Changing Slide Theme, Layout, and Text

Note: To complete this assignment, you will be required to use the Data Files for Students. See the inside back cover of this book for instructions on downloading the Data Files for Students, or contact your instructor for information about accessing the required files.

Instructions: Start PowerPoint. Open the presentation that you are going to prepare for your dental hygiene class, Extend 1–1 Winning Smile, from the Data Files for Students.
 You will choose a theme, format slides, and create a closing slide.

Perform the following tasks:
1. Apply an appropriate document theme.
2. On Slide 1, use your name in place of Student Name. Format the text on this slide using techniques you learned in this chapter, such as changing the font size and color and also bolding and italicizing words.
3. On Slide 2, change the slide layout and adjust the paragraph levels so that the lines of text are arranged under two headings: Discount Dental and Dental Insurance (Figure 1–78).
4. On Slide 3, create paragraphs and adjust the paragraph levels to create a bulleted list. Edit the text so that the slide meets the 7×7 rule, which states that each line should have a maximum of seven words, and each slide should have a maximum of seven lines.
5. Create an appropriate closing slide using the title slide as a guide.
6. The slides contain a variety of clips downloaded from the Microsoft Clip Organizer. Size and move them when necessary.
7. Apply an appropriate transition to all slides.
8. Change the document properties, as specified by your instructor. Save the presentation using the file name, Extend 1–1 Dental Plans.
9. Submit the revised document in the format specified by your instructor.

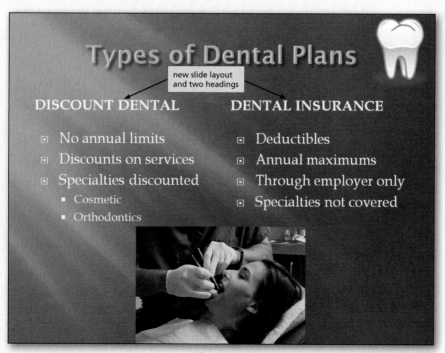

Figure 1–78

Make It Right

Analyze a presentation and correct all errors and/or improve the design.

Correcting Formatting and List Levels

Note: To complete this assignment, you will be required to use the Data Files for Students. See the inside back cover of this book for instructions on downloading the Data Files for Students, or contact your instructor for information about accessing the required files.

Instructions: Start PowerPoint. Open the presentation, Make It Right 1–1 Air Ducts, from the Data Files for Students.

Members of your homeowners' association are having their semiannual meeting, and each member of the board is required to give a short presentation on the subject of energy savings. You have decided to discuss the energy-saving benefits of maintaining the air ducts in your home. Correct the formatting problems and errors in the presentation while keeping in mind the guidelines presented in this chapter.

Perform the following tasks:

1. Change the document theme from Origin, shown in Figure 1–79, to Module.
2. On Slide 1, replace the words, Student Name, with your name. Format your name so that it displays prominently on the slide.
3. Increase the size of the clip on Slide 1 and move it to the upper-right corner.
4. Move Slide 2 to the end of the presentation so that it becomes the new Slide 3.
5. On Slide 2, correct the spelling errors and then increase the font size of the Slide 2 title text, Check Hidden Air Ducts, to 54 point. Increase the size of the clip and move it up to fill the white space on the right of the bulleted list.
6. On Slide 3, correct the spelling errors and then change the font size of the title text, Energy Savings, to 54 point. Increase the indent levels for paragraphs 2 and 4. Increase the size of the clips. Center the furnace clip at the bottom of the slide.
7. Change the document properties, as specified by your instructor. Save the presentation using the file name, Make It Right 1–1 Ducts Presentation.
8. Apply the same transition and duration to all slides.
9. Submit the revised document in the format specified by your instructor.

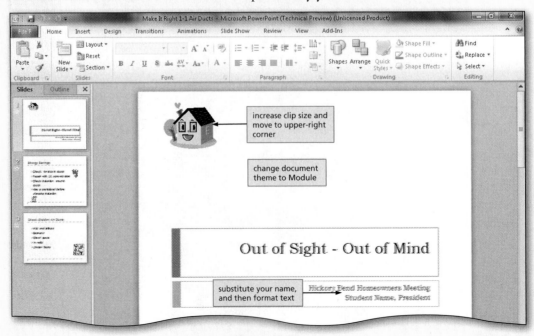

Figure 1–79

In the Lab

Design and/or create a presentation using the guidelines, concepts, and skills presented in this chapter. Labs 1, 2, and 3 are listed in order of increasing difficulty.

Lab1: Creating a Presentation with Bulleted Lists, a Closing Slide, and Clips

Problem: You are working with upper-level students to host a freshmen orientation seminar. When you attended this seminar, you received some helpful tips on studying for exams. Your contribution to this year's seminar is to prepare a short presentation on study skills. You develop the outline shown in Figure 1–80 and then prepare the PowerPoint presentation shown in Figures 1–81a through 1–81d.

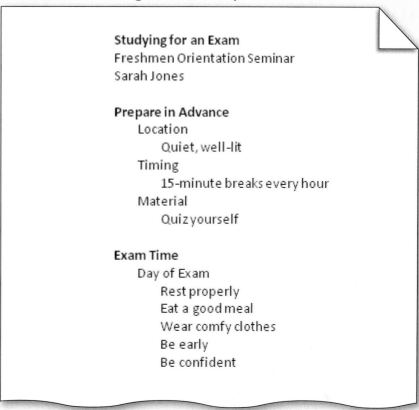

Studying for an Exam
Freshmen Orientation Seminar
Sarah Jones

Prepare in Advance
   Location
      Quiet, well-lit
   Timing
      15-minute breaks every hour
   Material
      Quiz yourself

Exam Time
   Day of Exam
      Rest properly
      Eat a good meal
      Wear comfy clothes
      Be early
      Be confident

Figure 1–80

Perform the following tasks:

1. Create a new presentation using the Aspect document theme.

2. Using the typed notes illustrated in Figure 1–80, create the title slide shown in Figure 1–81a, using your name in place of Sarah Jones. Italicize your name and increase the font size to 24 point. Increase the font size of the title text paragraph, Hit the Books, to 48 point. Increase the font size of the first paragraph of the subtitle text, Studying for an Exam, to 28 point.

(a) Slide 1 (Title Slide)
Figure 1–81

Continued >

In the Lab *continued*

3. Using the typed notes in Figure 1–80, create the two text slides with bulleted lists and find and insert clips from the Microsoft Clip Organizer, as shown in Figures 1–81b and 1–81c.

4. Create a closing slide by duplicating Slide 1, deleting your name, replacing the photograph with the photograph shown in Figure 1–81d, and moving the slide to the end of the presentation.

5. On Slide 3, change the font color of the words, Be confident, to Yellow (fourth color in the Standard Colors row).

6. Apply the Uncover transition in the Subtle category to all slides. Change the duration to 1.25 seconds.

7. Drag the scroll box to display Slide 1. Click the Slide Show button to start Slide Show view. Then click to display each slide.

8. Change the document properties, as specified by your instructor. Save the presentation using the file name, Lab 1–1 Study Skills.

9. Submit the document in the format specified by your instructor.

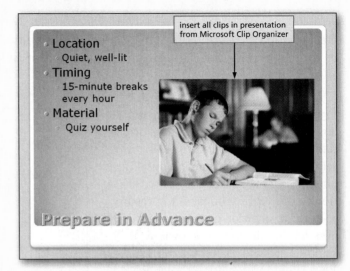

(b) Slide 2

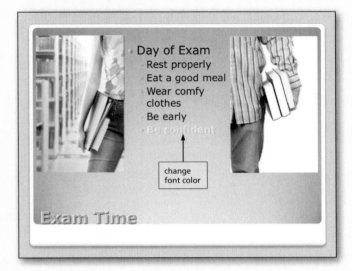

(c) Slide 3

(d) Slide 4 (Closing Slide)
Figure 1–81 (continued)

In the Lab

Lab 2: Creating a Presentation with Bulleted Lists and Clips

Problem: Your health class instructor has assigned every student a different vitamin to research. She hands you the outline shown in Figure 1–82 and asks you to create the presentation about Vitamin D shown in Figures 1–83a through 1–83d on pages PPT 62 and PPT 63.

Vitamin D

The Sunshine Vitamin
Are You D-ficient?
Presented by Jim Warner

Why Is Vitamin D Important?
  We need Vitamin D
    Vital to our bodies
        Promotes absorption of calcium and magnesium
          For healthy teeth and bones
        Maintains calcium and phosphorus in blood

  Daily Requirements
    How much do we need?
      Child: 5 mcg (200 IU)
      Adult: 10-20 mcg (400-600 IU)

Vitamin D Sources
  Sunshine
    Is our primary source
        Vitamin manufactured by our body after exposure
          Three times a week
          For 10-15 minutes
  Foods and Supplements
    Contained in few foods
        Some fish liver oils
        Flesh of fatty fish
    Fortified products
        Milk and cereals
    Available as supplement

Vitamin D History
  Research began in 1924
    Found to prevent rickets
  United States and Canada
    Instituted policy of fortifying foods with Vitamin D
        Milk – food of choice
  Other countries
    Fortified cereal, bread, margarine

Figure 1–82

Continued >

In the Lab *continued*

Perform the following tasks:

1. Create a new presentation using the Solstice document theme.

2. Using the typed notes illustrated in Figure 1–82, create the title slide shown in Figure 1–83a, using your name in place of Jim Warner. Italicize the title, The Sunshine Vitamin, and increase the font size to 48 point. Change the font size of the first line of the subtitle text, Are You D-ficient?, to 36 point. Change the font color of the title text to Orange (third color in the Standard Colors row) and both lines of the subtitle text to Light Blue (seventh color in the Standard Colors row).

3. Using the typed notes in Figure 1–82, create the three text slides with bulleted lists shown in Figures 1–83b through 1–83d. Change the color of the title text on all slides and the text above the bulleted lists on Slides 2 and 3 to Orange.

4. Add the photographs and clip art shown in Figures 1–83a through 1–83d from the Microsoft Clip Organizer. Adjust the clip sizes when necessary.

5. Apply the Ripple transition in the Exciting category to all slides. Change the duration to 2.00 seconds.

6. Drag the scroll box to display Slide 1. Click the Slide Show button to start Slide Show view. Then click to display each slide.

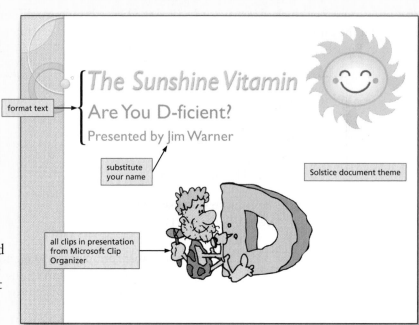

(a) Slide 1 (Title Slide)

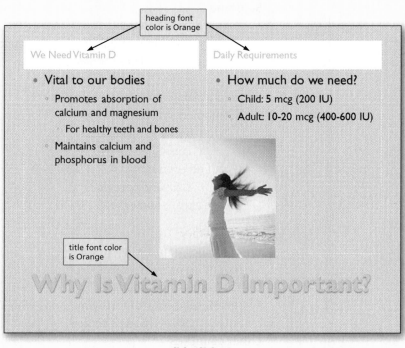

(b) Slide 2

Figure 1–83

7. Change the document properties, as specified by your instructor. Save the presentation using the file name, Lab 1–2 Vitamin D.

8. Submit the revised document in the format specified by your instructor.

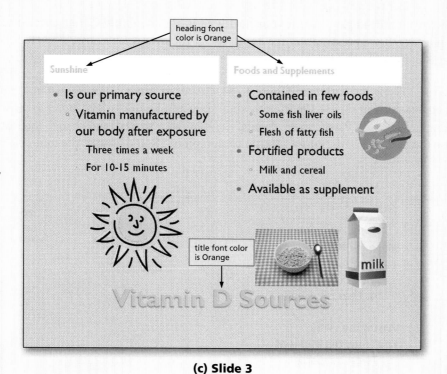

(c) Slide 3

(d) Slide 4

Figure 1–83 (continued)

In the Lab

Lab 3: Creating and Updating Presentations with Clip Art

Problem: You are employed part time at your health club, and the Child Care Center director has asked you to put together a presentation for her to use at the next open house. The club has a large playroom that is perfect for children's parties.

Instructions Part 1: Using the outline in Figure 1–84, create the presentation shown in Figure 1–85. Use the Office Theme document theme. On the title slide shown in Figure 1–85a, increase the font size of the title paragraph, Make It a Party!, to 48, change the font color to Red, and change the text font style to italic. Decrease the font size of the entire subtitle paragraph to 28, and change the font color to Blue.

Make It a Party!
Host Your Child's
Next Birthday Party
At The Oaks Health Club

We Do the Work
You Enjoy the Moment
Two-hour party
Two chaperones
Lunch & cake provided
Game or craft activity available
Decorations

Two Party Packages
Package No. 1 - $8/child
Lunch
Hot Dogs
Pizza
Package No. 2 - $12/child
Lunch including beverage
Hot Dogs
Pizza
Game
Craft (age appropriate)

Reserve Your Party Date
Reserve 2 weeks in advance
Deposit required
Party room can hold 20 children
Sign up in the Child Care Center

Figure 1–84

Create the three text slides with multi-level bulleted lists, photographs, and clip art shown in Figures 1–85b through 1–85d on the next page. Adjust the clip sizes when necessary. Apply the Vortex transition in the Exciting category to all slides and decrease the duration to 3.00 seconds. Change the document properties, as specified by your instructor. Save the presentation using the file name, Lab 1–3 Part One Child Party.

(a) Slide 1 (Title Slide)

(b) Slide 2
Figure 1–85

Continued >

In the Lab *continued*

Two Party Packages

Package No. 1 - $8/child

- Lunch
  - Hot Dogs
  - Pizza

Package No. 2 - $12/child

- Lunch including beverage
  - Hot Dogs
  - Pizza
- Game
- Craft (age appropriate)

(c) Slide 3

Reserve Your Party Date

- Reserve 2 weeks in advance
- Deposit required
- Party room can hold 20 children
- Sign up in the Child Care Center

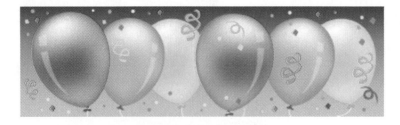

(d) Slide 4

Figure 1–85 (continued)

Instructions Part 2: The children's parties have proved to be a great perk for members of the health club. A large group of older adults work out at the club and also meet socially once a month. These members have asked about renting the playroom to hold a retirement party for some of their friends. You decide to modify the children's party presentation to promote retirement parties. Use the outline in Figure 1–86 to modify the presentation created in Part 1 to create the presentation shown in Figure 1–87 on the next page. Required changes are indicated by a yellow highlight.

To begin, save the current presentation with the new file name, Lab 1–3 Part Two Retirement Party. Change the document theme to Flow. On Slide 3, change the pianist's name from Ms. Winn to your name. Apply the Fade transition in the Subtle category to all slides and change the duration speed to 2.25 seconds. View the slide show. Change the document properties, as specified by your instructor. Submit both Part One and Part Two documents in the format specified by your instructor.

Make It a Party!
Host Your
Retirement Party
At The Oaks Health Club

We Do the Work
You Enjoy the Moment
Two-hour party

Lunch & cake provided

Decorations
Music

Two Party Packages
Package No. 1 - $9/person
Lunch
Lasagna
Salad & bread
Package No. 2 - $20/person
Lunch including beverage
Lasagna
Salad & bread
Ms. Winn on piano
Photo booth

Reserve Your Party Date
Reserve 2 weeks in advance
Deposit required
Party room can hold 15 adults
Sign up at the main desk

Figure 1–86

Continued >

(a) Slide 1 (Title Slide)

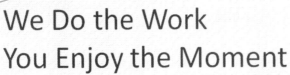

(b) Slide 2
Figure 1–87

(c) Slide 3

(d) Slide 4
Figure 1–87 (continued)

Cases and Places

Apply your creative thinking and problem-solving skills to design and implement a solution.

Note: To complete these assignments, you may be required to use the Data Files for Students. See the inside back cover of this book for instructions on downloading the Data Files for Students, or contact your instructor for information about accessing the required files.

As you design the presentations, remember to use the 7 × 7 rule: a maximum of seven words on a line and a maximum of seven lines on one slide.

1: Design and Create a Presentation about Galileo

Academic

Italian-born Galileo is said to be the father of modern science. After the invention of the telescope by a Dutch eyeglass maker named Hans Lippershey, Galileo made his own telescope and made many discoveries. You decide to prepare a PowerPoint presentation to accompany a speech that is required in your Astronomy class. You create the outline shown in Figure 1–88 about Galileo. Use this outline, along with the concepts and techniques presented in this chapter, to develop and format a slide show with a title slide and three text slides with bulleted lists. Add photographs and clip art from the Microsoft Clip Organizer and apply a transition. Submit your assignment in the format specified by your instructor.

Galileo Galilei
  Father of Modern Science
  Astronomy 201
  Sandy Wendt

Major Role in Scientific Revolution
February 15, 1564 – January 8, 1642
  Physicist
  Mathematician
  Astronomer
  Philosopher

Galileo's Research Years
  1581 – Studied medicine
  1589-1592 – Studied math and physics
  1592-1607 – Padua University
    Developed Law of Inertia
  1609 – Built telescope
    Earth's moon
    Jupiter's moons

Galileo's Later Years
  Dialogue – Two Chief World Systems
    Controversy develops
  1633 – Rome
    Heresy trial
    Imprisoned
  1642 – Dies

Figure 1–88

2: Design and Create a Presentation Promoting Hiking for Family Fitness

Personal

A great way for the entire family to get exercise is by participating in a hiking adventure. Employees at the local forest preserve district near your home have remodeled the nature center, and you have volunteered to give a presentation at the open house to help families plan their hikes. Use the outline shown in Figure 1–89 and then create an accompanying PowerPoint presentation. Use the concepts and techniques presented in this chapter to develop and format this slide show with a title slide, three text slides with bulleted lists, and clip art. Add photographs and clip art from the Microsoft Clip Organizer and apply a transition. Submit your assignment in the format specified by your instructor.

Take a Hike
   An Adventure with Kids
   Presented by Joshua Lind
   Pines Nature Center

Planning the Adventure
   Trail length — varies by child's age
      Ages 2 to 4: 1 to 2 miles
      Ages 5 to 7: 3 to 4 miles
      Ages 8 to 12: 5 to 7 miles
   Backpack — limit to 20 percent of child's weight

Packing Supplies
   Snacks and Drinks
      Child's favorite healthy foods
         Fruit and nuts
      Water
   Miscellaneous
      Sunscreen
      Insect repellent
      First-aid kit

Wearing the Right Clothes
   Dress in layers
      Children get cold quicker than adults
   Wear long pants and long-sleeved shirt
      Protect against insects and cuts
   Wear a hat and comfortable shoes
      Keep body warm

Figure 1–89

Continued >

Cases and Places continued

3: Design and Create a Landscaping Service Presentation

Professional

The home and garden center where you work is hosting weekend clinics for customers. The owner asks you to give a presentation about the center's new landscaping division and hands you the outline shown in Figure 1–90. Use the concepts and techniques presented in this chapter to develop and format a PowerPoint presentation with a title slide, three text slides with bulleted lists, and clip art. Add photographs and clip art from the Microsoft Clip Organizer and apply a transition. Submit your assignment in the format specified by your instructor.

Barry's Landscaping Service
Bensenville, Indiana

Full-Service Landscaping
    Initial design
    Installation
    Maintenance

Scope of Services
    Landscape design
    Irrigation
    Lighting
    Lawn-care programs
    Tree/shrub maintenance
    Masonry, carpentry
    Water features

Our Promise to You
    Deliver on-time service
    Provide highest level of workmanship
    Give maximum value for your dollar
    Install high-quality plants and materials
    Respond quickly to your needs

Figure 1–90

2 Enhancing a Presentation with Pictures, Shapes, and WordArt

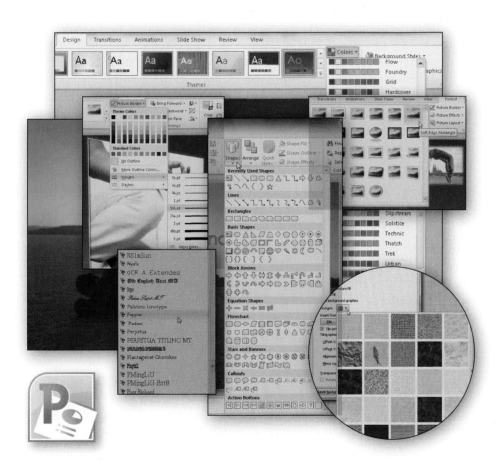

Objectives

You will have mastered the material in this chapter when you can:

- Change theme colors
- Insert a picture to create a background
- Format slide backgrounds
- Insert and size a shape
- Add text to a shape

- Apply effects to a shape
- Change the font and add a shadow
- Format pictures
- Apply a WordArt style
- Format WordArt
- Format text using the Format Painter

2 | Enhancing a Presentation with Pictures, Shapes, and WordArt

Introduction

In our visually oriented culture, audience members enjoy viewing effective graphics. Whether reading a document or viewing a PowerPoint presentation, people increasingly want to see photographs, artwork, graphics, and a variety of typefaces. Researchers have known for decades that documents with visual elements are more effective than those that consist of only text because the illustrations motivate audiences to study the material. People remember at least one-third more information when the document they are seeing or reading contains visual elements. These graphics help clarify and emphasize details, so they appeal to audience members with differing backgrounds, reading levels, attention spans, and motivations.

Project — Presentation with Pictures, Shapes, and WordArt

BTW
Yoga's Origins
The term, yoga, is derived from the Sanskrit word yuj, meaning to join or unite. Yogis have been practicing this system of exercises and philosophy of mental control for more than 26,000 years.

The project in this chapter follows graphical guidelines and uses PowerPoint to create the presentation shown in Figure 2–1. This slide show, which discusses yoga and meditation, has a variety of illustrations and visual elements. For example, pictures have particular shapes and effects. The enhanced type has a style that blends well with the background and illustrations. Pictures and type are formatted using Quick Styles and WordArt, which give your presentation a professional look.

Overview

As you read through this chapter, you will learn how to create the presentation shown in Figure 2–1 by performing these general tasks:

- Format slide backgrounds.
- Insert and format pictures by applying styles and effects.
- Insert and format shapes.
- Format text using WordArt.
- Print a handout of your slides.

(a) Slide 1 (Title Slide with Picture Background and Shapes)

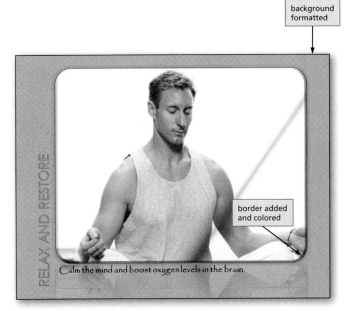

(b) Slide 2 (Formatted Picture)

(c) Slide 3 (Formatted Picture)

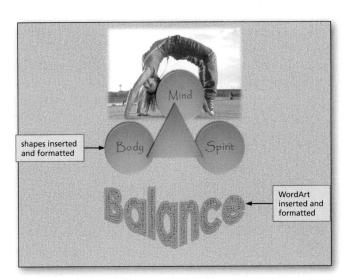

(d) Slide 4 (Inserted and Formatted Shapes)

Figure 2–1

Plan
Ahead

General Project Guidelines

When creating a PowerPoint presentation, the actions you perform and decisions you make will affect the appearance and characteristics of the finished document. As you create a presentation with illustrations, such as the project shown in Figure 2–1, you should follow these general guidelines:

1. **Focus on slide text content.** Give some careful thought to the words you choose. Some graphic designers advise starting with a blank screen so that the document theme does not distract from or influence the words.

2. **Apply style guidelines.** Many organizations and publishers establish guidelines for writing styles. These rules apply to capitalization, punctuation, word usage, and document formats. Ask your instructor or manager for a copy of these guidelines or use popular writing guides, such as the *The Chicago Manual of Style*, *The Associated Press Stylebook*, and *The Elements of Style*.

3. **Use color effectively.** Your audience's eyes are drawn to color on a slide. Used appropriately, color can create interest by emphasizing material and promoting understanding. Be aware of symbolic meanings attached to colors, such as red generally representing danger, electricity, and heat.

4. **Adhere to copyright regulations.** Copyright laws apply to printed and electronic materials. You can copy an existing photograph or artwork if it is in the public domain, if your company owns the graphic, or if you have obtained permission to use it. Be certain you have the legal right to use a desired graphic in your presentation.

5. **Consider graphics for multicultural audiences.** In today's intercultural society, your presentation might be viewed by people whose first language is different from yours. Some graphics have meanings specific to a culture, so be certain to learn about your intended audience and their views.

6. **Use WordArt in moderation.** Used correctly, the graphical nature of WordArt can add interest and set a tone. Format text with a WordArt style only when needed for special emphasis.

When necessary, more specific details concerning the above guidelines are presented at appropriate points in the chapter. The chapter also will identify the actions you perform and decisions made regarding these guidelines during the creation of the presentation shown in Figure 2–1.

Starting PowerPoint

For an introduction to Windows 7 and instruction about how to perform basic Windows 7 tasks, read the Office 2010 and Windows 7 chapter at the beginning of this book, where you can learn how to resize windows, change screen resolution, create folders, move and rename files, use Windows Help, and much more.

Chapter 1 introduced you to starting PowerPoint, selecting a document theme, creating slides with clip art and a bulleted list, and printing a presentation. The following steps, which assume Windows 7 is running, start PowerPoint. You may need to ask your instructor how to start PowerPoint for your computer. For a detailed example of the procedure summarized on the next page, refer to pages OFF 33 through OFF 35 in the Office 2010 and Windows 7 chapter.

To Start PowerPoint and Apply a Document Theme

1 Click the Start button on the Windows 7 taskbar to display the Start menu.

2 Type `Microsoft PowerPoint` as the search text in the 'Search programs and files' text box.

3 Click Microsoft PowerPoint 2010 in the search results on the Start menu to start PowerPoint and display a new blank document.

4 If the PowerPoint window is not maximized, click the Maximize button.

5 Apply the Verve document theme.

Focus on slide text content.
Once you have researched your presentation topic, many methods exist to begin developing slide content.

- Select a document theme and then enter text, illustration, and tables.

- Open an existing presentation and modify the slides and theme.

- Import an outline created in Microsoft Word.

- Start with a blank presentation that uses the default Office Theme. Consider this practice similar to an artist who begins creating a painting with a blank, white canvas.

Experiment using different methods of developing the initial content for slides. Experienced PowerPoint users sometimes find one technique works better than another to stimulate creativity or help them organize their ideas in a particular circumstance.

Plan Ahead

For an introduction to Office 2010 and instruction about how to perform basic tasks in Office 2010 programs, read the Office 2010 and Windows 7 chapter at the beginning of this book, where you can learn how to start a program, use the Ribbon, save a file, open a file, quit a program, use Help, and much more.

Creating Slides and Changing Font Colors and Background Style

In Chapter 1, you selected a document theme and then typed the content for the title and text slides. In this chapter, you will type the slide content for the title and text slides, select a background, insert and format pictures and shapes, and then insert and format WordArt. To begin creating the four slides in this presentation, you will enter text in four different layouts, change the theme colors, and then change the background style.

Apply style guidelines.
A good stylebook is useful to decide when to use numerals or words to represent numbers, as in the sentence, More than 25 students are waiting for the bus to arrive. Stylebooks also offer rules on forming possessives, capitalizing titles, and using commas. Once you decide on a style to use in your presentation, apply it consistently throughout your presentation.

Plan Ahead

To Create a Title Slide

Recall from Chapter 1 that the title slide introduces the presentation to the audience. In addition to introducing the presentation, this project uses the title slide to capture the audience's attention by using title text and a background picture. The following steps create the slide show's title slide.

1 Type `Yoga and Meditation` in the title text placeholder.

2 Type `Unify Your Mind,` in the subtitle text placeholder.

3 Press the ENTER key and then type `Body,` as the second line in the subtitle text placeholder.

4 Press the ENTER key and then type `and Spirit` as the third line in the subtitle text placeholder. Change the capital letter 'A' in the word, And, at the beginning of this line to a lowercase 'a' (Figure 2–2).

Q&A

Some stylebooks recommend using lowercase letters when using coordinating conjunctions (for, and, nor, but, or, yet, so) and also when using articles (a, an, the). Why is the case of the word, and, changed in the subtitle text?

By default, PowerPoint capitalizes the first word of each paragraph. For consistency, you can decide to lowercase this word to apply a particular style rule so that the word, and, is lowercase in both the title and subtitle text.

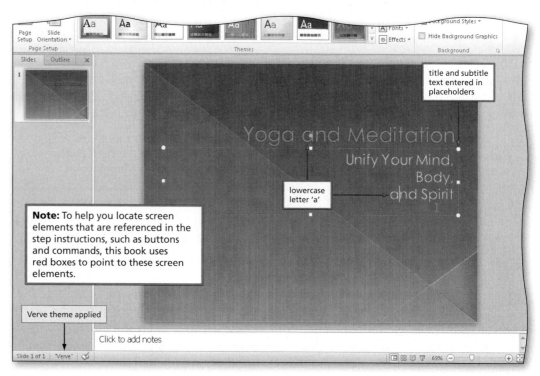

Figure 2–2

BTW

Q&As
For a complete list of the Q&As found in many of the step-by-step sequences in this book, visit the PowerPoint 2010 Q&A Web page (scsite.com/ppt2010/qa).

To Create the First Text Slide

The first text slide you create in Chapter 2 emphasizes the relaxation and restoration benefits derived from practicing yoga and meditation. The following steps add a new slide (Slide 2) and then create a text slide using the Picture with Caption layout.

1 Click Home on the Ribbon to display the Home tab, click the New Slide button arrow, and then click Picture with Caption in the Layout gallery to add a new slide with this layout.

2 Type `Relax and Restore` in the title text placeholder.

3 Press CTRL+ENTER to move to the caption placeholder and then type `Calm the mind and boost oxygen levels in the brain.` in this placeholder (Figure 2–3).

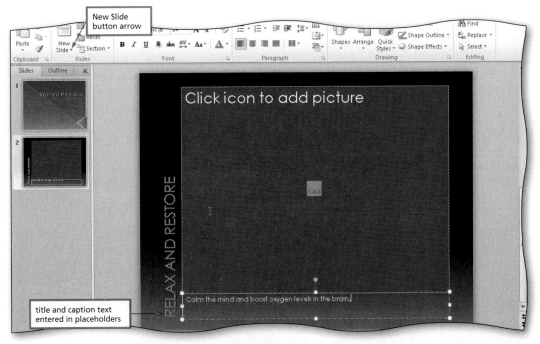

Figure 2–3

To Create the Second Text Slide

The second text slide you create stresses the fact that yoga and meditation strengthen the body in multiple ways. The following steps add a new text slide (Slide 3) that uses the Content with Caption layout.

1. Click the New Slide button arrow and then click Content with Caption in the Layout gallery to add a new slide with this layout.

2. Type **Strengthen Body** in the title text placeholder.

3. Press CTRL+ENTER and then type **Increase flexibility and tone muscles.** in the caption placeholder (Figure 2–4).

Q&A

Why does the text display with capital letters despite the fact I am typing uppercase and lowercase letters?

The Verve theme uses the All Caps effect for the title text. This effect converts lowercase letters to uppercase.

BTW

BTWs
For a complete list of the BTWs found in the margins of this book, visit the PowerPoint 2010 BTW Web page (scsite.com/ppt2010/btw).

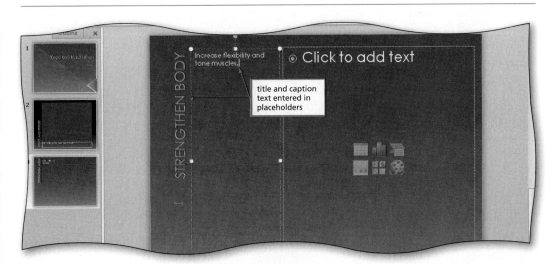

Figure 2–4

To Create the Third Text Slide

Yoga and meditation help create balance in an individual's life. The last slide you create uses graphics to depict the connection among the mind, body, and spirit. You will insert symbols later in this project to create this visual element. For now, you want to create the basic slide. The following step adds a new text slide (Slide 4) that uses the Blank layout.

1 Click the New Slide button arrow and then click Blank in the Layout gallery. (Figure 2–5).

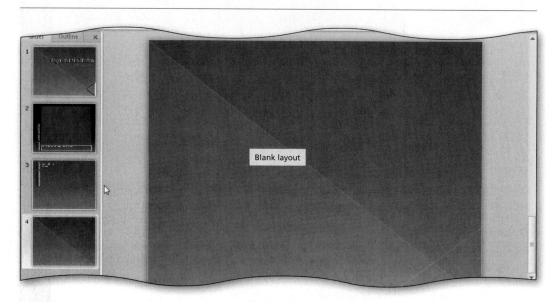

Figure 2–5

BTW

The Ribbon and Screen Resolution
PowerPoint may change how the groups and buttons within the groups appear on the Ribbon, depending on the computer's screen resolution. Thus, your Ribbon may look different from the ones in this book if you are using a screen resolution other than 1024 × 768.

Presentation Template Color Scheme

Each presentation template has 12 complementary colors, which collectively are called the **color scheme**. You can apply these colors to all slides, an individual slide, notes pages, or audience handouts. A color scheme consists of four colors for a background and text, six accent colors, and two hyperlink colors. The Theme Colors button on the Design tab contains a square with four colors; the top two colors indicate the primary text and background colors, and the bottom two colors indicate the accent colors. You also can customize the theme colors to create your own set and give them a unique name. Table 2–1 explains the components of a color scheme.

Table 2–1 Color Scheme Components

Component	Description
Background color	The background color is the fundamental color of a PowerPoint slide. For example, if the background color is black, you can place any other color on top of it, but the fundamental color remains black. The black background shows everywhere you do not add color or other objects.
Text color	The text color contrasts with the background color of the slide. As a default, the text border color is the same as the text color. Together with the background color, the text and border colors set the tone for a presentation. For example, a gray background with black text and border sets a dramatic tone. In contrast, a red background with yellow text and border sets a vibrant tone.
Accent colors	Accent colors are designed as colors for secondary features on a slide. They often are used as fill colors on graphs and as shadows.
Hyperlink colors	The default hyperlink color is set when you type the text. When you click the hyperlink text during a presentation, the color changes to the Followed Hyperlink color.

To Change the Presentation Theme Colors

The first modification to make is to change the color scheme throughout the presentation. The following steps change the color scheme for the template from a gray title slide background with pink text and accents to a blue background with pink and orange accents.

1

- Click Design on the Ribbon and then click the Theme Colors button (Design tab | Themes group) to display the Theme Colors gallery.

- Scroll down and then point to the Oriel built-in theme to display a live preview of this color scheme (Figure 2–6).

 **Experiment**

- Point to various themes in the Theme Colors gallery and watch the colors change on Slide 4.

 Why does a gold line surround the Verve color scheme in the Theme Colors gallery?

It shows the Verve document theme is applied, and those eight colors are associated with that theme.

Figure 2–6

2

- Click Oriel in the Theme Colors gallery to change the presentation theme colors to Oriel (Figure 2–7).

Q&A What if I want to return to the original theme color?

You would click the Theme Colors button and then click Verve in the Theme Colors gallery.

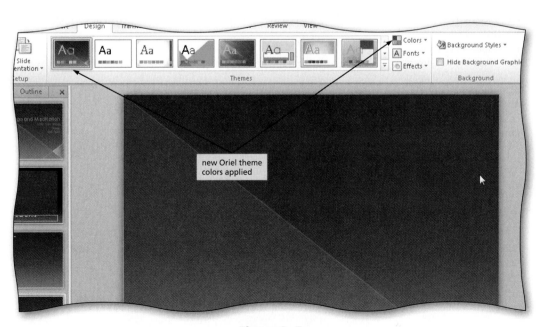

Figure 2–7

To Save a Presentation

You have performed many tasks while creating this slide and do not want to risk losing work completed thus far. Accordingly, you should save the document.

The following steps assume you already have created folders for storing your files, for example, a CIS 101 folder (for your class) that contains a PowerPoint folder (for your assignments). Thus, these steps save the document in the PowerPoint folder in the CIS 101 folder on a USB flash drive using the file name, Yoga. For a detailed example of the procedure summarized below, refer to pages OFF 27 through OFF 29 in the Office 2010 and Windows 7 chapter at the beginning of this book.

1 With a USB flash drive connected to one of the computer's USB ports, click the Save button on the Quick Access Toolbar to display the Save As dialog box.

2 Type **Yoga** in the File name text box to change the file name. Do not press the ENTER key after typing the file name because you do not want to close the dialog box at this time.

3 Navigate to the desired save location (in this case, the PowerPoint folder in the CIS 101 folder [or your class folder] on the USB flash drive).

4 Click the Save button (Save As dialog box) to save the document in the selected folder on the selected drive with the entered file name.

Inserting and Formatting Pictures in a Presentation

BTW

Inserting Watermarks
Checks, currency, business cards, and legal documents use watermarks to verify their authenticity. These semi-transparent images are visible when you hold this paper up to a light. You, likewise, can insert a clip art image or a picture as a watermark behind all or part of your slide to identify your unique PowerPoint presentation.

With the text entered and background formatted in the presentation, the next step is to insert digital pictures into the placeholders on Slides 2 and 3 and then format the pictures. These graphical images draw the viewers' eyes to the slides and help them retain the information presented.

In the following pages, you will perform these tasks:

1. Insert the first digital picture into Slide 3.
2. Insert the second digital picture into Slide 2.
3. Change the look of the first picture.
4. Change the look of the second picture.
5. Resize the second picture.
6. Insert a digital picture into the Slide 1 background.
7. Format slide backgrounds.

Plan
Ahead

To Insert a Picture

The next step in creating the presentation is to insert one of the digital yoga pictures in the picture placeholder in Slide 3. The picture is available on the Data Files for Students. See the inside back cover of this book for instructions on downloading the Data Files for Students, or contact your instructor for information about accessing the required files.

The following steps insert a picture, which, in this example, is located in the PowerPoint Chapter 02 folder on the same USB flash drive that contains the saved presentation, into Slide 3.

1
- With your USB flash drive connected to one of the computer's USB ports, click the Previous Slide button to display Slide 3.

- Click the Insert Picture from File icon in the content placeholder to display the Insert Picture dialog box.

2
- If Computer is not displayed in the navigation pane, drag the navigation pane scroll bar (Insert Picture dialog box) until Computer appears.

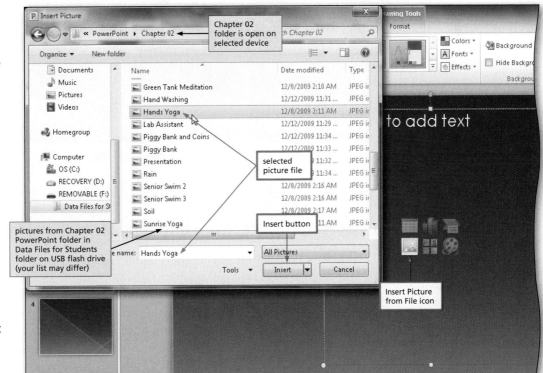

Figure 2–8

- Click Computer in the navigation pane to display a list of available storage devices in the Insert Picture dialog box. If necessary, scroll through the dialog box until your USB flash drive appears in the list of available storage devices.

- Double-click your USB flash drive in the list of available storage devices to display a list of files and folders on the selected USB flash drive. Double-click the Data Files for Students folder, double-click the PowerPoint folder, and then double-click the Chapter 02 folder to display a list of files in that folder.

- Scroll down and then click Hands Yoga to select the file name (Figure 2–8).

Q&A What if the picture is not on a USB flash drive?

Use the same process, but select the drive containing the picture.

3

- Click the Insert button (Insert Picture dialog box) to insert the picture into the content placeholder in Slide 3 (Figure 2–9).

Q&A

What are the symbols around the picture?

A selected graphic appears surrounded by a **selection rectangle**, which has small squares and circles, called **sizing handles**, at each corner and middle location.

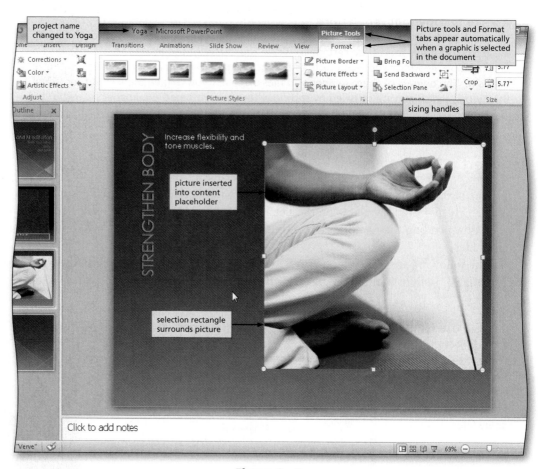

Figure 2 – 9

To Insert Another Picture into a Content Placeholder

BTW

Modernism's Effect on Graphic Design
The modernist movement of the late nineteenth and twentieth centuries influenced the design principles in use today. Artists and architects of that era simplified the world in terms of legible fonts, abstract shapes, and balanced layouts. Modernists sought to create works independent of language so their message could reach people throughout the world.

The next step is to insert another digital yoga picture into the Slide 2 content placeholder. This second picture also is available on the Data Files for Students. See the inside back cover of this book for instructions on downloading the Data Files for Students, or contact your instructor for information about accessing the required files.

The following steps insert a picture into Slide 2.

1 Click the Previous Slide button to display Slide 2.

2 With your USB flash drive connected to one of the computer's USB ports, click the Insert Picture from File icon in the content placeholder to display the Insert Picture dialog box.

3 If the list of files and folders on the selected USB flash drive are not displayed in the Insert Picture dialog box, double-click your USB flash drive to display them and then navigate to the PowerPoint Chapter 02 folder.

4 Scroll down and then click Green Tank Meditation to select the file name.

5 Click the Insert button (Insert Picture dialog box) to insert the picture into the Slide 2 content placeholder (Figure 2–10).

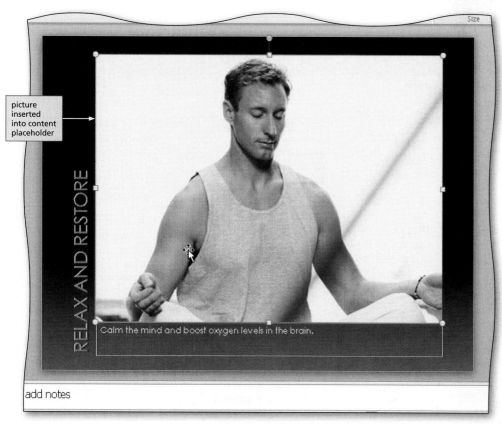

picture inserted into content placeholder

Figure 2–10

To Insert a Picture into a Slide without a Content Placeholder

In Chapter 1, you inserted a clip into a slide without a content placeholder. You also can insert a picture into a slide that does not have a content placeholder. The picture for Slide 4 is available on the Data Files for Students. See the inside back cover of this book for instructions on downloading the Data Files for Students, or contact your instructor for information about accessing the required files. The following steps insert a picture into Slide 4.

1
- Click the Next Slide button two times to display Slide 4.

- With your USB flash drive connected to one of the computer's USB ports, click Insert on the Ribbon (Figure 2–11).

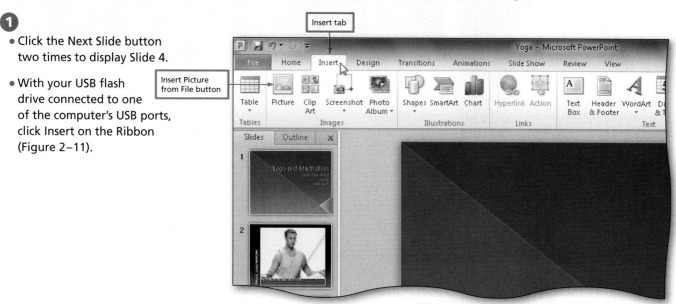

Insert tab

Insert Picture from File button

Figure 2–11

• Click Insert Picture from File (Insert tab | Images group) to display the Insert Picture dialog box. If the list of files and folders on the selected USB flash drive are not displayed in the Insert Picture dialog box, double-click your USB flash drive to display them and then navigate to the PowerPoint Chapter 02 folder.

• Click Arch Yoga to select the file name (Figure 2–12).

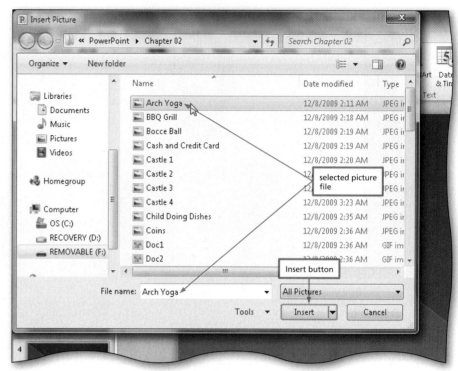

Figure 2–12

• Click the Insert button (Insert Picture dialog box) to insert the picture into the Slide 4 content placeholder.

• Move the picture so that it displays approximately as shown in Figure 2–13.

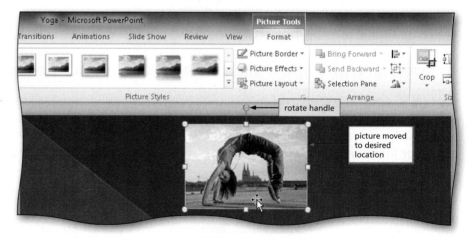

Figure 2–13

Q&A

What is the green circle attached to the selected graphic?

The green circle is a rotate handle. When you drag a graphic's rotate handle, the graphic moves in either a clockwise or counter clockwise direction.

To Correct a Picture

A photograph's color intensity can be modified by changing the brightness and contrast. **Brightness** determines the overall lightness or darkness of the entire image, whereas **contrast** is the difference between the darkest and lightest areas of the image. The brightness and contrast are changed in predefined percentage increments. The following step increases the brightness and decreases the contrast to intensify the picture colors.

1

- With the Arch Yoga picture on Slide 4 still selected, click the Corrections button (Picture Tools Format tab | Adjust group) to display the Corrections gallery.

- Point to Brightness: +20% Contrast: −40% (fourth picture in first row of Brightness and Contrast area) to display a live preview of these corrections on the picture (Figure 2–14).

Experiment

- Point to various pictures in the Brightness and Contrast area and watch the brightness and contrast change on the picture in Slide 4.

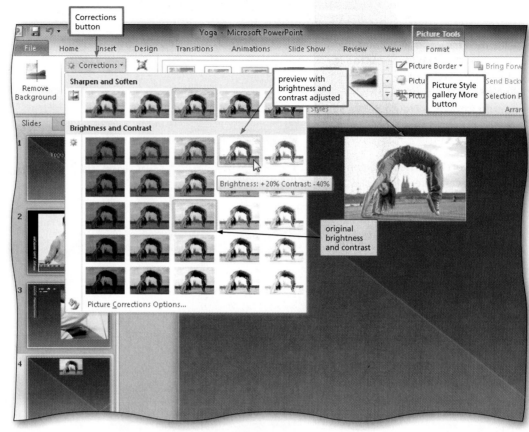

Figure 2–14

Q&A Why is a yellow border surrounding the picture in the center of the gallery?

The image on Slide 4 currently has normal brightness and contrast (0%), which is represented by this center image in the gallery.

- Click Brightness: +20% Contrast: −40% to apply this correction to the yoga picture.

Q&A How can I remove all effects from the picture?

Click the Reset Picture button (Picture Tools Format tab | Adjust group).

Other Ways	
1. Click Picture Corrections Options, move Brightness or Contrast sliders or enter	number in box next to slider (Format Picture dialog box)

To Apply a Picture Style

The pictures on Slides 2, 3, and 4 grasp the audience's attention, but you can increase their visual appeal by applying a style. A **style** is a named group of formatting characteristics. PowerPoint provides more than 25 picture styles that enable you easily to change a picture's look to a more visually appealing style, including a variety of shapes, angles, borders, and reflections. The photos in Slides 2, 3, and 4 in this chapter use styles that apply soft edges, reflections, or angled perspectives to the pictures. The following steps apply a picture style to the Slide 4 picture.

1

- With the Slide 4 picture selected, click the Picture Tools Format tab and then click the More button in the Picture Styles gallery (Picture Tools Format tab | Picture Styles group) (shown in Figure 2–14 on the previous page) to expand the gallery.

- Point to Soft Edge Rectangle in the Picture Styles gallery to display a live preview of that style applied to the picture in the document (Figure 2–15).

Experiment

- Point to various picture styles in the Picture Styles gallery and watch the style of the picture change in the document window.

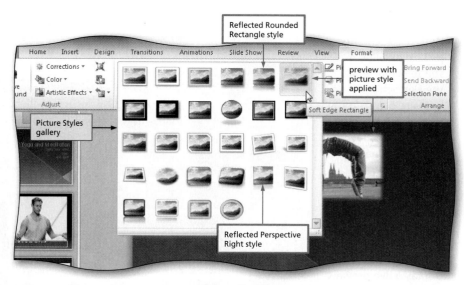

Figure 2–15

2

- Click Soft Edge Rectangle in the Picture Styles gallery to apply the style to the selected picture (Figure 2–16).

Figure 2–16

To Apply Other Picture Styles

The next step is to apply picture styles to the yoga pictures in Slides 3 and 2. To provide continuity, both of these styles will have a reflection. The following steps apply other picture styles to the Slide 3 and Slide 2 pictures.

1 Click the Previous Slide button to display Slide 3.

2 Click the Slide 3 picture to select it, click the Picture Tools Format tab, and then click the More button in the Picture Styles gallery to expand the gallery.

3 Click Reflected Perspective Right in the Picture Styles gallery to apply this style to the picture in Slide 3.

4 Click the Previous Slide button to display Slide 2.

5 Click the Slide 2 picture to select it, click the Picture Tools Format tab, and then click the More button in the Picture Styles gallery to expand the gallery.

6 Click Reflected Rounded Rectangle in the Picture Styles gallery to apply this style to the picture in Slide 2 (Figure 2–17).

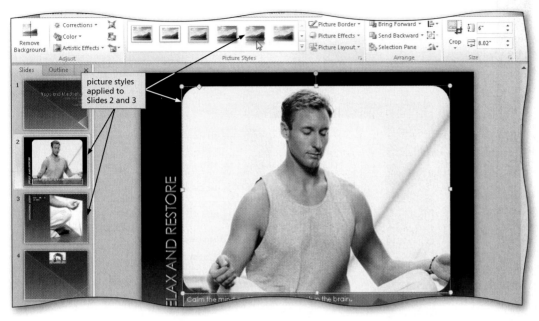

Figure 2–17

To Apply Picture Effects

PowerPoint provides a variety of picture effects so that you can further customize a picture. Effects include shadows, reflections, glow, soft edges, bevel, and 3-D rotation. The difference between the effects and the styles is that each effect has several options, providing you with more control over the exact look of the image.

In this presentation, the photos on Slides 2 and 3 have an orange glow effect and have a bevel applied to their edges. The following steps apply picture effects to the selected picture.

1

• With the Slide 2 picture selected, click the Picture Effects button (Picture Tools Format tab | Picture Styles group) to display the Picture Effects menu.

Q&A

What if the Picture Tools Format tab no longer is displayed on my Ribbon?

Double-click the picture to display the Picture Tools and Format tabs.

• Point to Glow on the Picture Effects menu to display the Glow gallery.

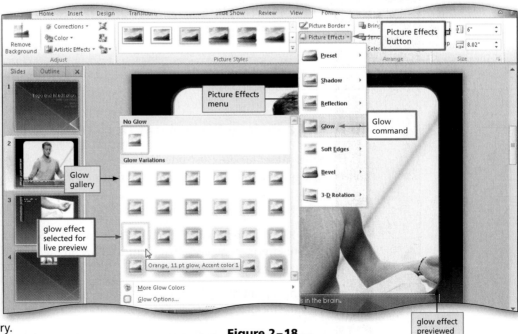

Figure 2–18

• Point to Orange, 11 pt glow, Accent color 1 in the Glow Variations area (leftmost glow in third row) to display a live preview of the selected glow effect applied to the picture in the document window (Figure 2–18).

Experiment

• Point to various glow effects in the Glow gallery and watch the picture change in the document window.

2

- Click Orange, 11 pt glow, Accent color 1 in the Glow gallery to apply the selected picture effect.

3

- Click the Picture Effects button (Picture Tools Format tab | Picture Styles group) to display the Picture Effects menu again.

- Point to Bevel on the Picture Effects menu to display the Bevel gallery.

- Point to Angle (leftmost bevel in second row) to display a live preview of the selected bevel effect applied to the Slide 2 picture (Figure 2–19).

⊘ **Experiment**

- Point to various bevel effects in the Bevel gallery and watch the picture change in the slide.

4

- Click Angle in the Bevel gallery to apply the selected picture effect.

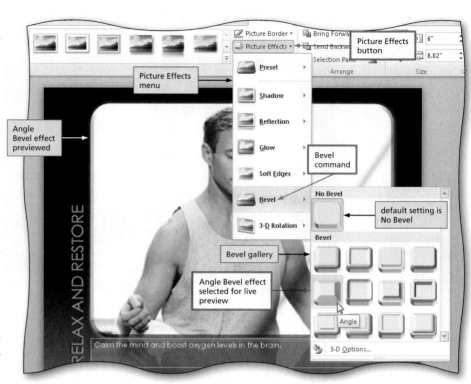

Figure 2–19

Other Ways
1. Right-click picture, click Format Picture on shortcut menu, select desired options (Format Picture dialog box), click Close button	Tools Format tab	Picture Styles group), select desired options (Format Picture dialog box), click Close button
2. Click Format Shape dialog box launcher (Picture	

To Apply a Picture Style and Effect to Another Picture

In this presentation, the Slide 3 picture also has orange glow and bevel effects. The following steps apply the picture style and picture effects to the picture.

1 Click the Next Slide button to display Slide 3 and then click the picture to select it.

2 Click the Picture Effects button (Picture Tools Format tab | Picture Styles group) to display the Picture Effects menu and then point to Glow on the Picture Effects menu to display the Glow gallery.

3 Click Orange, 11 pt glow, Accent color 1 (leftmost glow in third row) in the Glow gallery to apply the picture effect to the picture.

4 Click the Picture Effects button (Picture Tools Format tab | Picture Styles group) to display the Picture Effects menu again and then point to Bevel on the Picture Effects menu to display the Bevel gallery.

5 Click Convex (third bevel in second row) in the Bevel area to apply the picture effect to the selected picture (Figure 2–20).

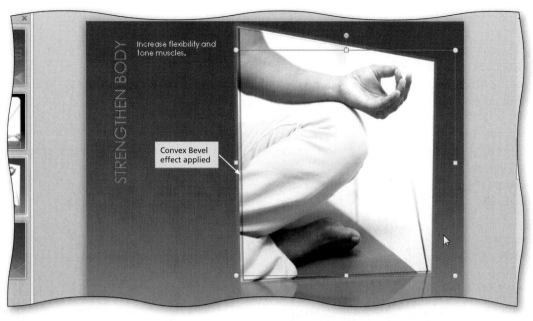

Figure 2–20

To Add a Picture Border

The next step is to add a small border to the Slide 3 picture. Some picture styles provide a border, but the Reflected Rounded Rectangle style you applied to this picture does not. The following steps add a border to the Slide 3 picture.

1

- With the Slide 3 picture still selected, click the Picture Border button (Picture Tools Format tab | Picture Styles group) to display the Picture Border gallery.

Q&A What if the Picture Tools Format tab no longer is displayed on my Ribbon?

Double-click the picture to display the Picture Tools and Format tabs.

2

- Point to Weight on the Picture Border gallery to display the Weight list.

- Point to 1½ pt to display a live preview of this line weight on the picture (Figure 2–21).

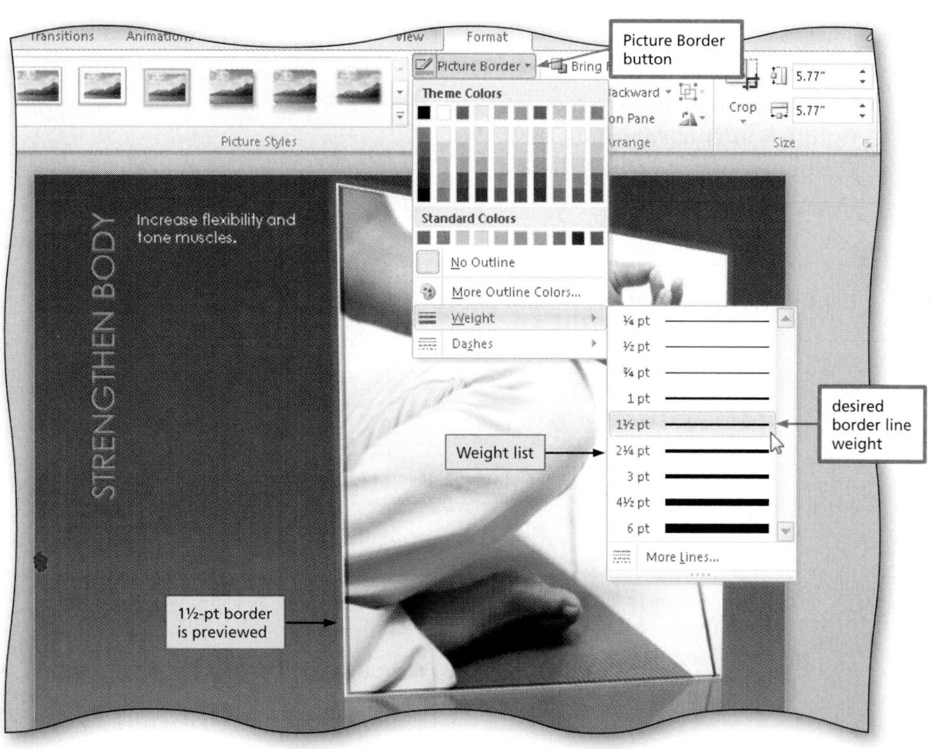

Experiment

- Point to various line weights in the Weight list and watch the line thickness change.

Q&A Can I make the line width more than 6 pt?

Yes. Click More Lines and then increase the amount in the Width box.

Figure 2–21

3

- Click 1½ pt to add this line weight to the picture.

To Change a Picture Border Color

The default color for the border you added to the Slide 3 picture is White. Earlier in this chapter, you changed the color scheme to Oriel. To coordinate the border color with the title text color and other elements of this theme, you will use a shade of red in the Oriel color scheme. Any color galleries you display show colors defined in this current color scheme. The following steps change the Slide 3 picture border color.

1

• With the Slide 3 photo still selected, click the Picture Border button (Picture Tools Format tab | Picture Styles group) to display the Picture Border gallery.

Q&A

What if the Picture Tools Format tab no longer is displayed on my Ribbon?

Double-click the picture to display the Picture Tools and Format tabs.

2

• Point to Red, Accent 3 (seventh theme color from left in first row) in the Picture Border gallery to display a live preview of that border color on the picture (Figure 2–22).

Experiment

• Point to various colors in the Picture Border gallery and watch the border on the picture change in the slide.

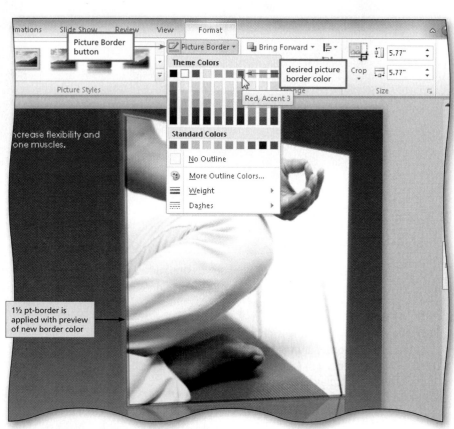

Figure 2–22

3

• Click Red, Accent 3 in the Picture Border gallery to change the picture border color.

To Add a Picture Border and Color to Another Picture

In this presentation, the Slide 2 picture does not have a border as part of the Reflected Perspective Right picture style. The following steps add a border to Slide 2 and change the color.

1 Click the Previous Slide button to display Slide 2 and then click the picture to select it.

2 Click the Picture Border button (Picture Tools Format tab | Picture Styles group) to display the Picture Border gallery.

3 Point to Weight on the Picture Border gallery to display the Weight list and then point to 1½ pt to display a live preview of this line weight on the picture.

4 Click 1½ pt to add this line weight to the picture.

5 Click the Picture Border button (Picture Tools Format tab | Picture Styles group) to display the Picture Border gallery again and then click Red, Accent 3 in the Picture Border gallery to change the picture border color (Figure 2–23).

Figure 2–23

To Resize a Graphic by Entering Exact Measurements

The next step is to resize the Slide 3 picture so that it fills much of the empty space in the slide. In Chapter 1, you resized clips by dragging the sizing handles. This technique also applies to changing the size of photos. You also can resize graphics by specifying exact height and width measurements. The yoga picture can be enlarged so that its height and width measurements are 6.0". When a graphic is selected, its height and width measurements show in the Size group of the Picture Tools Format tab. The following steps resize the Slide 3 picture by entering its desired exact measurements.

1

• Click the Next Slide button to display Slide 3 and then select the picture. Click the Shape Height text box (Picture Tools Format tab | Size group) to select the contents in the text box and then type   6 as the height (Figure 2–24).

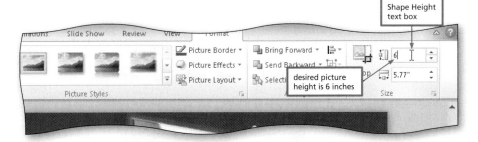

Figure 2–24

 What if the contents of the Shape Height text box are not selected?

Triple-click the Shape Height text box.

 Why did the width size also change?

PowerPoint kept the photo in proportion so that the width changed the same amount as the height changed.

2
- Click the Shape Width text box (Picture Tools Format tab | Size group) to select the contents in the text box and then type 6 as the width if this number does not display automatically.

- If necessary, move the photo to the location shown in Figure 2–25.

Q&A What if I want to return a graphic to its original size and start again?

With the graphic selected, click the Size and Position dialog box launcher (Picture Tools Format tab | Size group), if necessary click the Size tab (Format Picture dialog box), click the Reset button, and then click the Close button.

Other Ways

1. Right-click picture, enter shape height and width values in text boxes on shortcut menu
2. Right-click picture, click Format Picture

   on shortcut menu, click Size (Format Picture dialog box), enter shape height and width values in text boxes, click Close button

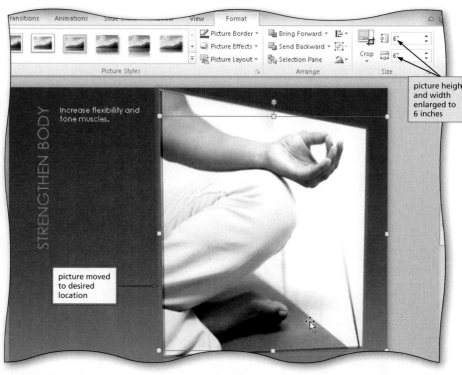

Figure 2–25

To Resize Another Graphic Using Exact Measurements

The Arch Yoga picture on Slide 4 also can be enlarged to fill space at the top of the slide. The yoga picture can be enlarged so that its height and width measurements are 3" and 4.48", respectively. The following steps resize the Slide 4 picture.

1 Click the Next Slide button to display Slide 4 and then select the picture. Click the Shape Height text box (Picture Tools Format tab | Size group) to select the contents in the text box and type 3 as the height.

2 Move the photo to the location shown in Figure 2–26.

Figure 2–26

To Save an Existing Document with the Same File Name

You have made several modifications to the document since you last saved it. Thus, you should save it again. The following step saves the document again. For an example of the step listed below, refer to page OFF 51 in the Office 2010 and Windows 7 chapter at the beginning of this book.

 Click the Save button on the Quick Access Toolbar to overwrite the previously saved file.

Break Point: If you wish to take a break, this is a good place to do so. You can quit PowerPoint now. To resume at a later time, start PowerPoint, open the file called Yoga, and continue following the steps from this location forward.

Formatting Slide Backgrounds

A slide's background is an integral part of a presentation because it can generate audience interest. Every slide can have the same background, or different backgrounds can be used in a presentation. This background is considered **fill**, which is the content that makes up the interior of a shape, line, or character. Three fills are available: solid, gradient, and picture or texture. **Solid fill** is one color used throughout the entire slide. **Gradient fill** is one color shade gradually progressing to another shade of the same color or one color progressing to another color. **Picture or texture fill** uses a specific file or an image that simulates a material, such as cork, granite, marble, or canvas.

Once you add a fill, you can adjust its appearance. For example, you can adjust its **transparency**, which allows you to see through the background, so that any text on the slide is visible. You also can select a color that is part of the theme or a custom color. You can use **offsets**, another background feature, to move the background from the slide borders in varying distances by percentage. **Tiling options** repeat the background image many times vertically and horizontally on the slide; the smaller the tiling percentage, the greater the number of times the image is repeated.

BTW

Resetting Backgrounds
If you have made many changes to the background and want to start the process over, click the Reset Background button in the Format Background dialog box.

To Insert a Texture Fill

A wide variety of texture fills are available to give your presentation a unique look. The 24 pictures in the Textures gallery give the appearance of a physical object, such as water drops, sand, tissue paper, and a paper bag. You also can use your own texture pictures for custom backgrounds. When you insert a fill, PowerPoint assumes you want this custom background on only the current slide displayed. To make this background appear on all slides in the presentation, click the Apply to All button in the Format Background dialog box. The following steps insert the Sand fill on Slide 4 in the presentation.

• Right-click anywhere on the Slide 4 blue background to display the shortcut menu (Figure 2–27).

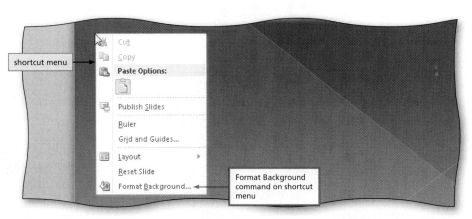

Figure 2–27

2

- Click Format Background on the shortcut menu to display the Format Background dialog box.

- With the Fill pane displaying, click 'Picture or texture fill' to expand the fill options (Figure 2–28).

Q&A Why did the background change to a yellow texture?

This texture is the Papyrus background, which is the default texture fill.

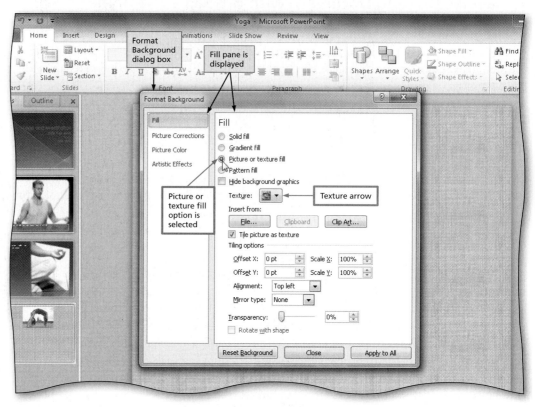

Figure 2–28

3

- Click the Texture arrow to display the Texture gallery (Figure 2–29).

Q&A Is a live preview available to see the various textures on this slide?

No. Live preview is not an option with the background textures and fills.

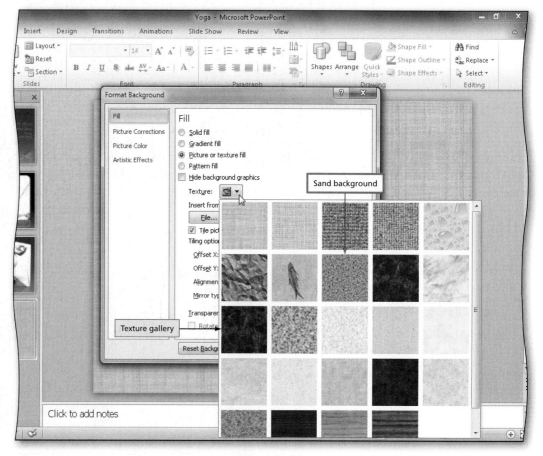

Figure 2–29

4

- Click the Sand background (third texture in second row) to insert this background on Slide 4 (Figure 2–30).

Q&A The Format Background dialog box is covering part of the slide. Can I move this box?

Yes. Click the dialog box title and drag it to a different location so that you can view the slide.

Q&A Could I insert this background on all four slides simultaneously?

Yes. You would click the Apply to All button to insert the Sand background on all slides.

Other Ways

1. Click Design tab, Background Styles, click Format Background (Design tab | Background group)

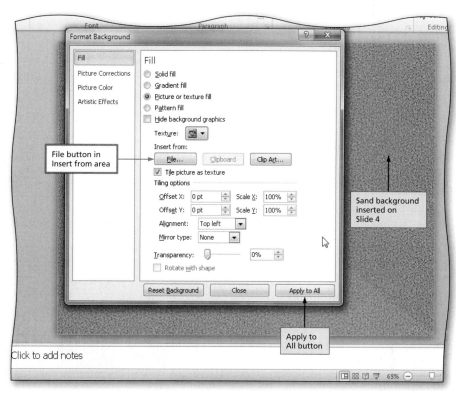

Figure 2–30

To Insert a Picture to Create a Background

For variety and interest, you want to use another yoga picture as the Slide 1 background. This picture is stored on the Data Files for Students. PowerPoint will stretch the height and width of this picture to fill the slide area. The following steps insert the picture, Sunrise Yoga, on only Slide 1.

1

- Click the Previous Slide button three times to display Slide 1.

- With the Fill pane displaying (Format Background dialog box), click 'Picture or texture fill'.

- Click the File button in the Insert from area (shown in Figure 2–30) to display the Insert Picture dialog box.

- If necessary, double-click your USB flash drive in the list of available storage devices to display a list of files and folders on the selected USB flash drive and then navigate to the PowerPoint Chapter 02 folder.

- Scroll down and then click Sunrise Yoga to select the file name (Figure 2–31).

Q&A What if the picture is not on a USB flash drive?

Use the same process, but select the drive containing the picture.

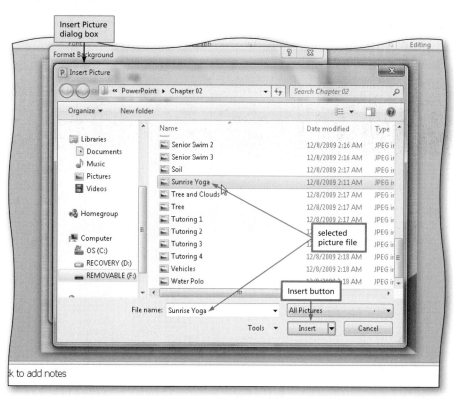

Figure 2–31

2

- Click the Insert button (Insert Picture dialog box) to insert the Sunrise Yoga picture as the Slide 1 background (Figure 2–32).

Q&A What if I do not want to use this picture?

Click the Undo button on the Quick Access Toolbar.

Q&A Why do the Left and Right offsets in the Stretch options area show a −6% value?

PowerPoint automatically reduced the photograph slightly so that it fills the entire slide.

Q&A Can I move the Format Background dialog box to the left so that I can see more of the subtitle text?

Yes. Click the dialog box title and then drag the box to the desired location on the slide.

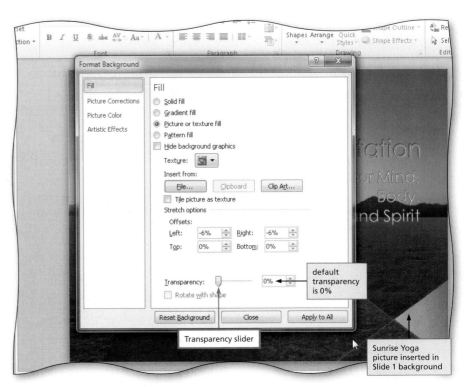

Figure 2–32

To Format the Background Picture Fill Transparency

The Sunrise Yoga picture on Slide 1 is a rich color and conflicts with the title and subtitle text. One method of reducing this richness is to change the transparency. The **Transparency slider** indicates the amount of opaqueness. The default setting is 0, which is fully opaque. The opposite extreme is 100%, which is fully transparent. To change the transparency, you can move the Transparency slider or enter a number in the text box next to the slider. The following step adjusts the transparency to 10%.

1

- Click the Transparency slider and drag it to the right until 10% is displayed in the Transparency text box (Figure 2–33).

Q&A Can I move the slider in small increments so that I can get a precise percentage easily?

Yes. Press the RIGHT ARROW or LEFT ARROW key to move the slider in one-percent increments.

Figure 2–33

To Format the Background Texture Fill Transparency

The Sand texture on Slide 4 is dark and may not offer sufficient contrast with the symbols and text you are going to insert on this slide. You can adjust the transparency of slide texture in the same manner that you change a picture transparency. The following steps adjust the texture transparency to 50%.

1

- Click the Next Slide button three times to display Slide 4.

- Click the Transparency slider and drag it to the right until 50% is displayed in the Transparency text box (Figure 2–34).

2

- Click the Close button (Format Background dialog box).

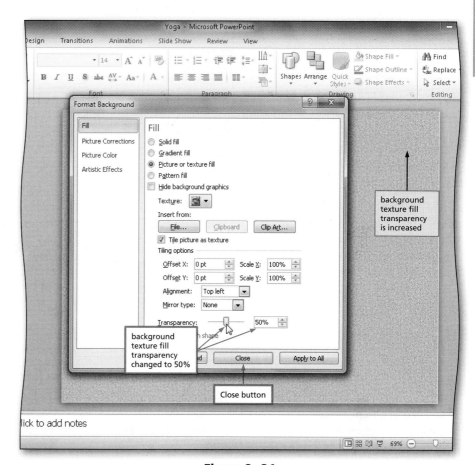

Figure 2–34

To Choose a Background Style

Now that the backgrounds for Slides 1 and 4 are set, and the title and text paragraphs for the presentation have been entered, you need to make design decisions for Slides 2 and 3. In this project, you will choose a background for these slides. For each theme, PowerPoint provides 12 **background styles** with designs that may include color, shading, patterns, and textures. **Fill effects** add pattern and texture to a background, which add depth to a slide. The following steps add a background style to Slides 2 and 3 in the presentation.

1

- Click the Previous Slide button once to display Slide 3 and then click the Design tab on the Ribbon.

- Click the Background Styles button (Design tab | Background group) to display the Background Styles gallery.

- Right-click Style 11 (third style in third row) to display the shortcut menu (Figure 2–35).

 **Experiment**

- Point to various styles themes in the Background Styles gallery and watch the backgrounds change on the slide.

Q&A Are the backgrounds displayed in a specific order?

Yes. They are arranged in order from light to dark running from left to right. The first row has solid backgrounds; the middle row has darker fills at the top and bottom; the bottom row has fill patterns. If you point to a background, a ScreenTip with the background's name appears on the screen.

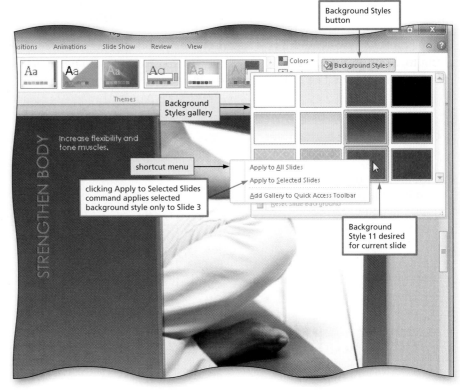

Figure 2–35

2

- Click Apply to Selected Slides to apply Style 11 to Slide 3 (Figure 2–36).

Q&A If I decide later that this background style does not fit the theme of my presentation, can I apply a different background?

Yes. You can repeat these steps at any time while creating your presentation.

Q&A What if I want to apply this background style to all slides in the presentation?

Click the desired style or click Apply to All Slides in the shortcut menu.

Other Ways

1. Click Background Styles, right-click desired background, press S

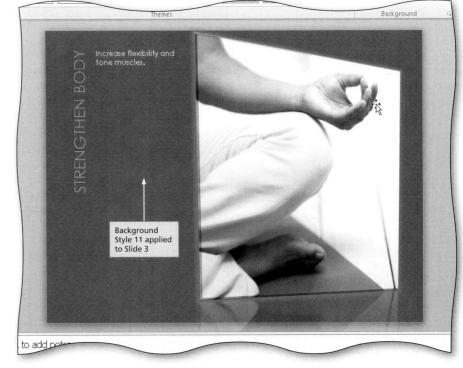

Figure 2–36

To Choose Another Background Style

In this presentation, the Slide 2 background can have a coordinating background to complement the yoga picture. The following steps add a background to Slide 2.

1 Click the Previous Slide button to display Slide 2. Click the Background Styles button (Design tab | Background group) and then right-click Style 10 (second style in third row) to display the shortcut menu.

2 Click Apply to Selected Slides to apply this background style to Slide 2 (Figure 2–37).

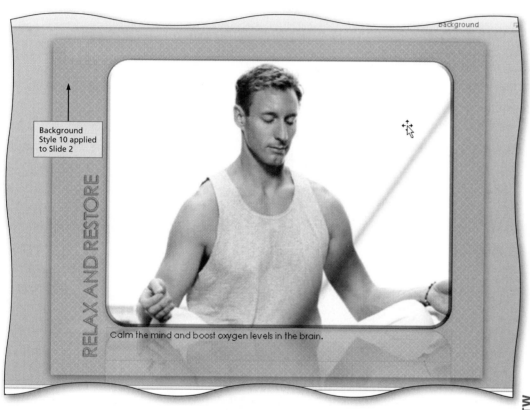

Background Style 10 applied to Slide 2

RELAX AND RESTORE

Calm the mind and boost oxygen levels in the brain.

Figure 2–37

Formatting Title and Content Text

Choosing well-coordinated colors and styles for text and objects in a presentation is possible. Once you select a particular Quick Style and make any other font changes, you then can copy these changes to other text using the **Format Painter**. The Format Painter allows you to copy all formatting changes from one object to another.

To Change the Subtitle and Caption Font

The default Verve theme heading, subtitle, and caption text font is Century Gothic. To draw more attention to subtitle and caption text and to help differentiate these slide elements from the title text, you want to change the font from Century Gothic to Papyrus. To change the font, you must select the letters you want to format. In Chapter 1, you selected a paragraph and then formatted the characters. To format the text in multiple paragraphs quickly and simultaneously, you can select all the paragraphs to be formatted and then apply formatting changes. The following steps change the subtitle and caption font.

BTW

Introducing the Presentation
Before your audience enters the room, start the presentation and then display Slide 1. This slide should be visually appealing and provide general interest in the presentation. An effective title slide gives a good first impression.

- Click the Previous Slide button to display Slide 1. Move the mouse pointer to the left of the first subtitle paragraph, Unify Your Mind, until the mouse pointer changes to an I-beam (Figure 2–38).

Figure 2–38

- Drag downward to select all three subtitle lines that will be formatted (Figure 2–39).

Figure 2–39

- With the text selected, click Home on the Ribbon and then click the Font box arrow (Home tab | Font group) to display the Font gallery (Figure 2–40).

Q&A Will the fonts in my Font gallery be the same as those shown in Figure 2–40?

Your list of available fonts may differ, depending on what fonts you have installed and the type of printer you are using.

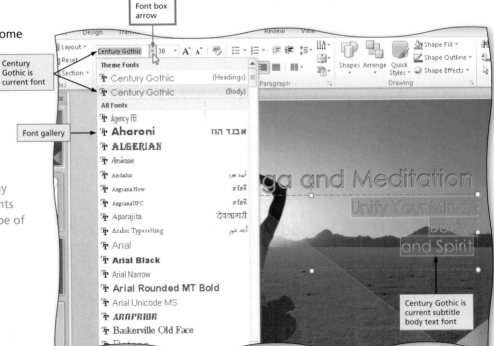

Figure 2–40

4

- Scroll through the Font gallery and then point to Papyrus (or a similar font) to display a live preview of the title text in the Papyrus font (Figure 2–41).

🔎 **Experiment**

- Point to various fonts in the Font gallery and watch the subtitle text font change in the slide.

- Click Papyrus (or a similar font) to change the font of the selected text to Papyrus.

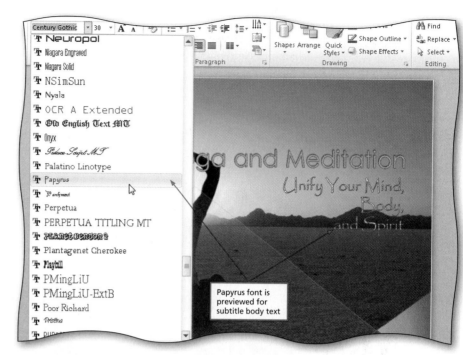

Figure 2–41

Other Ways
1. Click Font box arrow on Mini toolbar, click desired font in Font gallery 2. Right-click selected text, click Font on shortcut menu (Font dialog box), click	Font tab, select desired font in Font list, click OK button 3. Click Font dialog box launcher (Home tab | Font group), click Font tab (Font dialog box), select	desired font in Font list, click OK button 4. Press CTRL+SHIFT+F, click Font tab (Font dialog box), select desired font in the Font list, click OK button

To Shadow Text

A **shadow** helps letters display prominently by adding a shadow behind the text. The following step adds a shadow to the selected subtitle text, Unify Your Mind, Body, and Spirit.

1

- With the subtitle text selected, click the Text Shadow button (Home tab | Font group) to add a shadow to the selected text (Figure 2–42).

Q&A How would I remove a shadow?

You would click the Shadow button a second time, or you immediately could click the Undo button on the Quick Access Toolbar.

Figure 2–42

To Format the Subtitle Text

To increase readability, you can format the Slide 1 subtitle text by bolding the characters and changing the font color to yellow. The following steps format the Slide 1 subtitle text.

1 With the subtitle text selected, click the Bold button (Home tab | Font group) to bold the text.

2 Click the Font Color arrow and change the color to Light Yellow, Text 2 (fourth color in first row) (Figure 2–43).

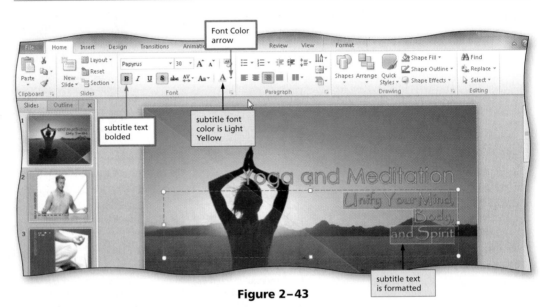

Figure 2–43

Decreasing Font Size
The Increase Font Size buttons on the Mini toolbar and in the Font group (Home tab) enlarge the selected characters in predetermined amounts. The Decrease Font Size buttons, which appear to the right of the Increase Font Size buttons, reduce the characters' size in the same predetermined point sizes.

To Format the Slide 2 Caption

The caption on a slide should be large enough for audience members to read easily and should coordinate with the font styles in other parts of the presentation. The caption on Slide 2 can be enhanced by changing the font, the font color, and the font size. The following steps format the Slide 2 caption text.

1 Click the Next Slide button to display Slide 2. Triple-click the caption text to select all the characters, click the Font box arrow on the Mini toolbar, and then scroll down and click Papyrus.

2 Click the Increase Font Size button on the Mini toolbar three times to increase the font size to 20 point.

3 Click the Bold button on the Mini toolbar to bold the text (Figure 2–44).

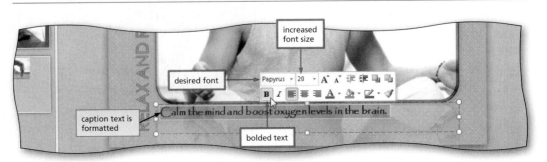

Figure 2–44

Format Painter

To save time and avoid formatting errors, you can use the Format Painter to apply custom formatting to other places in your presentation quickly and easily. You can use this feature in three ways:

- To copy only character attributes, such as font and font effects, select text that has these qualities.
- To copy both paragraph attributes, such as alignment and indentation and character attributes, select the entire paragraph.
- To apply the same formatting to multiple words, phrases, or paragraphs, double-click the Format Painter button and then select each item you want to format. You then can press the ESC key or click the Format Painter button to turn off this feature.

To Format Text Using the Format Painter

To save time and duplicated effort, you quickly can use the Format Painter to copy formatting attributes from the Slide 2 caption text and apply them to Slide 3. The following steps use the Format Painter to copy formatting features.

1
- With the Slide 2 caption text still selected, double-click the Format Painter button (Home tab | Clipboard group).
- Move the mouse pointer off the Ribbon (Figure 2–45).

Q&A Why did my mouse pointer change shape?

The mouse pointer changed shape by adding a paintbrush to indicate that the Format Painter function is active.

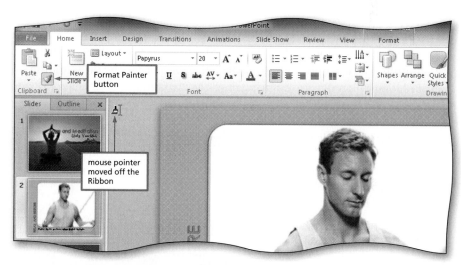

Figure 2–45

2
- Click the Next Slide button to display Slide 3. Triple-click the caption placeholder to apply the format to all the caption text (Figure 2–46).
- Press the ESC key to turn off the Format Painter feature.

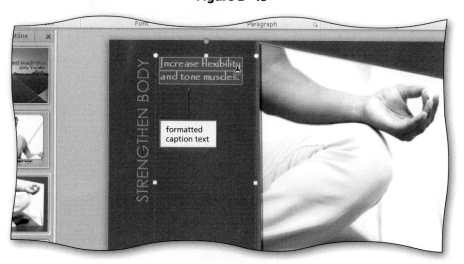

Other Ways
1. Click Format Painter button on Mini toolbar

Figure 2–46

Break Point: If you wish to take a break, this is a good place to do so. Be sure to save the Yoga file again and then you can quit PowerPoint. To resume at a later time, start PowerPoint, open the file called Yoga, and continue following the steps from this location forward.

BTW

Sizing Shapes
PowerPoint's Shapes gallery provides a wide variety of symbols that can help emphasize your major points on each slide. As you select the shapes and then size them, keep in mind that your audience will focus on the largest shapes first. The most important information, therefore, should be placed in or near the shapes with the most visual size.

Adding and Formatting a Shape

One method of getting the audience's attention and reinforcing the major concepts being presented is to have graphical elements on the title slide. PowerPoint provides a wide variety of predefined shapes that can add visual interest to a slide. Shape elements include lines, basic geometrical shapes, arrows, equation shapes, flowchart symbols, stars, banners, and callouts. After adding a shape to a slide, you can change its default characteristics by adding text, bullets, numbers, and styles. You also can combine multiple shapes to create a more complex graphic.

Slides 1 and 4 in this presentation are enhanced in a variety of ways. First, a sun shape is added to the Slide 1 title text in place of the letter o. Then a circle shape is inserted on Slide 4 and copied twice, and text is added to each circle and then formatted. Finally, a triangle is inserted on top of the three circle shapes on Slide 4.

To Add a Shape

Many of the shapes included in the Shapes gallery can direct the viewer to important aspects of the presentation. For example, the sun shape helps emphasize the presentation's theme of practicing yoga and meditation, and it complements the Sunrise Yoga background picture. The following steps add the Sun shape to Slide 1.

1
- Click the Previous Slide button two times to display Slide 1. Click the Shapes button (Home tab | Drawing group) to display the Shapes gallery (Figure 2–47).

Figure 2–47

Q&A

I do not see a Shapes button in the Drawing group. Instead, I have three rows of the shapes I have used recently in presentations. Why?

Monitor dimensions and resolution affect how buttons display on the Ribbon. Click the Shapes More button to display the entire Shapes gallery.

2

- Click the Sun shape in the Basic Shapes area of the Shapes gallery.

Q&A Why did my pointer change shape?

The pointer changed to a plus shape to indicate the Sun shape has been added to the Clipboard.

- Position the mouse pointer (a crosshair) above the person's hands in the picture, as shown in Figure 2–48.

Figure 2–48

3

- Click Slide 1 to insert the Sun shape (Figure 2–49).

Figure 2–49

Other Ways

1. Click More button (Drawing Tools Format tab | Insert Shapes group)

To Resize a Shape

The next step is to resize the Sun shape. The shape should be reduced so that it is approximately the same size as the letter o in the words Yoga and Meditation. The following steps resize the selected Sun shape.

1

- With the mouse pointer appearing as two-headed arrow, drag a corner sizing handle on the picture diagonally inward until the Sun shape is resized approximately as shown in Figure 2–50.

Q&A What if my shape is not selected?

To select a shape, click it.

Q&A What if the shape is the wrong size?

Repeat Steps 1 and 2.

Figure 2–50

2

- Release the mouse button to resize the shape.

- Drag the Sun shape on top of the letter o in the word, Yoga (Figure 2–51).

Q&A What if I want to move the shape to a precise location on the slide?

With the shape selected, press the ARROW keys or the CTRL+ARROW keys to move the shape to the desired location.

Figure 2–51

Other Ways

1. Enter shape height and width in Height and Width text boxes (Drawing Tools Format tab | Size group)
2. Click Size and Position dialog box launcher

(Drawing Tools Format tab | Size group), click Size tab, enter desired height and width values in text boxes, click Close button

To Copy and Paste a Shape

The next step is to copy the Sun shape. The duplicate shape will be placed over the letter 'o' in the word, Meditation. The following steps copy and move the identical second Sun shape.

1

- With the Sun shape still selected, click the Copy button (Home tab | Clipboard group) (Figure 2–52).

Q&A What if my shape is not selected?

To select a shape, click it.

Figure 2–52

2

- Click the Paste button on the Home tab to insert a duplicate Sun shape on Slide 1.

- Drag the Sun shape on top of the letter o in the word, Meditation, and release the mouse button when a dashed line connects this Sun shape to the Sun shape that is displaying in the word, Yoga (Figure 2–53).

Q&A What does the dashed line represent?

PowerPoint displays this Smart Guide when two shapes are aligned precisely. In this case, the two Sun shapes are centered horizontally.

Figure 2–53

Other Ways

1. Right-click selected shape, click Copy on shortcut menu, right-click, click Paste on shortcut menu

2. Select shape, press CTRL+C, press CTRL+V

To Add Other Shapes

Circles, squares, and triangles are among the geometric shapes included in the Shapes gallery. These shapes can be combined to show relationships among the elements, and they can help illustrate the basic concepts presented in your slide show. The following steps add the Oval and Isosceles Triangle shapes to Slide 4.

1

- Click the Next Slide button three times to display Slide 4 and then click the Shapes button (Home tab | Drawing group) to display the Shapes gallery (Figure 2–54).

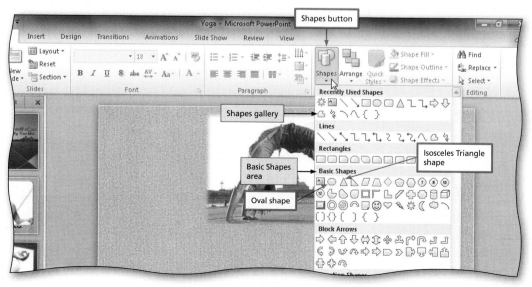

Figure 2–54

- Click the Oval shape in the Basic Shapes area of the Shapes gallery.

- Position the mouse pointer in the center of Slide 4 and then click to insert the Oval shape.

- Press and hold down the SHIFT key and then drag a corner sizing handle until the Oval shape forms a circle and is the size shown in Figure 2–55.

Q&A Why did I need to press the SHIFT key while enlarging the shape?

Holding down the SHIFT key while dragging draws a perfect circle.

- Move the shape so it is positioned approximately as shown in the figure.

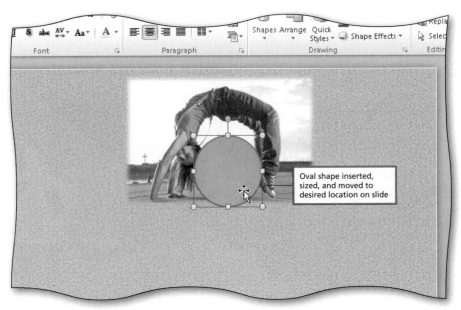

Figure 2–55

- Click the Shapes button (Home tab | Drawing group) and then click the Isosceles Triangle shape in the Basic Shapes area of the Shapes gallery.

- Position the mouse pointer in the right side of Slide 4 and then click to insert the Isosceles Triangle shape.

- Resize the shape so that it displays approximately as shown in Figure 2–56.

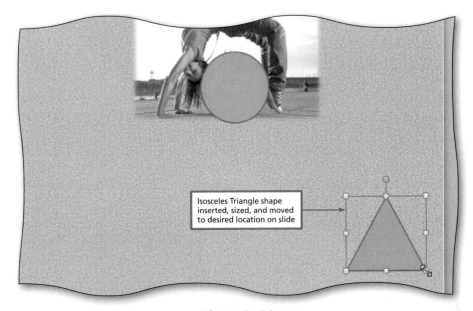

Figure 2–56

To Apply a Shape Style

Formatting text in a shape follows the same techniques as formatting text in a placeholder. You can change font, font color and size, and alignment. The next step is to apply a shape style to the oval so that it appears to have depth. The Shape Styles gallery has a variety of styles that change depending upon the theme applied to the presentation. The following steps apply a style to the Oval shape.

1

- Click the Oval shape to select it and then display the Drawing Tools Format tab (Figure 2–57).

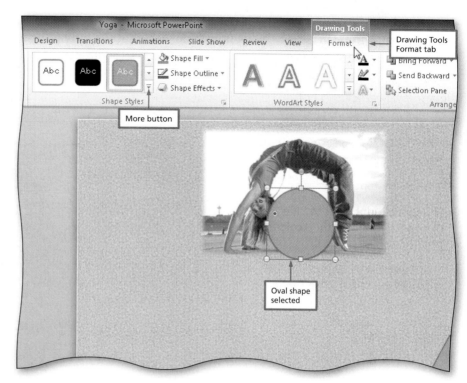

Figure 2–57

2

- Click the More button in the Shape Styles gallery (Drawing Tools Format tab | Shape Styles group) to expand the Shape Styles gallery.

- Point to Intense Effect – Orange, Accent 1 in the Shape Styles gallery (second shape in last row) to display a live preview of that style applied to the shape in the slide (Figure 2–58).

 Experiment

- Point to various styles in the Shape Styles gallery and watch the style of the shape change.

3

- Click Intense Effect – Orange, Accent 1 in the Shape Styles gallery to apply the selected style to the Oval shape.

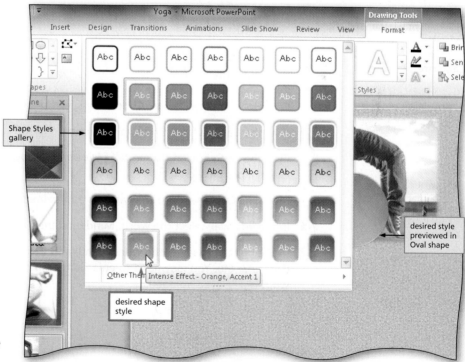

Figure 2–58

Other Ways

1. Click Format Shape dialog box launcher (Drawing Tools Format tab | Shape Styles group), select desired colors (Format Shape dialog box), click Close button

2. Right-click shape, click Format Shape on shortcut menu, select desired colors (Format Shape dialog box), click Close button

To Add Formatted Text to a Shape

Formatting text in a shape follows the same techniques as formatting text in a placeholder. You can change font, font color and size, and alignment. The next step is to add the word, Mind, to the shape, change the font to Papyrus and the font color to Blue-Gray, center and bold the text, and increase the font size to 24 point. The following step adds text to the Oval shape.

- With the Oval shape selected, type **Mind** in the shape.

- Change the font to Papyrus.

- Change the font color to Blue-Gray, Background 2 (third color in first Theme Colors row).

- Change the font size to 24 point and bold the text (Figure 2–59).

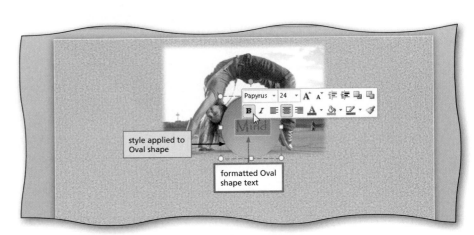

Figure 2–59

To Copy a Shape

Your presentation emphasizes that mind, body, and spirit are equal components in finding balance in life. Each of these elements can be represented by an oval. The following steps copy the Oval shape.

1 Click Home on the Ribbon. Click the edge of the Oval shape so that it is a solid line.

2 Click the Copy button (Home tab | Clipboard group).

3 Click the Paste button (Home tab | Clipboard group) two times to insert two duplicate Oval shapes on Slide 4.

4 Move the Oval shapes so they appear approximately as shown in Figure 2–60.

5 In the left oval, select the word, Mind, and then type the word, **Body**, in the oval.

6 In the right oval, select the word, Mind, and then type the word, **Spirit**, in the oval (Figure 2–60). You may need to enlarge the size of the oval shapes slightly so that each word is displayed on one line.

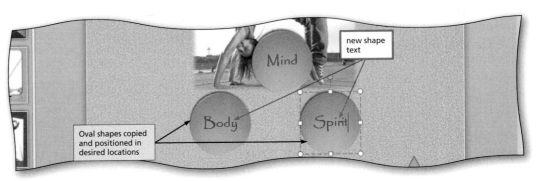

Figure 2–60

To Apply Another Style

The triangle shape helps show the unity among body, mind, and spirit. You can apply a coordinating shape style to the isosceles triangle and then place it on top of the three ovals. The following steps apply a style to the Isosceles Triangle shape.

1 Display the Drawing Tools Format tab. Click the Isosceles Triangle shape on Slide 4 to select it.

2 Click the More button in the Shape Styles gallery (Drawing Tools Format tab | Shape Styles group) to expand the Shape Styles gallery and then click Intense Effect – Blue, Accent 2 (third style in last row) to apply that style to the triangle.

3 Move the triangle shape to the center of the Ovals.

4 Click the Bring Forward button twice (Drawing Tools Format tab | Arrange group) to display the triangle on top of the ovals. Resize the triangle if necessary so that it displays as shown in Figure 2–61.

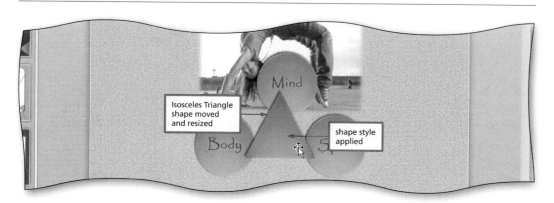

Figure 2–61

Break Point: If you wish to take a break, this is a good place to do so. Be sure to save the Yoga file again and then you can quit PowerPoint. To resume at a later time, start PowerPoint, open the file called Yoga, and continue following the steps from this location forward.

Using WordArt

One method of adding appealing visual elements to a presentation is by using **WordArt** styles. This feature is found in other Microsoft Office applications, including Word and Excel. This gallery of decorative effects allows you to type new text or convert existing text to WordArt. You then can add elements such as fills, outlines, and effects.

As with slide backgrounds, WordArt fill in the interior of a letter can consist of a solid color, texture, picture, or gradient. The WordArt **outline** is the exterior border surrounding each letter or symbol. PowerPoint allows you to change the outline color, weight, and style. You also can add an **effect**, which helps add emphasis or depth to the characters. Some effects are shadows, reflections, glows, bevels, and 3-D rotations.

BTW

Creating Logos
Many companies without graphic arts departments create their logos using WordArt. The bevels, glows, and shadows allow corporate designers to develop unique images with 3-D effects that give depth to their companies' emblems.

Plan Ahead

Use WordArt in moderation.
Some WordArt styles are bold and detailed, and they can detract from the message you are trying to present if not used carefully. Select a WordArt style when needed for special emphasis, such as a title slide that audience members will see when they enter the room. WordArt can have a powerful effect, so do not overuse it.

To Insert WordArt

Yoga and meditation can help individuals find balance among the mind, body, and spirit. The symbols on Slide 4 emphasize this relationship, and you want to call attention to the concept. You quickly can add a visual element to the slide by selecting a WordArt style from the WordArt Styles gallery and then applying it to a word. The following steps insert WordArt.

1

- With Slide 4 displaying, click Insert on the Ribbon.
- Click the WordArt button (Insert tab | Text group) to display the WordArt gallery (Figure 2–62).

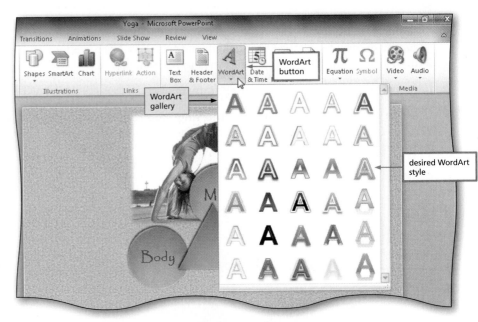

Figure 2–62

2

- Click Fill – Blue, Accent 2, Double Outline – Accent 2 (last letter A in third row) to display the WordArt text box (Figure 2–63).

Q&A What is a matte bevel style that is part of some of the styles in the gallery?

A matte finish gives a dull and rough effect. A bevel edge is angled or sloped and gives the effect of a three-dimensional object.

Figure 2–63

3

- Type **Balance** in the text box, as the WordArt text (Figure 2–64).

Q&A Why did the Format tab appear automatically in the Ribbon?

It appears when you select text to which you could add a WordArt style or other effect.

Figure 2–64

To Change the WordArt Shape

The WordArt text is useful to emphasize the harmony among the mind, body, and spirit. You can further emphasize this word by changing its shape. PowerPoint provides a variety of graphical shapes that add interest to text. The following steps change the WordArt to Triangle Down shape.

1
- With the Slide 4 text still selected, click the Text Effects button (Drawing Tools Format tab | WordArt Styles group) to display the Text Effects menu (Figure 2–65).

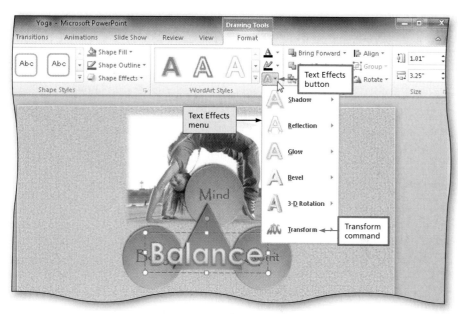

Figure 2–65

2
- Point to Transform in the Text Effects menu to display the WordArt Transform gallery (Figure 2–66).

 Experiment
- Point to various styles in the Transform gallery and watch the format of the text and borders change.

Q&A

How can I see the preview of a Transform effect if the gallery is overlaying the WordArt letters?

Move the WordArt text box to the left or right side of the slide and then repeat Steps 1 and 2.

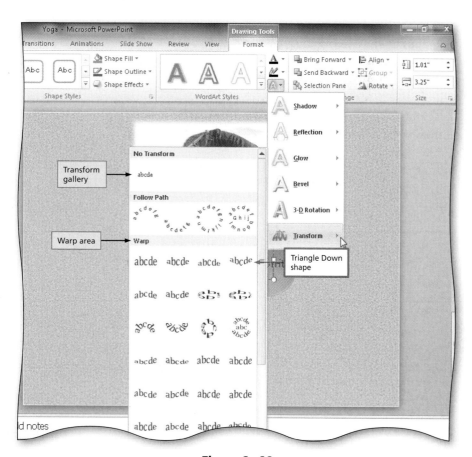

Figure 2–66

3

- Click the Triangle Down shape in the Warp area to apply the Triangle Down shape to the WordArt text (Figure 2–67).

Q&A Can I change the shape I applied to the WordArt?

Yes. Position the insertion point in the text box and then repeat Steps 1 and 2.

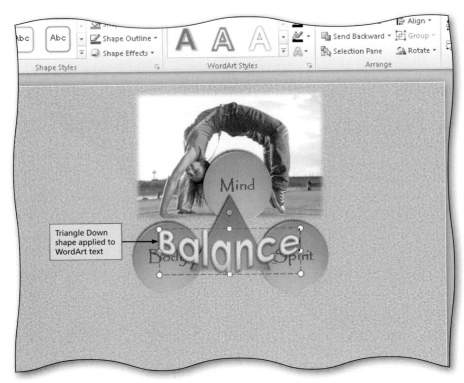

Figure 2–67

4

- Drag the WordArt downward until it is positioned approximately as shown in Figure 2–68.

- Drag a corner sizing handle diagonally outward until the WordArt is resized approximately as shown in the figure.

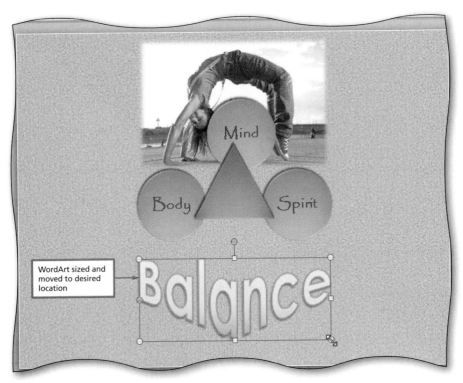

Figure 2–68

To Apply a WordArt Text Fill

The Slide 4 background has a Sand texture for the background, and you want to coordinate the WordArt fill with a similar texture. The following steps add the Denim texture as a fill for the WordArt characters.

1

- With the WordArt text selected, click the Text Fill button arrow (Drawing Tools Format tab | WordArt Styles group) to display the Text Fill gallery.

Q&A

The Text Fill gallery did not display. Why not?

Be sure you click the Text Fill button arrow, which is to the right of the Text Fill button. If you mistakenly click the Text Fill button, PowerPoint places the default fill in the WordArt instead of displaying the Text Fill gallery.

- Point to Texture in the Text Fill gallery to display the Texture gallery (Figure 2–69).

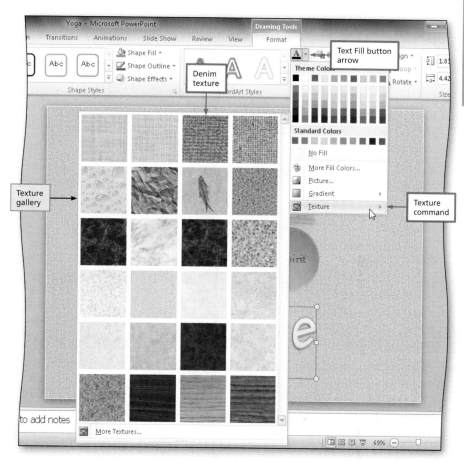

Figure 2–69

Experiment

- Point to various styles in the Text Fill gallery and watch the fill change.

Q&A

How can I see the preview of a fill if the gallery is overlaying the WordArt letters?

Move the WordArt text box to the left or right side of the slide and then repeat Step 1.

2

- Click the Denim texture (third texture in first row) to apply this texture as the fill for the WordArt.

Q&A

Can I apply this texture simultaneously to text that appears in more than one place on my slide?

Yes. Select one area of text, press and then hold the CTRL key while you select the other text, and then apply the texture.

To Change the Weight of the WordArt Outline

The letters in the WordArt style applied have a double outline around the edges. To emphasize this characteristic, you can increase the width of the lines. As with font size, lines also are measured in point size, and PowerPoint gives you the option to change the line **weight**, or thickness, starting with ¼ point (pt) and increasing in one-fourth–point increments. Other outline options include modifying the color and the line style, such as changing to dots or dashes or a combination of dots and dashes. The following steps change the WordArt outline weight to 6 pt.

1

- With the WordArt still selected, click the Text Outline button arrow (Drawing Tools Format tab | WordArt Styles group) to display the Text Outline gallery.

- Point to Weight in the gallery to display the Weight list.

- Point to 6 pt to display a live preview of this line weight on the WordArt text outline (Figure 2–70).

Experiment

- Point to various line weights in the Weight list and watch the line thickness change.

Q&A Can I make the line width more than 6 pt?

Yes. Click More Lines and increase the amount in the Width box.

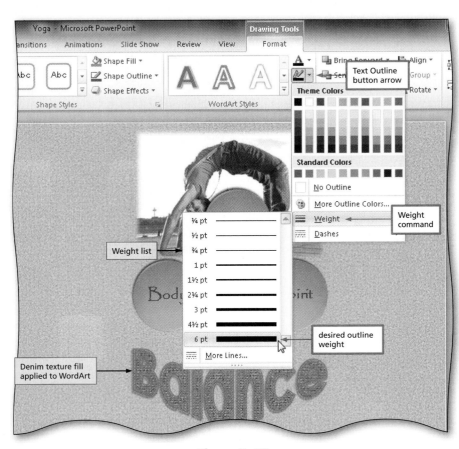

Figure 2–70

2

- Click 6 pt to apply this line weight to the title text outline.

Q&A Must my text have an outline?

No. To delete the outline, click No Outline in the Text Outline gallery.

To Change the Color of the WordArt Outline

The WordArt outline color is similar to the Denim fill color. To add variety, you can change the outline color. The following steps change the WordArt outline color.

1

- With the WordArt still selected, click the Text Outline button arrow (Drawing Tools Format tab | WordArt Styles group) to display the Text Outline gallery.

- Point to Orange, Accent 1 (fifth color in first row) to display a live preview of this outline color (Figure 2–71).

Experiment

- Point to various colors in the gallery and watch the outline colors change.

2

- Click Orange, Accent 1 to apply this color to the WordArt outline.

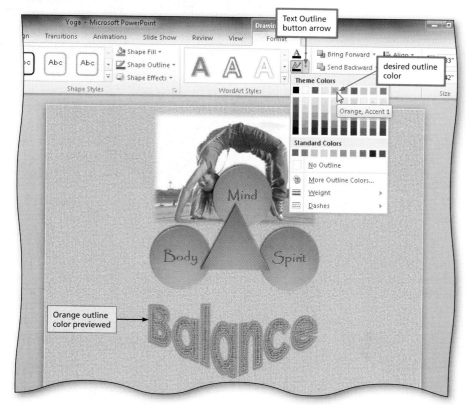

Figure 2–71

To Add a Transition between Slides

A final enhancement you will make in this presentation is to apply the Rotate transition in the Dynamic Content category to all slides and change the transition speed to Slow. The following steps apply this transition to the presentation.

1 Click Transitions on the Ribbon. Click the More button (Transitions tab | Transition to This Slide group) to expand the Transitions gallery.

2 Click the Rotate transition in the Dynamic Content category to apply this transition to Slide 4.

3 Click the Duration up arrow in the Timing group four times to change the transition speed from 02.00 to 03.00.

4 Click the Preview Transitions button (Transitions tab | Preview area) to view the new transition time.

5 Click the Apply To All button (Transitions tab | Timing group) to apply this transition and speed to all four slides in the presentation (Figure 2–72 on the next page).

BTW

Selecting Effect Options
Many PowerPoint transitions have options that you can customize to give your presentation a unique look. When you click the Effect Options button (Transitions tab | Transition to This Slide group), you can, for example, select the option to have a slide appear on the screen from the left or the right, or the screen can fade to black before the next slide is displayed.

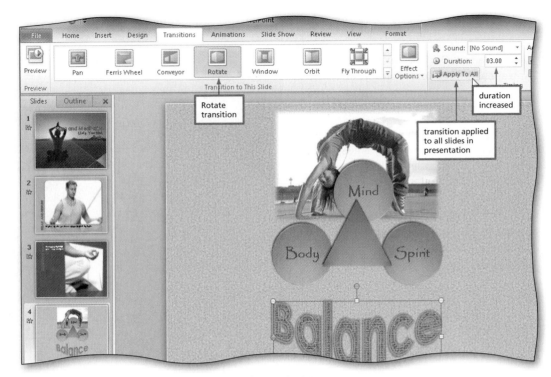

Figure 2–72

To Change Document Properties

Before saving the presentation again, you want to add your name, class name, and some keywords as document properties. The following steps use the Document Information Panel to change document properties.

1 Click File on the Ribbon to open the Backstage view. If necessary, click the Info tab.

2 Click the Properties button in the right pane of the Info gallery.

3 Click Show Document Panel on the Properties menu to close the Backstage view and display the Document Information Panel.

4 Click the Author box, if necessary, and then type your name as the Author property.

5 Click the Subject text box and then type your course and section as the Subject property.

6 Click the Keywords text box and then type `yoga, meditation` as the Keywords property.

7 Click the Close the Document Information Panel button so that the Document Information Panel no longer is displayed.

BTW

Certification
The Microsoft Office Specialist (MOS) program provides an opportunity for you to obtain a valuable industry credential — proof that you have the PowerPoint 2010 skills required by employers. For more information, visit the PowerPoint 2010 Certification Web page (scsite.com/ppt2010/cert).

To Print a Presentation

With the completed presentation saved, you may want to print it. If copies of the presentation are being distributed to audience members, you will print a hard copy of each individual slide on a printer. The following steps print a hard copy of the contents of the saved Yoga presentation.

1 Click File on the Ribbon to open the Backstage view. Click the Print tab in the Backstage view to display the Print gallery.

2 Verify the printer name in the Printer box will print a hard copy of the document. If necessary, click the Printer box arrow to display a list of available Printer options and then click the desired printer to change the currently selected printer.

3 Click the Print button in the Print gallery to print the document on the currently selected printer. When the printer stops, retrieve the hard copy (Figure 2–73).

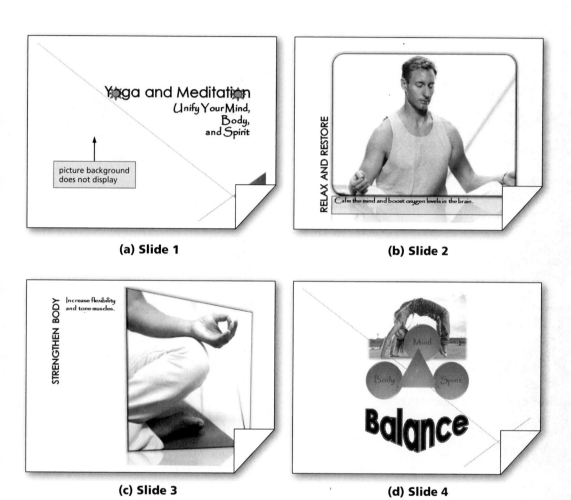

(a) Slide 1

(b) Slide 2

(c) Slide 3

(d) Slide 4

Figure 2–73   (Handouts printed using a black-and-white printer)

To Save an Existing Presentation with the Same File Name

You have made several changes to the presentation since you last saved it. Thus, you should save it again. The following step saves the document again.

1 Click the Save button on the Quick Access Toolbar to overwrite the previously saved file.

BTW

Quick Reference
For a table that lists how to complete the tasks covered in this book using the mouse, Ribbon, shortcut menu, and keyboard, see the Quick Reference Summary at the back of this book, or visit the PowerPoint 2010 Quick Reference Web page (scsite.com/ppt2010/qr).

To Run an Animated Slide Show

All changes are complete, and the presentation is saved. You now can view the Yoga presentation. The following steps start Slide Show view.

1 Click the Slide 1 thumbnail in the Slides tab to select and display Slide 1.

2 Click the Slide Show button to display the title slide and then click each slide to view the transition effect and slides.

To Quit PowerPoint

This project is complete. The following steps quit PowerPoint.

1 If you have one PowerPoint document open, click the Close Button on the right side of the title bar to close the document and then quit PowerPoint; or if you have multiple PowerPoint documents open, click File on the Ribbon to open the Backstage view and then click Exit in the Backstage view to close all open documents and quit PowerPoint.

2 If a Microsoft PowerPoint dialog box appears, click the Save button to save any changes made to the presentation since the last save.

Chapter Summary

In this chapter you have learned how to add a background style, insert and format pictures, add shapes, size graphic elements, apply styles, and insert WordArt. The items listed below include all the new PowerPoint skills you have learned in this chapter.

1. Change the Presentation Theme Colors (PPT 81)
2. Insert a Picture (PPT 83)
3. Insert a Picture into a Slide without a Content Placeholder (PPT 85)
4. Correct a Picture (PPT 86)
5. Apply a Picture Style (PPT 87)
6. Apply Picture Effects (PPT 89)
7. Add a Picture Border (PPT 91)
8. Change a Picture Border Color (PPT 92)
9. Resize a Graphic by Entering Exact Measurements (PPT 93)
10. Insert a Texture Fill (PPT 95)
11. Insert a Picture to Create a Background (PPT 97)
12. Format the Background Picture Fill Transparency (PPT 98)
13. Format the Background Texture Fill Transparency (PPT 99)
14. Choose a Background Style (PPT 99)
15. Change the Subtitle and Caption Font (PPT 101)
16. Shadow Text (PPT 103)
17. Format Caption Text Using the Format Painter (PPT 105)
18. Add a Shape (PPT 106)
19. Resize a Shape (PPT 107)
20. Copy and Paste a Shape (PPT 108)
21. Add Other Shapes (PPT 109)
22. Apply a Shape Style (PPT 110)
23. Add Formatted Text to a Shape (PPT 112)
24. Insert WordArt (PPT 114)
25. Change the WordArt Shape (PPT 115)
26. Apply a WordArt Text Fill (PPT 117)
27. Change the Weight of the WordArt Outline (PPT 118)
28. Change the Color of the WordArt Outline (PPT 118)

If you have a SAM 2010 user profile, your instructor may have assigned an autogradable version of this assignment. If so, log into the SAM 2010 Web site at www.cengage.com/sam2010 to download the instruction and start files.

Learn It Online

Test your knowledge of chapter content and key terms.

Instructions: To complete the Learn It Online exercises, start your browser, click the Address bar, and then enter the Web address **scsite.com/ppt2010/learn**. When the PowerPoint 2010 Learn It Online page is displayed, click the link for the exercise you want to complete and then read the instructions.

Chapter Reinforcement TF, MC, and SA
A series of true/false, multiple choice, and short answer questions that test your knowledge of the chapter content.

Flash Cards
An interactive learning environment where you identify chapter key terms associated with displayed definitions.

Practice Test
A series of multiple choice questions that test your knowledge of chapter content and key terms.

Who Wants To Be a Computer Genius?
An interactive game that challenges your knowledge of chapter content in the style of a television quiz show.

Wheel of Terms
An interactive game that challenges your knowledge of chapter key terms in the style of the television show *Wheel of Fortune.*

Crossword Puzzle Challenge
A crossword puzzle that challenges your knowledge of key terms presented in the chapter.

Apply Your Knowledge

Reinforce the skills and apply the concepts you learned in this chapter.

Changing the Background and Adding Photographs, WordArt, and a Shape Quick Style
Note: To complete this assignment, you will be required to use the Data Files for Students. See the inside back cover of this book for instructions on downloading the Data Files for Students, or contact your instructor for information about accessing the required files.

Instructions: Start PowerPoint. Open the presentation, Apply 2-1 Lab Procedures, from the Data Files for Students.

The four slides in the presentation present laboratory safety procedures for your chemistry class. The document you open is an unformatted presentation. You are to add pictures, which are available on the Data Files for Students. You also will change the background style, change slide layouts, apply a transition, and use the Format Painter so the slides look like Figure 2–74.

Perform the following tasks:

1. Change the background style to Style 5 (row 2, column 1).

2. On the title slide (Figure 2–74a), create a background by inserting the picture called Lab Assistant. Change the transparency to 30%.

3. Apply the WordArt style, Fill – Red, Accent 2, Matte Bevel (row 6, column 3) to the title text and increase the font size to 54 point. Also, apply the WordArt Transform text effect, Chevron Up (row 2, column 1 in the Warp area) to this text.

4. In the Slide 1 subtitle area, replace the words, Student Name, with your name. Bold and italicize your name and the words, Presented by, and then apply the WordArt style, Fill – Red, Accent 2, Warm Matte Bevel (row 5, column 3). Position this subtitle text and the title text as shown in Figure 2–74a.

Continued >

Apply Your Knowledge *continued*

5. On Slide 2, change the layout to Two Content and insert the pictures shown in Figure 2–74b called Female in Lab Coat and Female with Goggles. In the left placeholder, apply the Rotated, White picture style to the inserted picture. In the right placeholder, apply the Reflected Bevel, Black picture style to the inserted picture and then change the picture border color to Purple.

6. On Slide 3, change the layout to Two Content and insert the Fire Extinguisher picture shown in Figure 2–74c. Apply the Soft Edge Oval picture style and change the picture brightness to +20% (row 3, column 4 in the Brightness and Contrast area).

7. On Slide 4, change the layout to Picture with Caption and then insert the picture, Hand Washing shown in Figure 2–74d. Increase the subtitle text font size to 18 point. Change the title text font size to 28 point, add a shadow, change font to Algerian, and change the font color to Purple.

(a) Slide 1

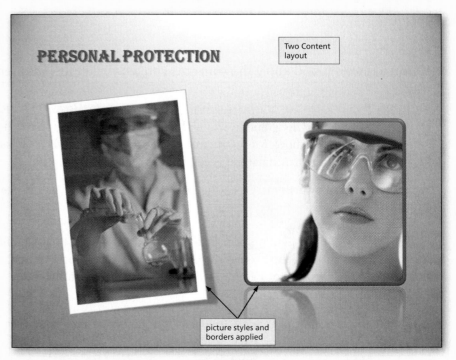

(b) Slide 2

Figure 2 – 74

8. Use the Format Painter to format the title text on Slides 2 and 3 with the same features as the title text on Slide 4.

9. Apply the Wipe transition in the Subtle category to all slides. Change the duration to 2.00 seconds.

10. Change the document properties, as specified by your instructor. Save the presentation using the file name, Apply 2-1 Chemistry Lab Safety. Submit the revised document in the format specified by your instructor.

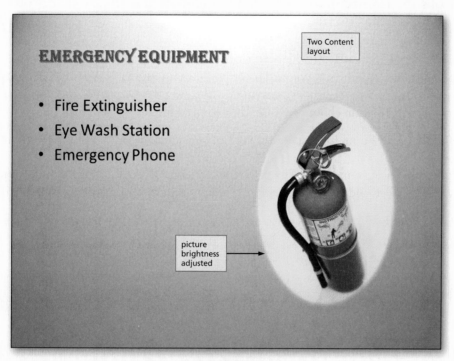

(c) Slide 3

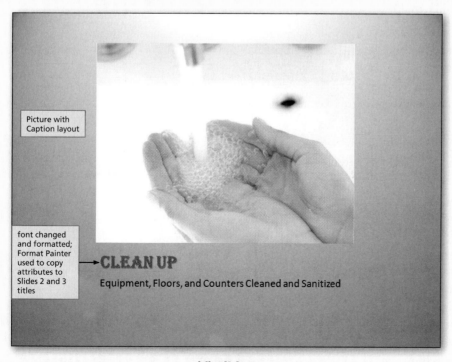

(d) Slide 4

Figure 2 – 74 (Continued)

Extend Your Knowledge

Extend the skills you learned in this chapter and experiment with new skills. You may need to use Help to complete the assignment.

Changing Slide Backgrounds and Picture Contrast, and Inserting Shapes and WordArt

Note: To complete this assignment, you will be required to use the Data Files for Students. See the inside back cover of this book for instructions on downloading the Data Files for Students, or contact your instructor for information about accessing the required files.

Instructions: Start PowerPoint. Open the presentation, Extend 2-1 Smith Family Reunion, from the Data Files for Students.

You will create backgrounds including inserting a picture to create a background, apply a WordArt Style and Effect, and add shapes to create the presentation shown in Figure 2–75.

Perform the following tasks:

1. Change the background style to Denim (row 1, column 3) and change the transparency to 48%. On Slides 2 through 5, change the title text to bold.

2. On the title slide (Figure 2–75a), create a background by inserting the picture called Tree, which is available on the Data Files for Students. Change the transparency to 40%.

3. Apply the WordArt style, Gradient Fill – Blue, Accent 1, to the title text and increase the font size to 66 point. Also, apply the WordArt Transform text effect, Arch Up (row 1, column 1 in the Follow Path area), to this text.

4. In the Slide 1 subtitle area, insert the Wave shape in the Stars and Banners area. Also, apply the Shape Style, Subtle Effect – Orange, Accent 6 to the Wave shape. Type **Highlights From Our Last Reunion** and increase the font size to 40 point, change the text to bold italic and change the color to Green. Position the shape as shown in Figure 2–75a.

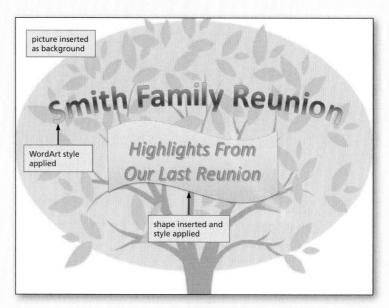

(a) Slide 1

(b) Slide 2

Figure 2–75

5. On Slide 2, change the layout to Two Content and insert the pictures shown in Figure 2–75b. The pictures to be inserted are called Bocce Ball and Frisbee Catcher and are available on the Data Files for Students. In the left placeholder, apply the Rotated White picture style to the inserted picture and change the picture border to Light Green. In the right placeholder, apply the Beveled Oval Black picture style to the inserted picture.

6. Insert the Plaque shape in the Basic Shapes area. Also, apply the Shape Style, Subtle Effect, Olive Green, Accent 3 and apply the Shape Effect, 3-D Rotation, Parallel, Off Axis 1 Right. Type **Cousin Tom & His Frisbee Moves** and increase the font size to 28 point. Move the shape as shown in Figure 2–75b.

(c) **Slide 3**

7. On Slide 3, change the layout to Picture with Caption and insert the picture shown in Figure 2–75c. The picture to be inserted is called BBQ Grill. Increase the title font size to 44 point. Also, increase the subtitle font size to 32 point, and then bold and italicize this text.

8. On Slide 4, change the layout to Two Content and insert the pictures shown in Figure 2–75d. The pictures to be inserted are called Reunion Boys and Reunion Toddler. In the left placeholder, apply the Rotated, White picture effect to the picture. In the right placeholder, apply the Bevel Perspective picture effect. Move the pictures as shown in Figure 2–75d.

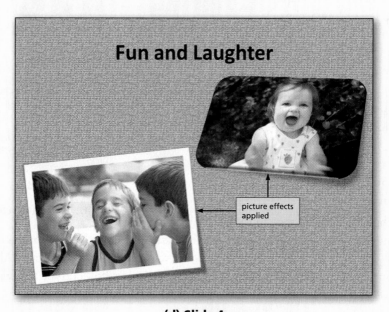

(d) **Slide 4**

Figure 2–75 (Continued)

Continued >

Extend Your Knowledge *continued*

9. On Slide 5, change the layout to Title and Content and insert the picture shown in Figure 2–75e. The picture to be inserted is called Reunion. Enlarge the picture as shown.

10. Insert the Oval Callout and Cloud Callout shapes in the Callouts area. In the Oval Callout shape, type `I hope Grandma makes cookies!` and change the font size to 24 point bold italic. Also add a Shape Style, Moderate Effect – Olive Green Accent 3 to this shape. In the Cloud Callout shape, type `I'm looking forward to our next reunion!` and change the font size to 24 point and the style to bold italic. Move the shapes as shown in Figure 2–75e. Use the adjustment handles (the yellow diamond below each shape) to move the callout arrows as shown in Figure 2–75e. You may need to use Help to learn how to move these arrows.

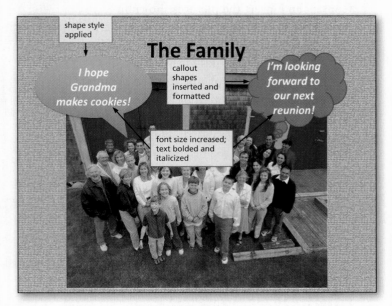

(e) Slide 5

11. On Slide 6, change the layout to Picture with Caption and insert the picture shown in Figure 2–75f and change the picture contrast to +20. The picture to be inserted is called Reunion Tree.

(f) Slide 6

Figure 2 – 75 (Continued)

12. Insert the Up Ribbon shape in the Stars and Banners area and type the words `Announcing Our Next Reunion`. Change the font color to Green, the font size to 32 point, and the style to bold italic. Also, apply the Shape Style, Subtle Effect – Orange Accent 6. In the title placeholder, type `Save the date – June 20, 2012` and change the font size to 28 point. Bold this text.

13. Add the Orbit transition under the Dynamic Content section to Slide 6 only. You may need to use Help to learn how to apply the transition to only one slide. Change the duration to 2.00 seconds.

14. Change the document properties, as specified by your instructor. Save the presentation using the file name, Extend 2-1 Smith Reunion.

15. Submit the revised document in the format specified by your instructor.

Make It Right

Analyze a presentation and correct all errors and/or improve the design.

Changing a Theme and Background Style

Note: To complete this assignment, you will be required to use the Data Files for Students. See the inside back cover of this book for instructions on downloading the Data Files for Students, or contact your instructor for information about accessing the required files.

Instructions: Start PowerPoint. Open the presentation, Make It Right 2-1 New Aerobics Classes, from the Data Files for Students.

Correct the formatting problems and errors in the presentation while keeping in mind the guidelines presented in this chapter.

Perform the following tasks:

1. Change the document theme from Flow, shown in Figure 2–76, to Waveform. Apply the Background Style 10 (row 3, column 2) to Slide 5 only.

2. On the title slide, change the title from New Aerobics Classes to New Pool Programs. Type your name in place of Northlake Fitness Center and change the font to bold italic.

3. Move Slide 2 to the end of the presentation so that it becomes the new Slide 5.

4. Adjust the picture sizes, font sizes, and shapes so they do not overlap text and are the appropriate dimensions for the slide content.

5. Apply the Ripple transition to all slides. Change the duration to 02.00.

6. Change the document properties, as specified by your instructor. Save the presentation using the file name, Make It Right 2-1 New Pool Programs.

7. Submit the revised document in the format specified by your instructor.

Figure 2 – 76

In the Lab

Design and/or create a presentation using the guidelines, concepts, and skills presented in this chapter. Labs 1, 2, and 3 are listed in order of increasing difficulty.

Lab 1: Creating a Presentation Inserting Pictures and Applying Picture Styles

Problem: You are studying German operas in your Music Appreciation class. Wilhelm Richard Wagner (pronounced 'va:gner') lived from 1813 to 1883 and was a composer, conductor, theatre director, and essayist known for his operas. Wagner wrote and composed many operas, and King Ludwig II of Bavaria was one of his biggest supporters. Because you recently visited southern Germany and toured King Ludwig's castles, you decide to create a PowerPoint presentation with some of your photos to accompany your class presentation. These pictures are available on the Data Files for Students. Create the slides shown in Figure 2–77 from a blank presentation using the Office Theme document theme.

Note: To complete this assignment, you will be required to use the Data Files for Students. See the inside back cover of this book for instructions on downloading the Data Files for Students, or contact your instructor for information about accessing the required files.

Instructions: Perform the following tasks:

1. On Slide 1, create a background by inserting the picture called Castle 1, which is available on the Data Files for Students.

2. Type **Fairy Tale Trip to Germany** as the Slide 1 title text. Apply the WordArt style, Fill – Tan, Text 2, Outline – Background 2, and increase the font size to 60 point. Change the text fill to the Papyrus texture, and then change the text outline weight to 1½ pt. Also, apply the Transform text effect, Arch Up (in the Follow Path area), to this text. Position this WordArt as shown in Figure 2–77a.

3. Type the title and content for the four text slides shown in Figure 2–77. Apply the Two Content layout to Slides 2 and 3 and the Picture with Caption layout to Slides 4 and 5.

4. On Slide 2, insert the picture called Castle 2 from the Data Files for Students in the right placeholder. Apply the Bevel Perspective picture style. Resize the picture so that it is approximately 4.5" × 6", change the border color to Purple, change the border weight to 6 pt, and then move the picture, as shown in Figure 2–77b.

5. On Slide 3, insert the picture called Castle 3 from the Data Files for Students. Apply the Reflected Bevel, Black picture style and then change the border color to Green. Do not change the border weight.

6. On Slide 4, insert the picture called Castle 4 from the Data Files for Students. Apply the Beveled Oval, Black picture style, change the border color to Blue, and then change the border weight to 6 pt.

7. On Slide 5, insert the picture called Castle 5 from the Data Files for Students. Apply the Moderate Frame, Black picture style, change the border color to Purple, and then change the border weight to 6 pt.

8. For both Slides 4 and 5, increase the title text size to 28 point and the caption text size to 24 point.

9. On Slide 2, change the title text font to Algerian, change the color to purple, and bold this text. Use the Format Painter to apply these formatting changes to the Slide 3 title text. In Slide 3, insert the Vertical Scroll shape located in the Stars and Banners area, apply the Subtle Effect – Purple, Accent 4 shape style, and change the shape outline weight to 3 pt. Type the text, **Inspiration for Disney's Sleeping Beauty Castle**, and then change the font to Curlz MT, or a similar font. Bold this text, change the color to Dark Blue, and then change the size to 28 point. Increase the scroll shape size, as shown in Figure 2–77c.

10. On Slides 2, 3, 4, and 5, change the background style to the White marble fill texture (row 2, column 5) and change the transparency to 35%. Apply the Glitter transition to all slides. Change the duration to 04.50.

11. Change the document properties, as specified by your instructor. Save the presentation using the file name, Lab 2-1 Trip to Germany.

12. Submit the revised document in the format specified by your instructor.

picture inserted as background

WordArt style, texture fill, and effect applied

(a) Slide 1

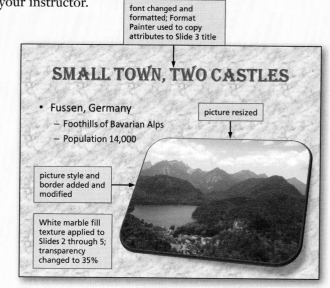

font changed and formatted; Format Painter used to copy attributes to Slide 3 title

picture resized

picture style and border added and modified

White marble fill texture applied to Slides 2 through 5; transparency changed to 35%

(b) Slide 2

picture style applied and border color changed to Green

shape inserted and formatted

font changed to Curlz MT and formatted

(c) Slide 3

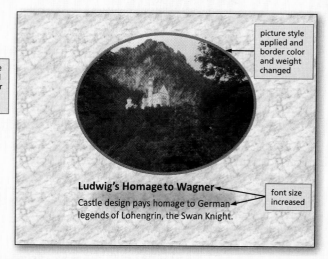

picture style applied and border color and weight changed

font size increased

(d) Slide 4

picture style applied and border color and weight changed

font size increased

(e) Slide 5

Figure 2–77

In the Lab

Lab 2: Creating a Presentation with a Shape and with WordArt

Problem: With the economy showing some improvement, many small businesses are approaching lending institutions for loans to expand their businesses. You work part-time for Loans Are Us, and your manager asked you to prepare a PowerPoint presentation for the upcoming Small Business Fair in your community. The pictures for this presentation are available on the Data Files for Students.

Note: To complete this assignment, you will be required to use the Data Files for Students. See the inside back cover of this book for instructions on downloading the Data Files for Students, or contact your instructor for information about accessing the required files.

Instructions: Perform the following tasks:

1. Create a new presentation using the Austin document theme.

2. Type the title and content for the title slide and the three text slides shown in Figure 2–78a–d. Apply the Title Only layout to Slide 2, the Two Content layout to Slide 3, and the Picture with Caption layout to Slide 4.

3. On both Slides 2 and 4, create a background by inserting the picture called Money. Change the transparency to 35%.

4. On Slide 1, insert the picture called Meeting. Apply the Reflected Bevel, White picture style. Resize the picture so that it is approximately 3.76" × 4.7", change the border color to Dark Blue, change the border weight to 3 pt, and then move the picture, as shown in Figure 2–78a. Increase the title text font size to 60 point, and then apply the WordArt style, Fill – Orange, Accent 6, Warm Matte Bevel.

5. Increase the subtitle text, Loans Are Us, font size to 28 point and then bold and italicize this text. Apply the WordArt style, Fill – Green, Accent 1, Metal Bevel, Reflection.

6. On Slide 2, bold the title text. Insert the pictures called Doc1, Doc2, and Doc3. Resize these pictures so they are approximately 3" x 2.7" and then move them to the locations shown in Figure 2–78b. Insert the Flowchart: Decision shape located in the Flowchart area, apply the Subtle Effect – Orange, Accent 6 shape style, and then resize the shape so that it is approximately 1.5" × 5.83". Change the shape outline weight to 6 pt. Type **Assets, Liabilities & Sales Reports** as the shape text, change the font to Aharoni, or a similar font, change the color to Dark Blue, and then change the size to 24 point.

7. On Slide 3, bold the title text. Insert the picture called Presentation into the right placeholder, apply the Beveled Oval, Black shape picture style, resize the picture so that it is approximately 3.5" × 5.25", and then sharpen the picture 50%.

8. On Slide 4, insert the picture called Cash and Credit Card. Change the title text font size to 36 point and bold this text. Change the subtitle text font size to 24 point and then bold and italicize these words.

9. Apply the Shape transition to all slides. Change the duration to 01.25.

10. Change the document properties, as specified by your instructor. Save the presentation using the file name, Lab 2-2 Small Business Loans.

11. Submit the document in the format specified by your instructor.

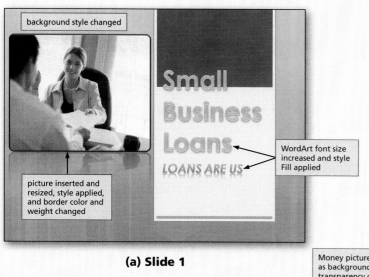

(a) Slide 1

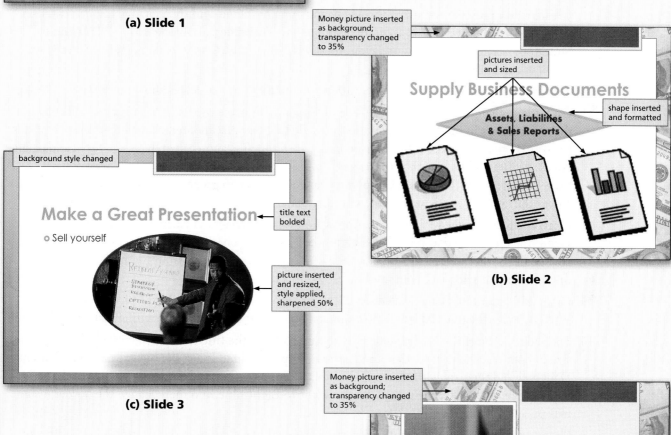

(b) Slide 2

(c) Slide 3

(d) Slide 4

Figure 2–78

In the Lab

Lab 3: Creating a Presentation with Pictures and Shapes

Problem: One of your assignments in your child development class is to give a speech about teaching children the value of money, so you decide to create a PowerPoint presentation to add a little interest to your speech. Prepare the slides shown in Figures 2–79a through 2–79e. The pictures for this presentation are available on the Data Files for Students.

Note: To complete this assignment, you will be required to use the Data Files for Students. See the inside back cover of this book for instructions on downloading the Data Files for Students, or contact your instructor for information about accessing the required files.

Instructions: Perform the following tasks:

1. Create a new presentation using the Median document theme, and then change the presentation theme colors to Flow. This presentation should have five slides; apply the Title Slide layout to Slide 1, the Picture with Caption layout to Slides 2 and 5, the Comparison layout to Slide 3, and the Blank layout to Slide 4.

2. Type the title and content text for the title slide and the four text slides shown in Figure 2–79a–d.

3. On Slide 1, change the title text font size to 54 point. To make the letter 's' appear smaller than the other letters in the first word of the title slide title text placeholder, change the font size of this letter to 44 point. Insert the Oval shape, resize it so that it is approximately 0.5" × 0.5", and change the shape fill to white, which is the second color in the first row of the Theme Colors gallery. Type **$**, increase the font size to 48 point, change the color to green, and bold this dollar sign. Cover the letter 'o' in the word, Do, with this shape.

4. Insert the picture called Piggy Bank. Apply the Rounded Diagonal Corner, White picture style. Resize the picture so that it is approximately 4.4" × 5.03", change the border color to Light Blue, change the border weight to 3 pt, and then move the picture, as shown in Figure 2–79a. Change the subtitle font size to 32 point and then bold this text.

5. On Slide 2, insert the picture called Child Doing Dishes and then decrease the picture's contrast to −20%. Change the title text size to 36 point and bold this text. Change the caption text size to 32 point.

6. On Slide 3, change the background style to Style 6. Bold the title text. Change the heading title text size in both placeholders to 32 point. In the right placeholder, insert the picture called Father and Daughter and then apply the Reflected Bevel, White picture style. Resize the picture so that it is approximately 3" × 4", change the border color to Light Blue, and then change the border weight to 3 pt, as shown in Figure 2–79c.

7. On Slide 4, create a background by inserting the picture called Piggy Bank and Coins. Insert the Cloud shape located in the Basic Shapes area and then increase the cloud shape size so that it is approximately 3" × 5.6". Change the shape outline color to Yellow and then change the shape outline weight to 3 pt. Type **Teach your children to save for a big purchase.** as the shape text, and then change the font to Comic Sans MS. Bold and italicize this text and then change the font size to 32 point.

8. On Slide 5, create a background by inserting the picture called Coins. Insert the picture called Father and Child Shopping and then decrease the picture's brightness to −20%. Change the title text font size to 36 point and bold this text.

9. Apply the Box transition to all slides. Change the duration to 02.00. Check the spelling and correct any errors.

10. Change the document properties, as specified by your instructor. Save the presentation using the file name, Lab 2-3 ABCs of Money.

11. Submit the revised document in the format specified by your instructor.

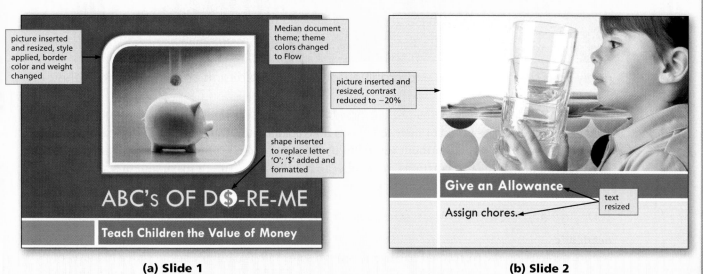

(a) Slide 1

(b) Slide 2

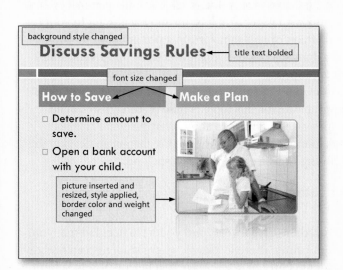

(c) Slide 3

(d) Slide 4

(e) Slide 5

Figure 2–79

Cases and Places

Apply your creative thinking and problem-solving skills to design and implement a solution.

Note: To complete these assignments, you may be required to use the Data Files for Students. See the inside back cover of this book for instructions on downloading the Data Files for Students, or contact your instructor for information about accessing the required files.

As you design the presentations, remember to use the 7 × 7 rule: a maximum of seven words on a line and a maximum of seven lines on one slide.

1: Design and Create a Presentation about Acid Rain

Academic

Nature depends on the correct pH balance. Although some rain is naturally acidic with a pH level of around 5.0, human activities have increased the amount of acid in this water. Burning fossil fuels, including coal, oil, and natural gas, produces sulfur dioxide. Exhaust from vehicles releases nitrogen oxides. Both of these gases, when released into the atmosphere, mix with water droplets, forming acid rain. In your science class, you are studying about the causes and effects of acid rain. Create a presentation to show what causes acid rain and what effects it can have on humans, animals, plant life, lakes, and rivers. The presentation should contain at least three pictures appropriately resized. The Data Files for Students contains five pictures called Factory, Rain, Soil, Tree and Clouds, and Vehicles; you can use your own digital pictures or pictures from Office.com if they are appropriate for this topic. These pictures also should have appropriate styles and border colors. Use shapes such as arrows to show what gases are released into the atmosphere. Apply at least three objectives found at the beginning of this chapter to develop the presentation. Add a title slide with a shape and a closing slide. Be sure to check spelling.

2: Design and Create a Presentation about Tutoring

Personal

You have been helping some of your classmates with their schoolwork, and you have decided that you should start a small tutoring business. In the student center, there is a kiosk where students can find out about programs and activities on campus. The student center manager gave you permission to submit a short PowerPoint presentation promoting your tutoring business; this presentation will be added to the kiosk. The presentation should contain pictures appropriately resized. The Data Files for Students contains four pictures called Tutoring 1, Tutoring 2, Tutoring 3, and Tutoring 4, or you can use your own digital pictures or pictures from Office.com if they are appropriate for this topic. Change the contrast and brightness for at least one picture. Insert shapes and WordArt to enhance your presentation. Apply a transition in the Subtle area to all slides and increase the duration. Be sure to check spelling.

3: Design and Create a Presentation on Setting Up Children's Fish Tanks

Professional

Fish make great pets for young children, but there is a lot to learn before they can set up a fish tank properly. The owner of the pet store where you work has asked you to create a presentation for the store to give parents an idea of what they need to purchase and consider when setting up a fish tank. He would like you to cover the main points such as the appropriate size bowl or tank, setup procedures, filtration, water quality, types of fish, care, and feeding. The presentation should contain pictures appropriately resized. The Data Files for Students contains five pictures called Fish 1, Fish 2, Fish 3, Fish 4, and Fish 5, or you can use your own digital pictures or pictures from Office.com if they are appropriate for this topic. Add a title slide and closing slide to complete your presentation. Format the title slide with a shape and change the theme color scheme. Change the title text font on the title slide. Format the background with at least one picture and apply a background texture to at least one slide. This presentation is geared to parents of young children, so keep it colorful, simple, and fun.

3 | Reusing a Presentation and Adding Media

Objectives

You will have mastered the material in this chapter when you can:

- Color a picture
- Add an artistic effect to a picture
- Delete and move placeholders
- Align paragraph text
- Copy a slide element from one slide to another

- Ungroup, change the color, and regroup a clip
- Insert and edit a video clip
- Insert audio
- Control audio and video clips
- Check for spelling errors
- Print a presentation as a handout

3 | Reusing a Presentation and Adding Media

Introduction

At times, you will need to revise a PowerPoint presentation. Changes may include inserting and adding effects to pictures, altering the colors of clips and pictures, and updating visual elements displayed on a slide. Applying a different theme, changing fonts, and substituting graphical elements can give a slide show an entirely new look. Adding media, including sounds, video, and music, can enhance a presentation and help audience members retain the information being presented.

Project — Presentation with Video, Audio, and Pictures with Effects

BTW

PowerPoint 2010 Video Enhancements
New video tools in PowerPoint 2010 enable you to develop a presentation filled with professional-quality features. You now can embed and edit videos from within PowerPoint instead of needing to use a separate program to customize your media files. You can add fades and effects to captivate your audience, and you can trim specific pieces of the video file to show the exact scenes needed to make a point. Video and audio files now are embedded in your PowerPoint file, so they become part of the entire presentation. These enhanced features help make your media fit the message you are sending to your audience.

The project in this chapter follows graphical guidelines and uses PowerPoint to create the presentation shown in Figure 3–1. The slides in this revised presentation, which discusses Bird Migration, have a variety of audio and visual elements. For example, the pictures have artistic effects applied that soften the pictures and help the audience focus on other elements on the slides. The bird clip has colors that blend well with the background. The video has been edited to play only the portion with Bird Migration and has effects to add audience interest. Bird calls integrate with the visual elements. Overall, the slides have myriad media elements and effects that are exciting for your audience to watch and hear.

Overview

As you read through this chapter, you will learn how to create the presentation shown in Figure 3–1 by performing these general tasks:

- Format pictures by recoloring and adding artistic effects.
- Insert and format video and audio clips.
- Modify clip art.
- Vary paragraph alignment.
- Check a presentation for spelling errors.
- Print a handout of your slides.

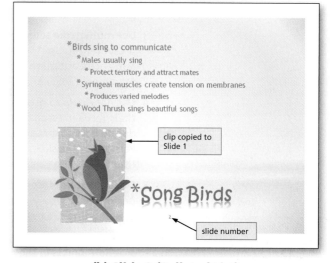

(a) Slide 1 (Title Slide with Picture Background, Modified Clip, and Animated Clip)

(b) Slide 2 (Bulleted List)

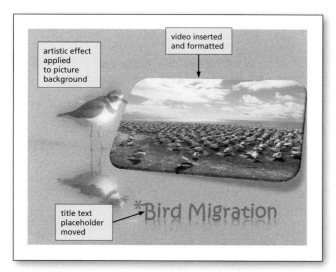

(c) Slide 3 (Picture Background and Video Clip)

(d) Slide 4 (Video Playing Full Screen)

Figure 3–1

Plan Ahead

General Project Guidelines

When creating a PowerPoint presentation, the actions you perform and the decisions you make will affect the appearance and characteristics of the finished document. As you create a presentation with illustrations, such as the project shown in Figure 3–1, you should follow these general guidelines:

1. **Use the color wheel to determine color choices.** Warm colors and cool colors evoke opposite effects on audience members. As you make decisions to color pictures, consider the emotions you want to generate and choose colors that match these sentiments.

2. **Vary paragraph alignment.** Different effects are achieved when text alignment shifts in a presentation. Themes dictate whether paragraph text is aligned left, center, or right in a placeholder, but you can modify these design decisions when necessary.

3. **Use multimedia selectively.** Video, music, and sound files can add interest to your presentation. Use these files only when necessary, however, because they draw the audience's attention away from the presenter and toward the slides. Using too many multimedia files can be overwhelming.

4. **Use handouts to organize your speech.** Effective speakers take much time to prepare their verbal message that will accompany each slide. They practice their speeches and decide how to integrate the material displayed. Viewing the thumbnails, or miniature versions of the slides, will help you associate the slide image with the script. These thumbnails also can be cut out and arranged when organizing the presentation.

5. **Evaluate your presentation.** As soon as you finish your presentation, critique your performance. You will improve your communication skills by eliminating the flaws and accentuating the positives.

When necessary, more specific details concerning the above guidelines are presented at appropriate points in the chapter. The chapter also will identify the actions performed and decisions made regarding these guidelines during the creation of the presentation shown in Figure 3–1.

For an introduction to Windows 7 and instruction about how to perform basic Windows 7 tasks, read the Office 2010 and Windows 7 chapter at the beginning of this book, where you can learn how to resize windows, change screen resolution, create folders, move and rename files, use Windows Help, and much more.

Starting PowerPoint

Chapter 1 introduced you to starting PowerPoint, selecting a document theme, creating slides with clip art and a bulleted list, and printing a presentation. Chapter 2 enhanced slides by adding pictures, shapes, and WordArt. The following steps, which assume Windows 7 is running, start PowerPoint and open the Birds presentation. For a detailed example of the procedure summarized below, refer to the Office 2010 and Windows 7 chapter at the beginning of this book.

To Start PowerPoint and Open and Save a Presentation

BTW

The Ribbon and Screen Resolution
PowerPoint may change how the groups and buttons within the groups appear on the Ribbon, depending on the computer's screen resolution. Thus, your Ribbon may look different from the ones in this book if you are using a screen resolution other than 1024 × 768.

1. Click the Start button on the Windows 7 taskbar to display the Start menu, type `Microsoft PowerPoint` as the search text in the 'Search programs and files' text box, and then click Microsoft PowerPoint 2010 in the search results on the Start menu to start PowerPoint and display a new blank document.

2. If the PowerPoint window is not maximized, click the Maximize button.

3. Open the presentation, Birds, from the Data Files for Students. See the inside back cover of this book for instructions on downloading the Data Files for Students, or contact your instructor for more information on accessing the required files.

4. Save the presentation using the file name, Bird Migration.

Inserting Pictures and Adding Effects

The Bird Migration presentation consists of four slides that have some text, a clip art image, a formatted background, and a transition applied to all slides. You will insert pictures into two slides and then modify them by adding artistic effects and recoloring. You also will copy the clip art from Slide 2 to Slide 1 and modify the objects in this clip. In Chapter 2, you inserted pictures, made corrections, and added styles and effects; the new effects you apply in this chapter will add to your repertoire of picture enhancements that increase interest in your presentation.

In the following pages, you will perform these tasks:

1. Insert the first digital picture into Slide 1.
2. Insert the second digital picture into Slide 3.
3. Recolor the Slide 3 picture.
4. Recolor and add an artistic effect to the Slide 1 picture.
5. Add an artistic effect to the Slide 3 picture.
6. Send the Slide 3 picture back behind all other slide objects.
7. Send the Slide 1 picture back behind all other slide objects.

For an introduction to Office 2010 and instruction about how to perform basic tasks in Office 2010 programs, read the Office 2010 and Windows 7 chapter at the beginning of this book, where you can learn how to start a program, use the Ribbon, save a file, open a file, quit a program, use Help, and much more.

To Insert and Resize Pictures into Slides without Content Placeholders

The next step is to insert digital pictures into Slides 1 and 3. These pictures are available on the Data Files for Students. See the inside back cover of this book for instructions on downloading the Data Files for Students, or contact your instructor for information about accessing the required files.

The following steps insert pictures into Slides 1 and 3.

1 With Slide 1 displaying and your USB flash drive connected to one of the computer's USB ports, click Insert on the Ribbon to display the Insert tab and then click the Picture button (Insert tab | Images group) to display the Insert Picture dialog box.

2 If necessary, navigate to the picture location (in this case, the PowerPoint folder in the CIS 101 folder [or your class folder] on the USB flash drive). For a detailed example of this procedure, refer to Steps 3a–3c on pages OFF 28 and OFF 29 in the Office 2010 and Windows 7 chapter at the beginning of this book.

3 Click Birds in Sky to select the file.

4 Click the Insert button (Insert Picture dialog box) to insert the picture into Slide 1.

5 Resize the picture so that it covers the entire slide (approximately 7.5" × 10").

6 Display Slide 3, display the Insert tab, click the Picture button to display the Insert Picture dialog box, and then insert the Bird Reflect picture into Slide 3.

7 Resize the picture so that it covers the entire slide (approximately 7.5" × 10") (Figure 3–2).

Q&A How do I resize the picture so that it maintains its proportions?

Press and hold the SHIFT key while dragging a sizing handle away from or toward the center of the picture. To maintain the picture's proportions and keep its center in the same location, press and hold down both the CTRL and SHIFT keys while you drag a sizing handle.

BTW

Inserting Text Boxes
If you want to add text in an area of the slide where a content placeholder is not located, you can insert a text box. This object allows you to emphasize or set off text that you consider important for your audience to read. To create a text box, click the Text Box button (Insert tab | Text group), click the slide, and then drag this object to the desired location on the slide. Click inside the text box to add or paste text. You also can change the look and style of the text box characters by using formatting features (Home tab | Font group).

picture inserted and sized to cover entire slide

Note: To help you locate screen elements that are referenced in the step instructions, such as buttons and commands, this book uses red boxes to point to these screen elements.

Figure 3–2

Plan Ahead

Use the color wheel to determine color choices.

The color wheel is one of designers' basic tools. Twelve colors on the wheel are arranged in a specific order, with the three primary colors — red, yellow, and blue — forming a triangle. Between the primary colors are the secondary colors that are formed when the primary colors are mixed. For example, red and yellow mixed together form orange; red and blue form purple; and yellow and blue form green. The six other colors on the wheel are formed when the primary colors are mixed with the secondary colors.

Red, orange, and yellow are considered warm colors, and they display adjacent to each other on one side of the wheel. They are bold and lively, so you should use them when your message is intended to invigorate an audience and create a pleasing effect. Opposite the warm colors are the cool colors: green, blue, and purple. They generate a relaxing, calming atmosphere.

If you put a primary and secondary color together, such as red and purple, your slide will make a very bold and vivid statement. Be certain that effect is one you intend when planning your message.

Adjusting Picture Colors

Q&As
For a complete list of the Q&As found in many of the step-by-step sequences in this book, visit the PowerPoint 2010 Q&A Web page (scsite.com/ ppt2010/qa).

PowerPoint allows you to adjust colors to match or add contrast to slide elements by coloring pictures. The Color Picture gallery has a wide variety of preset formatting combinations. The thumbnails in the gallery display the more common color saturation, color tone, and recolor adjustments. **Color saturation** changes the intensity of colors. High saturation produces vivid colors; low saturation produces gray tones. **Color tone** affects the coolness, called blue, or the warmness, called orange, of pictures. When a digital camera does not measure the tone correctly, a **color cast** occurs, and, as a result, one color dominates the picture. **Recolor** effects convert the picture into a wide variety of hues. The more common are **grayscale**, which changes the color picture into black, white, and shades of gray, and **sepia**, which changes the picture colors into brown, gold, and yellow, reminiscent of a faded photo. You also can fine-tune the color adjustments by clicking Picture Color Options and More Variations commands in the Color gallery.

To Color a Picture

The Slipstream theme and text on Slides 1 and 3 have many shades of blue. The inserted pictures, in addition, have blue backgrounds. The following steps recolor the Slide 3 picture to coordinate with the blue colors on the slide.

1

- With Slide 3 displaying and the Bird Reflect picture selected, click the Color button (Picture Tools Format tab | Adjust group) to display the Color gallery (Figure 3–3).

Q&A Why does the Adjust group look different on my screen?

Your monitor is set to a different resolution. See Chapter 1 for an explanation of screen resolution and the appearance of the Ribbon.

Q&A Why are yellow borders surrounding the thumbnails in the Color Saturation and Color Tone areas in the gallery?

The image on Slide 3 currently has normal color saturation and a normal color tone.

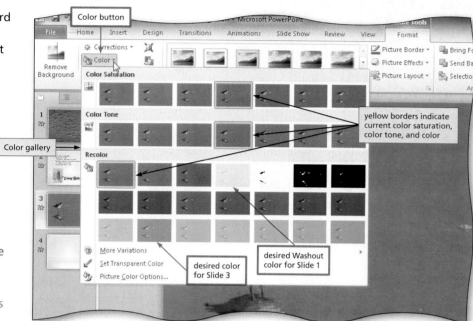

Figure 3–3

2

- Point to Blue, Accent color 1 Light (second picture in last row of Recolor area) to display a live preview of this adjustment on the picture.

Experiment

- Point to various thumbnails in the Recolor area and watch the hues change on the picture in Slide 3.

- Click Blue, Accent color 1 Light to apply this correction to the Bird Reflect picture (Figure 3–4).

Q&A Could I have applied this correction to the picture if it had been a background instead of a file inserted into the slide?

No. Artistic effects cannot be applied to backgrounds.

Figure 3–4

To Color a Second Picture

The Slide 1 picture has rich hues and is very prominent on the slide. To soften its appearance and to provide continuity with the Slide 3 picture, you can color this picture. The following steps color the picture on the title slide.

1 Display Slide 1 and then click the picture to select it. Click the Color button (Picture Tools Format tab | Adjust group) to display the Color gallery.

2 Click Washout (fourth picture in first row of Recolor area) to apply this correction to the Bird Reflect picture (Figure 3–5).

Figure 3–5

To Add an Artistic Effect to a Picture

Artists use a variety of techniques to create effects in their paintings. For example, they can vary the amount of paint on their brushstroke, use fine bristles to add details, mix colors to increase or decrease intensity, and smooth their paints together to blend the colors. You, likewise, can add similar effects to your pictures using PowerPoint's built-in artistic effects. The following steps add an artistic effect to the Slide 3 picture.

1

- With the Birds in Sky picture selected in Slide 1, click the Artistic Effects button (Picture Tools Format tab | Adjust group) to display the Artistic Effects gallery (Figure 3–6).

Q&A Why does the Adjust group look different on my screen?

Your monitor is set to a different resolution. See Chapter 1 for an explanation of screen resolution and the appearance of the Ribbon.

Q&A Why is a yellow border surrounding the first thumbnail in the gallery?

The first thumbnail shows a preview of the image on Slide 1 with no artistic effect applied.

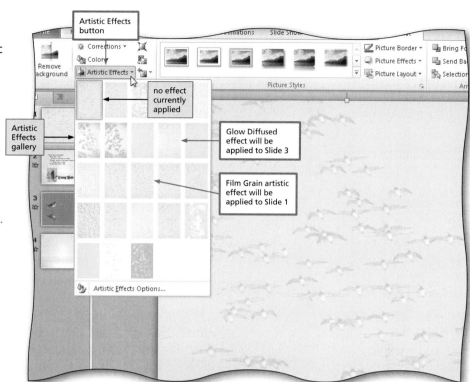

Figure 3–6

2

- Point to Film Grain (third picture in third row) to display a live preview of this adjustment on the picture.

Experiment

- Point to various thumbnails and watch the hues change on the picture in Slide 1.

- Click Film Grain to apply this correction to the Birds in Sky picture (Figure 3–7).

Q&A Must I adjust a picture by recoloring and applying an artistic effect?

No. You can apply either a color or an effect. You may prefer at times to mix these adjustments to create a unique image.

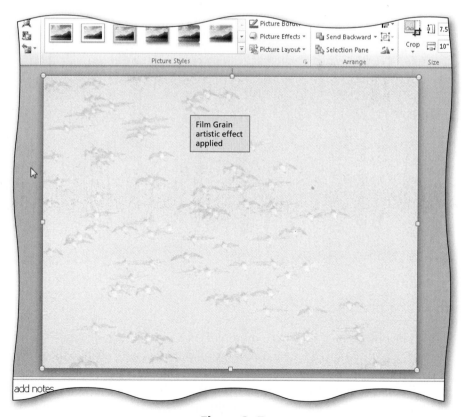

Figure 3–7

To Add an Artistic Effect to a Second Picture

The Slide 3 picture was softened when you applied a blue accent color. You can further change the images and provide continuity with the Slide 1 picture by applying an artistic effect. The following steps add an artistic effect to the Slide 3 picture.

1 Display Slide 3 and then click the picture to select it. If necessary, click the Picture Tools Format tab and then click the Artistic Effects button (Picture Tools Format tab | Adjust group) to display the Artistic Effects gallery.

2 Click Glow Diffused (fourth picture in second row) to apply this effect to the Bird Reflect picture (Figure 3–8).

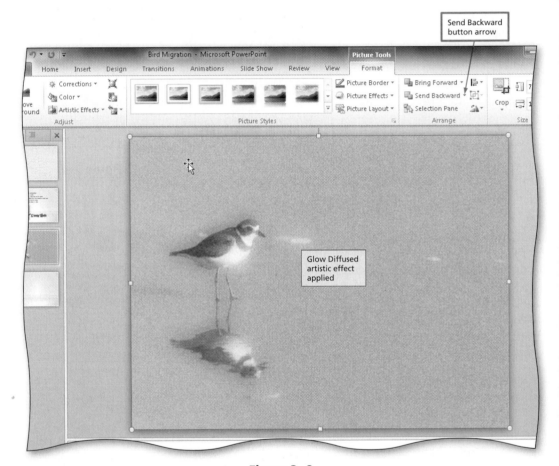

Figure 3–8

To Change the Stacking Order

The objects on a slide stack on top of each other, much like individual cards in a deck. On Slides 1 and 3, the pictures you inserted are on top of text placeholders. To change the order of these objects, you use the Bring Forward and Send Backward commands. **Bring Forward** moves an object toward the top of the stack, and **Send Backward** moves an object underneath another object. When you click the Bring Forward button arrow, PowerPoint displays a menu with an additional command, **Bring to Front**, which moves a selected object to the top of the stack. Likewise, when you click the Send Backward button arrow, the **Send to Back** button moves the selected object underneath all objects on the slide. The following steps arrange the Slide 3 and Slide 1 pictures by sending them to the bottom of the stack on each slide.

1

- With the Bird Reflect picture selected in Slide 3, click the Send Backward button arrow (Picture Tools Format tab | Arrange group) to display the Send Backward menu (Figure 3–9).

Q&A How can I see objects that are not on the top of the stack?

Press TAB or SHIFT+TAB to display each slide object.

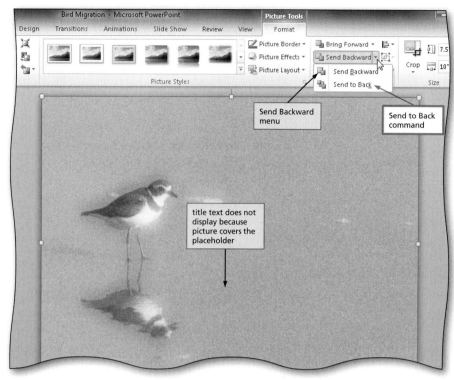

Figure 3–9

2

- Click Send to Back to move the picture underneath all slide objects (Figure 3–10).

Figure 3–10

3

- Display Slide 1, select the Birds in Sky picture, and then click the Send Backward button arrow (Picture Tools Format tab | Arrange group).
- Click Send to Back to move the picture underneath all slide objects (Figure 3–11).

Figure 3–11

Other Ways
1. Click Send to Back (Picture Tools Format tab | Arrange group), press K 2. Point to Send to Back on shortcut menu, click Send to Back

Modifying Placeholders and Deleting a Slide

BTW

BTWs
For a complete list of the BTWs found in the margins of this book, visit the PowerPoint 2010 BTW Web page (scsite.com/ppt2010/btw).

You have become familiar with inserting text and graphical content in the three types of placeholders: title, subtitle, and content. These placeholders can be moved, resized, and deleted to meet desired design requirements. In addition, placeholders can be added to a slide when needed. After you have modified the placeholder locations, you can view thumbnails of all your slides simultaneously by changing views.

In the following pages, you will perform these tasks:

1. Resize and move the Slide 1 title text placeholder.
2. Delete the Slide 1 subtitle text placeholder.
3. Align the Slide 1 and Slide 3 paragraph text.
4. Delete Slide 4.
5. Change views.

To Resize a Placeholder

The AutoFit button displays on the left side of the Slide 1 title text placeholder because the two lines of text exceed the placeholder's borders. PowerPoint attempts to reduce the font size when the text does not fit, and you can click this button to resize the existing text in the placeholder so the spillover text will fit within the borders. You also can resize the placeholder so that the letters fit within the rectangle. The following step increases the Slide 1 title text placeholder.

- With Slide 1 displaying, click somewhere in the title text paragraph to position the insertion point in the paragraph. Click the border of the title text placeholder to select it. Point to the bottom-middle sizing handle so that the mouse pointer changes to a two-headed arrow.

- Drag the bottom border downward to enlarge the text placeholder (Figure 3–12).

Q&A Can I drag other sizing handles to enlarge or shrink the placeholder?

Yes, you also can drag the left, right, top, and corner sizing handles to resize a placeholder.

Q&A How do the square sizing handles differ from circle sizing handles?

Dragging a square handle alters the shape of the text box so that it is wider or taller. Dragging a circle handle keeps the box in the same proportion and simply enlarges the overall shape.

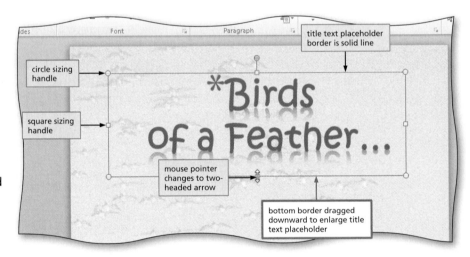

Figure 3–12

To Move a Placeholder

The theme layouts determine where the text and content placeholders display on the slide. If you desire to have a placeholder appear in a different area of the slide, you can move it to a new location. The Slide 1 title text placeholder currently displays in the upper third of the slide, but the text in this placeholder would be more aesthetically pleasing if it were moved toward the center of the slide. The following step moves the Slide 1 title text placeholder.

1

- With the Slide 1 title text placeholder border displaying as a solid line, point to an area of the bottom border between two sizing handles so that the mouse pointer changes to a four-headed arrow.

Q&A What if the placeholder border displays as a dotted line?

Click the border to change the line from dotted to solid.

Q&A Can I click any part of the border, or do I need to click the bottom edge?

You can click any of the four border lines.

- Drag the placeholder downward so that it overlaps part of the subtitle text placeholder (Figure 3–13).

- Click to set the placeholder in its new location.

Figure 3–13

To Delete a Placeholder

When you run a slide show, empty placeholders do not display. You may desire to delete unused placeholders from a slide so that they are not a distraction when you are designing slide content. The subtitle text placeholder on Slide 1 is not required for this presentation, so you can remove it. The following steps remove the Slide 1 subtitle text placeholder.

1 Click a border of the subtitle text placeholder so that it displays as a solid line or fine dots (Figure 3–14).

Q&A What if the placeholder border is displaying as a dotted line?

Click the border to change the line from dotted to solid or fine dots.

2 Press the DELETE key to remove the placeholder.

Q&A Can I click the Cut button (Home tab | Clipboard group) to delete the placeholder?

Yes. Clicking the Cut button deletes the placeholder if it does not contain any text.

BTW

Reusing Placeholders
If you need to show the same formatted placeholder on multiple slides, you may want to customize a slide master and insert a placeholder into a slide layout. Using a slide master saves you time because you do not need to type the same information in more than one slide. The slide master is useful when you have extremely long presentations. Every document theme has several slide masters that indicate the size and position of text and object placeholders. Any change you make to a slide master results in changing that component in every slide of the presentation.

Figure 3–14

Plan
Ahead

Vary paragraph alignment.
Designers use alignment within paragraphs to aid readability and to indicate relationships among slide elements. English language readers are accustomed to seeing paragraphs that are aligned left. When paragraphs are aligned right, the viewer's eyes are drawn to this unexpected text design. If your paragraph is short, consider centering or right-aligning the text for emphasis.

To Align Paragraph Text

The presentation theme determines the formatting characteristics of fonts and colors. It also establishes paragraph formatting, including the alignment of text. Some themes center the text paragraphs between the left and right placeholder borders, while others **left-align** the paragraph so that the first character of a text line is near the left border or **right-align** the paragraph so that the last character of a text line is near the right border. The paragraph also can be **justified** so that the text is aligned to both the left and right borders. When PowerPoint justifies text, it adds extras spaces between the words to fill the entire line.

The words, Birds of a Feather, are centered in the Slide 1 title text placeholder. Later, you will add clip art above the word, Feather, so you desire to left-align the paragraph to make room for this art. In addition, the words in the Slide 3 title text placeholder, Bird Migration, are covering the bird in the picture. You can right-align these words to uncover the bird in the lower-left corner. The following steps change the alignment of the Slide 1 and Slide 3 title placeholders.

1
- With the Home tab displayed, click somewhere in the title text paragraph of Slide 1 to position the insertion point in the paragraph to be formatted (Figure 3–15).

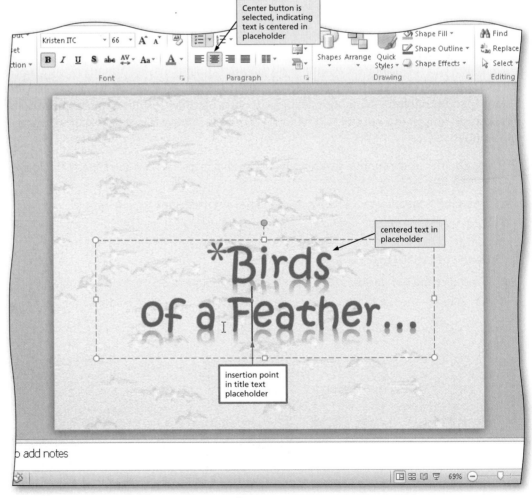

Figure 3–15

2

- Click the Align Text Left button (Home tab | Paragraph group) to left-align the paragraph (Figure 3–16).

Q&A What if I want to return the paragraph to center alignment?

Click the Center button (Home tab | Paragraph group).

3

- Display Slide 3. Click somewhere in the title text paragraph to position the insertion point in the paragraph to be formatted.

4

- Click the Align Text Right button (Home tab | Paragraph group) to right-align the paragraph.

Figure 3–16

5

- Move the Slide 3 title text placeholder downward so that it displays approximately as shown in Figure 3–17.

Figure 3–17

Other Ways		
1. Right-click paragraph, click Align Text Right button on Mini toolbar	Spacing tab (Paragraph dialog box), click Alignment box arrow, click Right, click OK button	Paragraph group), click Indents and Spacing tab (Paragraph dialog box), click Alignment box arrow, click Right, click OK button
2. Right-click paragraph, click Paragraph on shortcut menu, click Indents and	3. Click Paragraph Dialog Box Launcher (Home tab |	4. Press CTRL+R

To Delete a Slide

The Bird Migration presentation has a blank slide at the end. You decide that you will not use this slide, so you need to remove it from the file. The following steps delete Slide 4 from the presentation.

1

- Right-click the Slide 4 thumbnail in the Slides tab to display the shortcut menu (Figure 3–18).

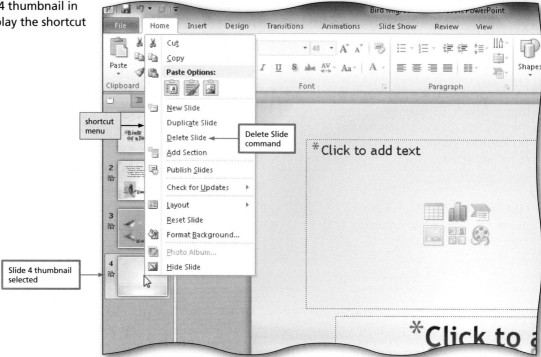

Figure 3–18

2

- Click Delete Slide to delete Slide 4 from the presentation (Figure 3–19).

Figure 3–19

Q&A

Can I delete multiple slides simultaneously?

Yes. If the slides are sequential, click the first slide you want to delete, press and hold the SHIFT key, click the last slide that you want to delete, right-click any selected slide, and then click Delete Slide on the shortcut menu. If the slides are not sequential, press and hold the CTRL key while you click each slide that you want to delete, right-click any selected slide, and then click Delete Slide on the shortcut menu.

Changing Views

You have been using Normal view to create and edit your slides. Once you completed your slides, you reviewed the final products by displaying each slide in Slide Show view, which occupies the full computer screen. You were able to view how the transitions, graphics, and effects will display in an actual presentation before an audience.

PowerPoint has other views to help review a presentation for content, organization, and overall appearance. Slide Sorter view allows you to look at several slides at one time. Reading view is similar to Slide Show view because each slide displays individually, but the slides do not fill the entire screen. Using this view, you easily can control the progression through the slides forward or backward with simple controls at the bottom of the window. Switching between Slide Sorter view, Reading view, and Normal view helps you review your presentation, assess whether the slides have an attractive design and adequate content, and make sure they are organized for the most impact. After reviewing the slides, you can change the view to Normal so that you may continue working on the presentation.

To Change Views

You have made several modifications to the slides, so you should check for balance and consistency. The following steps change the view from Normal view to Slide Sorter view, then Reading view, and back to Normal view.

1
• Click the Slide Sorter view button in the lower right of the PowerPoint window to display the presentation in Slide Sorter view (Figure 3–20).

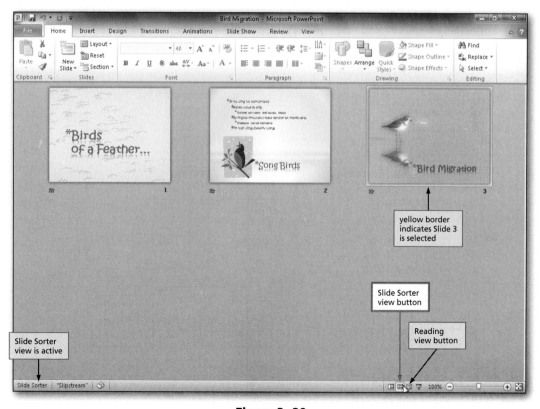

Figure 3–20

Q&A

Why is Slide 3 selected?

It is the current slide in the Slide pane.

- Click the Reading view button in the lower right of the PowerPoint window to display Slide 3 of the presentation in Reading view (Figure 3–21).

Figure 3–21

- Click the Previous button two times to display Slide 2 and then Slide 1.

- Click the Next button two times to advance through the presentation.

- Click the Menu button to display a menu of commonly used commands (Figure 3–22).

- Click End Show to return to Slide Sorter view, which is the view you were using before Reading view.

- Click the Normal view button to display the presentation in Normal view.

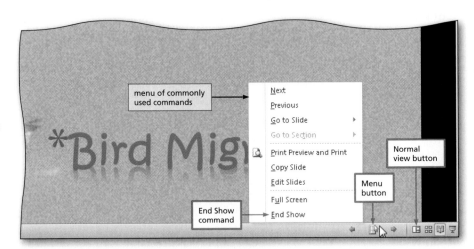

Figure 3–22

Copying and Modifying a Clip

Slide 1 (shown in Figure 3–1a on PPT 139) contains a modified version of a songbird. You may want to modify a clip art picture for various reasons. Many times, you cannot find a clip art picture that precisely illustrates your topic. For example, you want a picture of a red sports car, but the only available clip art picture is painted black.

Occasionally, you may want to remove or change a portion of a clip art picture or you might want to combine two or more clip art pictures. For example, you can use one clip art picture for the background and another picture as the foreground. Other times, you may want to combine a clip art picture with another type of object. In this presentation, the bird picture has a yellow background that is not required to display on the slide, so you will ungroup the clip art picture and remove the background.

Modifying the clip on Slide 1 requires several steps. You first must copy it using the Office Clipboard and then paste it in the desired location. The **Office Clipboard** is a temporary storage location that can hold a maximum of 24 text or graphics items copied from any Office program. The same procedure of copying and pasting objects works for copying and pasting text from one placeholder to another. In the following pages, you will perform these tasks:

1. Copy the clip from Slide 2 to Slide 1.
2. Zoom Slide 1 to examine the clip.
3. Ungroup the clip.
4. Edit and change the clip colors.
5. Delete a clip object.
6. Regroup the clip.

To Copy a Clip from One Slide to Another

The bird clip on Slide 2 also can display in a modified form on the title slide. The following steps copy this slide element from Slide 2 to Slide 1.

1

- Display Slide 2. With the Home tab displayed, click the bird clip to select it and then click the Copy button (Home tab | Clipboard group) (Figure 3–23).

Q&A Why are some words on Slide 2 underlined with red wavy lines?

Those words are not in PowerPoint's main or custom dictionaries, so PowerPoint indicates that they may be misspelled. For example, the word, Syringeal, is spelled correctly, but is not in PowerPoint's dictionaries.

2

- Display Slide 1 and then click the Paste button (Home tab | Clipboard group) to insert the bird clip into the title slide.

Q&A Is the clip deleted from the Office Clipboard when I paste it into the slide?

No.

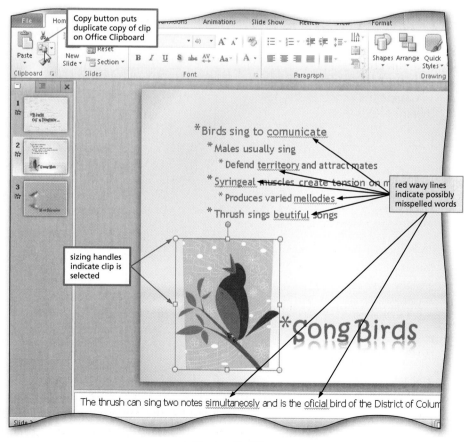

Figure 3–23

● Decrease the clip
size by dragging one
of the corner sizing
handles inward until
the clip is the size
shown in Figure 3–24.
Drag the clip to the
location shown in
this figure.

Figure 3–24

To Zoom a Slide

You will be modifying small areas of the clip, so it will help you select the relevant pieces if the graphic is
enlarged. The following step changes the zoom to 150 percent.

● Drag the Zoom slider to the right
to change the zoom level to 150%
(Figure 3–25).

Other Ways

1. Click Zoom button
   (View tab | Zoom
   group), change
   percentage in Percent
   text box (Zoom dialog
   box), click OK button

2. Click Zoom In button at
   end of slider

3. Click Zoom level on left
   side of slider, change
   percentage in Percent
   text box (Zoom dialog
   box), click OK button

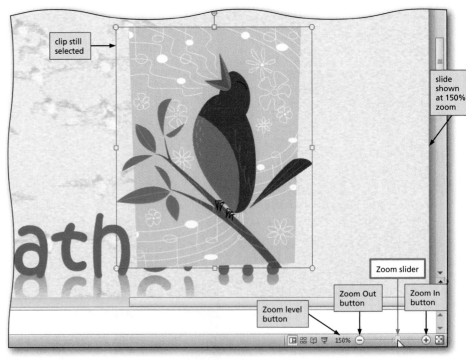

Figure 3–25

To Ungroup a Clip

The next step is to ungroup the bird clip on Slide 1. When you **ungroup** a clip art picture, PowerPoint breaks it into its component objects. A clip may be composed of a few individual objects or several complex groups of objects. These groups can be ungrouped repeatedly until they decompose into individual objects. Because a clip art picture is a collection of complex groups of objects, you may need to ungroup a complex object into less complex objects before being able to modify a specific object. When you ungroup a clip and click the Yes button in the Microsoft PowerPoint dialog box, PowerPoint converts the clip to a PowerPoint object. The following steps ungroup a clip.

1

- With the bird clip selected, click Format on the Ribbon to display the Picture Tools Format tab.

- Click the Group button (Picture Tools Format tab | Arrange group) to display the Group menu (Figure 3–26).

Q&A

Why does the Group button look different on my screen?

Your monitor is set to a different resolution. See Chapter 1 for an explanation of screen resolution and the appearance of the Ribbon.

Figure 3–26

2

- Click Ungroup on the Group menu to display the Microsoft PowerPoint dialog box (Figure 3–27).

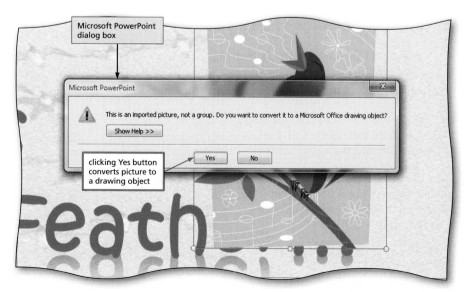

Figure 3–27

- Click the Yes button (Microsoft PowerPoint dialog box) to convert the clip to a Microsoft Office drawing.

Q&A What happens if I click the No button?

The clip will remain displayed on the slide as a clip art picture and will not ungroup.

- Click Format on the Ribbon to display the Drawing Tools Format tab. Click the Group button (Drawing Tools Format tab | Arrange group) and then click Ungroup again.

Q&A Why does the Drawing Tools Format tab show different options this time?

The clip has become a drawing object, so tools related to drawing now display.

- With the Drawing Tools Format tab displayed, click the Group button (Drawing Tools Format tab | Arrange group), and then click Ungroup a third time to display the objects that constitute the bird clip (Figure 3–28).

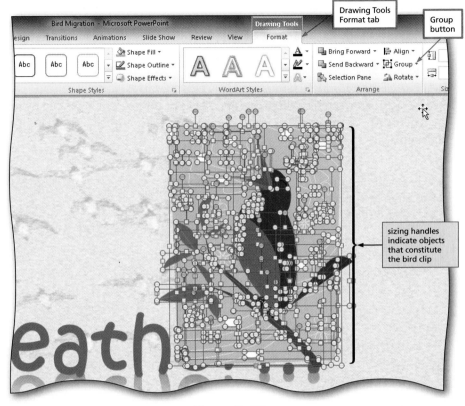

Figure 3–28

Q&A Why do all those circles and squares display in the clip?

The circles and squares are sizing handles for each of the clip's objects, which resemble pieces of a jigsaw puzzle.

Other Ways

1. Right-click clip, point to Group on shortcut menu, click Ungroup
2. Press SHIFT+CTRL+G

To Change the Color of a Clip Object

Now that the bird picture is ungrouped, you can change the color of the objects. The clip is composed of hundreds of objects, so you must exercise care when selecting the correct object to modify. The following steps change the color of the bird's mouth and the leaves.

- Click outside the clip area to display the clip without the sizing handles around the objects.

- Click the bird's mouth to display sizing handles around the colored area (Figure 3–29).

Q&A What if I selected a different area by mistake?

Click outside the clip and retry.

Figure 3–29

- Click the Shape Fill button arrow (Drawing Tools Format tab | Shape Styles group) to display the Shape Fill gallery.

- Point to Yellow in the Standard Colors area (fourth color) to display a live preview of the mouth color (Figure 3–30).

 **Experiment**

- Point to various colors and watch the bird's mouth color change.

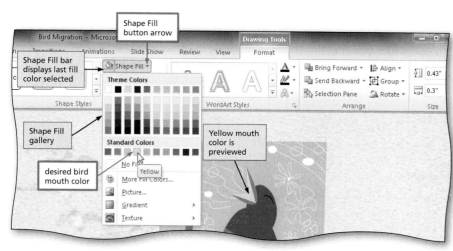

Figure 3–30

- Click the color Yellow to change the bird's mouth color.

Q&A Why is the bar under the Shape Fill button now yellow?

The button displays the last fill color selected.

- Click a leaf on the branch to display the sizing handles around the colored area (Figure 3–31).

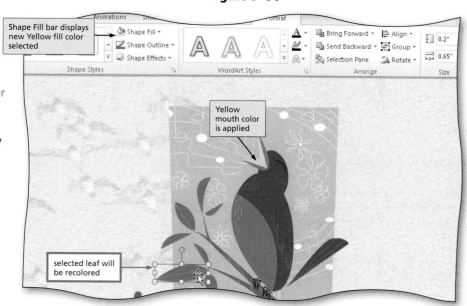

Figure 3–31

4

- Click the Shape Fill button arrow (Drawing Tools Format tab | Shape Styles group) and then point to Green, Accent 3 in the Theme Colors area (seventh color in first row) to display a live preview of the color of the selected leaf in the graphic (Figure 3–32).

 **Experiment**

- Point to various colors and watch the leaf color change.

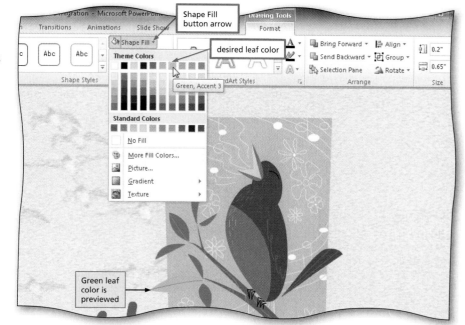

Figure 3–32

5

- Click the Green, Accent 3 color to change the leaf color.

6

- Click another leaf on the branch to select it.

- Click the Shape Fill button to change the leaf color to Green, Accent 3 (Figure 3–33).

Q&A Why did I not need to click the Shape Fill button arrow to select this color?

PowerPoint uses the last fill color selected. This color displays in the bar under the bucket icon on the button.

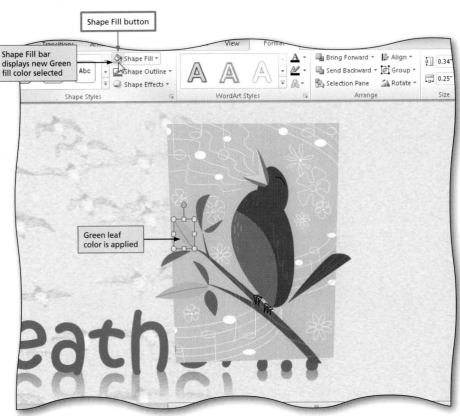

Figure 3–33

7

- Repeat Step 6 until all the leaves have been recolored (Figure 3–34).

Q&A Can I open the Microsoft Clip Organizer when I am not using PowerPoint?

Yes. On the Start menu, point to All Programs, point to Microsoft Office, point to Microsoft Office 2010 Tools, and then click Microsoft Clip Organizer.

Other Ways

1. Right-click object, click Format Shape on shortcut menu, click Color button

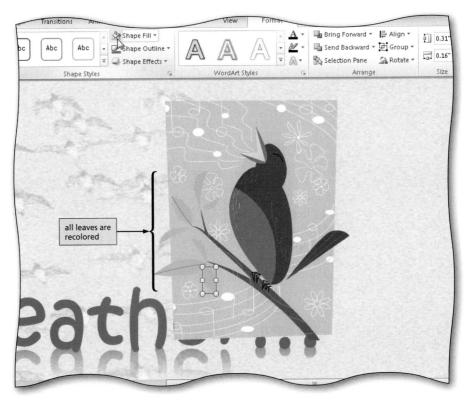

Figure 3–34

To Delete a Clip Object

With the bird mouth and leaf colors changed, you want to delete the gold background object. The following steps delete this object.

● Click the background in any area where the gold color displays to select this object (Figure 3–35).

Q&A   Can I select multiple objects so I can delete them simultaneously?

Yes. While pressing the SHIFT key, click the unwanted elements to select them.

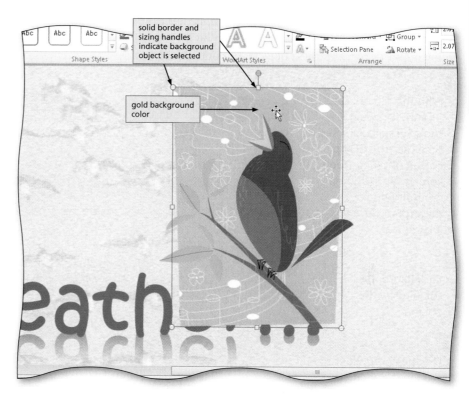

Figure 3–35

● Press the DELETE key to delete this object (Figure 3–36).

Q&A   Should the white musical staff display on the slide?

Yes. It is part of the bird clip.

Figure 3–36

To Regroup Objects

When you ungrouped the bird clip, you eliminated the embedding data or linking information that tied all the individual pieces together. If you attempt to move or size this clip now, you might encounter difficulties because it consists of hundreds of objects and is no longer one unified piece. Dragging or sizing affects only a selected object, not the entire collection of objects, so you must use caution when objects are not completely regrouped. All of the ungrouped objects in the bird clip must be regrouped so they are not accidentally moved or manipulated. The following steps regroup these objects into one object.

1

- With the clip selected, click the Drawing Tools Format tab and then click the Group button (Drawing Tools Format tab | Arrange group) to display the Group menu (Figure 3–37).

2

- Click Regroup to combine all the objects.

3

- Use the Zoom slider to change the zoom level to 69%.

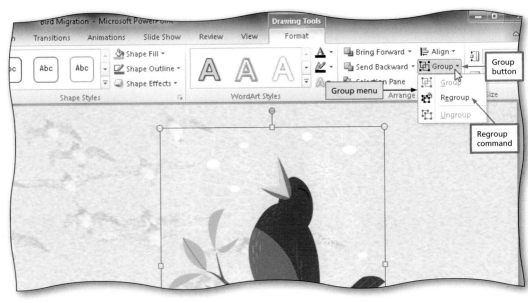

Figure 3–37

Other Ways
1. Right-click clip, point to Group on shortcut menu, click Regroup
2. Press CTRL+G

Plan Ahead

Use multimedia selectively.

PowerPoint makes it easy to insert multimedia into a presentation. Well-produced video clips add value when they help explain a procedure or show movement that cannot be captured in a photograph. Music can help calm or energize an audience, when appropriate. A sound, such as applause when a correct answer is given, can emphasize an action. Before you insert these files on a slide, however, consider whether they really add any value to your overall slide show. If you are inserting them just because you can, you might want to reconsider your decision. Audiences quickly tire of extraneous sounds and movement on slides, and they will find these media clips annoying. Keep in mind that the audience's attention should focus primarily on the presenter; extraneous or inappropriate media files may divert their attention and, in turn, decrease the quality of the presentation.

Break Point: If you wish to take a break, this is a good place to do so. Be sure to save the Bird Migration file again and then you can quit PowerPoint. To resume at a later time, start PowerPoint, open the file called Bird Migration, and continue following the steps from this location forward.

Adding Media to Slides

Media files can enrich a presentation if they are used correctly. Movies files can have two formats: digital video produced with a camera and editing software or animated GIF (Graphics Interchange Format) files composed of multiple images combined into a single file. Sound files can be from the Microsoft Clip Organizer, files stored on your computer, or an audio track on a CD. To hear the sounds, you need a sound card and speakers on your system.

In the following pages, you will perform these tasks:

1. Insert a video file into Slide 3.
2. Trim the video file so only the final few seconds play.
3. Add video options that determine the clip's appearance and playback.
4. Insert audio files.
5. Add audio options that determine the clips' appearance and playback.
6. Add a video style to the Slide 3 clip.
7. Resize the video.
8. Insert a movie clip into Slide 1.

To Insert a Video File

Slide 3 has the title, Bird Migration, and you have a video clip that is composed of many scenes featuring various animals and birds. A short segment of this clip shows a flock of birds on a beach, and you want to use only this part of the clip in your presentation. PowerPoint allows you to insert this clip into your slide and then trim the file so that just a portion will play when you preview the clip or run the slide show. This clip is available on the Data Files for Students. See the inside back cover of this book for instructions on downloading the Data Files for Students, or contact your instructor for more information about accessing the required file. The following steps insert this video clip into Slide 3.

1

- Display Slide 3 and then display the Insert tab. With your USB flash drive connected to one of the computer's USB ports, click the Insert Video button (Insert tab | Media group) to display the Insert Video dialog box.

- If the list of files and folders on the selected USB flash drive are not displayed in the Insert Video dialog box, double-click your USB flash drive to display them.

- Click Wildlife to select the file (Figure 3–38).

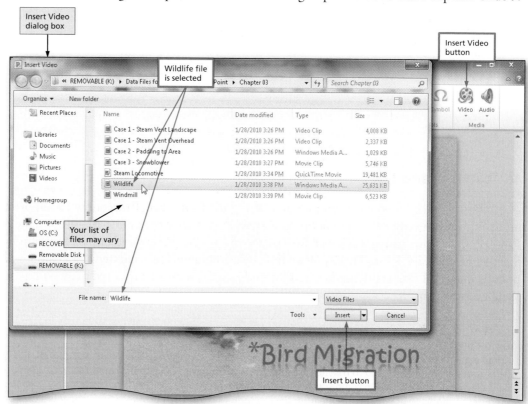

Figure 3–38

2

- Click the Insert button (Insert Video dialog box) to insert the movie clip into Slide 3 (Figure 3–39).

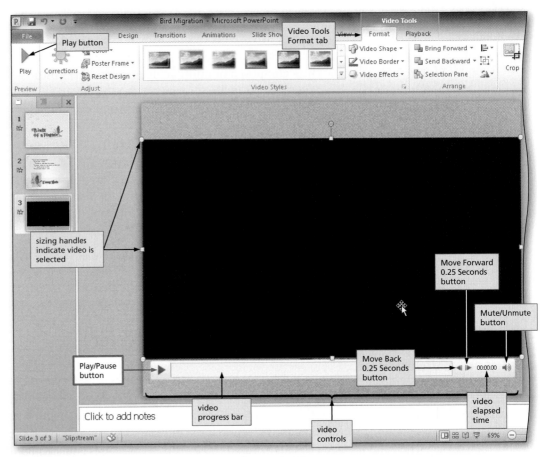

Figure 3–39

Q&A

Can I adjust the color of a video clip?

Yes. You correct the brightness and contrast, and you also recolor a video clip using the same methods you learned in this chapter to color a picture.

To Trim a Video File

The Wildlife video has a running time of slightly more than 30 seconds. The approximately six-second segment that you want to use in your presentation begins 24 seconds into the file and finishes at the end of the clip. PowerPoint's **Trim Video** feature allows you to trim the beginning and end of your clip by designating your desired Start Time and End Time. These precise time measurements are accurate to one-thousandth of a second. The start point is indicated by a green marker, and the end point is indicated by a red marker. The following steps trim the Wildlife video clip.

BTW

Using Codecs

Digital media file sizes often are quite large, so video and audio content developers use a codec (**co**mpressor/**dec**ompressor) to reduce the required storage space and to transfer the files across the Internet quickly and smoothly. Your computer can play any compressed file if the specific codec used to compress the file is available on your computer. If the codec is not installed or is not recognized, your computer attempts to download this file from the Internet. Microsoft Windows Media Encoder is a free program that makes some media files compatible with PowerPoint.

1

- With the video clip selected on Slide 3, click the Play/Pause button to play the entire video.

Q&A Can I play the video by clicking the Play button in the Preview group?

Yes. This Play button plays the entire clip. You may prefer to click the Play/Pause button displayed in the Video Controls to stop the video and examine one of the frames.

- Click Playback on the Ribbon to display the Video Tools Playback tab. Click the Trim Video button (Editing group) to display the Trim Video dialog box (Figure 3–40).

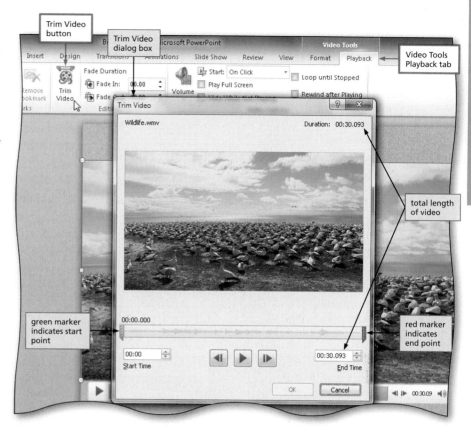

Figure 3–40

2

- Point to the start point, which is indicated by the green marker on the left side, so that the mouse pointer changes to a two-headed arrow.

- Drag the green marker to the right until the Start Time is 00:24:634 (Figure 3–41).

Q&A Can I specify the start or end times without dragging the markers?

Yes. You can enter the time in the Start Time or End Time boxes, or you can click the Start Time or End Time box arrows. You also can click the Next Frame and Previous Frame buttons (Trim Video dialog box).

Q&A How would I indicate an end point if I want the clip to end at a time other than at the end of the clip?

You would drag the red marker to the left until the desired end time displays.

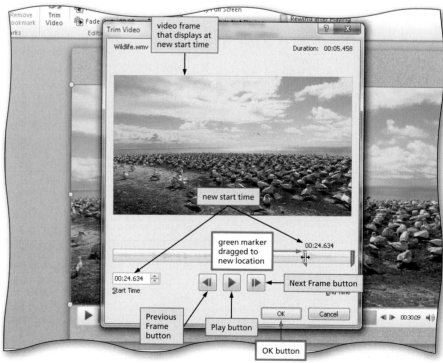

Figure 3–41

3

- Click the Play button (Trim Video dialog box) to review the shortened video clip.

- Click the OK button to set the Start Time and End Time and to close the Trim Video dialog box.

Other Ways

1. Right-click clip, click Trim Video on shortcut menu

To Add Video Options

Once the video clip is inserted into Slide 3, you can specify options that affect how the file is displayed and played. For example, you can have the video play automatically when the slide is displayed, or you can click the slide when you are ready to start the playback. You also can have the video fill the entire slide, which is referred to as **full screen**. If you decide to play the slide show automatically and have it display full screen, you can drag the video frame to the gray area off the slide so that it does not display briefly before going to full screen. You can select the Loop until Stopped option to have the video repeat until you click the next slide, or you can choose to not have the video frame display on the slide until you click the slide.

If your video clip has recorded sounds, the volume controls give you the option to set how loudly this audio will play. They also allow you to mute the sound so that your audience will hear no background noise or music.

The following steps add the options of playing the video full screen automatically when Slide 3 is displayed and also mutes the background music recorded on the video clip.

1
- If necessary, click Playback on the Ribbon to display the Video Tools Playback tab. Click the Start box (Video Tools Playback tab | Video Options group) to view the Start menu (Figure 3–42).

Q&A

What does the On Click option do?

The video clip would begin playing when a presenter clicks the slide during the slide show.

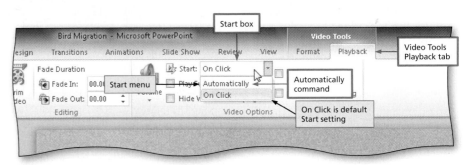

Figure 3–42

2
- Click Automatically in the Start menu (Figure 3–43).

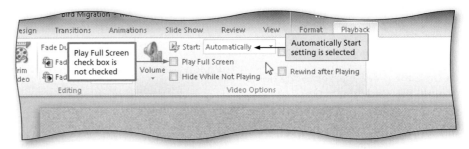

Figure 3–43

3
- Click the Play Full Screen check box (Video Tools Playback tab | Video Options group) to place a check mark in it.

- Click the Volume button (Video Tools Playback tab | Video Options group) to display the Volume menu (Figure 3–44).

4
- Click Mute in the Volume menu.

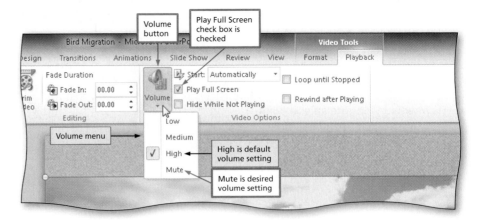

Figure 3–44

To Insert an Audio File

Avid bird watchers listen to the songs and calls birds make to each other. The Microsoft Clip Organizer and Office.com have several of these sounds in audio files that you can download and insert into your presentation. Once these audio files are inserted into a slide, you can add options that specify how long and how loudly the clip will play; these options are similar to the video options you just selected for the Wildlife video clip. The following steps insert an audio clip into Slide 3.

1

- With Slide 3 displaying, click Insert on the Ribbon to display the Insert tab and then click the Insert Audio button arrow (Insert tab | Media group) to display the Insert Audio menu (Figure 3–45).

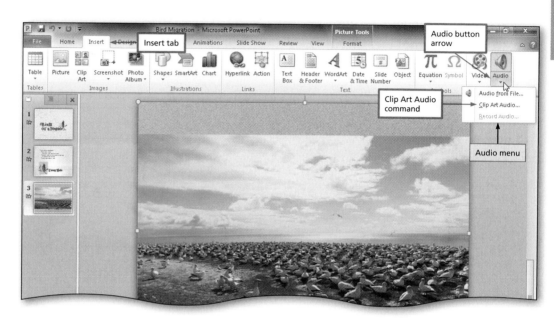

Figure 3–45

2

- Click Clip Art Audio in the Insert Audio menu to open the Clip Art task pane.

- Click the 'Results should be' box arrow and then click the 'All media types' check box to remove the check mark from each of the four types of media files.

- Click the Audio check box to place a check mark in it (Figure 3–46).

Q&A
Can I use this technique to search solely for videos, photographs, or illustrations?

Yes. You also can search for a combination of these file types, such as both video and audio files.

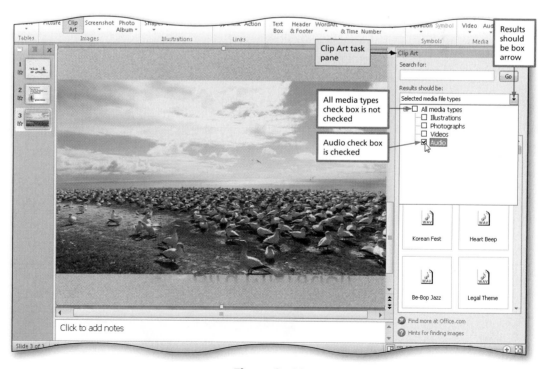

Figure 3–46

3

- If necessary, delete any letters that are present in the Search for text box and then type **Glade Birds** in the Search for text box. If necessary, click the 'Include Office.com content' check box to select it.

- Click the Go button so that the Microsoft Clip Organizer will search for and display all clips having the keyword or title, Glade Birds.

4

- Point to the Glade Birds clip to display the properties of this file (Figure 3–47).

Q&A
What if the Glade Birds audio clip is not shown in my Clip Art task pane?

Select a similar clip. Your clips may be different depending on the clips installed on your computer and if you have an active Internet connection.

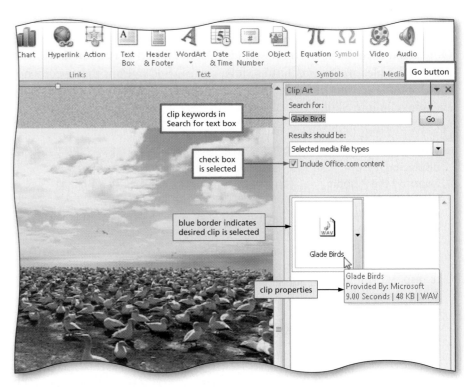

Figure 3–47

Q&A
What are the properties associated with this clip?

The properties include the number of seconds of playing time, the file size, and the type of audio file. This file is a **Windows waveform (.wav)** file, which uses a standard format to encode and communicate music and sound between computers, music synthesizers, and instruments.

5

- Right-click the Glade Birds clip to select the clip and to display the Edit menu (Figure 3–48).

Figure 3–48

6

- Click Preview/
  Properties to display
  the Preview/Properties
  dialog box and to hear
  the clip (Figure 3–49).

Q&A What are the
words listed in the
Keywords box?

Those words are the
search terms associated
with the file. If you
enter any of those
words in the Search for
text box, this audio file
would display in the
results list.

Q&A Can I preview the clip
again?

Yes. Click the Play
button in the Preview/
Properties dialog box.

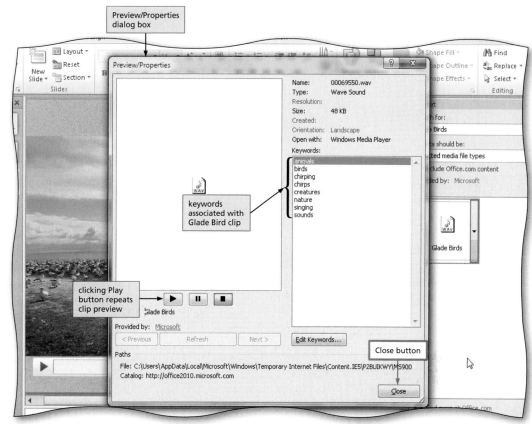

Figure 3–49

7

- Click the Close button
  (Preview/Properties
  dialog box) to close
  the dialog box.

- Click Glade Birds in
  the results list (Clip Art
  task pane) to insert
  that file into Slide 3
  (Figure 3–50).

Q&A Why does a sound icon
display in the video?

The icon indicates an
audio file is inserted.

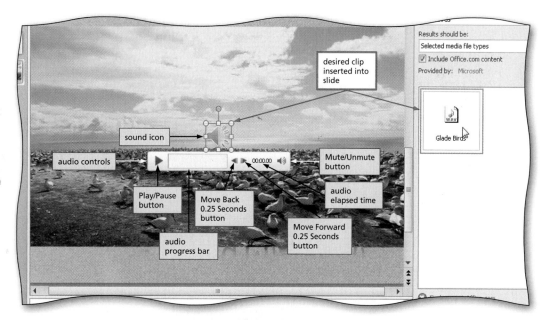

Figure 3–50

Q&A Do the Audio Controls buttons have the same functions as the Video Controls buttons that
displayed when I inserted the Wildlife clip?

Yes. The controls include playing and pausing the sound, moving back or forward 0.25
seconds, audio progress, elapsed time, and muting or unmuting the sound.

8
- Drag the sound icon to the upper-left corner of the slide (Figure 3–51).

Q&A Must I move the icon on the slide?

No. Although your audience will not see the icon when you run the slide show, it is easier for you to see the media elements when they are separated on the slide rather than stacked on top of each other.

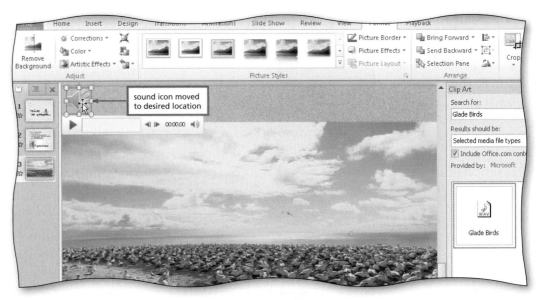

Figure 3–51

To Add Audio Options

Once an audio clip is inserted into a slide, you can specify options that control playback and appearance. As with the video options you applied to the Wildlife clip, the audio clip can play either automatically or when clicked, it can repeat the clip while a particular slide is displayed, and you can drag the sound icon off the slide and set the volume.

The following steps add the options of starting automatically and playing until the slide no longer is displayed, hiding the sound icon on the slide, and increasing the volume.

1
- Click Playback on the Ribbon to display the Audio Tools Playback tab. Click the Start box (Audio Tools Playback tab | Audio Options group) to display the Start box menu (Figure 3–52).

2
- Click Automatically in the Start menu.

Q&A Does the On Click option function the same way for an audio clip as On Click does for a video clip?

Yes. If you were to select On Click, the sound would begin playing only after the presenter clicks Slide 1 during a presentation.

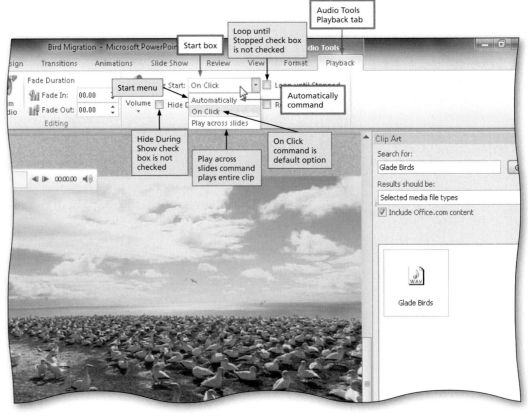

Figure 3–52

3

- Click the Loop until Stopped check box (Audio Tools Playback tab | Audio Options group) to place a check mark in it.

Q&A What is the difference between the Loop until Stopped option and the Play across slides option?

The audio clip in the Loop until Stopped option repeats for as long as one slide is displayed. In contrast, the Play across slides option clip would play only once, but it would continue to play while other slides in the presentation are displayed. Once the end of the clip is reached, the sound would end and not repeat.

4

- Click the Hide During Show check box (Video Tools Playback tab | Audio Options group) to place a check mark in it (Figure 3–53).

Q&A Why would I want the icon to display during the show?

If you had selected the On Click start option, you would need to find this icon on the slide and click it to start playing the clip.

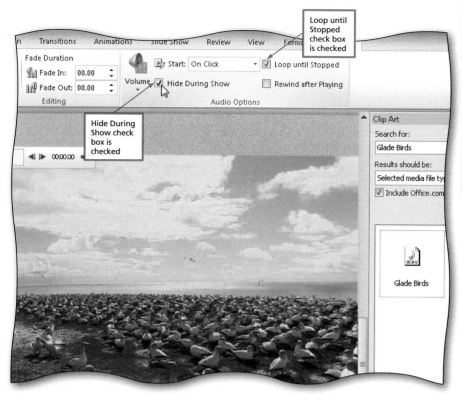

Figure 3–53

To Insert an Additional Audio File and Set Options

Having an audio clip play when Slide 1 is displayed would add interest and help set the tone of the presentation. Only one bird appears on that slide, and it appears to be singing heartily. A single bird singing would coordinate nicely with this clip art image. The following steps insert a songbird audio clip into Slide 1 and set playback options.

1 Display Slide 1, delete any letters that are present in the Search for text box, and then type **Birds at dawn** in the Search for text box (Clip Art task pane), and search for this audio clip.

2 Insert the Birds at dawn clip into Slide 1 and then drag the sound icon to the lower-left corner of the slide.

3 Close the Clip Art task pane.

4 Display the Audio Tools Playback tab. Click the Start box (Audio Tools Playback tab | Audio Options group) and then click Automatically in the Start menu.

5 Click the Loop until Stopped check box (Audio Tools Playback tab | Audio Options group) to place a check mark in it.

BTW

Playing Audio Continuously
You can play one audio file throughout an entire presentation instead of only when one individual slide is displayed. When you select the 'Play across slides' option in the Start box (Audio Tools Playback tab | Audio Options group), the audio clip will play continuously as you advance through the slides in your presentation. If you select this option, be certain the length of the clip exceeds the total time you will display all slides in your slide show.

6 Click the Hide During Show check box (Audio Tools Playback tab | Audio Options group).

7 Click the Volume button (Audio Tools Playback tab | Audio Options group) and then change the volume to Medium (Figure 3–54).

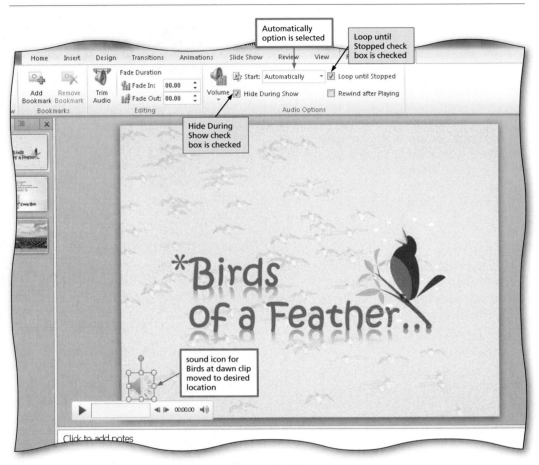

Figure 3–54

To Add a Video Style

The Wildlife video clip on Slide 3 displays full screen when it is playing, but you can increase the visual appeal of the clip when it is not playing by applying a video style. The video styles are similar to the picture styles you applied in Chapter 2 and include various shapes, angles, borders, and reflections. The following steps apply a video style to the Wildlife clip on Slide 3.

1

- Display Slide 3 and select the video. Click Format on the Ribbon to display the Video Tools Format tab (Figure 3–55).

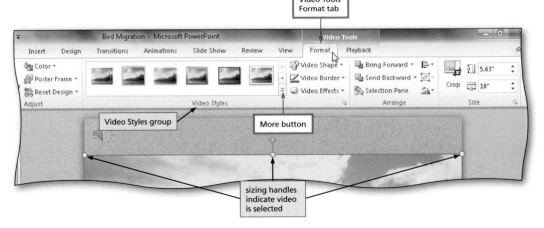

Figure 3–55

2

- With the video selected, click the More button in the Video Styles gallery (Video Tools Format tab | Video Styles group) (shown in Figure 3–55) to expand the gallery.

- Point to Bevel Perspective in the Intense area of the Video Styles gallery to display a live preview of that style applied to the video on the slide (Figure 3–56).

 Experiment

- Point to various picture styles in the Video Styles gallery and watch the style of the video frame change in the document window.

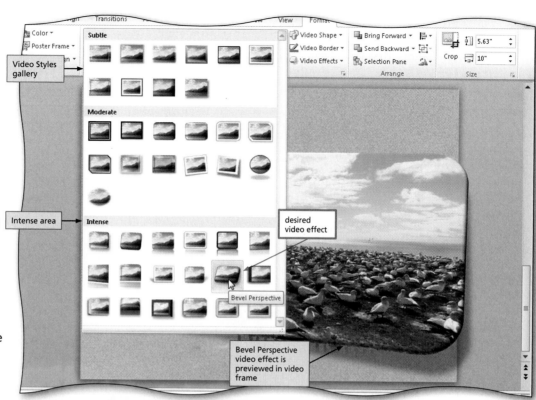

Figure 3–56

3

- Click Bevel Perspective in the Video Styles gallery to apply the style to the selected video (Figure 3–57).

Q&A Can I preview the movie clip?

Yes. Point to the clip and then click the Play/Pause button on the Video Controls below the video.

Q&A Can I add a border to a video style?

Yes. You add a border using the same method you learned in Chapter 2 to add a border to a picture. Click the Video Border button (Video Tools Format tab | Video Styles gallery) and then select a border line weight and color.

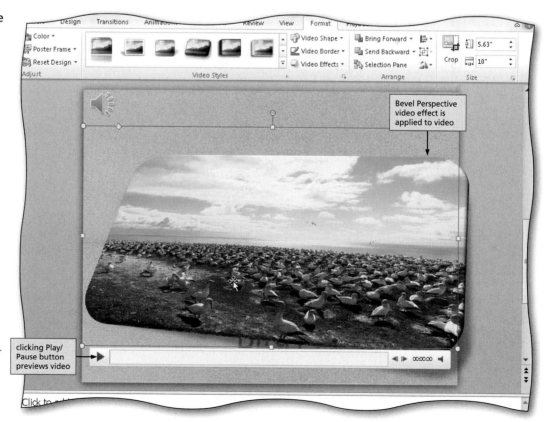

Figure 3–57

To Resize a Video

The Wildlife video size can be decreased to fill the space on the right side of the slide. You resize a video clip in the same manner that you resize clip art and pictures. The following steps resize this video using a sizing handle.

- With the video clip selected, drag the lower-left corner sizing handle on the photograph diagonally inward until the photograph is resized to approximately 3.9″ × 6.93″.

- Drag the clip to the location shown in Figure 3–58.

Figure 3–58

To Insert a Movie Clip

PowerPoint classifies animated GIF files as a type of video or movie because the clips have movement or action. These files are commonplace on Web sites. They also are found in PowerPoint presentations when you want to call attention to material on a particular slide. You can insert them into a PowerPoint presentation in the same manner that you insert video and audio files. They play automatically when the slide is displayed. The following steps insert a music notes video clip into Slide 1.

1

- Display Slide 1 and then display the Insert tab.

- Click the Picture button (Insert tab | Images group) to display the Insert Picture dialog box.

- If necessary, navigate to the Chapter 3 files on your USB drive.

- Click Music Notes to select the file (Figure 3–59).

 Why does my list of files look different?

The list of picture files can vary depending upon the contents of your USB drive and the organization of those files into folders for each chapter.

Q&A **Can I search for animated GIF files in the Microsoft Clip Organizer?**

Yes. Click the Video button arrow (Insert tab | Media group), click Clip Art Video, click the Videos check box (Clip Art task pane), type the search text, and then click the Go button.

Figure 3–59

2

- Click the Insert button (Insert Picture dialog box) to insert the Music Notes animated GIF clip into Slide 1.

- Resize the clip so that it is approximately 1" × 1.47".

- Drag the clip to the location shown in Figure 3–60.

Q&A **Why is the animation not showing?**

Animated GIF files move only in Slide Show view and Reading view.

Figure 3–60

Break Point: If you wish to take a break, this is a good place to do so. Be sure to save the Bird Migration file again and then you can quit PowerPoint. To resume at a later time, start PowerPoint, open the file called Bird Migration, and continue following the steps from this location forward.

BTW

Revising Your Text
Generating ideas, revising slides, editing graphics and text, and then proofreading all slide text are required as part of the development process. A good PowerPoint developer has the ability to write and then revise slide content. Multiple drafts generally are needed to complete a successful presentation. PowerPoint's Find and Replace feature is useful if you need to change all instances of a word throughout a large presentation when you are revising slides.

Reviewing and Revising Individual Slides

The text and graphics for all slides in the Bird Migration presentation have been entered. Once you complete a slide show, you might decide to change elements. PowerPoint provides several tools to assist you with making changes. They include finding and replacing text, inserting a synonym, and checking spelling. The following pages discuss these tools.

Replace Dialog Box

At times, you might want to change all occurrences of a word or phrase to another word or phrase. For example, an instructor may have one slide show to accompany a lecture for several introductory classes, and he wants to update slides with the particular class name and section that appear on several slides. He manually could change the characters, but PowerPoint includes an efficient method of replacing one word with another. The Find and Replace feature automatically locates specific text and then replaces it with desired text.

In some cases, you may want to replace only certain occurrences of a word or phrase, not all of them. To instruct PowerPoint to confirm each change, click the Find Next button in the Replace dialog box instead of the Replace All button. When PowerPoint locates an occurrence of the text, it pauses and waits for you to click either the Replace button or the Find Next button. Clicking the Replace button changes the text; clicking the Find Next button instructs PowerPoint to disregard that particular instance and look for the next occurrence of the Find what text.

To Find and Replace Text

While reviewing your slides, you realize that you could give more specific information regarding the type of thrush discussed in Slide 2. The Wood Thrush's songs especially are melodic and beautiful, so you decide to add the word, Wood, to the bird's name. In addition, you want to capitalize the word, Thrush, because it is a specific type of thrush. To perform this action, you can use PowerPoint's Find and Replace feature, which automatically locates each occurrence of a word or phrase and then replaces it with specified text. The word, thrush, displays twice on Slide 2. The following steps use Find and Replace to replace all occurrences of the word, thrush, with the words, Wood Thrush.

BTW

Matching Case and Finding Whole Words
Two options in the Replace dialog box are useful when revising slides. Match case maintains the upper- or lowercase letters within a word, such as a capitalized word at the beginning of a sentence. In addition, the 'Find whole words only' option specifies that PowerPoint makes replacements only when the word typed in the Find what box is a complete word and is not embedded within another word. For example, if you want to change the word 'diction' to 'pronunciation,' clicking the 'Find whole words only' option prevents PowerPoint from changing the word, dictionary, to 'pronunciationary.'

1

- Display the Home tab and then display Slide 2. Click the Replace button (Home tab | Editing group) to display the Replace dialog box.

- Type **thrush** in the Find what text box (Replace dialog box).

- Press the TAB key. Type **Wood Thrush** in the Replace with text box (Figure 3–61).

Do I need to display the slide that contains the words for which I want to search?

No. But to allow you to see the results of this search and replace action, you can display the slide where the changes will occur.

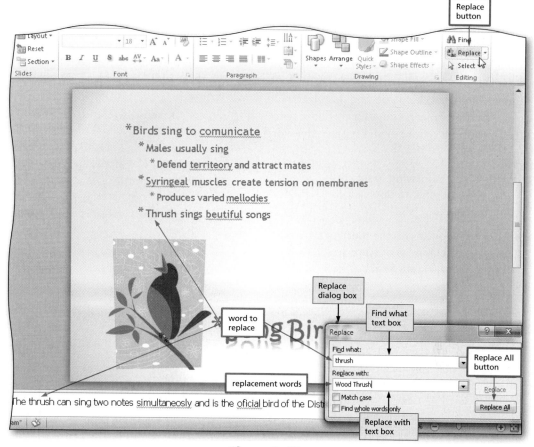

Figure 3–61

2

- Click the Replace All button (Replace dialog box) to instruct PowerPoint to replace all occurrences of the Find what word, thrush, with the Replace with words, Wood Thrush (Figure 3–62).

If I accidentally replaced the wrong text, can I undo this replacement?

Yes. Click the Undo button on the Quick Access Toolbar to undo all replacements. If you had clicked the Replace button instead of the Replace All button, PowerPoint would undo only the most recent replacement.

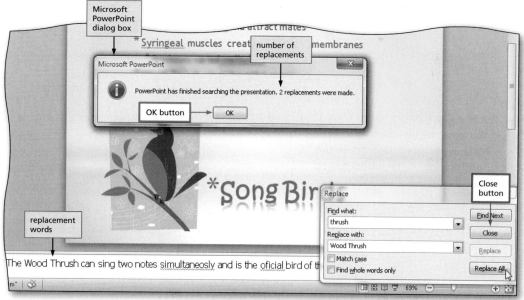

Figure 3–62

3

- Click the OK button (Microsoft PowerPoint dialog box).

- Click the Close button (Replace dialog box).

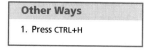

Other Ways

1. Press CTRL+H

To Find and Insert a Synonym

When reviewing your slide show, you may decide that a particular word does not express the exact usage you intended or that you used the same word on multiple slides. In these cases, you could find a **synonym**, or word similar in meaning, to replace the inappropriate or duplicate word. PowerPoint provides a **thesaurus**, which is a list of synonyms and antonyms, to help you find a replacement word.

In this project, you want to find a synonym to replace the word, Defend, on Slide 2. The following steps locate an appropriate synonym and replace the word.

1
- With Slide 2 displaying, right-click the word, Defend, to display a shortcut menu.

- Point to Synonyms on the shortcut menu to display a list of synonyms for this word (Figure 3–63).

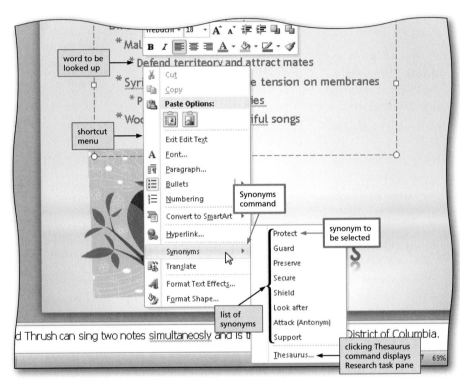

Figure 3–63

2
- Click the synonym you want (Protect) on the Synonyms submenu to replace the word, Defend, in the presentation with the word, Protect (Figure 3–64).

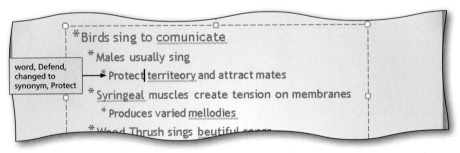

Figure 3–64

Q&A What if a suitable word does not display in the Synonyms submenu?

You can display the thesaurus in the Research task pane by clicking Thesaurus on the Synonyms submenu. A complete thesaurus with synonyms displays in the Research task pane along with an **antonym**, which is a word with an opposite meaning.

BTW

Foreign Language Synonyms
The thesaurus contains synonyms for languages other than English. To look up words in the thesaurus of another language, click the Thesaurus button (Review tab | Proofing group), click Research options (Research task pane), select the desired languages in the Reference Books area, and then click the OK button.

Other Ways

1. Click Thesaurus (Review tab | Proofing group)
2. Press SHIFT+F7

To Add Notes

As you create slides, you may find material you want to state verbally and do not want to include on the slide. You can type and format notes in the **Notes pane** as you work in Normal view and then print this information as **notes pages**. After adding comments, you can print a set of speaker notes. These notes will print below a small image of the slide. Charts, tables, and pictures added to the Notes pane also print on these pages. In this project, comments were included on Slide 2 when you opened that file. The following steps add text to the Notes pane on Slides 1 and 3.

1
- Display Slide 1, click the Notes pane, and then type `More than 10,000 species of birds exist in the world. The largest bird is the ostrich, and the smallest is the hummingbird. They generally live in small groups, but some form huge flocks with thousands of members and a variety of species. Flocks help keep the birds safe while they search for food.` (Figure 3–65).

Figure 3–65

What if I cannot see all the lines I typed?

You can drag the splitter bar up to enlarge the Notes pane. Clicking the Notes pane scroll arrows allows you to view the entire text.

2
- Display Slide 3, click the Notes pane, and then type `Birds migrate to benefit from warm weather. Some can fly more than 6,000 miles without stopping. We can help bird migration by providing food, shelters, nest sites, and water.` (Figure 3–66).

Figure 3–66

BTW

Using AutoCorrect Features
Microsoft Office programs use the AutoCorrect feature to correct typing mistakes and commonly misspelled words. When you install Microsoft Office, a default list of typical misspellings is created. You can modify the AutoCorrect list with words you are apt to misspell. The first column of this list contains the word that you often mistype, and the second column contains the replacement text. The AutoCorrect feature also inserts symbols, such as replacing (c) with the copyright symbol, ©.

Checking Spelling

After you create a presentation, you should check it visually for spelling errors and style consistency. In addition, you use PowerPoint's Spelling tool to identify possible misspellings on the slides and in the notes. Do not rely on the spelling checker to catch all your mistakes. Although PowerPoint's spelling checker is a valuable tool, it is not infallible. You should proofread your presentation carefully by pointing to each word and saying it aloud as you point to it. Be mindful of commonly misused words such as its and it's, through and though, and to and too.

PowerPoint checks the entire presentation for spelling mistakes using a standard dictionary contained in the Microsoft Office group. This dictionary is shared with the other Microsoft Office applications such as Word and Excel. A **custom dictionary** is available if you want to add special words such as proper names, cities, and acronyms. When checking a presentation for spelling errors, PowerPoint opens the standard dictionary and the custom dictionary file, if one exists. When a word appears in the Spelling dialog box, you can perform one of several actions, as described in Table 3–1.

Table 3–1 Spelling Dialog Box Buttons and Actions

Button Name	When To Use	Action
Ignore	Word is spelled correctly but not found in dictionaries	PowerPoint continues checking rest of the presentation but will flag that word again if it appears later in document.
Ignore All	Word is spelled correctly but not found in dictionaries	PowerPoint ignores all occurrences of the word and continues checking rest of presentation.
Change	Word is misspelled	Click proper spelling of the word in Suggestions list. PowerPoint corrects word, continues checking rest of presentation, but will flag that word again if it appears later in document.
Change All	Word is misspelled	Click proper spelling of word in Suggestions list. PowerPoint changes all occurrences of misspelled word and continues checking rest of presentation.
Add	Add word to custom dictionary	PowerPoint opens custom dictionary, adds word, and continues checking rest of presentation.
Suggest	Correct spelling is uncertain	Lists alternative spellings. Click the correct word from the Suggestions box or type the proper spelling. Corrects the word and continues checking the rest of the presentation.
AutoCorrect	Add spelling error to AutoCorrect list	PowerPoint adds spelling error and its correction to AutoCorrect list. Any future misspelling of word is corrected automatically as you type.
Close	Stop spelling checker	PowerPoint closes spelling checker and returns to PowerPoint window.

The standard dictionary contains commonly used English words. It does not, however, contain many proper names, abbreviations, technical terms, poetic contractions, or antiquated terms. PowerPoint treats words not found in the dictionaries as misspellings.

To Check Spelling

The following steps check the spelling on all slides in the Bird Migration presentation.

1

- Click Review on the Ribbon to display the Review tab.

- Click the Spelling button (Review Tab | Proofing group) to start the spelling checker and display the Spelling dialog box (Figure 3–67).

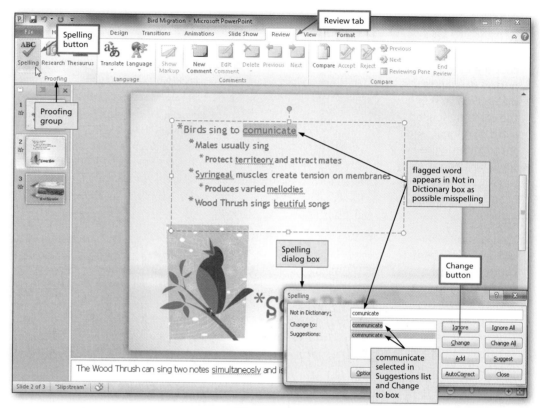

Figure 3–67

2

- With the word, communicate, selected in the Suggestions list, click the Change button (Spelling dialog box) to replace the misspelled flagged word, comunicate, with the selected correctly spelled word, communicate, and then continue the spelling check (Figure 3–68).

Q&A Could I have clicked the Change All button instead of the Change button?

Yes. When you click the Change All button, you change the current and future occurrences of the misspelled word.

The misspelled word, comunicate, appears only once in the presentation, so clicking the Change or the Change All button in this instance produces identical results.

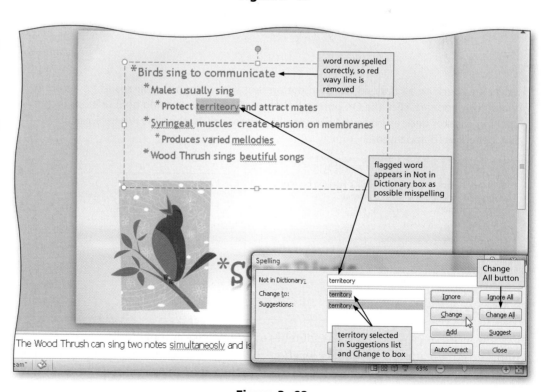

Figure 3–68

3

- Replace the misspelled word, territeory, with the word, territory (Figure 3–69).

- When the word, Syringeal, is flagged, click the Ignore button (Spelling dialog box) to skip the correctly spelled word, Syringeal, and then continue the spelling check.

Q&A

Syringeal is flagged as a possible misspelled word. Why?

Your custom dictionary does not contain the word, so it is recognized as spelled incorrectly. You can add this word to a custom dictionary to prevent the spelling checker from flagging it as a mistake.

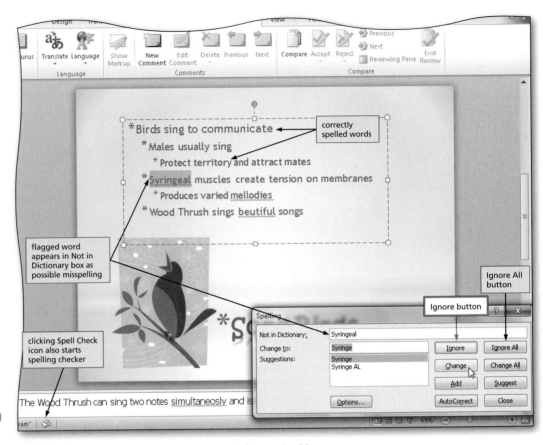

Figure 3–69

Q&A

Could I have clicked the Ignore All button instead of the Ignore button?

Yes. When you click the Ignore All button, you ignore the current and future occurrences of the word.

4

- Continue checking all flagged words in the presentation. When the Microsoft PowerPoint dialog box appears, click the OK button (Microsoft PowerPoint dialog box) to close the spelling checker and return to the current slide, Slide 2, or to the slide where a possible misspelled word appeared.

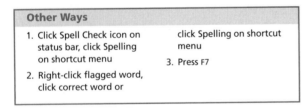

Other Ways

1. Click Spell Check icon on status bar, click Spelling on shortcut menu
2. Right-click flagged word, click correct word or

   click Spelling on shortcut menu
3. Press F7

To Insert a Slide Number

PowerPoint can insert the slide number on your slides automatically to indicate where the slide is positioned within the presentation. The number location on the slide is determined by the presentation theme. You have the option to not display this slide number on the title slide. The following steps insert the slide number on all slides except the title slide.

1

- If a word in the Notes pane is selected, click the Slide 2 Slide pane. Display the Insert tab and then click the Insert Slide Number button (Insert tab | Text group) to display the Header and Footer dialog box (Figure 3–70).

Q&A

Why did I need to click the Slide pane?

The page number would have been inserted in the Notes pane instead of on the slide.

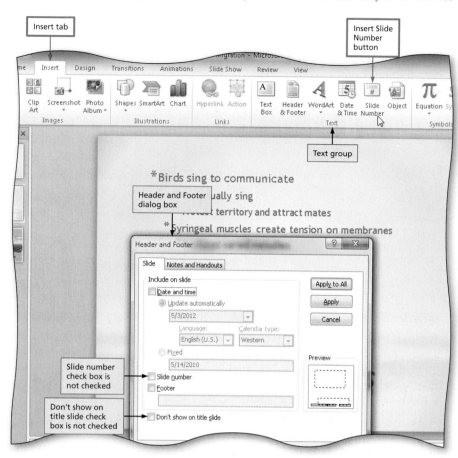

Figure 3–70

2

- Click the Slide number check box (Header and Footer dialog box) to place a check mark in it.

- Click the 'Don't show on title slide' check box (Header and Footer dialog box) to place a check mark in it (Figure 3–71).

Q&A

Where does the slide number display on the slide?

Each theme determines where the slide number is displayed in the footer. In the Slipstream theme, the slide number location is the center of the footer, as indicated by the black box at the bottom of the Preview area.

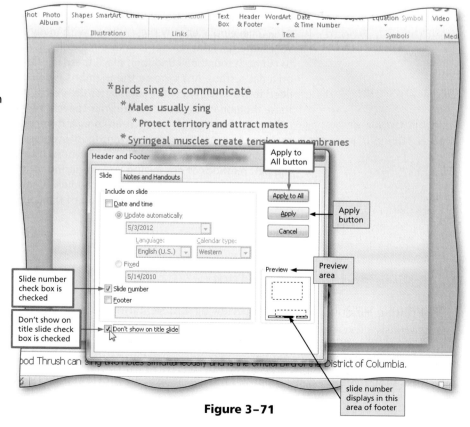

Figure 3–71

3
- Click the Apply to All button (Header and Footer dialog box) to close the dialog box and insert the slide number on all slides except Slide 1 (Figure 3–72).

Figure 3–72

Q&A

How does clicking the Apply to All button differ from clicking the Apply button?

The Apply button inserts the slide number only on the currently displayed slide whereas the Apply to All button inserts the slide number on every slide.

Other Ways

1. Click Header & Footer button (Insert tab | Text group), click Slide Number box (Header and Footer dialog box), click 'Slide number' and 'Don't show on title slide' boxes, click Apply to All button

---

Plan Ahead

Use handouts to organize your speech.

As you develop a lengthy presentation with many visuals, handouts may help you organize your material. Print handouts with the maximum number of slides per page. Use scissors to cut each thumbnail and then place these miniature slide images adjacent to each other on a flat surface. Any type on the thumbnails will be too small to read, so the images will need to work with only the support of the verbal message you provide. You can rearrange these thumbnails as you organize your speech. When you return to your computer, you can rearrange the slides on your screen to match the order of your thumbnail printouts. Begin speaking the actual words you want to incorporate in the body of the talk. This process of glancing at the thumbnails and hearing yourself say the key ideas of the speech is one of the best methods of organizing and preparing for the actual presentation. Ultimately, when you deliver your speech in front of an audience, the images on the slides or on your note cards should be sufficient to remind you of the accompanying verbal message.

To Preview and Print a Handout

Printing handouts is useful for reviewing a presentation because you can analyze several slides displayed simultaneously on one page. Additionally, many businesses distribute handouts of the slide show before or after a presentation so attendees can refer to a copy. Each page of the handout can contain reduced images of one, two, three, four, six, or nine slides. The three-slides-per-page handout includes lines beside each slide so that your audience can write notes conveniently. The following steps preview and print a presentation handout.

1

- Click File on the Ribbon to open the Backstage view and then click the Print tab to display Slide 2 in the Print gallery.

- Click Full Page Slides in the Settings area to display the Full Page Slides gallery (Figure 3–73).

 Q&A

Why does the preview of my slide appear in color?

Your printer determines how the preview appears. If your printer is not capable of printing color images, the preview will not appear in color.

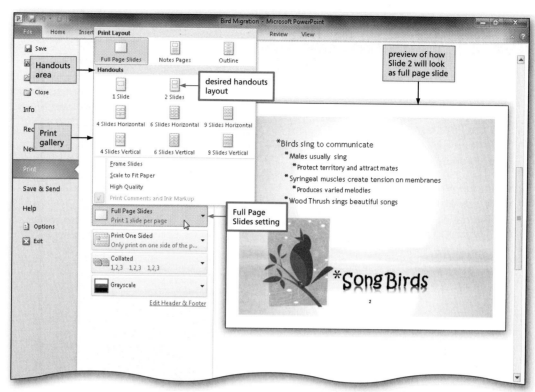

Figure 3–73

2

- Click 2 Slides in the Handouts area to select this option and display a preview of the handout (Figure 3–74).

Q&A

The current date displays in the upper-right corner of the handout, and the page number displays in the lower-right corner of the footer. Can I change their location or add other information to the header and footer?

Yes. Click the Edit Header & Footer link at the bottom of the Print gallery, click the Notes and Handouts tab (Header and Footer dialog box), and then decide what content to include on the handout page.

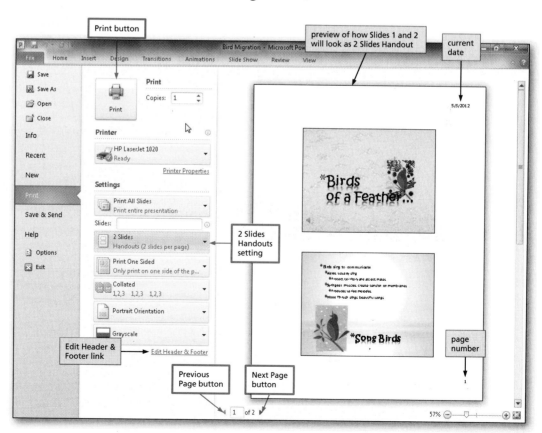

Figure 3–74

● Click the Next Page and Previous Page buttons to display previews of the two pages in the presentation.

● Click the Print button in the Print gallery to print the handout.

● When the printer stops, retrieve the printed handout (Figure 3–75).

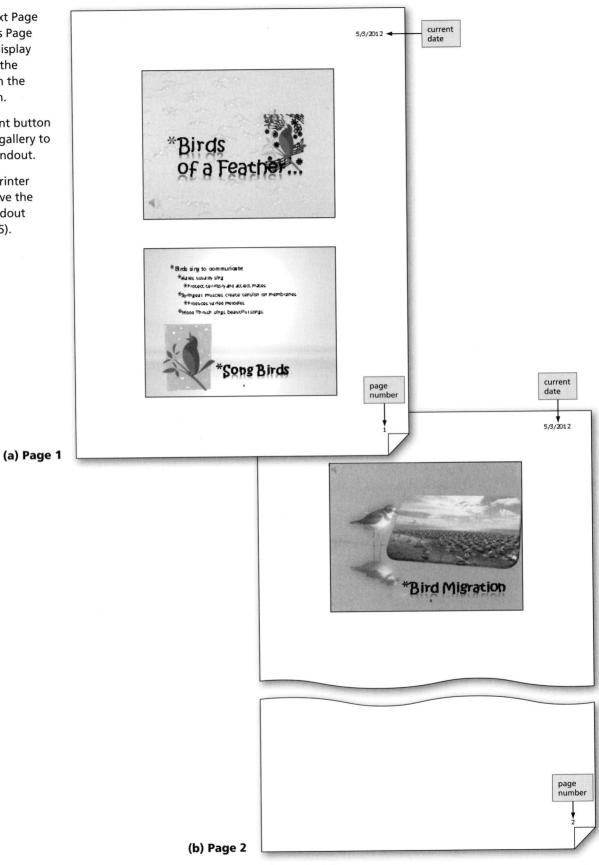

(a) Page 1

(b) Page 2

Figure 3–75

To Print Speaker Notes

Comments added to slides in the Notes pane give the speaker information that supplements the text on the slide. They will print with a small image at the top and the comments below the slide. The following steps print the speaker notes.

1

• Click the Print tab in the Backstage view and then click 2 Slides in the Settings area to display the gallery (Figure 3–76).

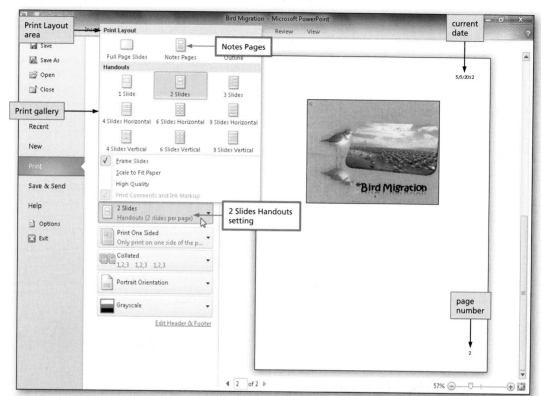

Figure 3–76

2

• Click Notes Pages in the Print Layout area to select this option and display a preview of the current page (Figure 3–77).

• Click the Previous Page and Next Page buttons to display previews of other pages in the presentation.

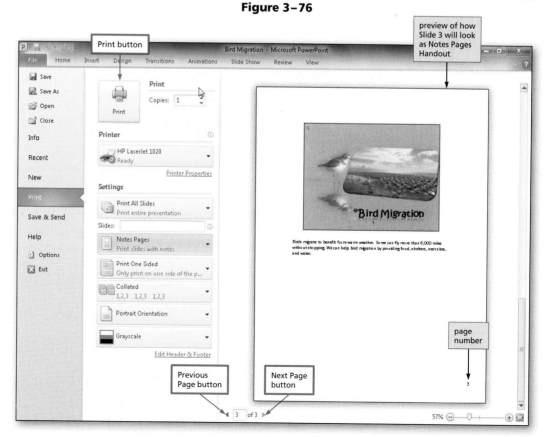

Figure 3–77

- Click the Print button in the Print gallery to print the notes.

- When the printer stops, retrieve the printed pages (Figure 3–78).

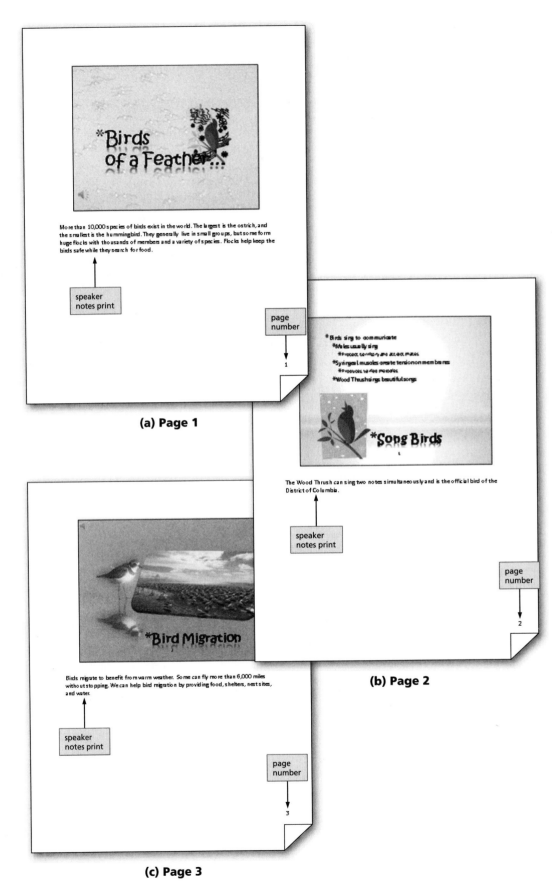

(a) Page 1

(b) Page 2

(c) Page 3

Figure 3–78

Evaluate your presentation.

One of the best methods of improving your communication skills is to focus on what you learned from the experience. Respond to these questions:

- How successfully do you feel you fulfilled your assignment?
- What strategies did you use to develop your slides and the accompanying oral presentation?
- What revisions did you make?
- If you could go back to the speaking engagement and change one thing, what would it be?
- What feedback did you receive from your instructor or audience?

To Change Document Properties

Before saving the presentation again, you want to add your name, class name, and some keywords as document properties. The following steps use the Document Information Panel to change document properties.

1 In the Backstage view, click the Properties button in the right pane of the Info gallery, and then click Show Document Panel on the Properties menu to close the Backstage view and display the Document Information Panel.

2 Enter your name in the Author text box. Enter your course and section in the Subject text box. Enter the text, `bird, migration, singing` in the Keywords text box.

3 Close the Document Information Panel.

4 Click the Save button on the Quick Access Toolbar to overwrite the previous Bird Migration file on the USB flash drive.

BTW

Quick Reference
For a table that lists how to complete the tasks covered in this book using the mouse, Ribbon, shortcut menu, and keyboard, see the Quick Reference Summary at the back of this book, or visit the PowerPoint 2010 Quick Reference Web page (scsite.com/ppt2010/qr).

To Run a Slide Show with Media

All changes are complete, and the presentation is saved. You now can view the Bird Migration presentation. The following steps start Slide Show view.

1 Click the Slide 1 thumbnail in the Slide pane to select and display Slide 1.

2 Click the Slide Show button to display the title slide, watch the animations, and listen to the bird calls. Allow the audio clip to repeat several times.

3 Press the SPACEBAR to display Slide 2.

4 Press the SPACEBAR to display Slide 3. Listen to the audio clip, watch the video clip, and then allow the audio clip to repeat several times.

5 Press the SPACEBAR to end the slide show and click to exit the slide show.

BTW

Certification
The Microsoft Office Specialist (MOS) program provides an opportunity for you to obtain a valuable industry credential — proof that you have the PowerPoint 2010 skills required by employers. For more information, visit the PowerPoint 2010 Certification Web page (scsite.com/ppt2010/cert).

To Quit PowerPoint

This project is complete. The following steps quit PowerPoint.

1 Click the Close button on the right side of the title bar to close the document and then quit PowerPoint.

2 If a Microsoft PowerPoint dialog box appears, click the Save button to save any changes made to the presentation since the last save.

Chapter Summary

In this chapter you have learned how to enhance an existing presentation by adding video, audio, and pictures with effects. You also learned to modify placeholders, align text, and review a presentation by checking spelling and creating handouts. The items listed below include all the new PowerPoint skills you have learned in this chapter.

1. Color a Picture (PPT 143)
2. Add an Artistic Effect to a Picture (144)
3. Change the Stacking Order (PPT 146)
4. Resize a Placeholder (PPT 148)
5. Move a Placeholder (PPT 148)
6. Delete a Placeholder (PPT 149)
7. Align Paragraph Text (PPT 150)
8. Delete a Slide (PPT 152)
9. Change Views (PPT 153)
10. Copy a Clip from One Slide to Another (PPT 155)
11. Zoom a Slide (PPT 156)
12. Ungroup a Clip (PPT 157)
13. Change the Color of a Clip Object (PPT 158)
14. Delete a Clip Object (PPT 161)
15. Regroup Objects (PPT 162)
16. Insert a Video File (PPT 163)
17. Trim a Video File (PPT 164)
18. Add Video Options (PPT 166)
19. Insert an Audio File (PPT 167)
20. Add Audio Options (PPT 170)
21. Add a Video Style (PPT 172)
22. Resize a Video (PPT 174)
23. Insert a Movie Clip (PPT 174)
24. Find and Replace Text (PPT 176)
25. Find and Insert a Synonym (PPT 178)
26. Add Notes (PPT 179)
27. Check Spelling (PPT 181)
28. Insert a Slide Number (PPT 182)
29. Preview and Print a Handout (PPT 184)
30. Print Speaker Notes (PPT 187)

If you have a SAM 2010 user profile, your instructor may have assigned an autogradable version of this assignment. If so, log into the SAM 2010 Web site at www.cengage.com/sam2010 to download the instruction and start files.

Learn It Online

Test your knowledge of chapter content and key terms.

Instructions: To complete the Learn It Online exercises, start your browser, click the Address bar, and then enter the Web address **scsite.com/ppt2010/learn**. When the PowerPoint 2010 Learn It Online page is displayed, click the link for the exercise you want to complete and then read the instructions.

Chapter Reinforcement TF, MC, and SA
A series of true/false, multiple choice, and short answer questions that test your knowledge of the chapter content.

Flash Cards
An interactive learning environment where you identify chapter key terms associated with displayed definitions.

Practice Test
A series of multiple choice questions that test your knowledge of chapter content and key terms.

Who Wants To Be a Computer Genius?
An interactive game that challenges your knowledge of chapter content in the style of a television quiz show.

Wheel of Terms
An interactive game that challenges your knowledge of chapter key terms in the style of the television show *Wheel of Fortune*.

Crossword Puzzle Challenge
A crossword puzzle that challenges your knowledge of key terms presented in the chapter.

Apply Your Knowledge

Reinforce the skills and apply the concepts you learned in this chapter.

Adding Artistic Effects to Pictures, Moving a Placeholder, and Inserting and Controlling Audio Clips

Note: To complete this assignment, you will be required to use the Data Files for Students. See the inside back cover of this book for instructions on downloading the Data Files for Students, or contact your instructor for information about accessing the required files.

Instructions: Start PowerPoint. Open the presentation, Apply 3-1 SAD, from the Data Files for Students.

The five slides in the presentation, shown in Figure 3–79, present information about Seasonal Affective Disorder, also known as SAD, which is a mood disorder that occurs generally during the winter months. The document you open is composed of slides containing pictures and clip art, and you will apply artistic effects or modify some of these graphic elements. You also will insert audio clips from Office.com. In addition, you will move the placeholder on the final slide.

Perform the following tasks:

1. Insert the audio clip, Sad Piano Music, into Slide 1 (Figure 3–79a). Change the volume to Medium, start the clip automatically, and hide the sound icon during the slide show. Then copy this audio clip to Slides 2, 3, and 4 with the same options. Insert the audio clip, Variety Hour, into Slide 5, change the volume to Medium, start the clip automatically, and hide the sound icon during the slide show.

2. On Slide 2, color the picture by selecting Yellow, Accent color 2 Dark from the Recolor area, as shown in Figure 3–79b.

3. On Slide 3, apply the Watercolor Sponge artistic effect to the picture, as shown in Figure 3–79c.

4. On Slide 4, select the lamp clip and then change the Zoom level to 120%. Ungroup the lamp clip and then recolor the arms to Dark Teal, Text 2, Lighter 10% (last color in fourth Theme Colors column), as shown in Figure 3–79d. Regroup the clip. Change the Zoom level to 69%.

5. On Slide 5, move the WordArt placeholder above the bird in the picture, as shown in Figure 3–79e.

6. On Slide 1, type `Up to 9 percent of U.S. adults may suffer from SAD.` in the Notes pane.

7. Check the slides for spelling errors and then run the revised presentation.

8. Change the document properties, as specified by your instructor. Save the presentation using the file name, Apply 3-1 Seasonal Affective Disorder.

9. Submit the revised document in the format specified by your instructor.

(a) Slide 1

(b) Slide 2

Figure 3–79

Continued >

Apply Your Knowledge *continued*

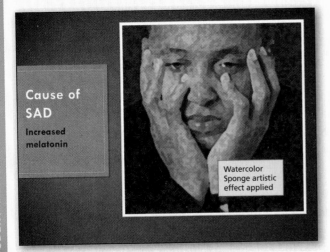

(c) Slide 3

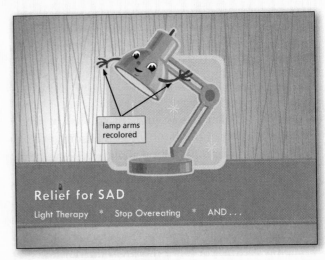

(d) Slide 4

(e) Slide 5

Figure 3–79 (Continued)

Extend Your Knowledge

Extend the skills you learned in this chapter and experiment with new skills. You may need to use Help to complete the assignment.

Formatting a Video Border, Deleting Audio, Adding a Font Effect, and Pausing and Resuming Video Playback

Note: To complete this assignment, you will be required to use the Data Files for Students. See the inside back cover of this book for instructions on downloading the Data Files for Students, or contact your instructor for information about accessing the required files.

Instructions: Start PowerPoint. Open the presentation, Extend 3-1 Nature, from the Data Files for Students. You will add the Small Caps font effect to the title text on the title slide, delete an audio clip, and format a video border, as shown in Figure 3–80a. While the slide show is running, you will adjust the video playback to pause and then resume playing the clip.

Perform the following tasks:

1. On Slide 1, move the title text placeholder up so that it is positioned in the upper-right corner of the slide, as shown in Figure 3–80a. Right-align the title text and then add the Small Caps font effect to these letters. *Hint:* Font effects are located in the Font dialog box (Home tab | Font group).

2. On the title slide, delete the audio clip positioned in the upper-left corner of the slide. The three audio clips on the right side of the slide will remain.

3. Change the video style from Soft Edge Oval to Beveled Oval, Black (in the Moderate area). Then change the video border color to Gold, Accent 2 and change the border weight to 10 pt. *Hint:* Click More Lines in the Video Border Weight gallery and then change the Border Style Width.

4. On Slide 2, add a border to each of the six pictures that surround the center deer video frame, and then change the border colors and the border weights. Use Figure 3–80b as a guide. Add the Compound Frame, Black video style (in the Moderate area) to the bird feeder clip.

5. Change the document properties, as specified by your instructor. Save the presentation using the file name, Extend 3-1 Observing Nature.

6. Start the slide show. When a few seconds of the video have elapsed, pause the video and then move your mouse pointer to an area other than the video and listen to the bird audio clips. Then move the mouse pointer over the video clip to display the Video Controls. Resume the video playback.

7. Submit the revised document in the format specified by your instructor.

(a) Slide 1

(b) Slide 2

Figure 3–80

Make It Right

Analyze a presentation and correct all errors and/or improve the design.

Editing Clips, Finding and Replacing Text, and Correcting Spelling

Note: To complete this assignment, you will be required to use the Data Files for Students. See the inside back cover of this book for instructions on downloading the Data Files for Students, or contact your instructor for information about accessing the required files.

Instructions: Start PowerPoint. Open the presentation, Make It Right 3-1 Flamingos, from the Data Files for Students.

Correct the formatting problems and errors in the presentation while keeping in mind the guidelines presented in this chapter.

Perform the following tasks:

1. On Slide 1 (Figure 3–81), change the audio clip volume to High and hide the sound icon during the show. Loop this clip for the duration of the slide show.

2. On Slide 2, add the Reflection video effect located in the Reflection Variations area, Tight Reflection 4 pt offset (first reflection in second row) to the video.

3. Trim the Slide 2 video so that the Start Time is 00:21.087 and the End Time is 01:44.273. The duration should be 01:23.186 minutes.

4. Copy the flamingo clip from Slide 4 to Slide 3 and then delete Slide 4. Place this clip on the left side of the picture frame and then adjust the picture frame size so it is the appropriate dimension for the slide content. Ungroup the flamingo clip and then recolor the flamingo to match the color of its legs, the palm tree leaves to a shade of green, and the bird to a shade of blue. Regroup the clip.

5. Find the word, Antarctica, in the Slide 1 Notes pane, and then replace it with the words, South America. Then find the number, 14, and replace it with the number, 4.

6. Check the slides for spelling errors and then run the revised presentation.

7. Change the document properties, as specified by your instructor. Save the presentation using the file name, Make It Right 3-1 Chilean Flamingos.

8. Submit the revised document in the format specified by your instructor.

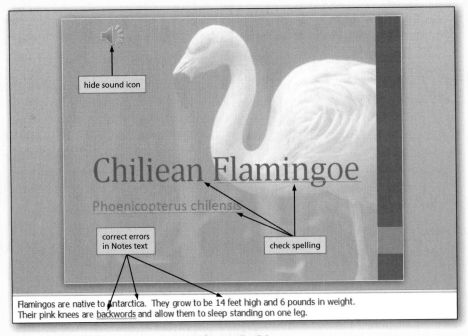

Figure 3–81

In the Lab

Design and/or create a presentation using the guidelines, concepts, and skills presented in this chapter. Labs 1, 2, and 3 are listed in order of increasing difficulty.

Lab 1: Inserting Audio Clips, Coloring a Picture, and Applying Artistic Effects to Pictures

Note: To complete this assignment, you will be required to use the Data Files for Students. See the inside back cover of this book for instructions on downloading the Data Files for Students, or contact your instructor for information about accessing the required files.

Problem: Start PowerPoint. Open the presentation, Lab 3-1 Cooking, from the Data Files for Students.
Your college has an outstanding culinary program, and you are preparing a PowerPoint presentation to promote an upcoming seafood cooking class. The slides will feature audio clips and graphics with applied effects. Create the slides shown in Figure 3–82.

Instructions: Perform the following tasks.

1. On Slide 1, insert the Mr. Light music audio clip from Office.com. Change the volume to Low, play across slides, and hide the sound icon during the show. Move the subtitle text placeholder downward to the location shown in Figure 3–82a and center both paragraphs.

2. On Slide 2, insert the picture called Blackboard and Chef, which is available on the Data Files for Students. Change the color of the picture to Gold, Accent color 3 Dark (Recolor area). Add a border to this picture using Dark Red, Accent 5, and then change the border weight to 6 pt., as shown in Figure 3–82b.

(a) Slide 1

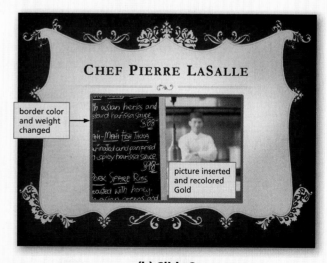

(b) Slide 2

Figure 3–82

Continued >

3. On Slide 3, right-align all the text. Insert the Chef video clip from Office.com and resize this clip so that it is approximately 4.08" × 3.99", as shown in Figure 3–82c. Insert the Pepper Grinder video clip from Office.com and resize this clip so that it is approximately 3.81" × 2.25". Move the Pepper Grinder video clip to the lower-left corner of the slide. Insert the audio clips, Pepper Grinder and Cartoon Crash, from Office.com. Start these clips automatically, hide the sound icons during the show, and loop until stopped.

4. On Slide 4, apply the Watercolor Sponge artistic effect to the lobster picture in the left content placeholder and the Plastic Wrap artistic effect to the paella picture in the right content placeholder, as shown in Figure 3–82d.

5. On Slide 5, insert the Bottle Open audio clip from Office.com. Move the sound icon to the lower-right corner of the slide. Start this clip on click. Center the text in the caption placeholder and then move this placeholder downward to the location shown in Figure 3–82e.

6. Review the slides in Slide Sorter view to check for consistency, and then change the view to Normal.

7. Drag the scroll box to display Slide 1. Start Slide Show view and display each slide.

8. Change the document properties, as specified by your instructor. Save the presentation using the file name, Lab 3-1 Cooking Classes.

9. Submit the revised document in the format specified by your instructor.

(c) Slide 3

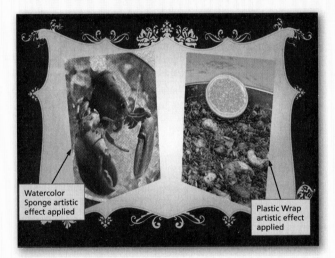

(d) Slide 4

(e) Slide 5

Figure 3–82 (Continued)

In the Lab

Lab 2: Adding Slide Numbers, Applying Artistic Effects to Pictures, and Recoloring a Video

Note: To complete this assignment, you will be required to use the Data Files for Students. See the inside back cover of this book for instructions on downloading the Data Files for Students, or contact your instructor for information about accessing the required files.

Problem: The Dutch tradition is continuing with Klompen dancers, who take their name from their traditional wooden clog shoes. You attended an annual festival this past spring and captured some video clips of teenagers dancing a traditional dance. In addition, you have some video of a hand-built windmill. In your speech class, you desire to inform your classmates of a few aspects of Dutch life, so you prepare the presentation shown in Figure 3–83.

Instructions: Perform the following tasks.

1. Start PowerPoint. Open the presentation, Lab 3-2 Dancers, from the Data Files for Students. On Slide 1, apply the Mosaic Bubbles artistic effect to the tulips picture, as shown in Figure 3–83a. Insert the audio clip, Spring Music, from Office.com. Start this clip automatically, hide the sound icon during the show, and change the volume to Medium.

2. On Slide 2, apply the Marker artistic effect to the wooden shoe picture, as shown in Figure 3–83b. Change the Start option for the video clip from On Click to Automatically. Apply the Rotated, Gradient video style (Moderate area) to the video clip, change the video border color to Tan, Accent 6, and then change the border width to 18 pt.

3. On Slide 2, type **Many dancers wear traditional, hand-sewn Dutch costumes. Dancers wear thick socks to make the wooden shoes comfortable during this annual event.** in the Notes pane.

(a) Slide 1

(b) Slide 2

Figure 3–83

Continued >

STUDENT ASSIGNMENTS

In the Lab *continued*

4. On Slide 3, insert the video clip called Windmill from the Data Files for Students. Apply the Reflected Bevel, White video style (Intense area). Change the color of the video to Dark Blue, Accent color 3 Dark (Recolor area). Start this clip automatically and loop until stopped. Center the text in the title placeholder, as shown in Figure 3–83c.

5. Use the thesaurus to change the word, Custom, to Tradition. Check the slides for spelling errors.

6. Add the slide number to all slides except the title slide.

7. Review the slides in Slide Sorter view to check for consistency. Then click the Reading view button to display the current slide and click the Next and Previous buttons to display each slide. Change the view to Normal.

8. Change the document properties, as specified by your instructor. Save the presentation using the file name, Lab 3-2 Klompen Dancers.

9. Submit the revised document in the format specified by your instructor.

(c) Slide 3

Figure 3–83 (Continued)

In the Lab

Lab 3: Applying Artistic Effects to and Recoloring Pictures, Inserting Audio, and Trimming Video

Note: To complete this assignment, you will be required to use the Data Files for Students. See the inside back cover of this book for instructions on downloading the Data Files for Students, or contact your instructor for information about accessing the required files.

Problem: Your Uncle Barney is an avid railroad buff, and he especially is interested in viewing steam locomotives. He has a collection of video clips and photographs of historic steam engines, and he asks you to create a presentation for the next Hessville Train Club meeting he is planning to attend. Start PowerPoint and then open the presentation, Lab 3-3 Locomotives, from the Data Files for Students. Prepare the slides shown in Figures 3–84a through 3–84c.

Instructions: Perform the following tasks.

1. Delete the subtitle text placeholder on Slide 1. Then insert the picture, Steamer 624, from the Data Files for Students and apply the Glow Diffused artistic effect. Position the picture as shown in Figure 3–84a. Center the title text. Insert the audio clip, Train Whistle By, from Office.com. Start this clip automatically, hide the sound icon during the show, and loop until stopped.

2. On Slide 2, insert the picture, Locomotive, from the Data Files for Students and resize it so that it fills the entire slide height and width (approximately 7.5" × 10"). Change the color of the picture to Tan, Accent color 1 Light (Recolor area), as shown in Figure 3–84b.

3. Insert the video clip, Steam Locomotive, from the Data Files for Students. Resize this clip to approximately 4.54" × 8.07" and move the clip to the location shown in Figure 3–84b. Apply the Metal Rounded Rectangle video style (Intense area). Change the color of the border to Olive Green, Accent 2. Trim the Slide 2 video so that the Start Time is 00:06.186 and the End Time is 00:23.432. The duration should be 00:17.246 seconds. Start this clip automatically and loop until stopped.

4. On Slide 3, insert the picture, Railroad Track Border, and the video clip, Red Locomotive, from the Data Files for Students. Resize the Red Locomotive clip to approximately 2.78" × 5.36" and move it to the location shown in Figure 3–84c. Also, insert the audio clip, Steam Train Pass, from Office. com, and move this sound icon to the lower-left corner of the slide. Copy the audio clip, Train Whistle By, from Slide 1 and then move the sound icon to the upper-right corner of the slide. Start both audio clips automatically, hide the sound icons during the show, and loop until stopped.

5. Review the slides in Slide Sorter view. Then click the Reading view button to display the current slide and click the Next and Previous buttons to display each slide. Change the view to Normal.

6. Change the document properties, as specified by your instructor. Save the presentation using the file name, Lab 3-3 Steam Locomotives.

7. Submit the revised document in the format specified by your instructor.

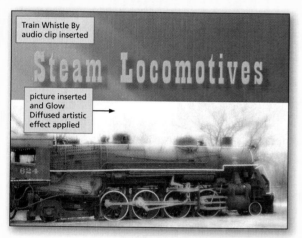

(a) Slide 1

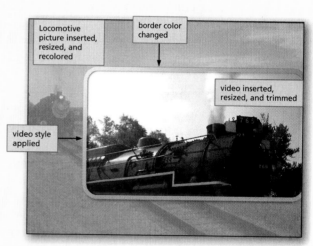

(b) Slide 2

(c) Slide 3

Figure 3–84

Cases and Places

Apply your creative thinking and problem-solving skills to design and implement a solution.

Note: To complete these assignments, you will be required to use the Data Files for Students. See the inside back cover of this book for instructions on downloading the Data Files for Students, or contact your instructor for information about accessing the required files.

As you design the presentations, remember to use the 7 × 7 rule: a maximum of seven words on a line and a maximum of seven lines on one slide.

1: Design and Create a Presentation about Kilauea Volcano

Academic

Most of the volcanic eruptions in Hawaii have occurred within Hawaii Volcanoes National Park. One of these volcanoes, Kilauea, has been erupting since 1983, and visitors to the National Park can drive on two roads to see lava tubes, steam vents, and plants returning to the barren landscape. Rainwater drains through cracks in the ground, is heated, and then is released through fissures and condenses in the cool air. Lava flows in underground tubes, and vents release volcanic gases that consist mainly of carbon dioxide, steam, and sulfur dioxide. During your recent trip to Hawaii Volcanoes National Park, you drove on these roads and captured these geological wonders with your video and digital cameras. You want to share your experience with your Geology 101 classmates. Create a presentation to show the pictures and video clips, which are located in the Data Files for Students and begin with the file name, Case 1. You also can use pictures from Office.com if they are appropriate for this topic. Apply appropriate styles and effects, and use at least three objectives found at the beginning of this chapter to develop the presentation. Be sure to check spelling.

2: Design and Create a Presentation about Surfing

Personal

During your summer vacation, you took surfing lessons and enjoyed the experience immensely. You now want to share your adventure with friends, so you decide to create a short PowerPoint presentation with video clips of the surf and of your paddling on your surfboard to the instruction area in the ocean. You also have pictures of your introductory lesson on shore and of your first successful run catching a wave. The Data Files for Students contains these media files that begin with the file name, Case 2. You also can use your own digital pictures or pictures from Office.com if they are appropriate for this topic. Use the clip, Case 2 - Yellow and Green Surfboard, on one slide, but ungroup this clip and then change the surfboard's colors to your school's team colors. Trim the video clips and apply appropriate styles and effects. Use at least three objectives found at the beginning of this chapter to develop the presentation. Be sure to check spelling.

3: Design and Create a Presentation to Promote Your Snow Removal Business

Professional

Record snowfalls have wreaked havoc in your neighborhood, so you have decided to earn tuition money by starting a snow removal business. You are willing to clear sidewalks and driveways when snowfall exceeds three inches. To promote your business, you desire to create a PowerPoint presentation to run behind the counter at the local hardware store. The Data Files for Students contains pictures and a video clip that begin with the file name, Case 3. You also can use your own digital pictures or pictures from Office.com if they are appropriate for this topic. Use the clip, Case 3 - Man Shoveling, on one slide, but ungroup this clip and then zoom in and delete the white area of the clip depicting the man's breath. Also, recolor at least one picture and apply an artistic effect. Be sure to check spelling.

NOTES

NOTES

NOTES

NOTES

Appendix A

Project Planning Guidelines

Using Project Planning Guidelines

The process of communicating specific information to others is a learned, rational skill. Computers and software, especially Microsoft Office 2010, can help you develop ideas and present detailed information to a particular audience.

Using Microsoft Office 2010, you can create projects such as Word documents, PowerPoint presentations, Excel spreadsheets, and Access databases. Productivity software such as Microsoft Office 2010 minimizes much of the laborious work of drafting and revising projects. Some communicators handwrite ideas in notebooks, others compose directly on the computer, and others have developed unique strategies that work for their own particular thinking and writing styles.

No matter what method you use to plan a project, follow specific guidelines to arrive at a final product that presents information correctly and effectively (Figure A–1). Use some aspects of these guidelines every time you undertake a project, and others as needed in specific instances. For example, in determining content for a project, you may decide that a chart communicates trends more effectively than a paragraph of text. If so, you would create this graphical element and insert it in an Excel spreadsheet, a Word document, or a PowerPoint slide.

Determine the Project's Purpose

Begin by clearly defining why you are undertaking this assignment. For example, you may want to track monetary donations collected for your club's fund-raising drive. Alternatively, you may be urging students to vote for a particular candidate in the next election. Once you clearly understand the purpose of your task, begin to draft ideas of how best to communicate this information.

Analyze Your Audience

Learn about the people who will read, analyze, or view your work. Where are they employed? What are their educational backgrounds? What are their expectations? What questions do they have?

PROJECT PLANNING GUIDELINES

1. DETERMINE THE PROJECT'S PURPOSE
Why are you undertaking the project?

2. ANALYZE YOUR AUDIENCE
Who are the people who will use your work?

3. GATHER POSSIBLE CONTENT
What information exists, and in what forms?

4. DETERMINE WHAT CONTENT TO PRESENT TO YOUR AUDIENCE
What information will best communicate the project's purpose to your audience?

Figure A–1

Design experts suggest drawing a mental picture of these people or finding photos of people who fit this profile so that you can develop a project with the audience in mind.

By knowing your audience members, you can tailor a project to meet their interests and needs. You will not present them with information they already possess, and you will not omit the information they need to know.

Example: Your assignment is to raise the profile of your college's nursing program in the community. How much do they know about your college and the nursing curriculum? What are the admission requirements? How many of the applicants admitted complete the program? What percent pass the state board exams?

Gather Possible Content

Rarely are you in a position to develop all the material for a project. Typically, you would begin by gathering existing information that may reside in spreadsheets or databases. Web sites, pamphlets, magazine and newspaper articles, and books could provide insights of how others have approached your topic. Personal interviews often provide perspectives not available by any other means. Consider video and audio clips as potential sources for material that might complement or support the factual data you uncover.

Determine What Content to Present to Your Audience

Experienced designers recommend writing three or four major ideas you want an audience member to remember after reading or viewing your project. It also is helpful to envision your project's endpoint, the key fact you wish to emphasize. All project elements should lead to this ending point.

As you make content decisions, you also need to think about other factors. Presentation of the project content is an important consideration. For example, will your brochure be printed on thick, colored paper or posted on the Web? Will your PowerPoint presentation be viewed in a classroom with excellent lighting and a bright projector, or will it be viewed on a notebook computer monitor? Determine relevant time factors, such as the length of time to develop the project, how long readers will spend reviewing your project, or the amount of time allocated for your speaking engagement. Your project will need to accommodate all of these constraints.

Decide whether a graph, photo, or artistic element can express or emphasize a particular concept. The right hemisphere of the brain processes images by attaching an emotion to them, so audience members are more apt to recall these graphics long term rather than just reading text.

As you select content, be mindful of the order in which you plan to present information. Readers and audience members generally remember the first and last pieces of information they see and hear, so you should place the most important information at the top or bottom of the page.

Summary

When creating a project, it is beneficial to follow some basic guidelines from the outset. By taking some time at the beginning of the process to determine the project's purpose, analyze the audience, gather possible content, and determine what content to present to the audience, you can produce a project that is informative, relevant, and effective.

Appendix B

Publishing Office 2010 Web Pages Online

With Office 2010 programs, you use the Save As command in the Backstage view to save a Web page to a Web site, network location, or FTP site. **File Transfer Protocol (FTP)** is an Internet standard that allows computers to exchange files with other computers on the Internet.

You should contact your network system administrator or technical support staff at your Internet access provider to determine if their Web server supports Web folders, FTP, or both, and to obtain necessary permissions to access the Web server.

Using an Office Program to Publish Office 2010 Web Pages

When publishing online, someone first must assign the necessary permissions for you to publish the Web page. If you are granted access to publish online, you must obtain the Web address of the Web server, a user name, and possibly a password that allows you to connect to the Web server. The steps in this appendix assume that you have access to an online location to which you can publish a Web page.

To Connect to an Online Location

To publish a Web page online, you first must connect to the online location. To connect to an online location using Windows 7, you would perform the following steps.

1. Click the Start button on the Windows 7 taskbar to display the Start menu.

2. Click Computer in the right pane of the Start menu to open the Computer window.

3. Click the 'Map network drive' button on the toolbar to display the Map Network Drive dialog box. (If the 'Map network drive' button is not visible on the toolbar, click the 'Display additional commands' button on the toolbar and then click 'Map network drive' in the list to display the Map Network Drive dialog box.)

4. Click the 'Connect to a Web site that you can use to store your documents and pictures' link (Map Network Drive dialog box) to start the Add Network Location wizard.

5. Click the Next button (Add Network Location dialog box).

6. Click 'Choose a custom network location' and then click the Next button.

7. Type the Internet or network address specified by your network or system administrator in the text box and then click the Next button.

8. Click 'Log on anonymously' to deselect the check box, type your user name in the User name text box, and then click the Next button.

9. If necessary, enter the name you want to assign to this online location and then click the Next button.

10. Click to deselect the Open this network location when I click Finish check box, and then click the Finish button.

11. Click the Cancel button to close the Map Network Drive dialog box.

12. Close the Computer window.

TO SAVE A WEB PAGE TO AN ONLINE LOCATION

The online location now can be accessed easily from Windows programs, including Microsoft Office programs. After creating a Microsoft Office file you wish to save as a Web page, you must save the file to the online location to which you connected in the previous steps. To save a Microsoft Word document as a Web page, for example, and publish it to the online location, you would perform the following steps.

1. Click File on the Ribbon to display the Backstage view and then click Save As in the Backstage view to display the Save As dialog box.

2. Type the Web page file name in the File name text box (Save As dialog box). Do not press the ENTER key because you do not want to close the dialog box at this time.

3. Click the 'Save as type' box arrow and then click Web Page to select the Web Page format.

4. If necessary, scroll to display the name of the online location in the navigation pane.

5. Double-click the online location name in the navigation pane to select that location as the new save location and display its contents in the right pane.

6. If a dialog box appears prompting you for a user name and password, type the user name and password in the respective text boxes and then click the Log On button.

7. Click the Save button (Save As dialog box).

The Web page now has been published online. To view the Web page using a Web browser, contact your network or system administrator for the Web address you should use to connect to the Web page.

Appendix C

Saving to the Web Using Windows Live SkyDrive

Introduction

Windows Live SkyDrive, also referred to as **SkyDrive**, is a free service that allows users to save files to the Web, such as documents, spreadsheets, databases, presentations, videos, and photos. Using SkyDrive, you also can save files in folders, providing for greater organization. You then can retrieve those files from any computer connected to the Internet. Some Office 2010 programs including Word, PowerPoint, and Excel can save files directly to an Internet location such as SkyDrive. SkyDrive also facilitates collaboration by allowing users to share files with other SkyDrive users (Figure C–1).

Figure C–1

Note: An Internet connection is required to perform the steps in this appendix.

To Save a File to Windows Live SkyDrive

You can save files directly to SkyDrive from within Word, PowerPoint, and Excel using the Backstage view. The following steps save an open PowerPoint presentation (Xanada Investment Corp, in this case) to SkyDrive. These steps require you to have a Windows Live account. Contact your instructor if you do not have a Windows Live account.

1

- Start PowerPoint and then open a document you want to save to the Web (in this case, the Xanada Investment Corp presentation).

- Click File on the Ribbon to display the Backstage view (Figure C–2).

Figure C–2

2

- Click the Save & Send tab to display the Save & Send gallery (Figure C–3).

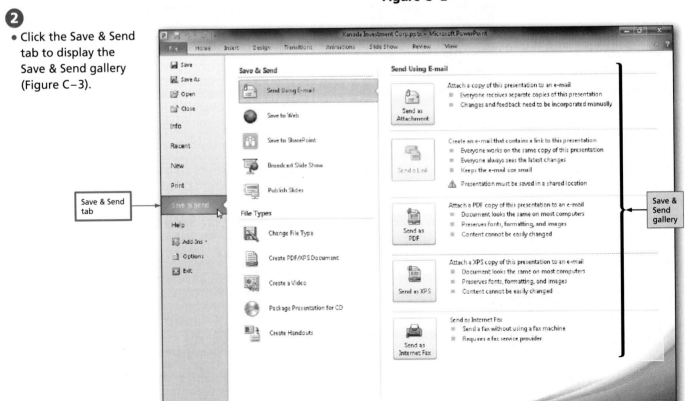

Figure C–3

• Click Save to Web in the Save & Send gallery to display information about saving a file to the Web (Figure C–4).

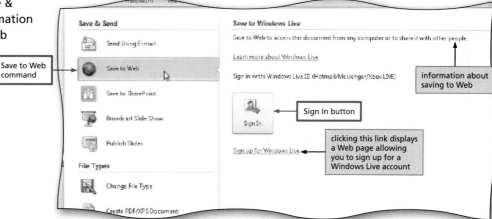

Figure C–4

• Click the Sign In button to display a Windows Live login dialog box that requests your e-mail address and password (Figure C–5).

Q&A

What if the Sign In button does not appear?

If you already are signed into Windows Live, the Sign In button will not be displayed. Instead, the contents of your Windows Live SkyDrive will be displayed. If you already are signed into Windows Live, proceed to Step 6.

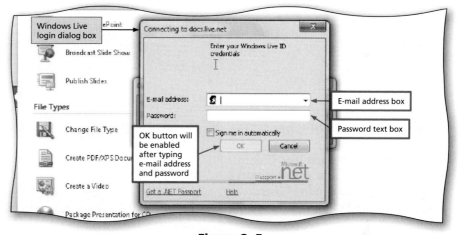

Figure C–5

• Enter your Windows Live e-mail address in the E-mail address box (Windows Live login dialog box).

• Enter your Windows Live password in the Password text box.

• Click the OK button to sign into Windows Live and display the contents of your Windows Live SkyDrive in right pane of the Save & Send gallery.

• If necessary, click the My Documents folder to set the save location for the document (Figure C–6).

Q&A

What if the My Documents folder does not exist?

Click another folder to select it as the save location. Record the name of this folder so that you can locate and retrieve the file later in this appendix.

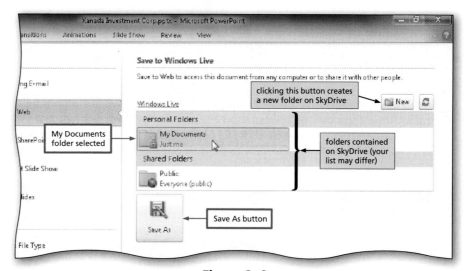

Figure C–6

Q&A

What is the difference between the personal folders and the shared folders?

Personal folders are private and are not shared with anyone. Shared folders can be viewed by SkyDrive users to whom you have assigned the necessary permissions.

- Click the Save As button in the right pane of the Save & Send gallery to contact the SkyDrive server (which may take some time, depending on the speed of your Internet connection) and then display the Save As dialog box (Figure C–7).

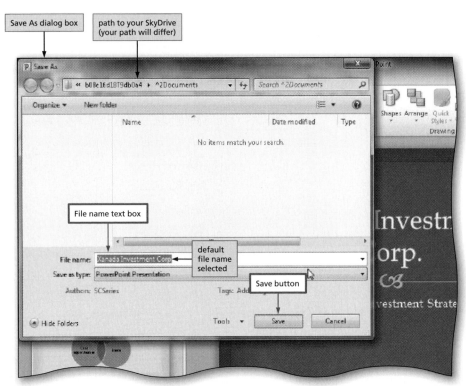

Figure C–7

- Type **Xanada Investment Web** in the File name text box to enter the file name and then click the Save button (Save As dialog box) to save the file to Windows Live SkyDrive (Figure C–8).

Q&A

Is it necessary to rename the file?

It is good practice to rename the file. If you download the file from SkyDrive to your computer, having a different file name will preserve the original file.

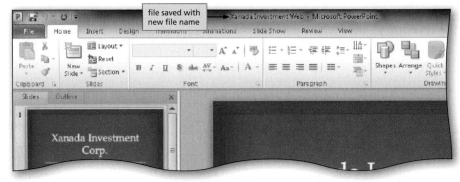

Figure C–8

- If you have one PowerPoint presentation open, click the Close button on the right side of the title bar to close the presentation and quit PowerPoint; or if you have multiple PowerPoint presentations open, click File on the Ribbon to open the Backstage view and then click Exit in the Backstage view to close all open presentations and quit PowerPoint.

Web Apps

Microsoft has created a scaled-down, Web-based version of its Microsoft Office suite, called **Microsoft Office Web Apps,** or **Web Apps**. Web Apps contains Web-based versions of Word, PowerPoint, Excel, and OneNote that can be used to view and edit files that are saved to SkyDrive. Web Apps allows users to continue working with their files even while they are not using a computer with Microsoft Office installed. In addition to working with files located on SkyDrive, Web Apps also enables users to create new Word documents, PowerPoint presentations, Excel spreadsheets, and OneNote notebooks. After returning to a computer with the Microsoft Office suite, some users choose to download files from SkyDrive and edit them using the associated Microsoft Office program.

To Open a File from Windows Live SkyDrive

Files saved to SkyDrive can be opened from a Web browser using any computer with an Internet connection. The following steps open the Xanada Investment Web file using a Web browser.

1

- Click the Internet Explorer program button pinned on the Windows 7 taskbar to start Internet Explorer.

- Type `skydrive.live.com` in the Address bar and then press the ENTER key to display a SkyDrive Web page requesting you sign in to your Windows Live account (Figure C–9).

Q&A Why does the Web address change after I enter it in the Address bar?

The Web address changes because you are being redirected to sign into Windows Live before you can access SkyDrive.

Q&A Can I open the file from Microsoft PowerPoint instead of using the Web browser?

If you are opening the file on the same computer from which you saved it to the SkyDrive, click File on the Ribbon to open the Backstage view. Click the Recent tab and then click the desired file name (Xanada Investment Web, in this case) in the Recent Presentations list, or click Open and then navigate to the location of the saved file (for a detailed example of this procedure, refer to the Office 2010 and Windows 7 chapter at the beginning of this book).

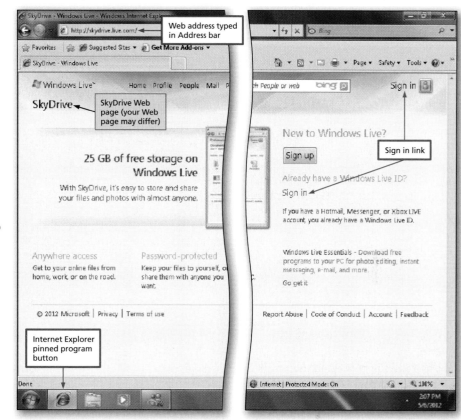

Figure C–9

2

- Click the Sign in link to display the Windows Live ID and Password text boxes (Figure C–10).

Q&A Why can I not locate the Sign in link?

If your computer remembers your Windows Live sign in credentials from a previous session, your e-mail address already may be displayed on the SkyDrive Web page. In this case, point to your e-mail address to display the Sign in button, click the Sign in button, and then proceed to Step 3. If you cannot locate your e-mail address or Sign in link, click the Sign in with a different Windows Live ID link and then proceed to Step 3.

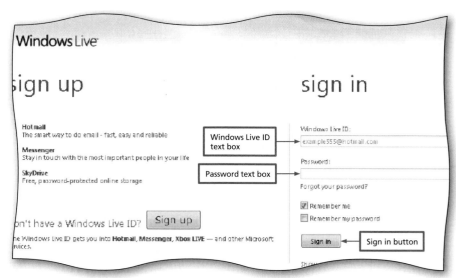

Figure C–10

• If necessary, enter your Windows Live ID and password in the appropriate text boxes and then click the Sign in button to sign into Windows Live and display the contents of your SkyDrive (Figure C–11).

Q&A

What do the icons beside the folders mean?

The lock icon indicates that the folder is private and is accessible only to you. The people icon signifies a folder that can be shared with SkyDrive users to whom you have assigned the necessary permissions. The globe icon denotes a folder accessible to anyone on the Internet.

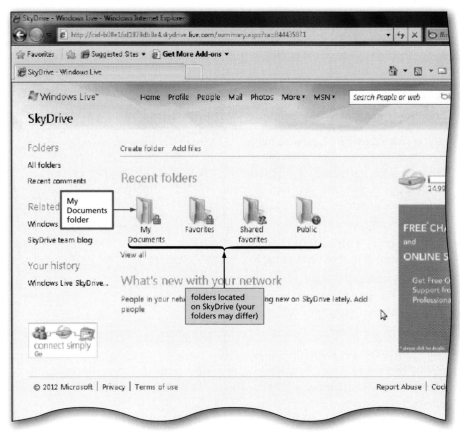

Figure C–11

• Click the My Documents folder, or the folder containing the file you wish to open, to select the folder and display its contents (Figure C–12).

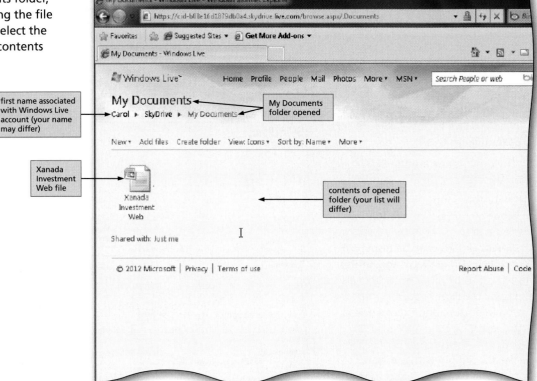

Figure C–12

5
- Click the Xanada Investment Web file to select the file and display information about it (Figure C–13).

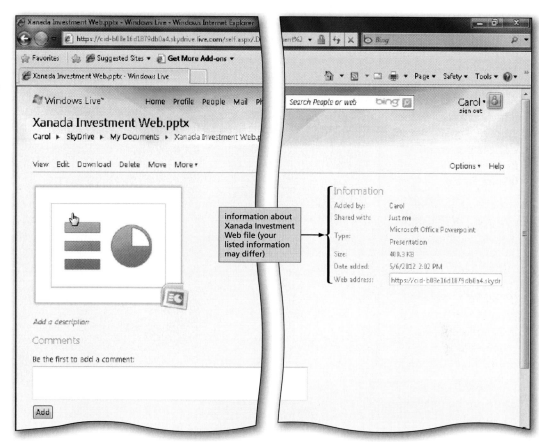

Figure C–13

6
- Click the Download link to display the File Download dialog box (Figure C–14).

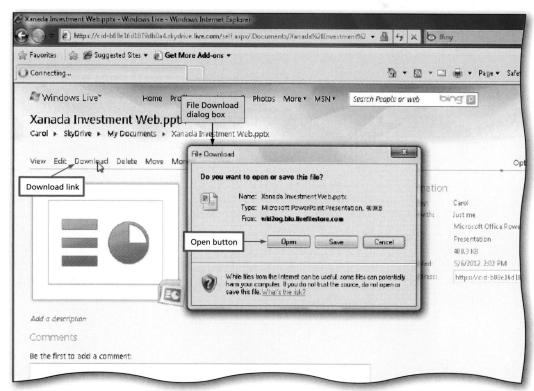

Figure C–14

7

- Click the Open button (File Download dialog box) to open the file in Microsoft PowerPoint. If necessary, click the Enable Editing button if it appears below the Ribbon so that you can edit the presentation in PowerPoint (Figure C–15).

Q&A

What if I want to save the file on my computer's hard disk?

Refer to the Office 2010 and Windows 7 chapter at the beginning of this book.

Q&A

Why does the file name on the title bar look different from the file name I typed when saving the document?

Because you are opening the file directly from SkyDrive without first saving it to your computer, the file name may differ slightly. For example, spaces may be replaced with "%20" and a number in parentheses at the end of the file name may indicate you are opening a copy of the original file that is stored online.

Figure C–15

Collaboration

In today's workplace, it is common to work with others on projects. Collaborating with the members of your team often requires sharing files. It also can involve multiple people editing and working with a certain set of files simultaneously. Placing files on SkyDrive in a public or shared folder enables others to view or modify the files. The members of the team then can view and edit the files simultaneously using Web Apps, enabling the team to work from one set of files. Collaboration using Web Apps not only enables multiple people to work together, it also can reduce the amount of time required to complete a project.

Index

Quick Reference Summary

Microsoft PowerPoint 2010 Quick Reference Summary

Task	Page Number	Mouse	Ribbon	Shortcut Menu	Keyboard Shortcut
Animated GIF (Movie), Insert	PPT 174		Picture button (Insert tab | Images group)		
Audio File, Insert	PPT 167		Insert Audio button (Insert tab | Media group)		
Audio Options, Add	PPT 170		Audio Tools Playback tab | Audio Options group		
Clip Art, Insert	PPT 27	Clip Art icon in slide	Clip Art button (Insert tab | Images group)		
Clip Art, Photo, or Shape, Move	PPT 36	Drag			ARROW KEYS move selected image in small increments
Clip Art, Regroup	PPT 162		Group button, Regroup command (Drawing Tools Format tab | Arrange group)	Group, Regroup	
Clip Art, Ungroup	PPT 157		Group button, Ungroup command (Picture Tools Format tab | Arrange group), click Yes to convert to Microsoft Office drawing, click Drawing Tools Format tab, Group button, Ungroup		
Clip Object, Recolor	PPT 158		Shape Fill button (Drawing Tools Format tab | Shape Styles group)	Format Shape, Color button (Format Shape dialog box)	
Copy	PPT 108, 155		Copy button (Home tab | Clipboard group)	Copy	CTRL+C
Document Properties, Change	PPT 46		Properties button (File tab | Info tab)		
Document Theme, Change Color	PPT 81		Colors button (Design tab | Themes group)		
Document Theme, Choose	PPT 5		More button (Design tab | Themes group)		
Font Size, Decrease	PPT 104	Decrease Font Size button or Font Size box arrow on Mini toolbar	Decrease Font Size button or Font Size box arrow (Home tab | Font group)		CTRL+SHIFT+<

Microsoft PowerPoint 2010 Quick Reference Summary *(continued)*

Task	Page Number	Mouse	Ribbon	Shortcut Menu	Keyboard Shortcut
Font Size, Increase	PPT 11	Increase Font Size button or Font Size box arrow on Mini toolbar	Increase Font Size button or Font Size box arrow (Home tab | Font group)		CTRL+SHIFT+>
Font, Change	PPT 102	Font box arrow on Mini toolbar	Font box arrow (Home tab | Font group)	Font, Font tab (Font dialog box)	CTRL+SHIFT+F
Font, Change Color	PPT 13	Font Color button or Font Color button arrow on Mini toolbar	Font Color button or Font Color button arrow (Home tab | Font group)	Font, Font tab (Font dialog box)	CTRL+SHIFT+F
Format Painter, Use	PPT 105	Format Painter button on Mini toolbar	Double-click Format Painter button (Home tab | Clipboard group), select text with format you want to copy, select text to apply previously selected format; press ESC to turn off Format Painter		
Handout, Print	PPT 184		Print button (File tab | Print tab)		
List Level, Increase	PPT 17	Increase List Level button on Mini toolbar	Increase List Level button (Home tab | Paragraph group)		TAB or ALT+SHIFT+RIGHT ARROW
List Level, Decrease	PPT 18	Decrease List Level button on Mini toolbar	Decrease List Level button (Home tab | Paragraph group)		SHIFT+TAB or ALT+SHIFT+LEFT ARROW
Next Slide	PPT 25	Next Slide button on vertical scroll bar or next slide thumbnail on Slides tab			PAGE DOWN
Normal View	PPT 153	Normal button at lower-right PowerPoint window	Normal View button (View tab | Presentation Views group)		
Open Presentation	PPT 50		Open (File tab)		CTRL+O
Paste	PPT 109		Paste button (Home tab | Clipboard group)	Paste	CTRL+V
Photo, Insert	PPT 32, 83	Insert Picture from File icon on slide or Insert Clip Art icon on slide	Picture button or Clip Art button (Insert tab | Images group)		
Picture, Add an Artistic Effect	PPT 145		Artistic Effects button (Picture Tools Format tab | Adjust group)	Format Picture, Artistic Effects (Format Picture dialog box)	
Picture, Add Border	PPT 91		Picture border button (Picture Tools Format tab | Picture Styles group)		
Picture, Correct	PPT 87		Corrections button (Picture Tools Format tab | Adjust group)	Format Picture, Picture Corrections (Format Picture dialog box)	
Picture, Recolor	PPT 143		Color button (Picture Tools Format tab | Adjust group)	Format Picture, Picture Color (Format Picture dialog box)	

Microsoft PowerPoint 2010 Quick Reference Summary *(continued)*

Task	Page Number	Mouse	Ribbon	Shortcut Menu	Keyboard Shortcut
Picture Border, Change Color	PPT 92		Picture border button (Picture Tools Format tab | Picture Styles group)		
Picture Effects, Apply	PPT 89		Picture Effects button (Picture Tools Format tab | Picture Styles group)	Format Picture	
Picture Style, Apply	PPT 87		More button (Picture Tools Format tab | Picture Styles group)		
Placeholder, Delete	PPT 149				Select placeholder, DELETE
Placeholder, Move	PPT 148	Drag			
Placeholder, Resize	PPT 148	Drag sizing handles			
Previous Slide	PPT 26	Previous Slide button on vertical scroll bar or click previous slide thumbnail on Slides tab			PAGE UP
Print a Presentation	PPT 51		Print button (File tab | Print tab)		CTRL+P
Quit PowerPoint	PPT 50	Close button on title bar	Exit (File tab)	Right-click Microsoft PowerPoint button on taskbar, click Close window	ALT+F4
Reading View	PPT 154	Reading View button at lower-right PowerPoint window	Reading View button (View tab | Presentation Views group)		
Resize	PPT 33, 93, 148	Drag sizing handles	Enter height and width values (Picture Tools Format tab | Size group or Drawing Tools Format tab | Size group)	Format Picture or Format Shape, Size tab; or enter height and width in Shape Height and Shape Width boxes	
Save a Presentation	PPT 14	Save button on Quick Access Toolbar	Save or Save As (File tab)		CTRL+S or F12
Shape, Apply Style	PPT 110		More button or Format Shape Dialog Box Launcher in Shapes Style gallery (Drawing Tools Format tab | Shape Styles group)	Format Shape	
Shape, Insert	PPT 106		Shapes button (Home tab | Drawing group); More button (Drawing Tools Format tab | Insert Shapes group)		
Slide, Add	PPT 14		New Slide button (Home tab | Slides group)		CTRL+M
Slide, Arrange	PPT 39	Drag slide in Slides tab or Outline tab to new position, or in Slide Sorter view drag to new position			

Microsoft PowerPoint 2010 Quick Reference Summary *(continued)*

Task	Page Number	Mouse	Ribbon	Shortcut Menu	Keyboard Shortcut
Slide, Delete	PPT 152			Delete Slide	DELETE
Slide, Duplicate	PPT 38		New Slide arrow (Home tab | Slides group), Duplicate Selected Slides		
Slide, Format Background	PPT 95		Background Styles button (Design tab | Background group)	Format Background	
Slide, Insert Picture as Background	PPT 97		Background Styles button (Design tab | Background group)	Format Background, Picture or Texture Fill, Insert from File (Format Background dialog box)	
Slide, Select Layout	PPT 21		Layout button or New Slide arrow (Home tab | Slides group)		
Slide Number, Insert	PPT 182		Insert Slide Number button (Insert tab | Text group) or Header & Footer button (Insert tab | Text group), click Slide number check box		
Slide Show View	PPT 47	Slide Show button at lower-right PowerPoint window	Slide Show button (Slide Show tab | Start Slide Show group)		F5
Slide Show, End	PPT 49	Click black ending slide		End Show	ESC or HYPHEN
Slide Sorter View	PPT 153	Slide Sorter button at lower-right PowerPoint window	Slide Sorter button (View tab | Presentation Views group)		
Speaker Notes, Add	PPT 179	In Normal view, click Notes pane and type notes			
Speaker Notes, Print	PPT 187		File tab, Print tab, click Notes Pages (Print Layout area), click Print button		
Spelling, Check	PPT 181		Spelling button (Review tab | Proofing group)	Spelling (or click correct word on shortcut menu)	F7
Stacking Order, Change	PPT 146		Bring Forward or Send Backward button (Picture Tools Format tab | Arrange group)	Send to Back or Bring to Front	
Synonym, Find and Insert	PPT 178		Thesaurus button (Review tab | Proofing group)	Right-click word, click desired synonym on Synonym submenu	SHIFT+F7
Text, Add Shadow	PPT 103		Text Shadow button (Home tab | Font group)		
Text, Align Horizontally	PPT 150	Align Text buttons on Mini toolbar	Align Text buttons (Home tab | Paragraph group)	Paragraph, Alignment box (Paragraph dialog box)	CTRL+R (right), CTRL+L (left), CTRL+E (center)

Microsoft PowerPoint 2010 Quick Reference Summary *(continued)*

Task	Page Number	Mouse	Ribbon	Shortcut Menu	Keyboard Shortcut
Text, Bold	PPT 20	Bold button on Mini toolbar	Bold button (Home tab | Font group)	Font, Font tab (Font dialog box)	CTRL+B
Text, Change Color	PPT 13	Font Color button or Font Color button arrow on Mini toolbar	Font Color button or Font Color button arrow (Home tab | Font group)	Font, Font tab (Font dialog box)	
Text, Delete	PPT 41		Cut button (Home tab | Clipboard group)	Cut	DELETE or CTRL+X or BACKSPACE
Text, Find and Replace	PPT 176		Replace button (Home tab | Editing group)		CTRL+H
Text, Italicize	PPT 11	Italic button on Mini toolbar	Italic button (Home tab | Font group)	Font, Font tab (Font dialog box)	CTRL+I
Text, Select Paragraph	PPT 10	Triple-click paragraph			SHIFT+DOWN ARROW or SHIFT+UP ARROW
Text, Select Word	PPT 12	Double-click word			CTRL+SHIFT+RIGHT ARROW or CTRL+SHIFT+LEFT ARROW
Transition, Add	PPT 43		Transitions tab | Transition to This Slide group		ALT+A , T
Transparency, Change	PPT 98		Background Styles button (Design tab | Background group), Format Background, move Transparency slider	Format Background, Transparency slider	
Video File, Insert	PPT 163		Insert Video button (Insert tab | Media group)		
Video File, Trim	PPT 165		Trim Video button (Video Tools Playback tab | Editing group), drag video start/end points or edit Start Time and End Time boxes		
Video Options	PPT 166		Video Tools Playback tab | Video Options group		
Video Style, Add	PPT 172		More button (Video Tools Format tab | Video Styles group)		
WordArt, Add Text Effects	PPT 115		Text Effects button (Drawing Tools Format tab | WordArt Styles group)		
WordArt, Insert	PPT 114		WordArt button (Insert tab | Text group)		
Zoom for Viewing Slides	PPT 156	Drag Zoom slider on status bar; click Zoom In or Zoom Out button on Zoom slider; change percentage in Zoom level box on left side of slider	Zoom button (View tab | Zoom group)		